ARCHIPELAGIC
MODERNISM

ARCHIPELAGIC MODERNISM

Literature in the Irish and British Isles, 1890–1970

John Brannigan

EDINBURGH
University Press

© John Brannigan, 2015

Edinburgh University Press Ltd
The Tun – Holyrood Road
12(2f) Jackson's Entry
Edinburgh EH8 8PJ
www.euppublishing.com

Typeset in 11/13pt Bembo by
Servis Filmsetting Ltd, Stockport, Cheshire
and printed and bound in Great Britain by
CPI Group (UK) Ltd, Croydon CR0 4YY

A CIP record for this book is available from the British Library

ISBN 978 0 7486 4336 3 (hardback)
ISBN 978 0 7486 4337 0 (webready PDF)
ISBN 978 0 7486 4335 6 (paperback)
ISBN 978 0 7486 9914 8 (epub)

Contents

Acknowledgements

Archipelagic Modernism is a book assembled from the fruits of many conversations, experiences, and adventures, mainly within and around the islands we still call 'Britain and Ireland', but sometimes further afield. Most of my intellectual debts are recorded in the references and bibliography, although I wish to acknowledge some more fully here. In my previous books I have scuttled between two national traditions, Irish literature and English literature, as if they could be kept apart, but it has always been clear that each tradition has informed and shaped the other profoundly and pervasively, as well as having similarly deep engagements with other national, regional, and transnational traditions. The cultivation of a full understanding of these literary interrelations, and of an archipelagic account of the literary histories of these islands, is an unassailable task for one scholar, but in this book I have sought to scout out some of the possibilities, and some of the problems, with which a more extensive archipelagic project would have to engage. I am deeply grateful to the commissioning editor at Edinburgh University Press, Jackie Jones, for inviting me to write a book which would explore the relations between the anglophone literatures of Scotland, Ireland, Wales, and England, without which invitation my archipelagic ambitions would have found expression only in a few expeditionary essays. Jackie, as well as her colleagues, including James Dale, Jen Daly, Cathy Falconer, Rebecca Mackenzie, Dhara Patel, and Kate Robertson, have patiently and kindly supported the book during its evolution.

I have been very fortunate to work with a group of similarly disposed and committed archipelagic scholars in building a collaborative scholarly network, the Atlantic Archipelagos Research Consortium, and I owe many of my heftiest intellectual debts to conversations I have enjoyed with Nicholas Allen, Nick Groom, Andrew McNeillie, and Jos Smith. Our forays into thinking together about Atlantic archipelagos have taken us to many places, actual and metaphorical, which have been highly significant for me in trying to follow the connections between literature, politics, and ecology. I am also grateful for their support for, and participation in, the events I have organised in University College Dublin on archipelagic and maritime themes, specifically the lecture series on 'Reconceiving the British Isles' (2009–10), the symposium on 'Over the Irish Sea' (2012), and the lecture series on 'The Literatures and Cultures of the Irish Sea' (2012–13). For inspiration, conversation, and collaboration, I would also like to thank the speakers and participants in all of those events, including Neal Alexander, Nicholas Allen, Jody Allen Randolph, Louise Chamberlain, Margaret Cohen, Claire Connolly, Amy Cutler, Alice Entwistle, Michael Gardiner, Andrew Gibson, Alan Gillis, Colin Graham, Nick Groom, Eamonn Hughes, Edna Longley, Peter Mackay, Andrew McNeillie, Kevin Mills, Conor O'Callaghan, Jos Smith, Fiona Stafford, Luke Thurston, Damian Walford Davies, and Julian Wolfreys. Thanks to the saintly efforts of P. J. Mathews and John Matthews, many of the lectures given by my colleagues above are available to download in audio and text formats from UCDscholarcast (<www.ucd.ie/scholarcast>).

I am grateful to UCD School of English, Drama and Film, UCD Humanities Institute, and UCD Research Seed Funding for small grants and big favours in support of this book and related endeavours. In particular, I have learned much and benefited greatly from discussions in seminar rooms and corridors with Ron Callan, Danielle Clarke, Catriona Clutterbuck, Lucy Collins, Gabriel Cooney, Luca Crispi, Tasman Crowe, Nick Daly, Sharae Deckard, Treasa de Loughry, Philip De Souza, Fionnuala Dillane, Porscha Fermanis, Anne Fogarty, Jane Grogan, Margaret Kelleher, Adam Kelly, P. J. Mathews, Frank McGuinness, Gerardine Meaney, Anne Mulhall, Diane Negra, Emilie Pine, Tony Roche, Maria Stuart, Fionnghuala Sweeney, and Nerys Williams. Various iterations of the chapters of this book were tentatively spoken as lectures, papers, and seminars at Anglia Ruskin University, Magdalene College in Cambridge, NUI Galway, University of Georgia in Athens, University of Glasgow, the Joyce Summer School at Trieste, Katholieke Universiteit Leuven, University of Loughborough, NUI Maynooth, University of Nottingham, Queen's University of Belfast, and University College Dublin. For encouraging suggestions, criticisms, and questions, as well as hospitality and kind invitations to speak, I am grateful to Neal Alexander, Matt Campbell, Brian Caraher, James Chandler, Eamonn Duffy, David Dwan, Anna Fenge, Anne Fogarty, Jane Goldman, Colin Graham, Hugh Haughton, Peter Hession, Geraldine Higgins, Keith Jeffrey, Mary Joannou, John Kenny,

John Kerrigan, Ed Larrissy, John McCourt, James Moran, Peter O'Neill, Eve Patten, Nels Pearson, Shaun Richards, Frank Shovlin, Moynagh Sullivan, Caroline Sumpter, and Clair Wills. I owe Julian Wolfreys an older debt: my first publication was an essay about Richard Jefferies written at his suggestion, and during twenty years of friendship he has always inspired me to try to think about Englishness differently and imaginatively. Some parts of the book have been tested in print, or are about to be, and for those opportunities, I am very grateful to the editors of the journal *Modernism/Modernity* and the edited collections *Regional Modernisms* (Neal Alexander and James Moran), *Literature of an Independent England* (Michael Gardiner and Claire Westall), and *Coastal Works* (Nicholas Allen, Nick Groom, Andrew McNeillie, and Jos Smith).

My biggest thanks go to my wife, Moyra, and our children, Conor, Owen, and Laura, who enjoyed and sometimes endured sharing holidays, day trips, and expeditions to seaside places which usually turned out somehow to have something to do with books and writers, and who, often with buckets and spades, helped me to make sense of the 'Signatures of all things I am here to read'.

Introduction: After London

In *After London* (1885), Richard Jefferies imagined a future in which the geography of England has been dramatically altered by an environmental catastrophe. Rising sea levels and the effects of human-made structures on water-courses combine to flood central and southern parts of England, resulting in a great lake which makes navigation by ship necessary around many of the surviving remnants of human settlement. London is buried under a 'vast stagnant swamp', formed by the debris of the city's collapse under water, and made poisonous by its own rotting cloacae.[1] Much of the remaining land around the city, which was once lush pasture, is now either marsh or overgrown woodland, dark and impenetrable. There is little by way of governance or protection, and social organisation has reverted to feudal forms of tyranny, slavery, and servitude. The technical innovations and industrial wealth of Victorian England are buried under water, and lost more deeply in the fables of the descendants of those survivors who can only pass on the names of 'the marvellous things which the ancients did'.[2] There is little communication with peoples outside of England, as the seaports have been wrecked or silted up, other than with the Irish, Scots, and Welsh who invade, harass, and plunder all along the settlements around the great lake, in 'direful acts of piracy'.[3] These acts are seen by the narrator as blameless, for 'the ancients from whom we are descended held them in subjection many hundred years, and took from them all their liberties'.[4]

The subtitle of *After London* is *Wild England*, and it is a Darwinian-inspired diluvian fantasy, or nightmare, of a 'relapse into barbarism'. The narrator's sympathetic explanation of acts of Irish, Scots, and Welsh piracy hints that the flood which has reduced England 'back' to its primitive origins might be seen as a kind of moral retribution for the injuries inflicted by England on other peoples. At the heart of this dark civilisation which subjugated other nations lay its capital city, now as foul and repugnant under water as it was above. Even the rats, prolific violators of boundaries, will not now approach the swamp which lies over the city's remains, and the inhabitants of 'Wild England' are superstitious that this swamp contains demons, as they avoid any place where there was once ancient habitation.[5] Jefferies can barely conceal his contempt for his contemporary society in this fantasy of the future, but there is nothing remotely utopian about the archipelagic England which takes the place of its drowned antecedent. Unlike William Morris, Jefferies did not imagine an ideal society rising to flourish in the wake of the old, just a rather familiar anarchic and violent past returning to haunt an English people who could now only dimly recall having been at the centre of a global empire, and the engine of industrial progress. Yet Morris found the book inspiring: 'absurd hopes curled round my heart as I read it,' he wrote; 'how often it consoles me to think of barbarism once more flooding the world'.[6] For Morris, *After London* suggested the possibility of beginning again, of resetting the terms upon which an English society might be founded, and of how it might relate to its neighbours.

The flood which scours a new archipelagic geography out of England is a revolutionary agent, purging the land of its industrial and commercial blight, even if it cannot usher in the new. In this sense, Jefferies's novel is also a proto-modernist, as well as an ecological, fantasy, a precursor to the modernist obsession with cataclysm and obliteration. T. S. Eliot's modernist poem *The Waste Land* (1922) imagines the catastrophe in terms of both drowning and drought, of the sailor who suffers 'death by water', and the cry for order in a dry, barren land.[7] There is both too much water and too little in Eliot's vision of an apocalyptic London on the brink of ruin, and London has sucked the life out of the crowd depicted flowing over London Bridge. Michael Gardiner reads Eliot's poem as an expression of anxiety about the loss of control over water as a signifier of 'the end of an Anglican, seafaring, imperialist aesthetics which had slid under Greater Britain'.[8] The desire to restore order, to 'shore up' the remnants of a decaying culture, pervades the poem, even if it takes some delight in ventriloquising the sounds of the debased present. In Eliot, perhaps the fantasy of sweeping away the past in one great tidal wash was no longer as desirable as it had been for Jefferies or Morris. Like Yeats, Woolf, and Lawrence, Eliot wrote as if the cataclysm had already happened, and the narratives of progress, expansion, and enlightenment which Jefferies and Morris despised had reached their bitter ends by 1922. Yet Jefferies's diluvian fantasy about the dissolution of Anglocentric power, and the 'absurd hopes' it inspired, contains no nostalgia for lost glories, just as it promises no certainties of a brighter future. It is unambiguous, however, in its implication that the social and political ills of Victorian Britain are the consequence of a ruthlessly centralised, metropolitan society, with London as its voracious Moloch.

After London is not unique in imagining a diluvian re-engineering of the geography of the British and Irish Isles. A similar vision is implicit in Hugh MacDiarmid's wish 'to speculate upon the very different course not only Scottish, and English, but world history would have taken if the whole of the mainland of Scotland had been severed from England and broken up into the component islands of a numerous archipelago'.[9] Lynette Roberts wrote of the rising sea levels which would one day 'leave nothing of Wales / But white island shining / The crest of Snowdon', but comforts her Welsh readers that this will only happen tomorrow, 'And before tomorrow / England will be / For thousands of years / Lying below us / A submerged village'.[10] In J. G. Ballard's *The Drowned World* (1962), the sea levels rise when solar radiation melts the polar ice caps, and new seas alter the shape of the continents. London is submerged, like all the low-lying cities, beneath a series of lagoons, its streets and buildings smothered in silt, and the higher land around it covered in tropical forests, 'a nightmare world of competing organic forms returning rapidly to their Paleozoic past'.[11] The scientists who return to this landscape to catalogue its life forms are haunted by nightmares of prehistoric swamps and Triassic reptiles, as the climatological changes awaken biological memories of our 'entire evolutionary past'.[12] None of the familiar geography exists any longer: London, England, Britain, the British Isles are distant memories in a planet in which the only permanently habitable places lie in the polar circles. In Eilís Ní Dhuibhne's *The Bray House* (1990), it is not the sea which alters the geography of the planet but a nuclear catastrophe which causes a chain of explosions when it reaches the water table, after an explosion in a nuclear plant in Islandmagee. As a result of environmental and nuclear disaster, 'South America is flooded, Africa is prey to drought, flood, famine, plagues of every kind. Half of western Europe has vanished.'[13] The novel follows a Swedish expedition of archaeologists to an Ireland covered in nuclear ash, in which every sign of life on land and water has been obliterated, and even the barest forms of vegetation have been stripped away. The leader of the expedition recalls seeing the British prime minister on television after the catastrophe, speaking tearfully from a mansion in Beverly Hills which she was visiting: '"We must now try to build on what we have left to us. We must not give in or despair, but remember that Great Britain has always been the leader among all nations. There will always be an England." She did not mention Ireland.'[14] For the archaeologist, who has fond memories of England, it is clear that England will now only exist as quaint memories of 'their corn flake breakfasts and their fish and chip suppers', Jane Austen and Charles Dickens novels, the

Queen Mother.[15] Ireland, on the other hand, subjected to the forensic analysis of the contents of the house the team excavate, is concluded to have been 'a country of poverty, violence and ignorance', 'a dying country', and a country as vulnerable to the depredations of neighbouring Britain as it was apathetic to its own fate.[16]

The utopian impulse underlying such fictions of submergence is not towards some ideal moment of *tabula rasa*, or clean slate, for remnants of the old geography, and the old social structures, remain. Rather, these fictional notions point towards a recalibration of relations between the regions and islands of the Irish and British archipelago, specifically of those social, political, and cultural relations which have been defined by Anglocentric identities so powerful that they have frequently been equated with the whole of the archipelago, and by nationalisms which, like Jefferies's pirates from the Celtic fringes, have been born and fuelled from their animosity towards an imperial centre. That this recalibration of relations takes the form of catastrophe, or obliteration, is perhaps indicative of the extent to which existing geopolitical identities are perceived to be unalterable. As Fredric Jameson argues, this is a familiar problem in utopian writing, that because 'even our wildest imaginings are all collages of experience . . . this means that our imaginations are hostages to our own mode of production (and perhaps to whatever remnants of past ones it has preserved)'.[17] Jameson thus distinguishes between the utopian vision, which he suggests has become since the middle of the twentieth century a synonym for totalitarian ideals of 'a perfect system that always had to be imposed by force on its imperfect and reluctant subjects', and the utopian desire, or yearning, which is a critical marker of both dissent from the existing structures of power and social organisation, and a kind of faith or hope in the possibility of alternatives.[18] The catastrophe functions, then, as the sign of such desire: the trope of a submerged archipelago, either by rising sea levels or by nuclear disaster, is the *deus ex machina* which compels an end to prevailing conditions in order to expose their contingency.

THE UNNAMEABLE ARCHIPELAGO

One argument of this book is that the writers identified as part of 'archipelagic modernism' were as much concerned with biopolitical, evolutionary, and eugenics debates about social organisation as they were preoccupied with the geopolitical landscape of the British and Irish archipelago. *After London* might be described as a devolutionary novel according to two different meanings of that term. It is devolutionary in the Darwinian sense of regression, in telling a story of the 'relapse into barbarism'. It is devolutionary also in depicting an archipelago no longer conjoined under political union but divided into 'numerous provinces, kingdoms, and republics', and in which each of the constituent regions and islands of the United Kingdom of Great Britain and Ireland is self-governing, or perhaps not governed at all.[19] Importantly, these two meanings are also interrelated, so that the return of Irish, Welsh, and Scottish political liberty is equated with the decline of 'British' civilisation, and with the vulnerability of a weakened and isolated England to attack from its vengeful neighbours.

Jefferies's novel was published at the height of the British Empire, the extent and power of which was believed to be evidence of both the success of the Union, and the superiority of the English who governed it (even when those English who governed it were also Scottish, Irish, or Welsh). Yet it was also a period of intense political debate about 'Home Rule', especially for Ireland, and intense philosophical debate about the implications of evolutionary science for social organisation, governance, and reproduction. Ulster Unionist objections to Home Rule were encapsulated in the famous quip that it would be 'Rome Rule', implying not just that it would be dominated by the Catholic Church, but also that the social and biopolitical structures of a devolved Ireland would depart from the forms which prevailed under the Union. The contests between Unionism and nationalism throughout the modern period have frequently involved strands of eugenic argument, even if often insidiously, about race, demography, and productivity. The anxieties about the loss of political power as a result of the Boer War and the First World War were accompanied by fears of racial degeneration, of an increasingly urban population which was producing weaker and smaller descendants. The reverberations from the Great Famine of the mid-nineteenth century meant that Irish nationalism had always been haunted by the redemptive hope that Irish sovereignty would prevent starvation, depopulation, and mass emigration. So, too, the growth of nationalist movements in Scotland and Wales from the mid-twentieth century onwards correlated closely with narratives of British decline, premised upon the idea that national biopolitical regimes could stem the tide of economic and social decay. Tom Nairn puts it succinctly in *After Britain*: 'Assimilation or subordination of the non-English periphery was a necessary condition of Britain's great-power phase and imperial ambitions. Their desubordination is an equally necessary accompaniment to that phase's end.'[20]

For this reason, perhaps, political devolution has almost always been seen as a matter of more concern to the 'periphery' than to the 'centre'. Ireland, Scotland, and Wales, demographically and economically, became more peripheral in the course of the nineteenth century to an increasingly Anglocentric Union, and therefore, with the decline of British power in the twentieth century, the causes of regional devolution and separatism became more compelling there than in England. Ireland was first to secede, and the legislative independence won for the Irish Free State in 1922 had already been preceded by partition into two states, with Ulster given its own devolved government in 1920. Successive campaigns for Welsh and Scottish independence eventually led to the devolution of power in 1998 to the Scottish Parliament and the Welsh Assembly, although devolution in these cases has always been a means of retaining the Union, of securing continuing consent to the supremacy of the United Kingdom rather than conceding to separatist arguments. Debates about the devolution of powers within England, despite serious inequities in power and wealth between the north of England and the south, especially the south-east, have rarely attracted much public interest. As Vernon Bogdanor argues, there are interesting legal and political reasons for this because 'constitutionally, England does not exist'.[21] There is no constitution founding the English state, and the people of England are represented only through the parliamentary institutions of Britain. Despite a shire system of local government which was in place for hundreds of years, in the modern period, especially, England has been ruled 'by a strong central government which left little room for provincial loyalties'.[22] Moreover, the very idea of England has been used to accommodate a vastly differing scale of territorial entities, from a very local vision of the rural south-east of England, to the British Isles as a whole, to the Empire, and arguably to a still powerful global constituency of 'English-speaking peoples'.

To use the word 'archipelago' to talk about the relations between the constituent parts of the British and Irish Isles implies a plural and connective vision quite at odds with the cultural and political homogenisation which lay at the heart of the Unionist project. It is also at odds with the nationalist project which, largely in reaction to Unionism, cherished exceptionalism and insularity. The recognition that alternative forms of political relationship which accommodated plural and contesting allegiances were a necessary condition for conflict resolution lay at the heart of the political negotiations in Northern Ireland in the late 1990s. The Belfast Agreement of 1998 envisioned a 'Council of the Isles', comprised of all the sovereign states, devolved governments, and island territories which make up the 'British Isles'. Although this has proved of limited significance to date as a political entity, Tom Nairn was right to note in 2000 that it marked a symbolic shift towards taking seriously an idea which was 'intended to modify – and possibly even to succeed – the United Kingdom'.[23] The devolution of governing powers to Scotland and Wales can be understood, at least from the perspective of their local advocates, as a means of enabling those constituencies to give political expression to relations with other nations and communities across the seas, beyond their landlocked union with England. The debates about an independent Scotland, seceded from the

Union, have raised a whole range of questions about what this means for both Scotland and Britain in terms of international relations, currency, economic policy, cultural identity, defence, European Union membership, and citizenship. The nomenclature spawned by these devolutionary processes, while casting around for neutral terms inoffensive to all its participant parties, stresses the archipelagic too: 'These Islands', 'Islands of the North Atlantic', 'North-Western European Archipelago', 'The Atlantic Archipelago', or, more simply, as in the title of Norman Davies's book, *The Isles*.

Davies describes his title as 'the simplest formula of all' to avoid confusion about terminology, and his introduction provides a thorough and amusing dissection of the anomalies, errors, ambiguities, and evasions which characterise how even the most professional and revered linguists, historians, and political scientists have referred to 'the isles'.[24] Yet none of the alternatives to our unsatisfactory existing terms is either sufficiently descriptive or sufficiently attractive to be viable. The political problem of devolution and conflict resolution resides precisely in this unnameability. As Andrew McNeillie suggests, the names we use to describe this 'unnameable constellation of islands on the Eastern Atlantic coast' belong to another age.[25] We do not yet have the vocabulary to describe what Tom Nairn called 'post-Ukanian' political identities in the archipelago, since all existing terms have been bound to the legacies of imperialism, nationalism, and unionism, and these identities are 'decreasingly useful lies' in an age in which the Empire has long been dissolved, nation-states are no longer sovereign actors, and the United Kingdom maps on to no consensual union of interests, allegiances, or aspirations. It was precisely this disparity between terminology and political reality which inspired the historian John Pocock to first use the phrase 'Atlantic archipelago' as a provisional name for these islands off the coast of North-West Europe. Writing in the early 1970s, with the death toll in Ulster rising, and Britain apparently abandoning the Commonwealth for the European Common Market, Pocock surmised 'that future historians may find themselves writing of a "Unionist" or even a "British" period in the history of the peoples inhabiting the Atlantic archipelago, and locating it between a date in the thirteenth, the seventeenth, or the nineteenth century and a date in the twentieth or the twenty-first'.[26] Pocock's contention was that the term 'British History' had in fact been rarely if ever used accurately, and usually meant English when it should have been used 'to denote the plural history of a group of cultures situated along an Anglo-Celtic frontier and marked by an increasing English political and cultural domination'.[27] That England was the dominant power did not obviate the need to understand the history of the archipelago as one of interaction and interdependence between its component kingdoms, nations, and peoples.

Pocock's analysis was influential upon the development of what has become known as the 'three kingdoms' or 'four nations' approach to the historiography of the 'British Isles', at least in certain of its phases. It took longer, however, for the archipelagic analysis of the political identities of 'these islands' to make an impact in studies of literature and culture. John Kerrigan's *Archipelagic English* (2008) made the case that despite the obvious significance of devolution for conceptions of literature within the isles, and indeed the influence of literary writing upon the devolutionary process itself, when it comes to how we study literature in the academy, 'the geopolitical parameters of enquiry remain substantially unrevised'.[28] England remains the central trunk, it seems, in our governing sense of what constitutes 'English literature' in the UK and Ireland, even if the exact horticultural relation to Irish, Scottish, Welsh, Caribbean, Canadian, Australian, or American literatures remains vague or unspoken. Kerrigan's book models an archipelagic understanding of how the anglophone literatures and cultures of the seventeenth century in these islands were plural, dynamic, and crucially interrelated. Yet, as Pocock perhaps implied when he observed the increasing Anglocentrism of the archipelago, in the twentieth century the risk of an archipelagic analysis which stresses connection and interrelation is that it may appear to underwrite a tacit unionism. Demographically and politically, it makes less sense to use a federal language of 'four nations' of the twentieth century than it does of the seventeenth, because of the disproportionate relations between those nations in terms of population and economic power. Such federal terms are especially inappropriate in relation to the Republic of Ireland, the people of which democratically mandated Sinn Fein in 1918 to sunder Ireland violently from the United Kingdom, and which therefore have perhaps little to gain from academic enquiry which situates Ireland culturally and politically back within the same island grouping. Yet as Brendan Behan observed in 1962, forty years after Irish independence, Ireland and Britain 'are inextricably mixed up and little in the way of national characteristics divide them. If you go into a pub in Manchester, Belfast, Dublin, Liverpool or London, you will hear people sing one song which might almost be their National Anthem: *I've got a lovely bunch of coconuts*, and their second favourite is *Nellie Dean*.'[29] He was observing, of course, the disparity between political rhetoric and social and cultural realities, a disparity which is pertinent not just to Ireland, but to the increasingly globalised franchising of cultural production. Both songs Behan cited were written and performed first in England, but in the postwar years were taken up by American artists and sold back to English audiences. It may also become more difficult in relation to the twentieth century to treat England as one element of a braided archipelago when it has been an even more hegemonic power than in the seventeenth. This is certainly the case in relation to language, and I echo here John Kerrigan's desire for a 'fully polyglot' study of the archipelago, to which this anglophone account is just one contribution.[30] In academic circles, the devolutionary imagination has given rise to Irish-Scottish research initiatives and to the Ireland-Wales research network, which serve to articulate the historical and cultural links between these nations, but the absence of any such forums for studying relations between England and its archipelagic neighbours is perhaps a sign of that English hegemony. It is arguably also a sign of a post-imperial phase of Englishness which, according to Simon Gikandi, has been characterised by an atrophic political discourse 'that seems to be generated by the need to take stock of that which no longer exists'.[31] England, it seems, remains securely wedded to a British and imperial identity which steadily ceased to exist in the course of the twentieth century, and it does so because the alternative is to think of itself as one small peripheral nation among others, or perhaps not even a nation at all.

SURROUNDED BY WATER

We use the term 'archipelago' to denote a group of islands, and to stress in neutral and plural terms the relationship between those islands. In the historical and political contexts of relations between the various nations, islands, and peoples in the Irish and British archipelago, this has obvious advantages in avoiding terms which are offensive, misrepresentative, or inaccurate. As John Kerrigan argues, the term is also a useful corrective to terrestrial scales of identity, since 'archipelago' refers nowhere in its etymology to islands but rather to an area of sea.[32] The *Oxford English Dictionary* shows the word emerging first in English to designate the Aegean Sea, and in more conventional modern usage, because the Aegean contains many islands, as 'Any sea, or sheet of water, in which there are numerous islands; and *transf.* a group of islands'. To think of the archipelago as a maritime space, in which lie a group of islands, places emphasis on how the seas and oceans surrounding the islands connect them to each other and to other land masses. 'The seas which we view on maps as surrounding and dividing the islands drew them together', Kerrigan argues, 'and opened them to continental and Atlantic worlds.'[33] Arguably this maritime conception has become more difficult to recognise since the advent of mass air travel, during which time, as Allan Sekula has made clear, the sea has both become 'the forgotten space' of modernity and at the same time has been transformed into a purely metaphorical realm of imaginary danger, or imaginary freedom, for capitalist consumers.[34]

One key focus for this book is literary representations of the seas and the islands within them as material spaces. The argument arising from that focus is that despite the general cultural tendency towards seeing islands and seas in figurative terms, there has been a strong counter-tradition in twentieth-century anglophone literature, perhaps especially in that modernist and late modernist literature associated with symbolism and metaphorical modes of representation, of reading them from resolutely material perspectives. This is not to deny that there continue to be important works of contemporary literature which read the sea as a psychological space, such as Iris Murdoch's *The Sea, The Sea* (1978) and more recently John Banville's *The Sea* (2005). But it is only by reading the sea as a material space that we can understand its importance as a global network for labour, trade, and migration, that we can see ports and coasts as conduits rather than borders, and that we can perceive islands as anything but insular. The materialist perspectives of this book, therefore, share some of the methodological frameworks of the recently emerged fields of oceanic studies or maritime studies in taking the sea, to use Hester Blum's terms, 'as a proprioceptive point of inquiry'.[35] Taking us out to sea, there is a rich body of maritime fiction which could be explored within the period investigated here, from Joseph Conrad, Richard Hughes, and James Hanley to popular series of novels published by C. S. Forester and Patrick O'Brian. However, my focus has remained fixed on the interaction between the land and the sea, and on how the maritime world, as Margaret Cohen argued, introduces geographic and spatial scales to literary studies which 'connect different kinds of landmasses and have histories of their own'.[36] The book which Cohen co-edited with Carolyn Dever, *The Literary Channel* (2002), which argues that the novel was invented by 'processes of literary and cultural exchange that occurred across the English Channel', is an exemplary investigation of the advantages of shifting focus from conventional national terrains of enquiry to a maritime zone of interaction.[37] Importantly, this re-scaling of the geographic terms of literary enquiry follows the flow of people and ideas across seas, as should be the case.

One implication of the arguments of this book is that the social and cultural connections of the people who live in the archipelago always exceed the limits of state or national formations, and that the spatial imagination of maritime zones may encompass some of those connections more fully than land zones. Is there a culture of the Atlantic seaboard which the peoples of Cornwall, Galway, and the Hebrides share, for example? What commonalities define the cities of the shipbuilding triangle formed on the estuarine banks of the Clyde, the Lagan, and the Mersey? How might it matter that Aberdeen is closer to Stavanger than it is to London? Is there some sense in which the Thames and the Rhine mingle more than water and silt in the southern reaches of the North Sea? What is the significance of seeing the Irish Sea as a kind of inland waterway of the archipelago, since it is the only sea bordered by Ireland, Scotland, Wales, and England, as well as containing the Isle of Man? As David

Brett argues in his intriguing book about the Irish Sea, 'Such a way of thinking – by way of shorelines – precedes the nations that squat along the shores.'[38] It may be argued that such thinking belongs to an age in which the boat was the fastest means of travel, and therefore that the nearest neighbours, markets, or employment lay across the adjacent sea rather than adjacent land. Modern transport infrastructures have a habit of funnelling people towards national or regional urban concentrations. Yet in our age, when the need to think in more local ecological scales of belonging and responsibility has become a matter of urgent necessity, thinking of the sea as a space of connection and communication has renewed importance.

It is important to revisit the sea as a space of alternate conceptions of the archipelago, because the sea was essential to the rise of England as a commercial and military empire, and to Scotland and Wales in their terrestrial and political union with England, as it was also essential to the imagination of the Irish nation as a 'whole island' which was 'surrounded by water'. At the same time, literary representations of the sea have more often been highly figurative, even wistfully romantic, to the point that one might argue they have obscured the very functional role of the sea in the maintenance of political power. Rudyard Kipling once described the maritime power of the British Empire as an intractable mystery, as he told junior naval officers, 'You'll win the world without anyone *caring* how you did it: you'll keep the world without anyone *knowing* how you did it: and you'll carry the world on your backs without anyone *seeing* how you did it.'[39] For George Orwell, the role of the navy in the conquest and rule of the Empire was a vital explanation of the 'sheer hypocrisy' towards the Empire which could be found in English people, who could continue to believe in themselves as a small island nation incapable of embracing militarism at the same time as ruling one quarter of the globe: 'A navy employs comparatively few people, and it is an external weapon that cannot affect home politics directly.'[40] Thus, Orwell argues, Britannia ruled the waves, but in a way which was almost invisible to the mass of British society. Orwell was writing of this hypocrisy during the Second World War, and he was attempting to explain the apparent paradox of a nation which could see itself in 1940, after the fall of France, as standing alone and isolated, when it continued to be supported by a global empire of several hundred million people. The material support of the maritime empire was easy to conceive for Virginia Woolf when she wrote her essay 'The Docks of London', in 1931, about the thousand ships which came to London port every week to anchor and unload their wares from around the world. Her account of the ceaseless swinging to and fro of the cranes, and the 'multitudinous products and waste products of the earth' which are hoisted on to the dockside to be graded and valued, is a materialist riposte to the 'romantic and free and fitful' ideas of the sea which have prevailed in literary representations.[41] Woolf begins her essay by quoting Robert Bridges's poem 'A Passer-by' (1879), which asks 'Whither, O splendid ship', and 'what thy quest?', even as the poem resolves to fancy the ship both beautiful and free.[42] Anchored in the docks of London, however, such ships are, in Woolf's eyes, tethered to a global system of commercial utility and value which extract every conceivable raw material from around the world so that it appears 'refined and transformed' in the 'garishness and gaudiness' of London's shops.[43]

Allan Sekula's 'forgotten space' of global capitalism was clearly preceded by, if not synonymous with, the maritime commercial and military system developed under the British Empire. Attending to the mechanics of this 'imperial archipelago' of trade and finance, and how it was experienced on a daily basis in material life, promises to open up global readings of even the most seemingly iconic national events or symbols, as Nicholas Allen demonstrates in his forthcoming book *1916: Ireland, Empire and Rebellion*.[44] The invisibility of the sea as a primary domain of power continues to obscure the ways in which we understand global geopolitics. As Peter Nolan has shown, we may appear to live in a post-imperial phase of British history, until we examine ownership of the sea. Under the UN Convention on the Law of the Sea, formalised in 1982, property rights over the sea were extended to an 'exclusive economic zone' (EEZ) of two hundred miles around sovereign territory. 'Thanks to their island holdings', Nolan writes, 'the EEZs of the US, UK and France dominate enormous stretches of the Pacific, Indian and South Atlantic Oceans . . . Indeed, the overseas EEZs of the United States, France and the UK vastly exceed those of their home territories.'[45] The island holdings themselves tend to be characterised by small populations, usually of white settlers, or have been cleared of civilian inhabitants to make way for military bases, research stations, or testing grounds.

Within the British and Irish archipelago, the sea has also been a space of conquest and conflict, long after the apparent demise of imperial rule. The uninhabited islet of Rockall, about three hundred miles west of the Hebrides, and slightly less from Donegal, was the last territory to be formally annexed as a colonial possession of the United Kingdom on 18 September 1955, when the Royal Navy landed a small party there to raise the Union flag and install a plaque claiming ownership.[46] Ireland has disputed ownership, but as the islet does not qualify as warranting its own EEZ, and it is incapable of sustaining life, there is little to be gained from pursuing the dispute. The Royal Navy was also at the centre of recurrent disputes between the United Kingdom and Iceland in the 'Cod Wars' of the 1950s and 1970s, when contested fishing rights in the North Atlantic led to clashes between naval vessels of both countries, as well as fishing vessels. The conflict arose out of the economic dependence of both Iceland and the UK upon extending and intensifying their respective fishing industries, in an age in which, as Callum Roberts has shown, successive centuries of mass exploitation of oceanic resources have led to fish stock depletion, destabilised marine ecosystems, and both anoxic and toxic marine environments.[47] The most toxic issue in Anglo-Irish relations of the late twentieth century, besides the conflict in Northern Ireland, was the pollution caused in the Irish Sea by the nuclear power and reprocessing plant in Sellafield in Cumbria. Thinking of the sea as a 'free space', without consequences, whether for waste dumping, overfishing, or most recently hydraulic fracture drilling, is clearly a major contributory factor in the environmental and social crises of our age. It is clearly also a by-product of that romanticism of the sea which Woolf critiqued.

MODERNIST ECOLOGIES

The account of modernism advanced in this book builds upon the expanded sense of that term in the 'new modernist studies' of the early twenty-first century. The archipelagic modernism of my title is one which encompasses an expanded chronology (partly because the later period does not equate with 'postmodernism', which has never been able to describe adequately the literature which came after the 1940s in the Irish and British archipelago), it comprises local as well as transnational geographies, and it prioritises a locational focus upon islands, coastlines, and the sea which reads against the metropolitan bias of the 'old' modernism. One effect of expanding the chronological and geographical scope of modernism, as Douglas Mao and Rebecca Walkowitz have argued, may be a weakening of the term as 'an evaluative and stylistic designation', although as they point out, it is a more productive exercise to focus on what happens when the qualitative and the chronological meanings of modernism are brought together.[48] It will be clear in the chapters that follow that Peadar O'Donnell and Elizabeth Taylor are not modernist to the same qualitative degree as James Joyce and Virginia Woolf, and yet the chronological framework establishes intriguing connections and comparisons between the evolutionary discourses evident in both O'Donnell and Joyce, or the materialist meanings of littoral spaces in both Woolf and Taylor. To different degrees also, and in different aesthetic modes, all the literary works discussed in this book share something of those adversarial, subversive and rejuvenative impulses which have been most persistently associated with modernism. If the archipelagic writings described here are not yet able to give a name or a shape to that new geography of identities, relations, and belongings which they anticipate, they are nonetheless consistent in deconstructing and exposing the crises and exhaustions of the old. They can thus be described as modernist on the same terms as Bradbury and McFarlane laid claim to the term, that 'it is the one art that responds to the scenario of our chaos'.[49]

The aesthetic and formal definition of modernism which gained currency in academic work of the postwar years emphasised, at least in some of its iterations, the autonomy of art from other spheres of knowledge and experience. Perhaps inadvertently, this definition generated the impression of an art which, for the sake of art, had to forsake science. This notion of modernism has not only compartmentalised it as an aesthetic phenomenon, but in cleaving off modernism from all other conceptions of society, ecology, and life, it deprived modernism of one of its most defining and sustaining characteristics, which was its transformative impulse. The impression is one which has been valuably and thoroughly undermined in the new modernist studies, a key focus of which has been to re-contextualise modernism as an art deeply immersed in, and informed by, contemporary scientific discourses. While modernist interest in the human sciences such as psychology, anthropology, and sociology has been recognised and analysed for some time, it is a more recent phenomenon to understand the extent to which modernist writers and artists were also preoccupied with a less anthropocentric science of the world. Oliver Botar and Isabel Wünsche make this case in particular in relation to biology and ecology: 'a closer examination of almost any genre of Modernist artistic and cultural production reveals an active interest in the categories of "life", the "organic", and even the destruction of the environment in modernity.'[50] Furthermore, they argue, 'many members of the various Modernist cultural movements were early adherents of the emergent environmental consciousness that permeated *fin de siècle* culture.'[51] In this book I set out to show that 'archipelagic modernism' is deeply concerned with understanding place and environment, and is richly engaged with life sciences as well as human sciences. This takes different forms, of course, for there is no single overarching scientific preoccupation which all modernist writers share, although much of what they do share might be captured in the term 'ecology'. As Timothy Morton has argued, 'Ecological thinking . . . isn't just to do with the sciences of ecology. Ecological thinking is to do with art, philosophy, literature, music, and culture . . . Ecology includes all the ways we imagine how we live together.'[52]

In the first chapter of this book, for example, I argue that the Atlantic islands which attracted the fascination of some of the key writers of the Celtic Revivals of the 1890s were not peripheral to the sciences of metropolitan modernity. Islands such as Aran, Iona, or Innisfree were synoptic models, whether historical or utopian, of the ecologies of human life. For J. M. Synge, for instance, his interests in the Aran islands as a society which operates according to alternative moral values from those of London or Paris were keyed to liberal Darwinist debates about the origins of morality and human compassion for others. The archipelagic periphery was in fact central to the contest between competing political ideologies about the social legacies of evolutionary theories. The 'Celticism' of the revival writers, which I argue might even include Thomas Hardy, seems less interested in racial discourses when put in such contexts than it is motivated by a concern for how human beings co-exist with each other in a shared environment, and by an anxiety about the transformative effects of a centralised, metropolitan society.

In chapter two, we turn from the lure of the western islands to James Joyce's preoccupation with the sea which forms the natural centre of the archipelago, the Irish Sea. The chapter charts a trajectory in Joyce's work from the hydrophasia of *Dubliners* to the headlong rush to embrace the sea with which *Finnegans Wake* concludes. Joyce's suspicion of the hermeneutics of maritime and littoral space is contextualised in relation to the developing coastal architecture and portal infrastructure of Dublin. A key focus for the chapter is to argue that although the sea and the coast have metaphorical functions in Joyce's work, they are also clearly intermeshed with the material histories and geographies of the port and the bay. Joyce uses tides and shifting sands as figures for Stephen's emotions, for example, in *A Portrait of the Artist as a Young Man*, but Stephen's vision of the transformation of the bird-girl takes place upon an island engineered from tides and shifting sands in resolutely material fashion. Like Synge, Joyce's work can be shown to be recurrently preoccupied with islands and coastlines as generative sites, associated throughout his work with questions of evolution, species differentiation, and biological origins. A materialist reading of Stephen's walk along the sands of Sandymount Strand, and of Leopold Bloom's consumption of the shore as a spectacle and entertainment, allows us to consider the function of the bay in the modern city. There is more at stake in Joyce's depiction of the shoreline than the reputed modernist disdain for the vulgar seaside. As both *Ulysses* and *Finnegans Wake* show, Joyce is concerned with the sea and the shoreline as social constructions of a territorial imagination, which are also material sites of resistance to myths of territorial insularity.

Chapter three addresses the fraught question of why Virginia Woolf deploys inexactitude in her geographical settings. This would seem to set her at odds with the locational politics of ecology, which tends to privilege an awareness of local and bioregional distinctiveness. In *To the Lighthouse*, however, Woolf sets her characters on Skye, an island she did not visit until more than ten years after she published the novel, and which critics have identified as a thinly veiled representation of St Ives in Cornwall. *Between the Acts* is set in some vague location in 'the heart of England', far from the sea. This chapter argues that far from signs of a disinterest or vagueness about geography, or a rootless cosmopolitanism, in Woolf, her settings are a vital part of how she understands and conceptualises the uneven social and political geography of the British Isles. It begins by arguing that Woolf's depictions of weather and geography thematise inaccuracy and error, exploring the limits of meteorological and topographical sciences. Woolf explores these limits as tropes of a hidden, peripheral Britain, in which imperialist and nationalist narratives of belonging are exhausted. This is particularly acute in her account of Englishness in *Between the Acts*, as Woolf is preoccupied with images of a land receding back to nature, a place which needs to be re-imagined. Woolf has no utopian vision of what will constitute post-imperial Englishness, but her work is a vital clearing of the imaginative space necessary to begin that vision.

A critical mass of archipelagic writing is most clearly discernible in what Jed Esty has characterised as the 'insular turn' of late modernism, although while Esty means the contraction of the British state within its 'insular borders', Chapter four explores how writers such as W. H. Auden, Louis MacNeice, Hugh MacDiarmid, Peadar O'Donnell, and Michael McLaverty were concerned with a northern archipelago on the peripheries of Britain and Ireland.[53] There are obvious connections between some of these writers and the island preoccupations of the Celtic Revival. Racial and eugenics discourses continue to underpin some of their literary explorations of island identities, yet it is also in these writings that the evolutionary sciences which informed eugenics can also be seen to morph into more broadly ecological theories of human interdependence and biotic co-existence. In some cases, this takes the form of a calculated rejection of the Robinsonian myth of insular individualism, while in others, islands are waypoints for thinking about the future shape of an archipelago off the coast of a Europe at war. The myth that islands could be 'places apart' proves unsustainable, and instead a new understanding of archipelagic commutuality begins to emerge in the wake of a dissolving Empire, and a weakening Union.

The limits of this emergent archipelagic literature of the interwar period are obvious when we think about how its bonds and borders are constituted. Chapter five begins with the recognition of how seas, coasts, and islands are already invested with particularly gendered meanings, as well as those of race, class, sexuality, and nation. The chapter first examines how women's writing of the postwar period in particular engages with the gendered spaces of the archipelago, and proceeds to consider the ways in which Caribbean writing interrogates the politics of a postcolonial archipelagic relationship stretching across the Atlantic. It concludes by probing the gendered literary culture of Northern Ireland at the outbreak of the conflict in 1969. Northern Ireland is one of the most complex and contested spaces of the archipelago for a post-imperial and post-national imagination, and the conflict has frequently disturbed critics and commentators in Britain and Ireland for whom it appeared to be fatally atavistic and violently obsessed with anachronistic identities. Yet perhaps the peace process in Northern Ireland has come close to exposing the lie of polarised identities in the archipelago, and to necessitating new plural, devolved, and connective narratives of life on these islands.

During the period examined in this book, from 1890 to 1970, many writers from the Irish and British archipelago began to write as if the dominant narratives of political identity in these islands were already exhausted, and they sought to explore their peripheries – their seas, coastlines, and islands – for the cultural resources with which to re-imagine and re-calibrate their identities, cartographies, and ecologies. As will be clear from the chapter descriptions above, the methodology of this book is necessarily prone towards a series of essays. The archipelago is plural, diverse, and abounds in local particularities, and any pretence of a comprehensive narrative of its anglophone literatures of the twentieth century would be misguided. There is no overriding historical narrative of archipelagic literary attempts and achievements offered in this book, nor would it be possible to argue that its chapters form a sequential, teleological narrative leading towards a brighter vision of the future. We may be no closer now, as I write, to an archipelagic conception of relations and identities on these islands than at any time examined in the book. Yet the writings discussed in this book do constitute evidence of the historical awareness of crises in the political identities of the states, nations, and peoples settled in these islands, as they also constitute evidence of the historical awareness of crises in the relations between human society and its environmental contexts. The book is focused upon that small group of islands off the north-west coast of Europe, not because these islands constitute an exceptional case, an anomalous condition at odds with global trends, but because in their local variation of those global trends, they may prove a fruitful and instructive means of thinking about locality, interconnectedness, and ecology more broadly.

I began this introduction with Richard Jefferies's apocalyptic vision of the archipelago relapsed into barbarism, but *After London* is an exception in Jefferies's oeuvre, which more characteristically registers the diversity, richness, and wonder of the natural world around him, and seeks to champion a more harmonious co-existence of human life with other forms of ecology. Writing in 1883, Jefferies understood something of the necessity of a new politics of planetary ecology, and understood too how ecology is inseparable from questions of social organisation:

> This our earth this day produces sufficient for our existence. This our earth produces not only a sufficiency, but a superabundance, and pours a cornucopia of good things down upon us. Further it produces sufficient

for stores and granaries to be filled to the roof-tree for years ahead. I verily believe that the earth in one year produces enough food to last for thirty. Why, then, have we not enough? Why do people die of starvation, or lead a miserable existence on the verge of it? Why have millions upon millions to toil from morning to evening just to gain a mere crust of bread? Because of the absolute lack of organisation by which such labour should produce its effect, the absolute lack of distribution, the absolute lack even of the very idea that such things are possible. Nay, even to mention such things, to say they are possible, is criminal with many. Madness could hardly go further.[54]

We might quibble with Jefferies's calculations, or with his benevolent interpretation of the reasons for starvation and poverty on an earth with sufficient resources to avoid them, but we still live in a world in which his questions are our questions, and his connection of ecology and social organisation around issues of the distribution, labour, and ideology of food production on our planet remains as pertinent today as it was in Jefferies's lifetime. Jefferies struggled to find the vocabulary to articulate what was needed to remedy the shortcomings of his own society, and to articulate a new relationship between human beings and ecology; he used words like 'soul', 'prayer', and a language of pilgrimage to describe what he knew was a post-theological and post-anthropocentric vision of humans-in-nature. We share this struggle to acquire the necessary literacy to surpass the exhausted narratives of society and belonging which continue to bind us, but the 'archipelagic modernism' which I describe in this book is a series of literary writings which have gone before us on that quest.

NOTES

1. Richard Jefferies, *After London: Wild England*. Oxford: Oxford World's Classics, 1980, 36–7.
2. Ibid. 17.
3. Ibid. 26–7.
4. Ibid. 27.
5. Ibid. 39.
6. J. W. Mackail, *The Life of William Morris*, vol. 2. London: Longman, Green and Co., 1899, 144.
7. T. S. Eliot, *Collected Poems 1909–1962*. London: Faber, 1974, 51–76.
8. Michael Gardiner, *The Cultural Roots of British Devolution*. Edinburgh: Edinburgh University Press, 2004, 31–2.
9. Hugh MacDiarmid, *The Islands of Scotland*. London: Batsford, 1939, 8.
10. Lynette Roberts, 'Fifth of the Strata', *Collected Poems*, ed. Patrick McGuinness. Manchester: Carcanet, 2005, 17.

11. J. G. Ballard, *The Drowned World*. London: HarperCollins, 2008, 19.
12. Ibid. 43–4.
13. Eilís Ní Dhuibhne, *The Bray House*. Dublin: Attic, 1990, 22.
14. Ibid. 64–5.
15. Ibid. 40–1.
16. Ibid. 167–8.
17. Fredric Jameson, *Archaeologies of the Future: The Desire Called Utopia and Other Science Fictions*. London: Verso, 2007, xiii.
18. Ibid. xi.
19. Jefferies, *After London*, 25.
20. Tom Nairn, *After Britain: New Labour and the Return of Scotland*. London: Granta, 2000, 5–6.
21. Vernon Bogdanor, *Devolution in the United Kingdom*. Oxford: Oxford University Press, 2001, 266.
22. Ibid. 5.
23. Nairn, *After Britain*, 4.
24. Norman Davies, *The Isles: A History*. London: Macmillan, 2000, xl.
25. Andrew McNeillie, 'Editorial', *Archipelago*, 1 (Summer 2007), vii (vii–viii).
26. J. G. A. Pocock, 'British History: A Plea for a New Subject', *Journal of Modern History*, 47.4 (December 1975), 603 (601–21).
27. Ibid. 605.
28. John Kerrigan, *Archipelagic English: Literature, History, and Politics 1603–1707*. Oxford: Oxford University Press, 2008, 2.
29. Brendan Behan, *Brendan Behan's Island*. London: Corgi, 1965, 190.
30. Kerrigan, *Archipelagic English*, 60.
31. Simon Gikandi, *Maps of Englishness: Writing Identity in the Culture of Colonialism*. New York: Columbia University Press, 1996, 21.
32. Kerrigan, *Archipelagic English*, 48.
33. Ibid. 48.
34. Allan Sekula, 'Between the Net and the Deep Blue Sea (Rethinking the Traffic in Photographs)', *October*, 102 (Autumn 2002), 3–34, and *The Forgotten Space: A Film Essay*, dir. Allan Sekula and Noël Burch. Amsterdam: Doc.Eye Film, 2010.
35. Hester Blum, 'The Prospect of Oceanic Studies', *PMLA*, 125.3 (May 2010), 671 (670–7).
36. Margaret Cohen, 'Literary Studies on the Terraqueous Globe', *PMLA*, 125.3 (May 2010), 658 (657–62).
37. Margaret Cohen and Carolyn Dever (eds), *The Literary Channel: The Inter-National Invention of the Novel*. Princeton: Princeton University Press, 2002, 2.
38. David Brett, *A Book Around the Irish Sea: History without Nations*. Dublin: Wordwell, 2009, 14.
39. Rudyard Kipling, *Kipling and the Sea: Voyages and Discoveries from North Atlantic to South Pacific*, ed. Andrew Lycett. London: I.B. Tauris, 2014, 218.
40. George Orwell, 'England Your England', *Inside the Whale and Other Essays*. London: Penguin, 1957, 69.

41. Virginia Woolf, 'The Docks of London', *The Essays of Virginia Woolf, Vol. 5: 1929–1932*, ed. Stuart N. Clarke. London: Hogarth, 2009, 275–82.

42. Robert Bridges, *The Shorter Poems*. London: George Bell, 1899, 24–5.

43. Virginia Woolf, 'Oxford Street Tide', *The Essays of Virginia Woolf, Vol. 5*, 283.

44. Nicholas Allen, *1916: Ireland, Empire and Rebellion*, forthcoming.

45. Peter Nolan, 'Imperial Archipelagos: China, Western Colonialism and the Law of the Sea', *New Left Review*, 80 (March/April 2013), 79 (77–95).

46. James Fisher, *Rockall*. London: Geoffrey Bles, 1956, 146–67.

47. Callum Roberts, *The Unnatural History of the Sea: The Past and Future of Humanity and Fishing*. London: Gaia, 2007.

48. Douglas Mao and Rebecca L. Walkowitz (eds), *Bad Modernisms*. Durham, NC: Duke University Press, 2006, 1–2.

49. Malcolm Bradbury and James McFarlane (eds), *Modernism: A Guide to European Literature 1890–1930*. London: Penguin, 1991, 27.

50. Oliver A. I. Botar and Isabel Wünsche (eds), *Biocentrism and Modernism*. Farnham, Surrey: Ashgate, 2011, 1.

51. Ibid. 2.

52. Timothy Morton, *The Ecological Thought*. Cambridge, MA: Harvard University Press, 2010, 4.

53. Jed Esty, *A Shrinking Island: Modernism and National Culture in England*. Princeton: Princeton University Press, 2004.

54. Richard Jefferies, *The Story of My Heart: My Autobiography*. Totnes, Devon: Green Books, 2002, 108–9.

1

Folk Revivals and Island Utopias

I will arise and go now, and go to Innisfree,
And a small cabin build there, of clay and wattles made;
Nine bean-rows will I have there, a hive for the honey-bee,
And live alone in the bee-loud glade.

And I shall have some peace there, for peace comes dropping slow,
Dropping from the veils of the morning to where the cricket sings;
There midnight's all a glimmer, and noon a purple glow,
And evening full of the linnet's wings.

I will arise and go now, for always night and day
I hear lake water lapping with low sounds by the shore;
While I stand on the roadway, or on pavements grey,
I hear it in the deep heart's core.

W. B. Yeats, 'The Lake Isle of Innisfree', 1893[1]

More than a century after it was first published, W. B. Yeats's 'The Lake Isle of Innisfree' became the poem from which to quote for politicians involved in the slow movement towards peace in Northern Ireland. An Taoiseach Albert Reynolds quoted from it in his speech in Washington on St Patrick's Day of 1994; David Trimble, the leader of the Ulster Unionist Party, used it in an article he wrote for the English newspaper *The Observer* on being awarded the Nobel Peace Prize with John Hume in 1998; An Taoiseach Bertie Ahern cited it in a speech in Sydney, Australia, in 2000; President Mary McAleese included it in her speech at the state banquet given in honour of the visit of Queen Elizabeth II to Dublin in 2011; and President Barack Obama had a line from it in his speech at the Waterfront Hall in Belfast in 2013. It is clear from these examples (and there are many more) that Yeats's poem travels well, that the poem is a kind of passport establishing the good credentials and intentions of the speaker, and accepted the world over. As Geraldine Higgins argues, 'Yeats has become the poet of choice for politicians seeking to engage in a type of literary shorthand.'[2] In these instances, Yeats's poem is clearly shorthand for many different, if related, meanings. It allows American presidents to suggest intimacy with Ireland, unionist politicians to evoke an idea of Irish Protestantism, Irish political leaders to call up the image of the national poet, and all of them to associate poetry with peace. In a place deeply divided by religion, culture, ethnicity, and nationality, of segregated lives and partitioned communities, 'peace' is inevitably a shorthand term for a political process in Northern Ireland which will take generations to result in an equitable, integrated society, and even then will be dependent upon how the political identities of the regions around it – England, Scotland, Ireland, Wales, Europe – evolve and change for a resolution of its own dilemma. But if 'The Lake Isle of Innisfree' is now eminently quotable as a model of peace and resolution, the history of its composition and publication reveals that the poem was instead born out of the fluid and dynamic interchange of plural identities which characterised the Irish and British Isles at the end of the nineteenth century.

In the first draft of 'The Lake Isle of Innisfree' in December 1888, there was no third verse, and no reference to the 'pavements grey' upon which the poem was first conceived.[3] As Yeats records in *Autobiographies*, the poem came from a 'sudden remembrance' of lake water inspired when 'walking through Fleet Street very homesick', and 'I heard a little tinkle of water and saw a fountain in a shop-window which balanced a little ball upon its jet'.[4] In the first published version of the poem in 1890, the allusion to 'pavements grey' place the speaker in this urban setting, a bare, dull 'here' to set against the imagined peace, freedom, and fulfilment of a future 'there'. The poem captures the sense of longing, the homesickness, the idyll of an island sanctuary, but it still shortchanges the reader about the flaneuresque encounter with the metropolitan spectacle, the Fleet Street stimulus which gave impetus to the poet's memory and desire. Yet it is, in one sense, a London poem, its speaker always 'on the roadway, or on pavements grey', its Thoreauvian vision of primitive perfection conceived as an imaginative space of retreat from the sounds and sights of the city. London, as a panoply of sensations and stimuli, found celebratory expression in the works of many of Yeats's Rhymers' Club associates, in Arthur Symons's *London Nights* (1895), John Davidson's *Fleet Street Eclogues* (1893), and Ernest Rhys's *A London Rose* (1894). Yeats penned no Baudelairean paeans to city streets or music halls, yet the movement between London and Sligo, physically and imaginatively, as it is embodied in 'The Lake Isle of Innisfree', was deeply formative of the aesthetic vision and cultural programme his work came to exemplify. With Symons, Lionel Johnson, and Ernest Dowson, he inhaled with the London air the influence of Walter Pater, Matthew Arnold, and the French symbolists, but as Louis MacNeice argued in his wartime study of Yeats's poetry, 'Most of the poets of the Nineties lost themselves in the sands. Yeats escaped because he harnessed the aesthetic doctrine to a force outside itself which he found in his own country.'[5]

'Innisfree' can often be reduced in readings of this poem to equate simply with Ireland, or biographically with Yeats's childhood home in Sligo, and, although it is the name of a small island on Lough Gill which Yeats visited as a child, undoubtedly the evocation of 'freedom' in its anglicised form gives the place-name a symbolic significance it does not have in Gaelic (Inis Fraoigh, meaning Island of Heather). The poem famously begins with a phrase from the Bible ('I will arise and go to my father', Luke 15: 18), and ends with a phrase from Shakespeare ('Give me that man / That is not passion's slave, and I will wear him / In my heart's core', *Hamlet*, III.ii.69–71). In between, Yeats conjures a sense of island life as ancient and primitive, in words associated with simple, rural living such as 'cabin', 'wattles', and 'glade', and in the natural sense of temporal rhythm in the second verse, where the allusions to dawn, 'noon', 'evening', and 'midnight', and the telling of the time by the lights and sounds of nature, place the poet far from the trading hours and railway time-tables of late Victorian London. The mythical time, or ancient time, coded into the poem, and deepened by the images associated with the lifestyle of a hermit, gives the sense of, but without making reference to, the legends connected with the island, legends of a 'buried city' beneath Lough Gill, for instance, and that two lovers had died in ancient times from eating the fruit grown on the island, which was known to be fit only for deities.[6]

'The Lake Isle of Innisfree' is Yeats's classic expression of belonging to a mythical, rural Ireland, borne in his 'deep heart's core' while in 'exile' in the drab streets of London. George Bornstein argued that this reading of the poem was carefully implied by the poet himself in the manner in which he placed the poem strategically in *Poems* (1895), suggesting to the reader a 'fictive Yeats', 'as an Irish poet devoted to tradition and rural Ireland, to leg-endary heroes and to the peasantry, and to esoteric pursuit of ideal Beauty'.[7] As Peter McDonald has shown in his more thorough survey, however, the early publication history of the poem reveals multiple and contending versions of the poet and his meanings. The poem was first published in 1890 in the *National Observer*, W. E. Henley's Scottish Unionist and pro-Empire journal to which Yeats contributed regularly, and in which, as McDonald writes, readers might have understood the poem, published alongside 'ultra-Tory' jibes about feckless Irish peasantry, as 'a judiciously "literary" celebration of the West of Ireland uneasily entangled in an otherwise hostile "political" portrayal of its destitution'.[8] In its appearance two years later in *The Book of the Rhymers' Club* (1892), the poem exemplified the manifesto commitments and the 'purist imperatives of a young group opposed to the English poetic establishment', tying Yeats's allegiances to a new English poetic avant-garde.[9] The poem was 'an expression of its author's racial origins', and more generally of 'the Celtic strain', in Elizabeth and William Sharp's *Lyra Celtica: An Anthology of Representative Celtic Poetry* (1896), published by the Scottish nationalist and pan-Celticist Patrick Geddes, which linked Yeats to ancient and modern Scottish, Welsh, Irish, Cornish, Breton, and Manx poets across a Celtic archipelago.[10] At the turn of the century, arguably as Yeats's own interests in Celticism were waning in favour of a national agenda, 'The Lake Isle of Innisfree' was again anthologised, in *A Treasury of Irish Poetry in the English Tongue* (1900), edited by Stopford A. Brooke and T. W. Rolleston, in which, as McDonald argues, Yeats was presented as the development of a distinctively Irish tradition in the English language, which was 'spiritual' and 'mystic', but at the same time 'reassuringly topographical'.[11]

It is clear from McDonald's essay not only that the publishing history of the poem in the 1890s legitimises many different readings, which may or may not be the intended consequences of the poet's strategic manoeuvres in the contemporary literary scene, but also that the poem's eventual iconic status in the Irish literary revival and beyond is only one of several positions with which the poem could be identified across the British and Irish archipelago. The point is not just that poems foster multiple and divergent readings, but that there is at work in the 1890s a political and cultural dynamic within which the same poem can be read as Irish, Celtic, and English, as 'West British' sentimentalism and emergent political nationalism, almost simultaneously. 'The Lake Isle of Innisfree' is an exemplary expression of longing for solitary life upon an idealised island, a figure which, as Jonathan Allison observes, recurs through Yeats's writings as a figure of desire for communion with landscape, but within protective, insulating boundaries.[12] The publication and circulation of the poem, however, tells a different story, one of overlapping and interconnecting contexts, in which no tradition or identification could be insulated from others, in which a poem embedded in the particular placelore of an island barely large enough to support nine bean-rows gestured outwards, to an emergent aestheticist avant-garde in London, to Thoreau in the woods of Massachusetts, and to the Atlantic shores of the Celtic fringe.

BOHEMIA IN THE ARCHIPELAGO

London is full of people who keep the country in their hearts, and the
life of studios, taverns, and newspaper offices is lived by many who
would scorn the name of a Londoner. One thinks himself a Devon man,
another is a Scot, another, though he works in London all the year, calls
the Lake Mountains home. It is so now; it has been so ever since the
green fields drew away from London, and made town and country two
hostile, different things.

> Arthur Ransome, *Bohemia in London*, 1907[13]

'The Lake Isle of Innisfree' is, of course, a metropolitan fancy, as much a toy of
the urban imagination as the shop-window fountain which inspired Yeats to
write the poem. It reverses, in fact, George Moore's pun that in Yeats, 'Sligo
turned into Fleet Street'.[14] Yeats might have longed for Sligo on Fleet Street,
but Fleet Street was the magnet of anglophone literary traffic in the 1890s. It
was thronged with writers working, or looking to work, for the national newspapers and journals, or meeting with editors, publishers, and printers located
there, or socialising in the public houses, clubs, and cafes which constituted
part of a bohemian London. For Richard Jefferies, it was 'the cerebellum of
the world', 'the thoughts of our time issue thence, like the radiating spokes of
a wheel, to all places of the earth'.[15] It was a street which was thronged too
with literary associations, as Arthur Ransome described, with the ghosts of
Lamb, Chaucer, Johnson, Richardson, Goldsmith, Shakespeare, Dickens, and
Ben Jonson discernible in 'a building here, an old doorway there, the name of
a side street'.[16] Through his father's artistic circle, Yeats was already well connected with writers and intellectuals in London when the Yeats family took
up residence in Bedford Park, a West London suburb, in 1887. Newly built
on the edge of London, Bedford Park would have symbolised all too clearly
the voracity of urban expansion, and the disappearance of rural cultures and
lore beneath bricks and slate. Against Yeats's homesick protest that London
could 'give me nothing', however, Roy Foster's biography has established the
importance of the friendships and influences Yeats found in London to his
emergence as a major writer.[17] Daniel Williams has also argued that London
was crucial to the formation of a pan-Celtic cultural movement in the 1890s,
and rightly criticises Irish Studies scholars for habitually equating 'Celtic' with
'Irish' in discussions of the period.[18] Yeats was drawn to the greater sense
of the 'Celtic', partly in racial terms, but also in more expansive terms as a
utopian discourse in opposition to the values he associated with the metropolis
and with Anglocentricity. He later characterised this period as dominated by
the tragic fall of Parnell, and the abeyance of the political movement for Irish

Home Rule, but as Foster shows, Parnell registers little in Yeats's writings of the time: 'his idea of a heroic leader was William Morris'.[19] The same note of disdain for the 'pavements grey' of the metropolis marks the opening of Morris's *News from Nowhere* (1891), with its glimpse of the 'vapour-bath of hurried and discontented humanity' on a 'stinking railway carriage', before it imagines a twenty-first-century utopia based on agrarian and communal values.[20] Innisfree is arguably Yeats's contemporaneous version of Morris's vision of harmony with nature, and creative labour, albeit a peculiarly solipsistic and hermetic one. Morris and Oscar Wilde were unacknowledged mentors to the emerging visionary poet of the Celtic Revival. Volumes of Morris's work adorned his bookcases, and he shared much of Morris's socialist critique of Victorian materialism; from Wilde, he learned the art of self-invention.

Yeats's invention of himself as the architect of the Irish literary revival evolved through the 1890s, but it depended throughout upon an experimental engagement with the wider cultural geographies of the archipelago. The Rhymers' Club which he founded with the Welsh poet and editor Ernest Rhys in May 1890 was renowned for its 'Celtic tone'.[21] There was a strong contingent of Irish contributors, including Yeats, T. W. Rolleston, and John Todhunter, as well as Rhys, a pioneer in modern 'self-consciously Anglo-Welsh literature',[22] and Scottish poet John Davidson, although Davidson did not consent to join the Rhymers in print. Even the English poets who joined the Rhymers' Club tended to have strong Celtic connections or affinities. Ernest Dowson was drawn to Breton culture; Arthur Symons had been born in Wales, of Cornish parentage; Lionel Johnson, although born in Kent, was heralded by Yeats as an Irish poet because of his Sligo ancestry. The Rhymers' Club met in the London pub 'Ye Old Cheshire Cheese', off Fleet Street, for beef pie, ale, wine, pipe-smoking, poetry readings and discussion. They were occasionally joined by Wilde, and also by Edward Garnett, later to become one of the foremost editors of the modernist fiction of Conrad, Ford, and Lawrence. Yeats, Dowson, and Davidson were probably the best poets among the club's members, although the club would become renowned more for its legacy in championing lyrical ballads, and as a Decadent prototype of avant-garde modernism, than for its own individual or collective achievements.[23] Ezra Pound moved to London to find the Yeats of the 'Cheshire Cheese'; T. S. Eliot's *The Waste Land* was partly influenced by Davidson's 'Thirty Bob a Week'.[24]

Yeats and Rhys collaborated first when Rhys, as editor of the 'Camelot' book series for a Newcastle publisher, Walter Scott, commissioned Yeats to compile his *Fairy and Folk Tales of the Irish Peasantry* (1888). Although Yeats published an edited collection of poems, *Poems and Ballads of Young Ireland* (1888), in the same year, and had already published two verse dramas, his Camelot book was arguably his first notable contribution to the Irish literary revival. Rhys published Yeats's volume to follow his own edition of Malory's *History of King Arthur*, as well as such volumes as an edition of Thoreau's *Walden*, Shelley's letters, Swift's essays, and Gilbert White's *Natural History of Selborne*, introduced by Richard Jefferies. Rhys's introduction to the series, which was published as a preface to his edition of Malory, set out its core principles as a determination to lay before the popular reader the best prose in the English language, to show the history of prose in English as one of perpetual assimilation, and, in the spirit of Caxton, to make such editions available for 'street and field'.[25] Malory's text was chosen as the most influential English-language version of Arthurian legend, evidently, but Rhys affirmed its origins in Welsh bardic myth, and saw an important dimension of the series as highlighting the roots of English prose in local folk traditions:

> The story of our prose is indeed most picturesque, full of folk-interest and local colour, as well as of wider historical suggestion. To read it aright we must go back farther even than the monk at his manuscript desk, – to the first life-springs of action, to the battle-field and the castle hall and the cottage hearth, where, on the very edge of adventure, men felt the stirring of that mental appetite which made them call for tale and song.[26]

Rhys's version of the history of English prose was oriented towards its oral, expressive, and topographical roots; the increasing domination of English as a global language of commerce and empire was a deviation from a 'right' course which was sourced in local and folk arts. Yeats's edition of fairy and folk tales was clearly valued for returning to the folk roots of prose, for in the western villages, Yeats asserted, far from the cities, lay a form of existence in which the fairies were 'still extant, giving gifts to the kindly, and plaguing the surly'.[27] Yeats wrote of a distinction between the Celt and the English, and between the remotely rural peasant and the irredeemably urban citizen, and of affinities between the Irish and the Scottish fairy tale which were unmatched in English writing. The fairies in English literature were 'mortals beautifully masquerading', and 'romantic bubbles from Provence', the remnants of an altogether different racial imaginary from the unbroken visionary tradition of the Celt.[28] Yet just as Rhys was keen to trace English prose back to its folk roots, there are hints in Yeats's introduction of connections, vestiges of a common ground, in the allusion to the romance tradition as a cultural imposition from Provence, perhaps, and also in Yeats's distinction that 'even a newspaper man, if you entice him into a cemetery at midnight, will believe in phantoms, for every one is a visionary, if you scratch him deep enough. But the Celt is a visionary without scratching.'[29] Yeats is suggesting here, in the spirit of Matthew Arnold, that his work is a kind of Celtic scratching of the materialist surface of Anglo-Saxon England, and such is its place in a series named after a legend which recalls the Celtic history of the British peoples.

The Rhymers' Club, then, emerging from the friendship and collaboration of Yeats and Rhys, was founded upon work of (at least vaguely) pan-Celtic ambitions. The club is chiefly renowned now as London's emulation of Parisian bohemia, as a conduit for French symbolism to work its way through to Anglo-American modernism, and as a late flowering of aestheticism. Its Celtic 'tone' has been noted in the birthplaces or ancestry of its contributors: Arthur Symons observed how 'few of us, as a matter of fact, were Anglo-Saxon'.[30] It is also in the literary output of individual contributors that one can take seriously a way of reading the Rhymers' Club as a manifestation of what Grant Allen called 'The return wave of Celtic influence over Teutonic or Teutonised England'.[31] The two anthologies, or rather miscellanies, published by the Rhymers offer some evidence of 'Celtic' preoccupations, but as neither *The Book of the Rhymers' Club* (1892) nor *The Second Book of the Rhymers' Club* (1894) is anything other than a platform for publishing the early work of a loose group of very different and unevenly gifted poets, the evidence lies in individual contributions rather than in any discernible collective programme.[32] Yeats's contributions are almost all drawn from Irish themes and sources; Rhys wrote ballads upon Welsh myth and history; Victor Plarr wrote of 'the glamour of the Celt' in his poem 'To a Breton Beggar', while his 'Deer in Greenwich Park' finds Celtic echoes in the woods at night; Lionel Johnson's first outings as a poet are full of Celtic twilight, music, and dreams. In his study of the Rhymers, Norman Alford notes that the impact of the group was diminished by the tendency of the lesser talented poets to suggest 'a kind of literary heartiness', or 'roystering fraternalism', which was 'by no means characteristic of a Yeats, Dowson, Johnson, or Symons'.[33] Yeats himself acknowledged the unevenness of the books, regretting in particular the inclusion of 'the Trinity College men, Rolleston, Hillier, Todhunter and Greene', who wrote mostly imitations of mid-century English verse.[34] The gender imbalance was even more striking: no women were admitted to, or associated with, the Rhymers' Club or its two collective publications.

The most obvious connection between the more gifted Rhymers in relation to 'the Celtic renaissance' which many of them openly professed to support was in their poetic affinity for popular forms such as the ballad. This can be seen in particular in the Welsh ballads and songs which constitute the major portion of Rhys's poetic output in the 1890s, in the significant number of ballads and songs in Yeats's early poems in *Poems* (1895), and in Davidson's *Ballads and Songs* (1894) and *The Last Ballad* (1899). One reviewer of *The Book of the Rhymers' Club* inadvertently raises a moot point about the provenance of the ballad form when he praises Rhys's 'The Wedding of Pale Bronwen' as 'a really fine ballad in the old English manner, a form much overworked'.[35] A few years later, the English critic George Saintsbury argued that the ballad quatrain 'is perhaps the most definitely English – blood and bone, flesh and marrow – of all English metres. It comes the most naturally of all to an English tongue and an English ear.'[36] Yet, as Linda K. Hughes argues in an essay on Davidson's 'A Ballad in Blank Verse', the provenance of ballads had been contested throughout the nineteenth century, with a substantial claim for Scotland registered in Walter Scott's *Minstrelsy of the Scottish Border* (1802–3) and Irish poet William Allingham's *The Ballad Book* (1864).[37] Due weight was given to both traditions, and crossings between them, in Francis James Child's ten-volume edition of *The English and Scottish Popular Ballads* (1882–98). Yeats had already edited a volume which advertised an Irish national tradition of the ballad in *Poems and Ballads of Young Ireland* (1888), the title of which echoed the earlier work of Charles Gavan Duffy, a leading member of the Young Ireland rebellion of 1848, who laid claim to an indigenous ballad tradition in his collection *The Ballad Poetry of Ireland* (1846). Yeats's own ballads placed him in the role of folklorist, gathering and preserving folk beliefs and tales in popular verse form, much the same role he adopted in collecting folk tales in prose for his Camelot volume, and *The Celtic Twilight* (1893). These ballads are, according to Terence Brown, experiments in seeking 'a tonal register that can suggest rustic authenticity without condescension', and imaginative in their 'apparently unself-conscious, subtly modulated reverence for the aural implications of Irish place-names, with their Gaelic language origins'.[38] As Hughes argues in relation to Davidson, to use the ballad form in the late nine-teenth century was to announce an engagement with the ideological registers of prosody:

> The ballad . . . could uphold national literary tradition and greatness, or splinter it according to whether England or Scotland commanded its site of origins. The ballad could invoke the cadences of sacred hymns and thereby inspire reverence, or unleash the relentless speed of supernatural or romantic ballads unfolding deeds of lawless passion and violence.[39]

Davidson's ballads complicate, and perhaps sometimes even subvert, these registers of national affiliation, but what his ballads share with Rhys and Yeats is a commitment to the ballad form as a locally adaptable (and translatable) folk art.

Rhys's 'An Autobiography' expressed in simple, if miscegenetic, terms the translations and crossings which comprised his complicated sense of belonging:

> Wales England wed; so I was bred. 'Twas merry
>   London gave me breath.

I dreamt of love, and fame: I strove. But Ireland
    taught me love was best;
And Irish eyes, and London cries, and streams of
    Wales, may tell the rest.
What more than these I asked of Life, I am
    content to have from Death.[40]

In a more dialogic form, John Davidson's eclogue 'St George's Day' dramatises a tension between Anglocentric and archipelagic perspectives upon
the British Isles. While English characters celebrate a 'Merry England', of
Shakespeare, law and order, and empire, the Scottish character, Menzies,
objects that 'Cockney and Celt and Scot are here, / And Democrats and
"ans" and "ists" / In clubs and cliques and divers lists; / But now we have no
Englishmen'.[41] Unaccountably, Menzies suddenly joins in with the chorus of
approval for 'Merry England' at the end, despite his distaste for 'the hackneyed
brag / About the famous English flag'.[42] Davidson's poem acknowledges, by
its unexpected haste in resolving tension into chorus, that 'Englishness' and
empire were inadequate, although durable, terms of association, terms which
were elastic but which in their elasticity masked dissent and disunity. When
the poem's speakers mention Cromwell, Bruce, Wallace, and Parnell, it is
clear that the folk myths of St George and 'Merry England' cannot conceal
the pains of history, and this makes the seemingly patriotic closure of the
poem ironic. 'Englishness' was forced, in the forge of an unequal and rapidly
divergent union, to bear tensions beyond its capacity; or, to adapt Yeats's later
terms, it was the centre which could not hold.

'St George's Day' was another in Davidson's series of *Fleet Street Eclogues*, an
attempt to imagine the meanings of Englishness, and Britishness, in a London
which reverberated with 'Celtic' voices. The persistence and surprise of the
folk voice in bohemian London is recalled by Arthur Ransome in his memoir,
in which he describes the happy 'breaking through' of rural, folk culture into
the 'gloom or weariness or excitement' of London life, when a young female
model from Gloucestershire shares with him the verses of a song she learned
from her grandmother:

Oh, it's of a fair damsel in Londin did dwell;
Oh, for wit and for beauty her none could excel.
With her mistress and her master she servèd seven year,
And what followed after you quickly shall hear.[43]

The song is a version of 'The Crafty Farmer', which was collected by Child
in *The English and Scottish Popular Ballads*, and in which Child traces variants

in Scotland, Yorkshire, Cheshire, and Norfolk.[44] Ransome's surprise is all the more for expecting a young artist's model to know only 'modern jingles', and instead finding a folk song set in London, 'yet its melody carried the very breath of the country into the room'.[45] When she leaves his room, Ransome laments that 'the afternoon was foggy London once again, and Gloucestershire seemed distant as the Pole'. A. E. Housman depicted the same tension between the metropolis and rural folk culture in *A Shropshire Lad* (1896), with memories of Shropshire figured in the poem as 'sighing winds' which 'out of the west land blow'.[46] Edward Thomas recalls a similar moment of rural folk life recollected in 'The Ash Grove' (1916), in which the poet remembers the tranquillity of the place, but it is 'as if I heard a girl sing / The song of the Ash Grove', the Welsh folk song, 'and then in a crowd or in distance it were lost'.[47] The folk revival was, perhaps inevitably, shaped by such a marked sense of the disappearance of rural and regional cultures, a process accelerated, of course, by the very newspaper and print technologies associated with Fleet Street, as well as by the transfer of economic power from the industrial north of England to the financial south. Jose Harris argues that the late nineteenth century marked a decisive shift 'in the balance of social life away from the locality to the metropolis and the nation', and that a British state which had been characterised politically by its dependence upon 'intense and variegated local and provincial culture' became centralised around the dominance of London.[48] The result was a metropolitan bias which marked the shape of cultural life in the British and Irish Isles throughout the twentieth century, in which the 'regions' are habitually relegated to the role of subordinated others orbiting around the hegemony of south-east England.

In this context, alternative geographies of the Celtic margins or the primitive depths of the British Isles acquired a particular significance in the literary cultures which were based in London in the 1890s. Arthur Symons's short-lived magazine *The Savoy*, named after one of London's most famous hotels, drew heavily from the Celtic fringes for its contributors and its subjects. Symons alone contributed three separate essays on his travels in the West of Ireland,[49] and Yeats was – not surprisingly, given the close friendship then enjoyed between Yeats and Symons in their shared rooms at the Temple – the most frequent contributor apart from Symons. A similar point might be made about the literary geography of the 'New Woman' writers: George Egerton grew up in Dublin, Sarah Grand was born in Donaghadee to English parents, and Mona Caird was a Scottish novelist, although born on the Isle of Wight. William and Elizabeth Sharp's *Lyra Celtica* was perhaps the principal venture to give expression to what Scott Ashley has called the 'Atlantic *fin de siècle*', 'a Celtic Baedecker to the cultural nationalisms of a *fin de siècle* gathered around the coasts of the North Atlantic'.[50] Like Yeats in his essay 'The Celtic Element in Literature', William Sharp in his introduction to *Lyra Celtica* seeks to divest the discourse of 'Celticism' of some of its racial meaning, and to champion instead 'the nationality of the brain', and thereby to trace the currents of Celtic literary history in Keats, Milton, perhaps even Shakespeare:

> The truth is, that just as in Scotland we may come upon a type which is unmistakably national without being either Anglo-Saxon or Celtic or Anglo-Celtic, but which, rightly or wrongly, we take to be Pictish (and possibly a survival of an older race still), throughout our whole country, and in Sussex and Hampshire, as well as in Connemara or Argyll, we may at any moment encounter the Celtic brain in the Anglo-Saxon flesh.[51]

Yeats in his essay would substitute the word 'primitive' for Arnold's argument that whatever was melancholic and magical in English literature derived from Celtic inspiration, but it was clear that Yeats believed that the primitive could be found most readily in the British Isles at its western extremities, along the shorelines of the Celtic remnants of Europe.[52] There it was, Yeats argued, 'among known woods and seas', that such primitive legends 'may well give the opening century its most memorable symbols'.[53]

Ironically, Yeats seemed to lose interest in the potential of pan-Celticism to generate the defining symbols of the twentieth century at precisely the point at which the Celtic archipelago might appear to have taken some cultural and political shape. In August 1901, Dublin hosted the first Pan-Celtic Congress, a meeting of representatives from organisations from Ireland, Brittany, Scotland, Wales, and the Isle of Man which was designed to show 'Celtic unity', and to address practical questions of development and revival. Much of the five-day congress was taken up with ceremonial and celebratory functions: an opening procession of delegates led by Druids, Bards, and officials in 'national costume', the laying of the Lia Cineil (five stones which denoted the Celtic nations), concerts of music and dancing, and exhibitions of Celtic artefacts and symbols.[54] There were also practical questions to address – 'Should a direct line of steamers be established between Ireland and Brittany?', 'How can Celtic art-forms be applied to modern native industries?', and 'In what directions should folk-lore researches be chiefly made in the immediate future?' – and proposals for adoption at the congress – 'That bi-lingual education, being the key to all linguistic attainments, should be made general in every Celtic country' and, less importantly, perhaps, 'That the heather be adopted as the symbolic flower of the Celtic Race'.[55] Cornish claims for admission to the rank of 'Celtic nation' were discussed, but deferred, and lively debate followed in the pages of *Celtia*, the journal of the Pan-Celtic Association. The Dublin congress, which was followed by one in Caernarfon (1904) and one in Edinburgh (1907), sought to imagine and realise a community of Celtic nations stretching from the Highlands of Scotland, down through Ireland, Man, and Wales around the Irish Sea, and stretching past Cornwall to Brittany. The congress, it could be argued, was the culmination of a decade and more of literary and cultural experimentation with an alternative geography of Europe's Celtic fringes, a geography which explicitly ran counter to the dominant Anglocentric perspective on the British Isles. Organised by the physicist E. E. Fournier, who also edited *Celtia*, and patronised by Lord Castletown, the Dublin congress was supported financially by some of the leading names in the cultural revivals of the Celtic nations, including Lady Gregory, Ernest Rhys, Patrick Pearse, Horace Plunkett, Patrick Geddes, and T. W. Rolleston. Yeats's contributions to the congress show a degree of reservation: he participated in discussions of language revival and national costume, and advertised the work of the Irish Literary Society and the newly formed Irish Literary Theatre, but his comments indicate that he saw himself speaking for Irish movements which could be examples to other Celtic nations. None of his comments indicate enthusiasm for pan-Celticism as a viable movement in itself. As Kaori Nagai has argued, the congress was easily ridiculed for its 'portentous ceremonies', it was boycotted by the Gaelic League, and its patron, Lord Castletown, as a soldier and conservative politician, represented the British establishment to many nationalists in Ireland.[56] Yeats had already, perhaps, foreseen that nation was to be the primary vehicle for folk revival, not the vague racial union represented in the strange costumes and sword-wielding Druids of the Pan-Celtic Congress.[57] In Roy Foster's words, 'the Celtic Revival became the Gaelic Revival, and was rapidly politicized'.[58] The Pan-Celtic Association was also ambivalent about literature in English: an editorial in March 1901 argued that 'Celtic literature must be in a Celtic language', and although Yeats's name was included among the 'brilliant and goodly company' of writers of the 'Celtic Note', with Sharp, Macleod, Munro, Russell, and Hopper, their work was too easily 'annexed' by Fleet Street journalists as '*English* literature', in the views of the editor.[59] But it was precisely the capacity of the metropolis to annex and absorb, to overwrite the historical and cultural specificity of its neighbours, which Yeats's commitment to a Celtic literature in English, so famously exemplified by 'The Lake Isle of Innisfree', had sought to contest.

ON A WET ROCK IN THE ATLANTIC

One does not enough reflect on how strange it is that an ancient race should continue down to our day, and almost under our eyes, in some islands and peninsulas of the West, its own life, more and more diverted

from it, it is true, by the noise from without, but still faithful to its language, its memories, its ideals and its genius. We are especially apt to
forget that this small race, contracted now to the extreme confines of
Europe, in the midst of those rocks and mountains where its enemies
have driven it, is in possession of a literature, which in the Middle Ages
exerted an immense influence, changed the current of European imagination, and imposed upon almost the whole of Christianity its poetical
motifs.

William Sharp, 'Introduction', *Lyra Celtica* (1896)[60]

London was the intellectual hub of the Celtic Revival; Dublin was to be, in
Lady Gregory's words, 'the Mecca of the Celt';[61] but it was to the western
margins of Ireland and Scotland, and the Atlantic fringes of Brittany, that
revival writers turned to connect with what they saw as the last surviving
remnants of an ancient Celtic culture which could be the source of a new art
and a new vision. Yeats visited the Aran islands for the first time in August
1896 with Arthur Symons, Edward Martyn, and George Moore. On the boat
out to the islands, he was reading Fiona Macleod's *The Washer of the Ford*.[62] He
was yet to learn that Macleod was the pseudonym of William Sharp, a pseudonym which was not simply a deception, but a complex adoption of another
personality, gender, and style.[63] Yeats would shortly champion her work as
exemplary of the Celtic literary movement, not just for its mythic and spiritual
subjects from the fractal coastlines of western Scotland, but for its 'absolute
absorption' in the lives and beliefs of Celtic peasants:

> It seemed to me that Miss Macleod had not, like the rest of us, taken a
> peasant legend and made it the symbol of some personal phantasy, but
> that she felt about the world, and the creatures of its winds and waters,
> emotions that were of one kind with the emotions of these grave peas-
> ants, the most purely Celtic peasants in Ireland, and that she had become
> their voice, not from any mere observation of their ways, but out of an
> absolute identity of nature.[64]

In this review, which appeared in *The Sketch* in April 1897, Yeats describes
having put Macleod's Hebridean tales to 'a hard test' by talking with the fishermen of the Aran islands of the legends contained in her book. What con-
vinces him of their veracity and their power is the uncanny correspondence
between Macleod's retelling of legends of talking seals, and men descended
from seals, and the beliefs and legends of the fishermen. Yeats's excitement
is palpable: Macleod's tales are set in a 'land tortured by the sea, scourged
by the sea-wind. A myriad lochs, fjords, inlets, passages serrate its broken
frontiers.'[65] Yeats had only to look up from his book as they left the coast of

Connemara to see such a landscape. 'The Washer of the Ford', the title story
of the volume, is exemplary of the Celtic spiritualism which Yeats celebrated
in legends of Oisin and Cuchulainn. 'Muime Chriosd', the story of St Bride
of the Isles, who is transported magically from Iona to Bethlehem to nurse the
infant Jesus, would have resonated with Yeats's passion for Blake's *Milton*, and
its idea of a spiritual resurrection of Jerusalem in 'England's green and pleasant
land', although evidently relocated to the Western Isles.

For Yeats, the dream of a 'Celtic Mystical Order', which would 'unite the
radical truths of Christianity to those of a more ancient world', became an
essential and far-reaching project.[66] Through a ritualistic order, which would
train an intellectual cadre in visionary and supernatural arts, Ireland would
be the first country to transform. William Halloran has shown that Yeats's
admiration for Fiona Macleod's work fuelled his commitment in the 1890s
that this should be a *Celtic* revival, and not just Irish, and thus he invited
Macleod's participation.[67] Yeats's plan for the order focused on yet another
utopian lake island, Castle Rock on Lough Key in Roscommon, 'a place of
great beauty', which he dreamed of making 'an Irish Eleusis or Samothrace'.[68]
Macleod's *The Washer of the Ford* drew its epigraphs from the writings of Yeats
and Geddes, twin patrons of the Celtic movement. In her preface, Macleod
alluded to an earlier manifestation of part of the legend of the 'washer of the
ford' in Samuel Ferguson's *Congal* (1872), in which the washerwoman is 'of
the Tuatha de Danaan line of Magi'.[69] In Macleod's version, however, the
washerwoman is both 'a terrible and sombre pagan goddess of death' and, as
Mary Magdalene, 'a symbolic figure in the new faith, foreshadowing spiritual
salvation and the mystery of resurrection'.[70] Halloran has charted how William
Sharp skilfully situated the work of his female alter ego to find favour with
Yeats, at the forefront of the Celtic Revival, so that for Yeats she became the
'woman who embodied the spirit of the surviving Celtic peoples on the shores
and off-shore islands of western Scotland'.[71] There is a danger, however, that
this approach reads Macleod's writings simply as deception and manipulation.
Macleod's work fitted Yeats's scheme for a Celtic Revival more completely
than any other he had encountered: more than Davidson, Geddes, or Sharp
himself, more than Rhys, or Dowson, or Johnson. Macleod's tales and poems
revealed an intimacy of myth, history, and landscape between the Gaels of
western Scotland and those of western Ireland, an intimacy which could be
explained for Yeats partly in racial terms, and partly (and increasingly towards
the end of the decade) in terms of primitivism and the survival in Christian
practices of Celtic pagan forms.

What Yeats celebrates most clearly in 'The Celtic Element in Literature',
which Halloran shows had contained high praise for Macleod in its 1897
redaction, was the love and worship of nature, which for Yeats is not the same

as Arnold's association of Celtic literature with 'natural magic'.[72] For Yeats, prevalent in all Celtic folk song and folk belief was 'the ancient worship of Nature', and 'that certainty of all beautiful places being haunted'. Macleod had written in her 'Prologue' to *The Washer of the Ford* of this intimacy with nature, of 'Man in subservient union with the life of nature',[73] and her stories abound with figures of such union in the 'wild places' of the Highlands and Islands, of seals conversing with men, birds brought into the chorus of a mass by the holy man of Iona, and a harper who plays 'what the wind sang, and the grass whispered, and the tree murmured, and the sea muttered or cried hollowly in the dark'.[74] She wrote of a relative who 'saw, in South Uist, less than twenty-five years ago, what may have been the last sun-sacrifice in Scotland', and that in the language of the islanders 'we breathe the air of that early day when the mind of man was attuned to a beautiful piety which was wrought into nature itself'.[75] Sharp's masquerade as Fiona made it easy for fellow travellers of pan-Celticism in later years to dismiss her work, as Ernest Rhys did, as 'romantic camouflage', as the work of a 'literary chameleon',[76] but no such retrospective denials of her talent could contest the esteem in which Yeats publicly valued her work as exemplary of the Celtic movement. Before Synge and Lady Gregory took her place, Fiona Macleod represented to Yeats the very spirit and style of what a Celtic Revival could be, and in their correspondence they affirmed with revolutionary fervour the sense of impending changes: 'we shall pioneer a wonderful marvellous new life for humanity,' wrote Macleod to Yeats on his return from Aran.[77]

It was Macleod's example, perhaps, which led Yeats to advise the young John Millington Synge, 'Go to the Aran Islands. Live there as if you were one of the people themselves; express a life that has never found expression.'[78] There are many reasons why critics doubt the credibility of Yeats's claim (although Yeats defended that he had published this account of their meeting in Synge's lifetime), and doubt the significance of the advice for Synge, who had already become well acquainted with the Gaelic language, and with antiquarian studies of Celtic cultures, and whose uncle had lived in Aran as a Church of Ireland missionary. It is perhaps clear that Yeats meant his accounts of his advice to Synge to be understood as prophetic of the uses to which Synge would put his five visits to Aran, of the transformation, as Greene and Stephens put it, of 'a man of ostensibly mediocre talent, a complete failure, in fact, into a writer of genius'.[79] Yeats's account invited scepticism not least because it was hardly credible in December 1896 to depict the Aran islands as a virgin territory which had 'never found expression'. As W. J. McCormack writes, 'there was a substantial body of prose (and factual) literature about Aran', including William Stokes's biography of George Petrie, with which Synge was very familiar.[80] The Aran islands became the site of intense popular and scholarly interest, in relation to language, culture, archaeology, literature, folklore, ethnology, economics, and politics.[81] Far from having 'never found expression', the islands arguably became the most over-signified, symbolically loaded location in Ireland, and perhaps even the British Isles.

Yeats records telling Synge, 'Give up Paris. You will never create anything by reading Racine, and Arthur Symons will always be a better critic of French literature,' before he advised him to go to Aran.[82] Yeats gave this now famous advice to Synge in December 1896, in the same month as Arthur Symons published his account of the islands in *The Savoy*.[83] As Declan Kiberd has suggested, Symons's text should be regarded as the unacknowledged model for Synge's book.[84] Symons saw the islands as if they were 'some strange, half-mythical, almost real dream', which persisted in his mind as the memory of having been 'so far from civilisation, so much further out of the world than I had ever been before'.[85] The word 'primitive' recurs in Symons's text, as in Synge's, and just as Synge tries to fix a hold on Aran by comparing the islands to Scotland and 'the East', so too Symons draws comparisons with Cornwall and 'the East'. Perhaps influenced by having Yeats alongside him, Symons writes that 'Since I have seen Aran and Sligo, I have never wondered that the Irish peasant still sees fairies about his path, that the boundaries of what we call the real, and of what is for us the unseen, are vague to him.'[86] Interestingly, Symons immediately links this blurring of boundaries to topography, to the mingling of 'land and sea and sky' on Aran's shores, but the effect on him anticipates the profound mystical impact the islands have on Synge: 'I have never believed less in the reality of the visible world, in the importance of all we are most serious about. One seems to wash off the dust of cities, the dust of beliefs, the dust of incredulities.' Symons was writing for the bohemian readers of *The Savoy*, and inviting the decadents of London to find their own remote, primitive islands from which to attack the metropolis. He published Joseph Conrad's first short story as a professional writer in *The Savoy* in the same year, after having read and admired *An Outcast of the Islands* (1896).[87]

The significance of Synge's *The Aran Islands* for the Celtic literary revival is readily apparent. Synge immersed himself over five summers, between 1898 and 1902, in the Gaelic-speaking culture of the islands he described as 'The Last Fortress of the Celt', and out of that experience came *The Aran Islands* (1907), which, according to Declan Kiberd, 'won a global audience for Gaelic lore by translating it into English'.[88] Synge's journey to Aran began in Paris, with his meeting of Yeats, perhaps, but also his reading books on Breton culture by Anatole Le Braz, Ernest Renan, and Pierre Loti.[89] In contrast to Le Braz, whose work he admired but found full of 'lingering regret', Synge saw in the primitivism of the islands their very excitement for revivalists: 'an Irishman of modern culture' who visits Aran, he writes, would have to 'yield himself up' to 'the entrancing newness of the old'.[90] *The Aran Islands* was Synge's first major piece of work, and through it, in Synge's own estimation, he learned to write the 'talk of the people and their stories', which became the material of his dramatic achievements in plays such as *Riders to the Sea* (1904) and *The Playboy of the Western World* (1907).[91] When Yeats accepted the Nobel Prize for Literature in 1923, he famously invoked the figure of Synge's ghost to stand beside him and Lady Gregory, and compared Synge's importance to Ireland to Burns's reputation as the national poet of Scotland.[92] He also recalls the advice he gave to Synge to leave Paris and go to the Aran islands, a move which he credits as the basis for Synge's future work in 'seeking foundations for an Ireland that can only come into existence in a Europe that is still but a dream'.[93]

In truth, of course, although Synge habitually depicts himself as the remote outsider visiting a primitive outlier of civilisation, the Aran islands were the destination of choice for many cultural and linguistic pilgrims in the 1890s. In 1898, when Synge first arrived, he unknowingly shared the boat back to the mainland with Lady Gregory. Patrick Pearse had visited the islands for the first time that summer also, and Agnes O'Farrelly recorded her stay on Aran in the same year in her *Smaointe Ar Árainn* (*Thoughts on Aran*), which was published in 1902.[94] Naturalists such as Nathanial Colgan and Robert Lloyd Praeger also made field trips to the islands in the early 1890s. It is difficult to determine exactly why the Aran islands became such a magnet for writers, linguists, folklorists, botanists, and anthropologists, but it is not accidental that these pilgrims gravitated towards the islands in the 1890s.[95] The islands were opening up to the connective technologies of modernity in the years before Synge's visit. Telegraph cables were laid to the island in 1892. The Connemara Railway was completed in 1895, connecting Galway to Oughterard and Clifden, and promised greater access to the railway for the Aran fishing and seaweed trade.[96] The Congested Districts Board, established in 1891 by Chief Secretary for Ireland Arthur J. Balfour, funded several transportation and communications schemes in the 1890s with the aim of connecting the Aran islands to centres of trade and industry, including the very steamship services Synge uses to travel to and from the islands.[97] The idea was even mooted in the *Freeman's Journal* in 1889 that, should Galway's harbour be improved sufficiently to make it a major transatlantic port, the Aran islands would provide a perfect location for 'mounting batteries of heavy ordinance on the commanding heights covering all the channels of approach', a sort of 'Guns of Navarone' of the Atlantic.[98] In an article published in 1912, James Joyce figured the islands in precisely such terms, not as primitive outliers, but as waypoints on an Atlantic highway.[99] Nicholas Allen argues that such a vision of the Aran islands as already globalised, as a 'node' in an 'unfinished circuit' of global communication, is evident in Synge's references to newspapers, yellowback novels, letters, and other forms of textual exchange, references which signal 'imaginative connections to other cultures – connections that depend on the very trade and contact that made English dominant'.[100] The poverty of the islands was indisputable, but the 'primitivism' of the islands is the product of the modernist imagination. The islands had been struck by famines several times in the late 1880s and early 1890s, reminders of the physical hardships of island life, but even these events brought the islands into the purview of modernity, with frequent appeals in Dublin and London newspapers for disaster relief. Far from being remote and unknown, therefore, the islands figured in public representations – nationalist, imperialist, and other discourses too – as both strategically important, and an object of concern and welfare. The islands became iconic of linguistic, cultural, and racial purity at the same time as new forms of connection and new patterns of travel made it clear that they were bound by trade, migration, and industry to coastal confederations which bore little relation to the conventional allegiances of nation, race, or religion.[101] As both Nicholas Grene and David Fitzpatrick have recently shown, Synge habitually conceals or obscures the extent to which the places he visits have been changed, or modernised, by new technologies, by new forms of transport, and by increased access to commercial goods, but there is no doubt that Synge's travels and travel writings were made possible by such changes.[102]

Not one of Yeats's biographers enquires in detail, or even speculates, as to what inspired Yeats to visit the Aran islands, or what significance the islands held for him. As Tony Roche shows, in all the accounts Yeats gave of his advice to Synge, he gave no reasons for his visit to Aran but that he was 'pursuing research for a book'.[103] He had planned to go to Tory island for 'local colour for a new story' in July of 1896.[104] With Macleod's work in his hand, he was undoubtedly reminded of the idea that islands were repositories of folklore and superstition, and, supposedly isolated from the ravages of modernity, might have preserved currency with ancient myths which had been long forgotten elsewhere. Synge would also have known from Irish language specialists of the significance the Aran islands had for language revivalists, who venerated the islands as a sort of linguistic ark from which a new Gaelic civilisation could emerge. But Yeats's recollections of the visit to Aran associate the island with neither the fairies nor the fada, but with an alternative morality. Yeats recalled the story that when he and Symons arrived on Aran, an old islander assured them that 'if any gentleman has done a crime we'll hide him. There was a gentleman that killed his father, and I had him in my own house six months till he got away to America.'[105]

Synge tells a similar story at greater length in his book, about 'a Connaught man who killed his father with the blow of a spade when he was in a passion, and then fled to this island and threw himself at the mercy of some of the natives'. The islanders then hid him when the police came searching, and resisted the temptation of a reward, until the man could be shipped off to America. Synge then explains that this is not the consequence of a rebellious streak in the islands, but rather an 'impulse' which is 'universal in the west', and is associated directly to 'the primitive feeling of these people': 'If a man has killed his father, and is already sick and broken with remorse, they can see no reason why he should be dragged away and killed by the law.'[106] The story is famously the basis for Synge's *The Playboy of the Western World*, but it shares currency with a more widespread association of the islands with an alternative morality. It should also be noted that 'remorse' is a central aspect of how William Morris's utopian society functions without law and without police: 'In a society where there is no punishment to evade, no law to triumph over, remorse will certainly follow transgression.'[107] Anthropological work by Alfred Cort Haddon and Charles Browne on the Aran islands in 1892 found similar accounts of the role of remorse in the relationship between islanders and the law:

> If any case deserved punishment [the magistrate] would say to the defendant, speaking in Irish, 'I must transport you to Galway jail for a month'. The defendant would beg hard not to be transported to Galway, promising good behaviour in future. If, however, his worship thought the case serious, he would draw his committal warrant, hand it to the defendant, who would, without the intervention of police or any one else, take the warrant, travel at his own expense to Galway, and deliver himself up, warrant in hand, at the county jail.[108]

Haddon and Browne sourced this story in Oliver Burke's account of the islands (1887), but it was also recounted in Emily Lawless's novel *Grania: The Story of an Island* (1891), which was set on Inishmaan.[109] Indeed, Lawless's novel makes a case for literary representations of Aran in terms which are interestingly close to Yeats's words to Synge, when she describes an old island peasant, old Durane, who had

> hidden away in the recesses of that old brain of his a whole phantasmagoria of recollections, beliefs, prejudices, traditions; bits of a bygone feudal world, with all its habits and customs; bits of a hardly more remote and forgotten legendary world; the world of the primitive Celt . . . [which had] never yet found expression in art.[110]

Was this, despite Yeats's critical view of Lawless as having 'an imperfect sympathy with the Celtic nature', also one of the sources of his advice to Synge to 'express a life that has never found expression'?[111] Symons recalls that on the crossing to Aran, 'we had time to read all that needed reading of *Grania*, Miss Emily Lawless's novel, which is supposed to be the classic of the islands'.[112] Was Yeats also reading *Grania* on the crossing? Synge's response to Lawless's novel was equally reticent: 'the real Aran spirit is not there,' he wrote. Lawless captured the 'pure and spiritual' side of the islanders, but not 'the healthy animal blood of a peasant', the 'delight in broad jests and deeds'. For a contrast to the 'lady' who 'does not appear to have lived here', Synge says, 'Compare the peasants of *Grania* with those of Fiona Macleod who I feel sure has a real deep knowledge.'[113] For Synge, as for Yeats, Macleod's tales of Hebridean peasants were a more truthful portrayal of life on the Aran islands than Lawless's *Grania*, which purports to be the story of Inishmaan. While both Yeats and Synge in their comments upon the novel snipe at the social status of its author, Gerardine Meaney has argued that a more cogent explanation of their antipathy lies in the fact that Grania, herself a model of 'linguistic purity and integrity of national character', is 'in many regards the antithesis of the degeneracy of those around her'.[114] Lawless's novel does not present the island in utopian terms; there is no spark of future redemption in the 'world of the primitive Celt' locked away in old Durane's head. Emblematic of the 'new woman', yet too of island wildness, Grania's fate is still sealed in the demise of the world around her. For Meaney, this makes the novel 'a startling, powerful, and still relevant exploration of the conflict between communal identity and feminine individuality'.[115] For Yeats and Synge, it was clearly a reason to mark the novel out as not sufficiently authentic to, or sympathetic with, 'Celtic nature'. Indeed, at just the time when Yeats may have learned of the forged identity of his ideal Celtic woman writer, Fiona Macleod, Lawless published an essay on 'literary forgery' in which she posed rather demanding questions of the Celtic movement, asking if the 'Celtic spirit . . . was not nearly as much a topographical as either a philological or an ethnological spirit? Certainly if "the breath of Celtic eloquence" is not also to some degree the breath of the Atlantic, I should be puzzled to define what it is.'[116]

Under the pretence of claims to authenticity, or degrees of sympathy, Yeats and Synge objected to Lawless's Aran islands because they were not sufficiently idyllic. That the alternative morality of the islands might be a useful basis for counter-cultural claims about an alternative, and revivable, Celtic civilisation was clearly an important part of Yeats's outlook. In this view, Yeats and Synge were supported by contemporary anthropological findings. Haddon and Browne observed that the Aran islanders are relatively free of 'idiocy', 'imbecility', 'insanity', and sexual 'irregularity', all of which were markers of racial health for physical anthropologists and eugenicists.[117] They draw upon other sources to inform their narrative regarding the relative lack of crime, and the absence of violence, although they are also sceptical of the appearance given by the islanders to the 'casual visitor' of being 'a kindly, courteous, and decidedly pleasing people'.[118]

Despite their scepticism, the islands depicted by Haddon and Browne exhibit the characteristics of a primitive and moral society. These are islands in which there are relatively few specialised trades, and the bulk of the male inhabitants are 'small farmers who do a little fishing'.[119] Synge's observations on the sociology of the islands are couched in terms which approximate to the agrarian idealism of Marx and Engels, emphasising the 'absence of any division of labour', the rhythm of labour closely allied to the seasons, and the aesthetic and emotional fulfilment of man's struggle with the elements to wrest from the land and the sea his daily needs.[120] Synge is describing a primitive society, of course, a society in which 'the claim of kinship' is 'more sacred than the claims of abstract truth', in which the law breeds violence and injustice because it is 'absurd' in relation to the 'natural' morality of the islanders.[121] It is more obvious in Synge's text than in Haddon and Browne's that the depiction of the 'natural' morality of a primitive society is an engagement with evolutionary arguments about the first emergence of morality.[122] This is made clearest in Synge's book when he discusses the sexualities of the islanders:

> The direct sexual instincts are not weak on the island, but they are so subordinated to the instincts of the family that they rarely lead to irregularity. The life here is still at an almost patriarchal stage, and the people are nearly as far from the romantic moods of love as they are from the impulsive life of the savage.[123]

This passage corresponds closely to the following passage in Haddon and Browne's essay:

> The men do not appear to have strong sexual passions, and any irregularity of conduct is excessively rare: only five cases of illegitimacy having been registered within the past ten years. There is no courtship or lovemaking, marriages being suddenly arranged for, mainly for unsentimental reasons.[124]

The key difference between the two accounts of island sexualities is that Synge is explicit in articulating the morality of the islanders as indicative of a distinct stage in human evolution, between the impulsive and the romantic, between savagery and modernity. This is to say that within evolutionary history, Synge equates the primitivism of island life with the first appearance of a life beyond animal impulse, with the first appearance of morality. Crucial to his depiction is what Garrigan Mattar sees as Synge's debt to Frazer's characterisation of 'primitive religion':

Synge's four-book narrative contains not one mention of the name of the Christian Saviour, nor of any Catholic saint. The divinity worshipped remains a vague and nameless one and (in keeping with the final trait Frazer outlined) there is no suggestion of any propitiatory rites being performed in his/her honour. The Catholic community described utters no prayer for the relief of their suffering from the elements, but rather to see their fate . . . as a fixed affair which no prayers can alleviate.[125]

The erasure of Christian religious practices from the life of the islanders in Synge's text may well be a consequence of Frazer's influence, but it also enables Synge to depict their moral virtues as inherent in primitive society. The superior morality of the islanders appears to be related directly to the primitive conditions of their existence. As Garrigan Mattar suggests, Synge is moulding an idea of the islands to suit his readings in anthropology, but it is not Frazer, one could argue, that is crucial here, but the influence of Spencer, Darwin, and, as McCormack suggests, a reaction against Nietzsche, in their various theories of the evolution of morality.[126]

Synge's text, like Haddon and Browne's essay, takes as its subject a group of islands already powerfully associated with a myth of primitivism, and an equally powerful myth of cultural and moral purity. The Aran islands are, in both texts, prelapsarian societies, remote from the corruptions of the mainland, and therefore ideal testing grounds of a philosophical theory of the nature of morality in a primitive culture. We might even read Synge's alternating image of the visibility and invisibility of the mist-bound islands on the opening page of his book as a figure of the mythical, vanishing island, of which Atlantis and Hy Brasil are the most prominent examples. It is not clear that Synge had read Haddon and Browne's study of the Aran islands. In his teenage years, however, Synge attended meetings of the Dublin Naturalists' Field Club, of which Haddon was a founding member, and he records notes from a lecture given by Haddon in December 1887 'on the supposed Atlantis or submerged continent which he proved never existed'.[127] From Synge's notes, which are brief and somewhat elliptical, it seems that Haddon extrapolated from scientific research of the flora and fauna of the Atlantic islands thought to be the likely locations of Atlantis, such as the Azores and Canaries, to show that the biological origins of life on these islands were European, and that the islands had not suffered from the catastrophic submergence or destruction that Atlantean myths supposed. The precise argument is unclear, but it is certain that Haddon was using the tools of natural science to dispel romantic myths of the island. Haddon was most likely responding, using the evidence of his own profession, to Ignatius Donnelly's *Atlantis: The Antediluvian World* (1882), which had purported to use scientific evidence to support the hypothesis that there had been a large island between Europe and America, and that it had been the first place upon which human beings had risen from barbarism into civilisation.[128] Donnelly was a lawyer and politician, not a scientist, and his book was not well received by academics. Hyde Clarke, discussing the legend of Atlantis in 1885, reminded his readers that both Charles Darwin and Alfred Wallace had already proved that, geologically and biologically, 'There is no evidence that such a continent ever did exist, nor is it even possible that it could.'[129] A review of Donnelly's book in *The American Naturalist* also indicated to readers that Edward Tylor's book *Anthropology* (1881) had already proved that the myth of Atlantis was impossible according to anthropological and ethnological research.[130] This is to say that Haddon's lecture was not doing anything especially novel with regard to the relationship between the mythology and the science of Atlantis, but it was very clearly placed in relation to contemporary discourses of cultural and moral evolution.

The most recent discussions of Atlantis had focused on questions of where and how human civilisation (and human morality) had first emerged, and indeed on questions of how to square evolutionary science with antediluvian myths of a moral society. Greta Jones has shown that in British culture of the 1880s and 1890s, there was 'a constant search for a scientific basis for moral and social obligation', including a search for the historical origins of morality.[131] It should be added that this preoccupation was evident in Irish culture too: T. W. Rolleston's *Parallel Paths* (1908) argues the case for a social basis for morality.[132] This was a particularly important strand within liberal social Darwinism, which had 'to demonstrate that rationality, even if it destroyed religious authority, was not subversive of morality and social order in general', that 'It was reasonable to be moral partly because it could be shown to be socially useful', and not just utilitarian.[133] As Jones suggests, this liberal interest in 'sociologising ethics' was a response to the adoption of Darwinism by advocates of individualism, who could argue that the intellectual creed of 'survival of the fittest' justified an economics and politics of aggressive self-interest. Patrick Geddes, at the forefront of the 'Celtic Renascence' in Scotland, and a pioneering biologist himself, supported a liberal social Darwinist outlook in his *The Evergreen: A Northern Seasonal*, the first issue of which contained an article which railed against the 'libel projected upon Nature' by the conservative individualist version of Darwinism, arguing that science had now 'shown how primordial, how organically imperative the social virtues are; how love, not egoism, is the motive which the final history of every species justifies'.[134]

In Irish responses to Darwinism, this question was particularly important in the work of Frances Power Cobbe, who objected to Darwin's treatment of morality chiefly on two grounds. The first was that Darwin's postulation that morality emerged instinctively under the conditions of the struggle for existence, under no external influence, meant that our moral sense was 'merely tentative and provisional, the provincial prejudice, as we may describe it, of this little world and its temporary inhabitants', and that, moreover, different races and different epochs would conceivably hold completely different senses of morality, depending upon their conditions of existence.[135] Cobbe also objected to Darwin's presumption that primitive humanity developed a clear sense of social feeling, which she found difficult to attribute to anything other than a religious doctrine such as Christianity:

> In what Island of the Blessed do people love all the way round their social circles, the mean and the vulgar, the disgusting, and the tiresome, not excepted? If such beings are entirely exceptional now, when the careful husbandry of Christianity has been employed for eighteen centuries in cultivating that virtue of mansuetude, of which the ancient world produced so limited a crop, how is it to be supposed that our hirsute and tusky progenitors of the Paleolithic or yet remoter age, were thoroughly imbued with such gentle sentiments?[136]

Cobbe was not objecting to Darwinism per se, and was not, despite the implied praise of Christianity's 'careful husbandry', raising religious objections to Darwinism. In fact, the Christian account of morality provides a very clear example of such an 'Island of the Blessed' in which human morality was at its most virtuous in the story of the Garden of Eden (an important dimension to Donnelly's account of Atlantis). Cobbe's objection to Darwin's account of the origins of morality, then, is that it is not evolutionary enough. One can see here what Thomas Duddy discusses as the paradoxical nature of Cobbe's arguments, and the reason why he characterises her work among those who 'compartmentalise' the clash between Darwinism and religious belief: Cobbe 'accepts Darwin's theory of evolution, yet criticizes it on moral grounds'.[137] But it is this anxiety about the unpalatable moral implications of Darwinism, and the attempt to negotiate a Darwinist history of human morality, which came to preoccupy much of the ethnographic interest in island and peripheral cultures in the 1890s.

Both Synge's text and Haddon and Browne's essay depict Aran as such an 'Island of the Blessed' as Cobbe dismisses. For Synge, the 'most primitive' society 'left in Europe' retains a sense of gentle nobility which belies the simplicity and poverty of its inhabitants.[138] Synge repeatedly figures the islanders as innocents, charming in their lack of self-consciousness, and their apparent freedom from the modern conventions of social and sexual morality. Differences between primitivism and modernity manifest themselves bodily, in the 'natural walk of man' when freed from 'the heavy boot of Europe', or the 'eyes and expression' which distinguish the people of Inishmaan from the more anxious look of their island and mainland neighbours, or the absence of conventionality among Aran women which paradoxically brings them closer to the 'liberal features' of the women of Paris and New York.[139] The passage quoted by many critics to indicate the affinities between Synge's text and ethnographic methods makes this visual association of the islanders with pre-modernity explicit:

> These strange men with their receding foreheads, high cheek-bones, and ungovernable eyes seem to represent some old type found on these few acres at the extreme border of Europe, where it is only in wild jests and laughter that they can express their loneliness and desolation.[140]

Synge appears to connect most closely with ethnographic discourse here in his reiteration of its association of distinctive facial and cranial features with a specific racial type made identifiable particularly through geographic isolation. Haddon and Browne's methods were more technically proficient, of course: they used a craniometer, a sliding rule first used in Francis Galton's anthropometrical laboratory, and index cards designed by John Beddoe.[141] Interestingly, however, their methods arrive at different conclusions about the physical characteristics of the islanders. Haddon and Browne find that in the 'typical' island man 'The forehead is broad, upright, and very rarely receding' and 'The cheek-bones are not prominent', and although, perhaps understandably, there is no indication of whether or not the eyes are 'ungovernable', they do find the eyes are 'rather small, close together' and 'marked at the outer corners by transverse wrinkles'.[142] The contradiction between the two accounts of the facial features of the islanders serves to illustrate the erroneous assumptions behind such ethnographic methods, of course. What they share, however, is the conviction that they are describing a racially definable type, distinctive to the Aran islands, and indicative of the geography of the islands and the history of their inhabitants.

Synge alluded to the science of craniometry, and its role in racial typology, in *The Playboy of the Western World*, when in Act III Jimmy asks Philly, 'Did you ever hear tell of the skulls they have in the city of Dublin, ranged out like blue jugs in a cabin of Connaught?' It is a sight he has not seen himself, but he has heard of it from a man returning through Dublin from harvesting work in England, who has described the display of skulls as 'making a show of the great people there was one time walking the world. White skulls and black skulls and yellow skulls, and some with full teeth and some haven't only but one.'[143] The implication of the scene is partly to mock the 'low' morals of Dubliners for making a spectacle of human remains (a point made more explicit in an earlier draft of the play),[144] but the discussion also centres upon a distinction between the 'great people' of the past, as evident from their skulls, and the suggestion that present inhabitants of the locality show physical signs of degeneration. At this point in the scene, Old Mahon directs their attention to his own 'skull', scarred by the blow of his son's spade, as an exceptional specimen. The scene demonstrates that 'skull-reading' as a measure of racial and physical characteristics is not confined to Dublin academics, but given that Haddon was particularly renowned for collecting and displaying skulls (some retrieved on his expeditions to western Ireland),[145] it is also possible to read this allusion to craniometry as corroborating evidence of Synge's awareness of Haddon's work.

Haddon and Browne were pioneering new methods of ethnographic field work, methods which Haddon would go on to make famous for the discipline of anthropology in his expedition to the Torres Straits in 1898.[146] The text of their essay on the Aran islands, however, jumbles together the pseudo-science of physical anthropometry with extensive quotations from a diverse range of antiquarian and historical sources to comment upon the sociological, psychological, linguistic, and folk history of the islanders. For Haddon and Browne, 'the ethnical characteristics of a people are to be found in their arts, habits, language, and beliefs as well as in their physical characters', yet access to a history of such characteristics is beyond the reach of a short anthropometric field trip.[147] The sources used by Haddon and Browne, which range from 1684 to 1892, and from the colonial racism of John Beddoe to the romantic nationalism of Samuel Ferguson, are a means of connecting the physical typology of the islanders to this wider sense of 'ethnical characteristics'. A lengthy quotation from John O'Flaherty identifies Aran as the 'Isle of Saints' of historical legend, with the people said to 'retain in language, habits and customs, beyond comparison, more of the primitive Celtic character than any of the contemporary tribes of that stock'.[148] Samuel Ferguson is quoted at length also to inform the sense of 'a very superior population – physically, morally, and even economically'.[149] O'Flaherty is cited again to testify to the 'simplicity' of the islanders in their religious and supernatural beliefs, and ample evidence is provided of the 'primitive' nature of the islanders' superstitions, which are at least partly understood to be a product of their isolation.[150] Had the chronology been reversed, Synge's book would have provided Haddon and Browne with a much richer and more contemporary source for their borrowed outline of the folklore and culture of the islands. Yet to speculate on a reversed chronology would be to miss the point that Synge's text comes in the wake of Haddon and Browne's call for further collecting of Aran folklore, which they write is 'fast disappearing from the folk, and . . . no time should be lost in recording the vanishing customs and beliefs of the old times'.[151] Indeed, Haddon made such a call also in a lecture he gave to the Belfast Naturalists' Field Club in January 1893, and in an article in *The Irish*

Naturalist in December 1893, which was an abbreviated version of the essay
he published with Browne.[152] Haddon was promoting Irish ethnographical
activity which would feed into the work of the ethnographical committee
of the British Association for the Advancement of Science, a committee of
which he was a leading member, and which was chaired by Francis Galton,
the founder of the field of eugenics. The committee was formed to plan and
co-ordinate an 'Ethnographical Survey of the British Isles', and it provided
participating members with forms for the collection of ethnographical data, as
well as a short handbook which gave detailed guidance on how to observe,
photograph, and interview subjects for the survey.[153] To speculate within the
bounds of chronology, then, might have us wonder what Synge might have
made of some of the topics and questions proposed for the budding ethnog-
rapher in the handbook which Haddon promoted in Ireland, topics such as
'Describe the customs of fishermen at launching their boats' and 'Explain the
popular belief in the object of each festival', and questions such as 'Are charms
used to find evil spirits and prevent their moving away?' and 'What superstitions are attached to the status of widowhood?'.[154]

Synge's *The Aran Islands* was not produced in response to such questions
(or at least to speculate so would go beyond any available evidence), but it
did clearly share the same ethnographical interests and categories of investigation as the survey Haddon was helping to organise. The committee divided
the work into five categories in particular – 'Physical types of the inhabitants,
Current traditions and beliefs, Peculiarities of dialect, Monuments and other
remains of ancient culture; and Historical evidence as to continuity of race' –
which are, to differing degrees, the subjects of both Synge's book and Haddon
and Browne's essay.[155] Synge's book is, of course, discernibly different in
its methodology at times from Haddon and Browne's, as many critics have
emphasised. It is clearly a more modernist work, as Garrigan Mattar argues, a
more autobiographical work in the way that Elaine Sisson describes,[156] and a
book which reflects Synge's emotional, intellectual, and sexual attraction to
the islanders, as Castle shows. But to distinguish it, as Castle does, as a work
of 'indigenous ethnography', situated within revival nationalism, compared
to the straightforward 'ethnography' of Haddon and Browne, the intention
of which is understood to be to 'serve colonial administrations and anthropological institutions in their efforts to regulate and stabilize colonial territories',
risks a misleading simplification of the role of ethnography in Ireland in the
1890s.[157] The Celtic Revival was steeped in ethnography, and in philosophical debates in the light of the work of Darwin, Wallace, and Spencer, as it was
in language, literature, or the arts. It owed as much to the Galapagos islands
as to the Aran islands. As Nicholas Whyte argues, studies of Irish culture have
been slow to recognise the significance of the history of science in Ireland to

literary and cultural debates, but recent scholarship on Irish science in the late nineteenth and early twentieth centuries, and a simultaneous re-contextualisation of the Revival period, have provided solid foundations for reviewing the close relationship between science and culture.[158]

The members of the Belfast Naturalists' Field Club, for example, who enthusiastically attended Haddon's lecture in 1893, and contributed for many years to Haddon's collection of information about Irish customs and beliefs, greeted Yeats's lecture on fairy tales and Hyde's lecture on Gaelic literature in the same year with equal fervour, and supported a programme of lectures and readings on Gaelic literature (with the programme published in Gaelic and English) in April 1894.[159] It was the Belfast Naturalists' Field Club, in fact, which fostered the formation of the Belfast branch of the Gaelic League in 1895. It is clear also that the Belfast Field Club maintained close links with the Dublin, Limerick, and Cork clubs, with which it shared similar programmes of lectures, classes, and excursions. In 1895, all four clubs, as associated societies of the Irish Field Club Union, held their annual conference in Galway, which included an excursion to the Aran islands. Haddon wrote the programme notes concerning ethnology for the excursion. As much as these Field Clubs promoted and participated in the work of an ethnographical survey, then (a survey organised by men such as Galton and Beddoe whose views were undoubtedly racist and linked to imperial authority), they were also involved in sponsoring and sustaining the growth of cultural nationalism in Ireland. Ethnography was not just a colonial discourse, nor was it incompatible with the aims and ideals of the various forms of nationalism taking shape in Ireland in the late nineteenth century and early twentieth.

As Greta Jones argues, by the 1890s the Aran islands had become 'the most important anthropological laboratory – as it were – available in Ireland and possibly Europe'.[160] Haddon began a project which he envisaged would encompass the whole of the British Isles in the Aran islands precisely because it was already invested with symbolic significance in contemporary discourses of race. But exactly the same argument could be made about the archipelagic preoccupations of Synge, Yeats, Macleod, and Geddes. In the cultural laboratories of Aran, or Iona, or Innisfree, such writers either found or invented models of alternative forms of living, alternative moralities, to cast against the values represented by the metropolis and the Empire. As Geddes wrote in a paper on Celtic art, 'it is not for London to educate Iona, but for Iona to educate London'.[161]

ON ENGLAND'S FOLKLORE REVIVAL

'Is not the evangel of folk-lore needed in England also?' asked Yeats in a review of Irish folk tales.[162] Yeats spent a good deal of his early career studying, collecting, and publishing folklore, and encouraging such work in others, most notably, as discussed above, Rhys, Sharp, Gregory, and Synge. The collection of folklore was not only a task oriented to preserving connections with historical cultures, but it was also a key source of inspiration for the poetry and drama of the Revival. In Yeats's distinction between Celtic, or primitive, and English cultures, this survival of remnants of the past in Celtic folklore was a key marker of difference. The question posed by Yeats reveals a curious blindness about the folk revival which had been taking place around him in England, however. Yeats can list the names of Douglas Hyde, Lady Wilde, Jeremiah Curtin, and William Larminie, among others, who were publishing collections of Irish folk tales and songs in the 1890s, but in his writings he shows little or no interest in a similar flourishing of English folk tales and lore. The Folk-Lore Society was founded in 1878 with the aim of preserving and publishing 'Popular Traditions, Legendary Ballads, Local Proverbial Sayings, Superstitions and Old Customs (British and foreign), and all subjects relating to them'.[163] From its inception, its journals – first *The Folk-Lore Record* (1878–82), then *The Folk-Lore Journal* (1883–9), and then *Folklore* (1890–) – published accounts and studies of various aspects of folklore in England, Ireland, Scotland, and Wales, and frequently too anthropological 'findings' from around the world. The corpus of folklore accumulated in the pages of *Notes and Queries* (1849–) should also be regarded, it has been argued, as 'a major source for English folklore studies', especially given 'the absence of any national folklore archive in England'.[164] From an anthology of such 'notes and queries' published in 1859, W. J. Thoms hoped the basis could be formed for 'a complete system of the ancient mythology of these islands'.[165] The publication of English folkloric tales and customs – such as fertility rituals, omens, pixies and fairies, wassailing, field names, cures, songs, and feasts – tended to be organised along county lines, even in books such as Northall's *English Folk-Rhymes* (1892), which appeared to be national. Antiquaries, garland books, and dialect books of the same period swell the volume of published material which gave expression to local English lore. Yeats certainly drew upon some of these scholarly and popular sources for his Irish fairy tales, but objected to the scientific discourse which accompanied them, specifically caricaturing such scientific folklorists as soulless: 'when he captures a folk-tale, nothing remains with him for all his trouble but a wretched lifeless thing with the down rubbed off and a pin thrust through its once-living body'.[166] 'What lover of Celtic lore', he asked, 'has not been filled with a sacred rage when he came upon some exquisite story, dear to him from childhood, written out in newspaper English and called science?'

Yeats failed to appreciate, however, the most imaginative and sympathetic engagement with folklore among his English contemporaries, in the novels of

Thomas Hardy. In commenting upon his friend Lionel Johnson's book about Thomas Hardy, the first critical study of Hardy's writings, Yeats professed his admiration of Johnson's gifts as a critic, but lamented that 'there is something wrong about praising Hardy in a style so much better than his own. I wish he had written instead of Dante or Milton.'[167] Yeats's recalcitrance towards Hardy, for whatever reasons, must have been strong, for he clearly failed to appreciate the implications of Johnson's argument that Hardy was essentially similar in his values and his 'gift of sight into the spirit of place' to any of the writers Yeats championed as part of the Celtic Revival.[168] Yeats memorably and publicly argued with Symons on this very point, when Symons advocated that writers should lead a nomadic life, against which Yeats declared 'that an artist worked best among his own folk and in the land of his fathers'.[169] Johnson celebrates Hardy's rootedness in the folklore of Wessex, in his sense of rustic religion as primitive and pagan veiled thinly by Christianity, in his understanding of landscape as 'filled with immemorial signs of age', and of place as haunted and palimpsestic. If this did not make Hardy sufficiently exemplary of the same values Yeats was espousing, Johnson also made clear the provincial directions and Celtic affinities of Hardy's work: 'There is one aspect of Mr Hardy's devotion to Wessex, upon which I must again touch: its example, in an English writer, of that spirit, which animates the *félibrige* of Provence, the Celtic gatherings of Brittany, the *Eisteddfod* of Wales.'[170]

Tess of the D'Urbervilles (1892) would certainly have brought such thoughts of Hardy's affinities to the Celtic Revival to the fore, not least for the climactic scene at Stonehenge in which Tess is encircled and captured. Hardy's novel abounds with ancient prophecies and superstitions which prove inescapable, and the 'heathen temple . . . Older than the centuries, older than the D'Urbervilles' is the culminating site of Tess's struggle to defy the curse placed upon her name.[171] Significantly, of course, she lies sleeping upon the sacrificial altar stone as the sun begins to rise between the solstitial pillars, and as dawn breaks the men hunting her for murder close in. The location allows Hardy to make the point, rather forcibly, that Tess is the sacrificial victim of the social conventions about women and class by which she is constantly defeated. In one sense, it is the 'fulfilment', as Hardy's section title has it, of a catalogue of personal and social injustices which seems to involve at every turn the clash of old folk rural ways and the brash materialism of the new. Tess is raped and left pregnant by Alec D'Urberville, son of the nouveau riche northern family who have usurped the ancient name of D'Urberville (of which Tess Durbeyfield is a true descendant) and built a shiny new house in 'one of the few remaining woodlands in England of undoubted primaeval date'.[172] In another sense, however, the 'fulfilment' scene also concludes a series of occurrences in which the primeval force of ancient myths is constantly shown to triumph. Such myths include those of witchcraft (Tess's mother insists upon the white magic of the *Compleat Fortune-Teller*, but keeps it outside the house for fear of black magic), pagan fertility rites (the May-Day dance and club-walking of chapter two), pagan beliefs in nature (Tess sings a paean of sun and moon worship, in Christian form, when she first walks down Froom Valley), ghosts (the legend of the D'Urbervilles' haunted coach and four), and the eerie presence of the past which haunts places such as Egdon Heath and The Chase (in both cases with suggestions of a 'Druidical' or 'British' prehistory).[173] Alec D'Urberville's insistence that Tess swear upon the 'Cross-in-hand', an old stone relic of various and uncertain myths of origin, reputed to be of 'ill-omen', combines several of these myths.[174] In the darkly primeval settings of The Chase (where Tess is raped) and Stonehenge (where she is captured during her final bid for escape), there is more than a suggestion that Tess's fate is determined not simply by property laws and social stigmas, but by savage gods and primitive forces more familiar from Celtic mythology than Marx's manifesto.

Ruth Firor's study of *Folkways in Thomas Hardy* (1931) provided an early and illuminating exploration of Hardy's rootedness in folklore, and his commitment to depicting the persistence of ancient beliefs and customs in an age abundant with invented traditions.[175] Firor shows that Hardy's novels do not simply collect and preserve folklore, as an anthropologist might, but rather they affirm the validity of folk wisdom and custom. In *Tess*, country superstitions invariably bear some truth, or come true: the butter churns only when Tess withdraws from the dairy, for example, and trouble does follow when the cock crows in the afternoon.[176] Yet Hardy also presents such superstition simply as a way of seeing the world, as when Tess looks into the mirror and remembers her mother's ballad of the 'mystic robe' in King Arthur's court that could tell if its wearer 'had once done amiss', wondering if her own robe would change colour and give her secret away.[177] The ballad is shown to maintain social conventions, or morals, and the superstition contained in it does not have to manifest itself in literal outcomes to have effect. Here, Hardy is showing the effective power of myth and superstition, even in a society undergoing a process of rapid modernisation. Hardy's peasants bear out the sentiment which Declan Kiberd has repeatedly associated with fairy lore in the West of Ireland, the story of the Connemara woman who, when asked by an American anthropologist if she believed in fairies, replied, 'I do not, sir, but they're there anyway.'[178] Andrew Radford has argued that Hardy's ironic portrayal of Angel Clare's idealism in *Tess* makes it 'impossible profoundly to entertain traditional mythological representation as a means of invigorating a late-Victorian milieu',[179] but his evidence for this consists of debunking Clare's predilection for idealising Tess in the names of Greek goddesses Artemis and Demeter, names 'which she did not like because she did not understand them'.[180] Hardy provides no names for the local deities, of whom Clare is unaware but Tess is ever watchful, but even the narrator defers to pagan tendencies at times:

> The sun, on account of the mist, had a curious, sentient, personal look, demanding the masculine pronoun for its adequate expression. His present aspect, coupled with the lack of all human forms in the scene, explained the old-time heliolatries in a moment. One could feel that a saner religion had never prevailed under the sky. The luminary was a golden-haired, beaming, mild-eyed, godlike creature, gazing down in vigour and intentness of youth upon an earth that was brimming with interest for him.[181]

There is scepticism and humour in Hardy's depiction of a sun-god, looking down upon 'his' earth on harvest day, of course, but it is not a depiction which dismisses or makes impossible the credibility of such pagan mythologies, or the survival of their force in modern times. As Julian Wolfreys argues, what cannot be dismissed easily from Hardy's narratives is the sense of 'an inhuman puissance' which provides 'both the potential for vision and the possibility of destruction'.[182]

Like Yeats, Synge, and Sharp, Hardy's interest in folklore emerged from the conflict between the residual persistence of old forms of cultural practice and the incursions of the new. Tess, in particular, is the focal point for this clash between the old and the new, and the survival of primitive myths in modern, rational society. She represents a new age, as Hardy contrasts her to her mother, Joan Durbeyfield:

> Between the mother, with her fast-perishing lumber of superstitions, folk-lore, dialect, and orally transmitted ballads, and the daughter, with her trained National teachings and Standard knowledge under an infinitely Revised Code, there was a gap of two hundred years as ordinarily understood. When they were together the Jacobean and the Victorian ages were juxtaposed.[183]

This feeling of proximity to the remote past is precisely what Synge sought in his encounters in the Aran islands, precisely what Yeats celebrated in the work of Fiona Macleod. In his obituary of the Dorset poet William Barnes, Hardy charted this transformation from primitivism to modernity in the scope of one man's life. His characterisation of Barnes begins with the poet as an old man who would trudge into Dorchester and set his old-fashioned watch by the public clock which told the newly appointed Greenwich Mean Time. Yet almost within the compass of Barnes's memory was the first time a stage coach came to the town nearest his birthplace, and within his lifetime, 'til quite recently', Hardy writes, there used to come to a little bridge, close to his father's door . . . a conjuror or 'white wizard', who cured afflicted persons by means of the toad-bag – a small piece of linen having a limb from a living toad sewn up inside, to be worn round the sufferer's neck and next his skin, the twitching movements of which limb gave, so it was said, 'a turn' to the blood of the wearer, and effected a radical change in his constitution.[184]

In *Tess*, the proximity of such practices and beliefs to a modern age defined by the spread of railways and the 'London time' which chimes from local town clocks suggests a model of culture which is heterogeneous and contestable. It is not that modernity has overcome folk mythologies, but rather that they might co-exist and contradict one another. The despotism of modern law may triumph in the spectre of the black flag which is the novel's only representation of Tess's execution at the end, but it is far from certain that Tess's fate has been determined by the judge whom Hardy sardonically characterises as 'President of the Immortals', and not the darker primeval forces which have haunted her throughout the novel. Hardy's novel belongs precisely to the folk tradition Yeats reveres in 'The Celtic Element in Literature' in its depiction of 'a world where anything might flow and change, and become any other thing; and among great gods whose passions were in the flaming sunset, and in the thunder and the thunder-shower'.[185] Just as Synge's characters fall foul of curses, or forgotten blessings, Tess's end can be traced to the accidental death of her family's horse, or the curse which seems to lie in her family name.

There are glimpses of possible salvation in the novel, if she could escape the conventionality of others and herself. Hardy conjures the image of a desert island as a utopian refuge from social conventions:

alone in a desert island would she have been wretched at what had happened to her? Not greatly. If she could have just been created, to discover herself as a spouseless mother, with no experience of life except as the parent of a nameless child, would the position have caused her to despair? No, she would have taken it calmly, and found pleasures therein. Most of the misery had been generated by her conventional aspect, and not by her innate sensations.[186]

The figure of the desert island comes shortly after Tess comes close to a feeling of liberation from the 'moral hobgoblins' of society in her twilight walk in the hills and dales around her home, when the narrator makes clear that Tess's perception of herself as a 'figure of Guilt intruding into the haunts of innocence' is based upon 'an accepted social law, but no law known to the environment in which she fancied herself such an anomaly'.[187] The desert island is a powerful figure in literatures in English, of course, in Stevenson's

Treasure Island (1883), Defoe's *Robinson Crusoe* (1719), or Shakespeare's *The Tempest* (1611). It serves to equate territorial integrity with human individuality or isolation, using natural boundaries as a trope of the human returned to nature, much as Yeats does with Innisfree. Hardy brings this trope into play much more widely than his solitary reference to the 'desert island' suggests, through figures of the homely and the anomalous, and through figures of the landscape as insulated in discrete regions by natural features. The 'bio-region', as Kirkpatrick Sale called it,[188] recurs in Hardy's novel whenever a significant natural boundary is crossed, such as his depiction of the 'Vale of Blakemore or Blackmoor':

> This fertile and sheltered tract of country, in which the fields are never brown and the springs never dry, is bounded on the south by the bold chalk ridge that embraces the prominences of Hambledon Hill, Bulbarrow, Nettlecombe-Tout, Dogbury, High-Stoy, and Bubb-Down. The traveller from the coast who, after plodding northward for a score of miles over calcareous downs and corn-lands, suddenly reaches the verge of one of these escarpments, is surprised and delighted to behold, extended like a map beneath him, a country differing absolutely from that which he has passed through. Behind him the hills are open, the sun blazes down upon fields so large as to give an unenclosed character to the landscape, the lanes are white, the hedges low and plashed, the atmosphere colourless. Here in the valley, the world seems to be constructed upon a smaller and more delicate scale; the hedges are mere paddocks, so reduced that from this height their hedgerows appear a network of dark green threads overspreading the paler green of the grass. The atmosphere beneath is languorous, and is so tinged with azure that what artists call the middle-distance partakes also of that hue, while the horizon beyond is of the deepest ultramarine. Arable lands are few and limited; with but slight exceptions the prospect is a broad rich mass of grass and trees, mantling minor hills and dales within the major. Such is the Vale of Blackmoor.[189]

The plot of *Tess* is resolved through a series of journeys which Tess undertakes across Wessex, each journey taking her across physical boundaries which mark more significant regional identities than county or national borders. In this, the first such passage of extended topographical description of many in the novel, even the narrative is premised upon the motion of a traveller across the terrain. In each distinct locality, Hardy identifies landscape with character, and prepares the reader for good or ill omen by relating Tess's feelings of being 'akin' or 'strange' to the landscape. Sale defines a bioregion as an ecological and political unit which is discernible from geological and natural features – mountain ranges, watersheds, or ecosystems – while also mapping on to the territorial homelands of indigenous communities. Islands are obvious exemplars of the bioregion, for according to R. J. Berry in his naturalist history of the British Isles 'The two defining traits of islands are "boundedness" and isolation', and by isolation Berry means both geographic and genetic isolation.[190] Hardy wrote about the 'Isle of Slingers', or Portland Isle, in *The Well-Beloved* (1897) in terms of its primitive isolation, but Hardy's vales resemble islands too. When Tess returns from Trantridge, for example, the narrator remarks upon the insularity of one vale from another, 'despite the amalgamating effects of a roundabout railway'.[191] Each vale is connected to others, and to the world beyond, by trade, migration, and transport, but although it is understood to be on the cusp of change, each is also understood to be 'shut in', or 'bounded': 'The Vale of Blackmoor was to her the world, and its inhabitants the races thereof.'[192]

Hardy's rural localities are as isolated and primitive as Synge's Aran: the railways (milk is traded by rail to London), the global migration of capital and labour (Angel's venture in Brazil), and national government (Tess's education) have all encroached to some degree, but not, it seems, any more deeply than Synge finds in the steamers, tourism, national school, and trade which were changing Aran. Richard Jefferies testified to this sentiment in his many writings on the southern counties of England: there was a 'primitive England' to be found, Jefferies argued, just a few hours outside its great cities, and even 'where the steam ploughing engine has left the mark of its wide wheels on the dust', there still 'old manners and customs linger'.[193] The 'frontier line to civilisation', as Jefferies termed it, was 'in this country yet', in his home country of North Wiltshire, in the Sussex Downs, as much as it might lie at the western edges of the British Isles, or further afield in the exoticised places of the Empire. In Hardy, in Jefferies, in William Barnes, in Sheila Kaye-Smith, and the work of many other English writers of the period who were 'rooted' in some provincial locality or other, there was as strong a recalcitrance towards the generalising tendencies of metropolitan and imperial discourses as anything in Yeats. Lionel Johnson, in celebrating Hardy's intimate use of Wessex dialect, argued that such recalcitrance grew out of reaction to the ways in which 'the barbarous and Gothic peasantry of England, in the north and west countries' had their share of the same 'horrified curiosity' which 'Our antiquarian ancestors' bestowed upon the 'wild Irish' and 'Highland savages'.[194] Against such metropolitan disdain, Johnson champions Hardy as a writer who 'shows how to write of provincial ways without provincialism'.[195]

In his comparison of Hardy and Yeats, Edward Alexander argued that 'Hardy was not a *fin de siècle* writer in the sense that Yeats was, because he could find no consolation for present evil in the prospect that the century's end would bring cataclysm and a new revelation'.[196] Yeats first stirred the fire of a Celtic revival, before committing to an Irish national revival which would have decisive consequences for the failed project of political union in the British Isles. The elegant simplicity of his own narratives of the gestation of the Irish state out of the first seeds of cultural revival may leave them open to challenge, but Yeats did write himself and his revival contemporaries into the mythology of the foundation of the Irish Free State in 1922. He took his place in its upper chamber as a senator, and continued to speak of the ways in which the state might give expression to its cultural distinctiveness. It might be said that he struggled to find viable literary nationalisms in Wales and Scotland in the 1890s on which to build the pan-Celtic alliance of his dreams, but the voices of Welsh and Scottish literary nationalism did emerge, partly spurred on by the success of the Irish example, in the work of Caradoc Evans, Saunders Lewis, Hugh MacDiarmid, and Lewis Grassic Gibbon. Yeats neither looked for, nor was able to recognise, comparable signs of cultural resistance among English writers. He revered Morris and Shelley, for example, and strangely lamented that they did not set their work upon Welsh or Scottish scenes, where 'their art would have entered more intimately, more micro-scopically, as it were, into our thought and given perhaps to modern poetry a breadth and stability like that of ancient poetry'.[197] The possibility that English settings might provide a basis for local or regional recalcitrance to Victorian materialism and the dreaded prospect of cultural homogeneity seems to have been unthinkable to Yeats. Yet, as Alexander argues, 'the nationalist passion that made Yeats deplore Irish subservience to English culture finds its analogue in Hardy's rootedness in Dorset'.[198] MacNeice was right to argue that one reason for Yeats's success was his attachment to the juggernaut of nationalism, yet the nation-state which his work helped to found proved to be far short of his ideal vision. It is the cultural geographies which Yeats dis-carded – the possibilities of a Celtic archipelago, the regional devolution of the England he loved to hate, a folk revival of local cultures which might have had political consequences for all regions of the Irish and British Isles – which seem in retrospect to demand more searching questions about the geopolitics of literature in the 1890s.

NOTES

1. W. B. Yeats, 'The Lake Isle of Innisfree', *Yeats's Poems*, ed. A. Norman Jeffares. Dublin: Gill and Macmillan, 1989, 74.
2. Geraldine Higgins, 'The Quotable Yeats: Modified in the Guts of the Living', *South Carolina Review*, 32.1 (Fall 1999), 184 (184–92).
3. R. F. Foster, *W. B. Yeats: A Life – I. The Apprentice Mage*. Oxford: Oxford University Press, 1997, 78–9.

4. W. B. Yeats, *Autobiographies*. Dublin: Gill and Macmillan, 1955, 153.
5. Louis MacNeice, *The Poetry of W. B. Yeats* [1941]. London: Faber, 1967, 45.
6. See W. G. Wood-Martin, *The Lake Dwellings of Ireland: Or Ancient Lacustrine Habitations of Erin, Commonly Called Crannogs*. Dublin: Hodges, Figgis and Co., 1886, 248–9, and *History of Sligo, County and Town, from the Earliest Ages to the Close of the Reign of Queen Elizabeth*. Dublin: Hodges, Figgis and Co., 1882, 63–4. Yeats certainly knew of Wood-Martin's 'county history', and retells the story of the lovers briefly as a possible inspiration for his dream of living on Innisfree in *Autobiographies*, 72.
7. George Bornstein, 'Remaking Himself: Yeats's Revisions of His Early Canon', *Text*, 5 (1991), 351 (339–58).
8. Peter McDonald, 'A Poem for All Seasons: Yeats, Meaning, and the Publishing History of "The Lake Isle of Innisfree" in the 1890s', *The Yearbook of English Studies*, 29 (1999), 229 (202–30).
9. Ibid. 229.
10. Ibid. 221.
11. Ibid. 227.
12. Jonathan Allison, 'W. B. Yeats, Space, and Cultural Nationalism', *ANQ*, 14.4 (Fall 2001), 55–67.
13. Arthur Ransome, *Bohemia in London*. New York: Dodd, Mead and Co., 1907, 83.
14. George Moore, *Hail and Farewell*, ed. Richard Cave. Gerrards Cross: Colin Smythe, 1976, 205.
15. Richard Jefferies, *Amaryllis at the Fair*. London: Sampson Low, Marston, Searle, and Rivington, 1887, 219.
16. Ransome, *Bohemia in London*, 156 (153–71).
17. Foster, *W. B. Yeats: A Life – I*, 81 (59–111).
18. Daniel G. Williams, *Ethnicity and Cultural Authority: From Arnold to Du Bois*. Edinburgh: Edinburgh University Press, 2006, 124, 153 (121–75).
19. Foster, *W. B. Yeats: A Life – I*, 59.
20. William Morris, *News from Nowhere*. Oxford: Oxford World's Classics, 2003, 3.
21. Daniel Rutenberg, 'A Study of Rhymers' Club Poetry'. Unpublished PhD dissertation, University of Florida, 1967, 20.
22. See J. Kimberley Roberts, *Ernest Rhys*. Writers of Wales Series. Cardiff: University of Wales Press, 1983.
23. Rutenberg, 'A Study of Rhymers' Club Poetry', 166–76.
24. See Peter Brooker, *Bohemia in London: The Social Scene of Early Modernism*. Basingstoke: Palgrave, 2004, 27–51.
25. Ernest Rhys (ed.), *Malory's History of King Arthur and the Quest of the Holy Grail*. London: Walter Scott, 1886, v–xxxv.
26. Ibid. xi.
27. W. B. Yeats (ed.), *Fairy and Folk Tales of the Irish Peasantry*. London: Walter Scott, 1888, ix.
28. Ibid. xvi.

29. Ibid. x.

30. Arthur Symons, 'Memoir', in *The Poems and Prose of Ernest Dowson*. New York: Modern Library, 1919, 3 (1–16).

31. Quoted in Holbrook Jackson, *The Eighteen Nineties: A Review of Art and Ideas at the Close of the Nineteenth Century*. London: Grant Richards, 1922, 147.

32. *The Book of the Rhymers' Club*. London: Elkin Mathews, 1892, and *The Second Book of the Rhymers' Club*. London: Elkin Mathews, 1894.

33. Norman Alford, *The Rhymers' Club*. Victoria, BC: Cormorant Press, 1980, 32.

34. Quoted in Alford, *The Rhymers' Club*, 41.

35. Quoted in Alford, *The Rhymers' Club*, 28.

36. George Saintsbury, *A History of English Prosody from the Twelfth Century to the Present Day, Vol. 1: From the Origins to Spenser*. London: Macmillan, 1906, 247.

37. Linda K. Hughes, 'Ironizing Prosody in John Davidson's "A Ballad in Blank Verse"', *Victorian Poetry*, 49.2 (Summer 2011), 161–78.

38. Terence Brown, *The Life of W. B. Yeats: A Critical Biography*. Dublin: Gill and Macmillan, 1999, 81.

39. Hughes, 'Ironizing Prosody', 165.

40. Ernest Rhys, 'An Autobiography', *A London Rose and Other Poems*. London: Elkin Mathews, 1894, 97.

41. John Davidson, *St George's Day: A Fleet Street Eclogue*. London: John Lane, 1895, 9.

42. Ibid. 14, 16.

43. Ransome, *Bohemia in London*, 95.

44. Francis James Child (ed.), *The English and Scottish Popular Ballads*, Part IX. Boston: Houghton, Mifflin and Co., 1894, 128–30.

45. Ransome, *Bohemia in London*, 97.

46. A. E. Housman, *A Shropshire Lad*. New York: John Lane, 1917, 55.

47. Edward Thomas, 'The Ash Grove', *The Annotated Collected Poems*, ed. Edna Longley. Tarset: Bloodaxe, 2008, 108.

48. Jose Harris, *Private Lives, Public Spirit: Britain 1870–1914*. London: Penguin, 1994, 19.

49. Arthur Symons, 'A Causerie: From a Castle in Ireland', *The Savoy*, 6 (October 1896), 93–5; 'In Sligo: Rosses Point and Glencar', *The Savoy*, 7 (November 1896), 55–61; 'The Isles of Aran', *The Savoy*, 8 (December 1896), 73–86.

50. Scott Ashley, 'Primitivism, Celticism and Morbidity in the Atlantic *fin de siècle*', in Patrick McGuinness (ed.), *Symbolism, Decadence and the Fin de Siècle: French and European Perspectives*. Exeter: University of Exeter Press, 2000, 177 (175–93).

51. William Sharp, 'Introduction', in Elizabeth Sharp and William Sharp (eds), *Lyra Celtica: An Anthology of Representative Celtic Poetry*. Edinburgh: Patrick Geddes, 1896, xxiv–xxv.

52. W. B. Yeats, 'The Celtic Element in Literature', *Essays and Introductions*. London: Macmillan, 1961, 173–88.

53. Ibid. 187.

54. *Celtia: A Pan-Celtic Monthly Magazine*, 1.9 (September 1901), 129–48.

55. *Celtia*, 1.8 (August 1901), 123.

56. Kaori Nagai, ""'Tis Optophone with Optophanes": Race, the Modern, and Irish Revivalism', in Len Platt (ed.), *Modernism and Race*. Cambridge: Cambridge University Press, 2011, 58–76.

57. It should also be noted that Yeats may have had more personal reasons for falling out of love with pan-Celticism: his relationships with contemporary Scottish writers in particular seem often fraught. He did not get on well with John Davidson after misattributing a bad review of *The Countess Cathleen* in 1892 to Davidson. See John Sloan, *John Davidson: First of the Moderns*. Oxford: Oxford University Press, 1995, viii. Foster charts Yeats's initial enthusiasm for William Sharp and his pseudonymous writings as Fiona Macleod, but by 1900 he had distanced himself from Sharp for his 'Celtic unionism', and Macleod after he learned of Sharp's deception, and his extensive plagiarism. See Foster, *W. B. Yeats: A Life – I*, 197, 237–8. Andrew Lang, whose books of fairy tales and folklore were admired by Yeats, wrote what Yeats described as a 'hardly civil' review of his first book (*Fairy and Folk Tales*) and a 'very uncivil' review of *The Book of the Rhymers' Club*. See *The Letters of W. B. Yeats*, ed. Allan Wade. London: Rupert Hart-Davis, 1954, 474.

58. R. F. Foster, *The Irish Story: Telling Tales and Making It Up in Ireland*. London: Penguin, 2001, 99.

59. *Celtia*, 1.3 (March 1901), 36.

60. Sharp, 'Introduction', *Lyra Celtica*, xlix.

61. James Pethica (ed.), *Lady Gregory's Diaries: 1892–1902*. Gerrards Cross: Colin Smythe, 1996, 153.

62. Fiona Macleod, *The Washer of the Ford, and Other Legendary Moralities*. Edinburgh: Patrick Geddes, 1896.

63. See William F. Halloran, 'W. B. Yeats, William Sharp, and Fiona Macleod: A Celtic Drama, 1887–1897', in Warwick Gould (ed.), *Yeats Annual No. 13*. Basingstoke: Palgrave, 1998, 62–109. See also Flavia Alaya, *William Sharp – 'Fiona Macleod': 1855–1905*. Cambridge, MA: Harvard University Press, 1970. Alaya makes a strong case for treating the work of Macleod and Sharp as a single oeuvre, and for recognising the merits of that work beyond the controversy of concealed identity.

64. W. B. Yeats, 'Miss Fiona Macleod', *Uncollected Prose, Vol. 2: Reviews, Articles and Other Miscellaneous Prose 1897–1939*, ed. John P. Frayne and Colton Johnson. London: Macmillan, 1975, 42–5.

65. Macleod, 'The Dark Nameless One', *The Washer of the Ford*, 131–2.

66. W. B. Yeats, *Memoirs*, ed. Denis Donoghue. London: Macmillan, 1972, 124.

67. William F. Halloran, 'W. B. Yeats, William Sharp, and Fiona Macleod: A Celtic Drama, 1897', in Warwick Gould (ed.), *Yeats Annual No. 14: Yeats and the Nineties – A Special Number*. Basingstoke: Palgrave, 2001, 159–208.

68. Yeats, *Memoirs*, 123.

69. Samuel Ferguson, *Congal: A Poem in Five Books*. Dublin: Edward Ponsonby, 1872, 57.

70. Macleod, 'Prologue', *The Washer of the Ford*, 10.

71. Halloran, 'W. B. Yeats, William Sharp, and Fiona Macleod', *Yeats Annual No. 13*, 63.

72. Yeats, 'The Celtic Element in Literature', 176; Halloran, 'W. B. Yeats, William Sharp, and Fiona Macleod', *Yeats Annual No. 14*, 198.

73. Macleod, 'Prologue', *The Washer of the Ford*, 13.

74. Macleod, *The Washer of the Ford*, 138, 153, 27.

75. Macleod, 'Prologue', *The Washer of the Ford*, 7–9.

76. Quoted in Alaya, *William Sharp – 'Fiona Macleod'*, 5–6.

77. Quoted in Halloran, 'W. B. Yeats, William Sharp, and Fiona Macleod', *Yeats Annual No. 13*, 85.

78. W. B. Yeats, 'Preface to the First Edition of *The Well of the Saints*', in J. M. Synge, *Collected Works, Vol. 3: Plays Book 1*, ed. Ann Saddlemyer. Gerrards Cross: Colin Smythe, 1982, 63.

79. David H. Greene and Edward M. Stephens, *J. M. Synge, 1871–1909*. New York: Collier, 1961, 83.

80. W. J. McCormack, *Fool of the Family: A Life of J. M. Synge*. London: Weidenfeld and Nicolson, 2000, 194.

81. Ríona Nic Congáil provides an excellent overview of the symbolic significance of the Aran islands for any writer visiting them in the summer of 1898 in the introduction to her edition of Agnes O'Farrelly's *Smaointe ar Árainn* (*Thoughts on Aran*). Dublin: Arlen House, 2010.

82. Yeats, 'Preface to the First Edition of *The Well of the Saints*', 63.

83. Symons, 'The Isles of Aran', 73–86.

84. Declan Kiberd, 'Synge, Symons, and the Isles of Aran', *Notes on Modern Irish Literature*, 1 (1989), 32 (32–9).

85. Symons, 'The Isles of Aran', 73.

86. Ibid. 79.

87. Karl Beckson, *Arthur Symons: A Life*. Oxford: Clarendon Press, 1987, 152.

88. Declan Kiberd, *Synge and the Irish Language*. Dublin: Gill and Macmillan, 1993, 31.

89. Greene and Stephens, *J. M. Synge, 1871–1909*, 73.

90. J. M. Synge, 'Anatole Le Braz', *Collected Works, Vol. 2: Prose*, ed. Alan Price. Gerrards Cross: Colin Smythe, 1982, 394.

91. Quoted in Kiberd, *Synge and the Irish Language*, 215.

92. Yeats, *Autobiographies*, 559–72.

93. Ibid. 554.

94. Agnes O'Farrelly, *Smaointe Ar Árainn* (*Thoughts on Aran*), ed. Ríona Nic Congáil. Dublin: Arlen House, 2010.

95. It is even more difficult to ascertain why the Aran islands have a longer and deeper appeal than is explained by technological developments, but Tim Robinson's fascinating meditation upon the history, culture, folklore,

topography, geology, and botany of the islands in the two volumes of *Stones of Aran* (1986, 1995) comes closest to providing such an explanation.

96. Tom Ferris, *Irish Railways: A New History*. Dublin: Gill and Macmillan, 2008, 148.
97. Fraser MacHaffie, 'Facilities for Transit: The Congested Districts Board and Steamship Services', *Irish Geography*, 28.2 (1995), 91–104.
98. 'The Connemara Railway', *Freeman's Journal*, 10 October 1889, 6.
99. James Joyce, 'The Mirage of the Fisherman of Aran', *James Joyce: The Critical Writings*, ed. Ellsworth Mason and Richard Ellmann. Ithaca, NY: Cornell University Press, 1989, 234–7.
100. Nicholas Allen, 'Synge, Reading, and Archipelago', in Brian Cliff and Nicholas Grene (eds), *Synge and Edwardian Ireland*. Oxford: Oxford University Press, 2012, 159–71.
101. John Kerrigan's influential analysis of archipelagic conceptions of seventeenth-century writing in the British and Irish Isles is a notable model of how we might re-think the cultural dynamics of the British-Irish archipelago beyond the terms of nation, race, or religion. See *Archipelagic English: Literature, History, and Politics 1603–1707*. Oxford: Oxford University Press, 2008, especially 1–90.
102. See J. M. Synge, *Travelling Ireland: Essays 1898–1908*, ed. Nicholas Grene. Dublin: Lilliput, 2009, xiii–xlix, and David Fitzpatrick, 'Synge and Modernity in *The Aran Islands*', in Brian Cliff and Nicholas Grene (eds), *Synge and Edwardian Ireland*. Oxford: Oxford University Press, 2012, 121–58.
103. Anthony Roche, 'Yeats, Synge, and an Emerging Irish Drama', *Yeats: An Annual of Critical and Textual Studies*, vol. 10. Ann Arbor: University of Michigan Press, 1992, 37 (32–55).
104. Foster, *W. B. Yeats: A Life – I*, 164, 167.
105. Yeats, 'J. M. Synge and the Ireland of his Time', *Essays and Introductions*, 338.
106. J. M. Synge, *The Aran Islands*. London: Penguin, 1992, 50.
107. Morris, *News from Nowhere*, 71.
108. A. C. Haddon and C. R. Browne, 'The Ethnography of the Aran Islands, County Galway', *Proceedings of the Royal Irish Academy (1889–1901)*, vol. 2 (1891–1893), 803 (768–830).
109. Oliver J. Burke, *The South Isles of Aran (County Galway)*. London: Kegan Paul, Trench and Co., 1887, 60; Emily Lawless, *Grania: The Story of an Island*. London: Macmillan, 1892, 214.
110. Lawless, *Grania*, 216–17.
111. W. B. Yeats, 'Irish National Literature, II: Contemporary Prose Writers', *Uncollected Prose, Vol. 1: First Reviews and Articles 1886–1896*, ed. John P. Frayne. New York: Columbia University Press, 1970, 369.
112. Symons, 'The Isles of Aran', 74.
113. Synge, *Collected Works, Vol. 2: Prose*, 102–3, n. 1.
114. Gerardine Meaney, 'Decadence, Degeneration and Revolting Aesthetics: The Fiction of Emily Lawless and Katherine Cecil Thurston', *Colby Quarterly*, 36.2 (June 2000), 165 (157–75).

115. Ibid. 168.
116. Emily Lawless, 'A Note on the Ethics of Literary Forgery', *The Nineteenth Century* (January 1897), 92 (84–95).
117. Haddon and Browne, 'The Ethnography of the Aran Islands', 798–800. Haddon and Browne's accounts of the relative absence of insanity, idiocy, and criminality among the Aran islanders should also be contextualised in relation to the widespread anxieties among the medical profession in Britain that Irish migrants had racially-inherited tendencies towards insanity, idiocy, and criminality.
118. Ibid. 800.
119. Ibid. 811.
120. Synge, *The Aran Islands*, 84. Such a vision of ancient, 'primitive' Ireland as an ideal, communal society was also important to James Connolly. See for example the opening paragraphs of Connolly's 1910 pamphlet on *Labour in Irish History*, and his 1915 pamphlet, *The Re-Conquest of Ireland*, although Connolly had articulated idyllic views of ancient Ireland under the Brehon laws as early as 1896. See also David Lloyd's discussion of Connolly's understanding of the persistence of a 'counter-cultural consciousness' of alternative forms of social organisation in 'Rethinking National Marxism: James Connolly and "Celtic Communism"', *Interventions*, 5.3 (2003), 345–70. Lloyd attributes Connolly's conception of the communism of ancient society to Engels's *Origin of the Family, Private Property, and the State* (351).
121. Synge, *The Aran Islands*, 51.
122. Synge's interest in this question of the origins of human morality can be traced in his notebooks. In the pages of a notebook he kept while a student at Trinity College Dublin, where he was a student between 1888 and 1892, he wrote, 'The first moral philosophy unconnected with religion was Esop's fables.' He also made extensive notes from John Locke's *An Essay Concerning Human Understanding*, a key work of liberal and empiricist thought, which offers a rational explanation for the existence of God, and the foundations of moral philosophy. See TCD MS 4371, 4373, and 4374.
123. Synge, *The Aran Islands*, 96.
124. Haddon and Browne, 'The Ethnography of the Aran Islands', 800.
125. Sinead Garrigan Mattar, *Primitivism, Science, and the Irish Revival*. Oxford: Oxford University Press, 2004, 159.
126. On Nietzsche's influence on Synge, see McCormack's cautionary suggestion, *Fool of the Family*, 203.
127. TCD MS 4370, 43v–45v.
128. Ignatius Donnelly, *Atlantis: The Antediluvian World*. New York: Harper and Brothers, 1882.
129. Hyde Clarke, 'Examination of the Legend of Atlantis in Reference to Protohistoric Communication with America', *Transactions of the Royal Historical Society*, 3 (1886), 16 (1–46).
130. 'Donnelly's Atlantis', *The American Naturalist*, 16.9 (September 1882), 729–31.

131. Greta Jones, *Social Darwinism and English Thought: The Interaction Between Biological and Social Theory*. Sussex: Harvester, 1980, 47.

132. T. W. Rolleston, *Parallel Paths: A Study in Biology, Ethics and Art*. London: Duckworth, 1908.

133. Jones, *Social Darwinism and English Thought*, 45.

134. 'Proem', *The Evergreen: A Northern Seasonal*, 1 (Spring 1895), 11. The contents assigns authorship of 'Proem' to W. Macdonald and J. Arthur Thomson, but interestingly Cairns Craig in *The Edinburgh Companion to Twentieth-Century Scottish Literature* seems to assign authorship to Patrick Geddes: see Craig, 'Arcades – The Turning of the Nineteenth Century', in Ian Brown and Alan Riach (eds), *The Edinburgh Companion to Twentieth-Century Scottish Literature*. Edinburgh: Edinburgh University Press, 2009, 22 (15–24). For a detailed appraisal of Geddes's creative endeavours in the Celtic Renascence in Edinburgh, see Megan C. Ferguson, 'Patrick Geddes and the Celtic Renascence in the 1890s'. Unpublished PhD thesis, University of Dundee, January 2011.

135. Frances Power Cobbe, *Darwinism in Morals and Other Essays*. London: Williams and Norgate, 1872, 10. For a thorough and sympathetic account of Cobbe's interventions in moral and theological debates, see Sandra J. Peacock, *The Theological and Ethical Writings of Frances Power Cobbe, 1822–1904*. Lewiston, NY: Edwin Mellen Press, 2002.

136. Ibid. 21–2.

137. Thomas Duddy, 'The Irish Response to Darwinism', in Juliana Adelman and Éadaoin Agnew (eds), *Science and Technology in Nineteenth-Century Ireland*. Dublin: Four Courts Press, 2011, 30 (18–31).

138. Synge, *The Aran Islands*, 10.

139. Ibid. 21, 69, 95.

140. Ibid. 93.

141. Haddon and Browne, 'The Ethnography of the Aran Islands', 772, 776.

142. Ibid. 778–9.

143. J. M. Synge, *The Playboy of the Western World, Collected Works, Vol. 4: Plays Book 2*, ed. Ann Saddlemyer. Gerrards Cross: Colin Smythe, 1982, 133–5.

144. Ibid. 134n.

145. A. Hingston Quiggin's biography of Haddon is even titled *Haddon the Head Hunter* in acknowledgement of his reputation for skull collecting. An account of one expedition in which Haddon stole skulls from a graveyard in Inishboffin for his collection is given in his journal of a voyage in 1890 down the west coast of Ireland. MS Haddon, Cambridge University Library, Envelope 22, 'Journal on board the SS Fingal', 1890, 30.

146. See A. Hingston Quiggin, *Haddon the Head Hunter*. Cambridge: Cambridge University Press, 1942, 81–109.

147. Haddon and Browne, 'The Ethnography of the Aran Islands', 769.

148. Ibid. 816.

149. Ibid. 781.

150. Ibid. 817–20.

151. Ibid. 816.

152. The lecture given in Belfast on 17 January 1893 shares the same title as the article, namely 'The Aran Islands: A Study in Irish Ethnography', *The Irish Naturalist*, 2.12 (December 1893), 303–8. The Belfast Naturalists' Field Club applied an admission charge to the lecture because of the high level of interest, and used the lecture as an opportunity to launch a local committee to co-ordinate work for the survey of the ethnography of the British Isles. See Haddon MS 3058, Cambridge University Library.

153. Copies of the forms and handbook used in the ethnographical survey of the British Isles are contained in Haddon MS 4061 and 4061A, Cambridge University Library.

154. Haddon MS 4061A, Cambridge University Library.

155. Haddon MS 4061A, Cambridge University Library.

156. See Elaine Sisson, '*The Aran Islands* and the Travel Essays', in P. J. Mathews (ed.), *The Cambridge Companion to J. M. Synge*. Cambridge: Cambridge University Press, 2009, 52–63.

157. Gregory Castle, *Modernism and the Celtic Revival*. Cambridge: Cambridge University Press, 2001, 101–7.

158. Nicholas Whyte, *Science, Colonialism and Ireland*. Cork: Cork University Press, 1999. For recent scholarship on the history of science in Ireland, see Adelman and Agnew (eds), *Science and Technology in Nineteenth-Century Ireland*; David Attis and Charles Mollan (eds), *Science and Irish Culture: Why the History of Science Matters in Ireland*. Dublin: Royal Dublin Society, 2004; Charles Mollan (ed.), *Science and Ireland: Value for Society*. Dublin: Royal Dublin Society, 2005; Charles Mollan, William Davis, and Brendan Finucane (eds), *Irish Innovators in Science and Technology*. Dublin: Royal Irish Academy, 2002; Don O'Leary, *Irish Catholicism and Science*. Cork: Cork University Press, 2012; and Marc Caball and Clara Cullen (eds), *Communities of Knowledge in Nineteenth-Century Ireland*. Dublin: Four Courts Press, 2013. Gregory Castle observes that revival studies in the twenty-first century has been marked by a new attention to cultural and intellectual movements and institutions, which has led to recognition of the importance of scientific discourses and schemes to cultural revivalists. See Gregory Castle, 'Irish Revivalism: Critical Trends and New Directions', *Literature Compass*, 8.5 (2011), 291–303, and for examples of such revival re-contextualisations, see Castle's own *Modernism and the Celtic Revival*; Garrigan Mattar's *Primitivism, Science, and the Irish Revival*; P. J. Mathews's *Revival*. Cork: Cork University Press, 2003; Nicholas Allen's *George Russell (AE) and the New Ireland, 1905–1930*. Dublin: Four Courts Press, 2003; and the special issue of the *Irish University Review*, *New Perspectives on the Irish Literary Revival: Special Issue*, ed. Margaret Kelleher, 33.1 (Spring/Summer 2003).

159. See Haddon MS 3058, Cambridge University Library, and Greta Jones, 'Contested Territories: Alfred Cort Haddon, Progressive Evolutionism and Ireland', *History of European Ideas*, 24.3 (1998), 201 (195–211).

160. Jones, 'Contested Territories', 202.

161. Quoted in Ferguson, 'Patrick Geddes and the Celtic Renascence in the 1890s', 136.
162. Yeats, 'The Evangel of Folk-Lore', *Uncollected Prose, Vol. 1*, 327.
163. 'The Folk-Lore Society: Rules', *The Folk-Lore Record*, 1 (1878), viii.
164. Jonathan Roper, 'Thoms and the Unachieved "Folk-lore of England"', *Folklore*, 118.2 (August 2007), 210 (203–16).
165. W. J. Thoms, *Choice Notes from* Notes and Queries: *Folklore*. London: Bell and Daldy, 1859, vi.
166. Yeats, 'Poetry and Science in Folk-lore', *Uncollected Prose, Vol. 1*, 174.
167. W. B. Yeats, 'To Olivia Shakespear, 28 November 1894', *The Collected Letters of W. B. Yeats, Vol. 1: 1865–1895*, ed. John Kelly. Oxford: Clarendon Press, 1986, 416. Yeats indicates that Olivia Shakespear had expressed this opinion herself.
168. Lionel Johnson, *The Art of Thomas Hardy*. London: Elkin Mathews and John Lane, 1894, 68.
169. Beckson, *Arthur Symons: A Life*, 132. Beckson is quoting here from Max Beerbohm's account of the argument in *Mainly on the Air* (1957).
170. Johnson, *The Art of Thomas Hardy*, 129.
171. Thomas Hardy, *Tess of the D'Urbervilles* [1892]. Oxford: Oxford World's Classics, 2005, 416.
172. Ibid. 44.
173. Ibid. 28–9, 19, 120, 398, 44.
174. Ibid. 330–1.
175. Ruth A. Firor, *Folkways in Thomas Hardy*. New York: Perpetua, 1962.
176. Hardy, *Tess of the D'Urbervilles*, 148–50, 234.
177. Ibid. 225.
178. Declan Kiberd, *Inventing Ireland: The Literature of the Modern Nation*. London: Jonathan Cape, 1995, 3. See also Kiberd, *Irish Classics*. London: Granta, 2000, 511, and Kiberd, *The Irish Writer and the World*. Cambridge: Cambridge University Press, 2005, 280. The latter gives the fullest and most detailed account of this anecdote.
179. Andrew Radford, *Thomas Hardy and the Survivals of Time*. Aldershot: Ashgate, 2003, 176.
180. Hardy, *Tess of the D'Urbervilles*, 146.
181. Ibid. 99.
182. Julian Wolfreys, *Thomas Hardy*. Basingstoke: Palgrave Macmillan, 2009, 209.
183. Hardy, *Tess of the D'Urbervilles*, 29.
184. Thomas Hardy, 'The Rev. William Barnes B.D.', in Johnson, *The Art of Thomas Hardy*, xlix–l (xlix–lviii).
185. Yeats, 'The Celtic Element in Literature', 178.
186. Hardy, *Tess of the D'Urbervilles*, 104.
187. Ibid. 97–8.
188. Kirkpatrick Sale, *Dwellers in the Land: The Bioregional Vision*. San Francisco: Sierra Club, 1985.

189. Hardy, *Tess of the D'Urbervilles*, 18.

190. R. J. Berry, *Islands*. New Naturalist Library. London: HarperCollins, 2009, 49.

191. Hardy, *Tess of the D'Urbervilles*, 87.

192. Ibid. 87, 18, 42.

193. Richard Jefferies, *Wild Life in a Southern County* [1879]. Stanbridge, Dorset: Little Toller Books, 2011, 15.

194. Johnson, *The Art of Thomas Hardy*, 176–7.

195. Ibid. 130.

196. Edward Alexander, 'Fin de Siècle, Fin du Globe: Yeats and Hardy in the Nineties', *Bucknell Review*, 23.2 (1977), 162 (142–63).

197. Yeats, *Autobiographies*, 150.

198. Alexander, 'Fin de Siècle, Fin du Globe', 157.

2

James Joyce and the Irish Sea

One key question for archipelagic studies of the Irish and British Isles concerns the sea which lies at the geographical centre of the archipelago. How does the Irish Sea connect or divide the people who live on its shores? Halford Mackinder, the English geographer, writing in 1902, regarded the Irish Sea as a 'truly inland' waterway, the entry points of which were mountainous gateposts, giving way to a heartland of flat shores and protected harbours: 'The Irish Sea is a British Mediterranean, a land-girt quadrilateral, wholly British, whose four sides are England, Scotland, Ireland, and Wales.'[1] When Buck Mulligan mounts the parapet of the Martello tower in the opening scene of *Ulysses* and hails the sea in Greek, '*Thalatta! Thalatta!*', and conjoins Stephen to 'Hellenise' the island with him, it is this 'British Mediterranean' which they gaze upon.[2] The 'mythic method' of *Ulysses* might be regarded in such terms not simply as the projection of the Mediterranean of the *Odyssey* upon the backcloth of Dublin in 1904, but as a materialist reading of the Irish Sea as a British transcription of the Mediterranean onto the cartography of the Unionist state. As Mackinder's proto-Braudelian analysis suggests, it is the natural shape and forms of the Irish Sea and its coastline which seem to suggest that it is, as the archaeologist Gordon Childe put it, 'the natural centre of a province whose several parts it unites rather than divides'.[3] This is the context in which much of Joyce's work can be read for its preoccupation with the signs of nature, and with the question of how natural forms might or might not imply correlation with cultural identities. What does it mean to declare the shore as a boundary of a political state? What does it mean to make the sea a territory?

For Jacques Rancière, the same Greece which is a founding space of

Western philosophy and democracy is also the cradle of 'an anti-maritime polemic': 'Athens has a disease that comes from its port, from the predominance of maritime enterprise governed entirely by profit and survival.'[4] The treacherous boundaries of the political are imagined as island shores, riverbanks, and abysses. Its enemies are the mutinous waves and the drunken sailor. 'In order to save politics', writes Rancière, 'it must be pulled aground among the shepherds.' And yet, as Rancière points out, this always entails the paradox that to found a new utopian island, safe from the perils of sailors and the sea, means crossing the sea once more.[5] Writing in the midst of utopian dreams of founding new states in the crumbling ruins of falling empires, James Joyce considered the material meanings of the shoreline and the sea to a politics which sought the illusion of 'terra firma'. This chapter follows the journey Joyce made in the course of his work about how to read the 'ground' of the emergent new political geography of the Irish and British Isles.

'A GOOD CROSSING': *DUBLINERS* AT SEA

Much has been written about the turn westwards in Joyce's *Dubliners*, the turn which most emphatically takes place in 'The Dead', in which Gabriel Conroy is drawn imaginatively away from his 'West Briton' preoccupations with continental fashions, and towards Miss Ivors' beacons of Irishness, Galway and the Aran islands, which lie beyond the 'dark mutinous Shannon waves'.[6] Joyce's collection ends, famously, perhaps triumphantly, with Gabriel's resolution 'to set out on his journey westwards'.[7] Yet, it is almost wholly unremarked how the sea which lies to Gabriel's east is a source of recurrent, almost pathological, phasia, for the characters of Joyce's stories.[8] It is the sea upon which Dublin depends, for its origins as a settlement, and as a port, as well as for its livelihood. There are allusions to this archipelagic dependence of the city upon its hintersea throughout the stories, of course. Gabriel's father was 'of the Port and Docks',[9] Mrs Kernan's eldest sons are now 'launched' in careers in the neighbouring ports of Glasgow and Belfast,[10] Mrs Sinico's husband was 'captain of a mercantile boat plying between Dublin and Holland',[11] Mrs Mooney's boarding house is described as consisting of 'a floating population made up of tourists from Liverpool and the Isle of Man and, occasionally, *artistes* from the music halls',[12] and the boys in 'An Encounter' mitch their way through the wharfs, docks, and canals which mark the nodes and flows of maritime commerce and down towards the 'brown fishing fleet beyond Ringsend'.[13] Yet, whenever any of Joyce's principal characters approach the Irish Sea, or consider its shores and crossings, they turn back, and cannot look upon what 'After the Race' calls 'its darkened mirror'.[14]

The 'mirror' image of the sea is by no means unusual as a literary trope, although it could be argued that it has particular significance to the geography of Dublin's situation as the one major natural inlet along the Leinster coast, an inlet which frames and calms the sea between Howth and Dun Laoghaire. It was the image George Moore used to describe the waters of Dublin Bay in the opening passage of his charismatic book *Parnell and his Island* (1886):

> This is Dalkey, a suburb of Dublin. From where I stand I look down upon the sea as on a cup of blue water; it lies two hundred feet below me like a great smooth mirror; it lies beneath the blue sky as calm, as mysteriously still, as an enchanted glass in which we may read the secrets of the future. How perfectly cuplike is the bay! Blue mountains, blue embaying mountains, rise on every side, and amorously the sea rises up to the lip of the land. These mountains of the north, these Turner-like mountains, with their innumerable aspects, hazy perspectives lost in delicate grey, large and trenchant masses standing out brutally in the strength of the sun, are as the mailed arms of a knight leaning to a float-ing siren whose flight he would detain and of whom he asks still an hour of love. I hear the liquid murmur of the sea; it sings to the shore as softly as a turtle-dove to its mate.[15]

Moore's metaphors for the relationship between the sea and the land are principally romantic and chivalric, the embrace of the sea by the outreaching arms of the land met by the amorous rise of the sea 'to the lip of the land', and culminating in a vision of a mating song. The relationship is clearly generative, with the 'enchanted glass' of the sea a mirror of a future born from the kiss of the waves against the shore. In *Dubliners*, however, the coastline is treacher-ous, and maritime metaphors and images signify corruption and sterility. In 'After the Race', for example, Dublin is merely a conduit of transnational capital, a 'channel of poverty and inaction' through which 'the Continent sped its wealth and industry'.[16] The 'cargo of hilarious youth' which races incongruously through Dublin's streets ends up in a yacht anchored in Kingstown harbour, with the only Dubliner in the party, Jimmy, sinking into a 'dark stupor' which would hide his gambling losses. The story closes with the image of the 'grey light' of dawn cast through the cabin door, and with Jimmy's painful recognition of the disparity between the apparent resem-blance of Dublin to 'a capital' (with capital) and the actuality of a city which can only wear the mask of capital. Even the name of the harbour town, in this instance, is a reminder of its ransomed status, its dependence upon the flows and tides of wealth and prestige from elsewhere. The sea, in other words, is the 'darkened mirror' through which Jimmy is brought to see the image of Dublin's peripheral and provincial role in an Atlantic arc of capital, trade, and labour.

Far from amorous, Joyce's images of the Irish Sea in 'Eveline' signal an anti-maritime polemic. Pitted against the exotic 'tales of distant countries' which Frank tells Eveline, and the prospect of a new and prosperous life in Argentina, it is the terror of the sea which foils Eveline's dream of romance. The 'black mass of the boat', the 'swaying crowd', the mist on the quay: all engender 'nausea', 'distress', 'frenzy', bodily sensations which deprive Eveline of agency and make her 'passive, like a helpless animal', like the cattle herded down the Dublin quays to the same North Wall dock on their way to slaughter. In Hugh Kenner's influential reading of 'Eveline', Eveline's refusal to go with Frank is a lucky escape from a dubious fantasy about a new life in Buenos Aires, a fantasy which, as the 'night-boat' from the North Wall goes to Liverpool, and not Buenos Aires, would have resulted instead in a quick consummation 'in an English seaport'.[17] Kenner's argument hinges on the currency of maritime romance, and suspicion of the tales and songs of a sailor, with Eveline's father's dismissive reaction to the news of her planned elopement with Frank – 'I know these sailor chaps' – compelling the reader to cast doubt upon Frank's 'tales of distant countries', 'stories of the terrible Patagonians', and his too eager catalogue of 'the names of the ships he had been on and the names of the different services'.[18] But Eveline's turn against Frank only begins with the nausea induced by her littoral surroundings: 'All the seas of the world tumbled about her heart. He was drawing her into them: he would drown her . . . Amid the seas she sent a cry of anguish!'[19] Eveline's sudden turn from the prospects of a new life seems to be a revulsion from the worldliness of the seas, not just from the passage across the Irish Sea, or the credibility or otherwise of the sea-stories of her lover, but from her queasy proximity to the global web of ports and crossings which the 'night-boat' signifies. This passage, across to Liverpool, would be the end of Eveline's rootedness, the end of place and belonging, and the beginning of a cosmopolitan subjectivity which would be defined by sensations of tumbling, anguish, and drowning. The seas are emblematic for Eveline of a globalised modernity of migration and disruption which repel her as much as the terror of 'that life of commonplace sacrifices closing in final craziness' which her mother's life of keeping 'the home together' represented.[20]

In Moore's vision of Dublin Bay, his thoughts 'turn involuntarily to the Bay of Naples', not simply for comparison, but as if one bay necessarily evokes the image of and connection to others.[21] Ports and shorelines are cultural meeting places, the leavings of one life, and the beginnings of others. This recognition causes Eveline to grip the iron railings of the quayside in terror, seizing up in the liminal space of the dockside. In 'An Encounter', Joyce associates the dockside again with the thwarted promise of escape, and the grim realisation of the shoreline as a dangerously transitional space. Two schoolboys, filled with tales of 'the Wild West' of cowboys and Indians, and bored of school lessons about Roman history, abscond from the classroom and venture down to the quays. Here, Joyce has his characters enjoy 'the spectacle of Dublin's commerce', surrounded by barges, carts, cranes, big ships, and the high masts, through which images the narrator 'saw, or imagined, the geography which had been scantily dosed to me at school gradually taking substance under my eyes'.[22] It is the portal consciousness of Dublin which is at stake in this vision of the quays, and their openness to a global imagination. The exposure to dime novels of American frontier mythology, to the imperial chronicles of Rome, and to the romance of the freedom of the seas is a condition of portal life, the consequence of migration, conquest, trade. At the dockside, the narrator 'examined the foreign sailors to see had any of them green eyes for I had some confused notion . . .'. The incomplete sentence signifies the narrator's dawning recognition of the dockside as a schooling of its own kind, a place in which the plurality of the sea-borne world makes visible the fictions of the classroom. It is a dawning which becomes troublesome as the boys abandon their adventure to reach Pigeon House beyond Ringsend, and stray into conversation with the 'queer old josser', whose talk of sweethearts and whipping rough boys alerts the narrator that he has entered a perilous and liminal space. The boys retreat from the coast, chastened from their adventure, and their dreams of running away to sea. The 'bottle-green eyes' of the old man equate him to the mythic green-eyed sailor of the narrator's 'confused notion', and hence sea life becomes associated with dark secrets of violence and perversion, the kind of grim, ritual abuse which James Hanley would controversially chart in *Boy* (1935). So too, as Marilyn Reizbaum argues, the 'odd' detail that the two boys crossed over the Liffey on a ferry 'in the company of two labourers and a little jew with a bag' marks the quays out as a transitional, rootless space, since Jewish figures in Joyce are always 'quintessential deracinated urbanites', embodiments of a cosmopolitan geography of uncertain boundaries.[23]

It is worth noting also that the abandonment of the quest to reach Pigeon House is itself somewhat mysterious. The narrator records that it 'was too late and we were too tired', yet at Ringsend, they are within a few minutes' walk of Pigeon House. As an article in the *Irish Times* in 1902 records, Pigeon House had been transformed in the minds of Dubliners from being synonymous with a military fort guarding the entrance to the Liffey pool, to being the site of an electric lighting station and the pumping station of the drainage works: 'Darkness and disease will be combated by these new erections, and greater enemies warded off, let us hope, from Dublin's inhabitants than the guns of the fort could have vanquished if they had ever been called upon for active service.'[24] The coastline has long figured as a line of defence, and Joyce's story does not specify whether the boys are intent on Pigeon House as a remnant of military history, or as a symbol of Dublin's embrace of modern technological methods of making the city clean and bright. In either case, however, and without a cogent reason for the aborted journey, the story connects this abandoned pilgrimage to the site of Dublin's defences to the boys' vulnerability to the approaches of a dangerous old man. It is a connection which seems to implicate proximity to the shore as an encroachment upon other boundaries, boundaries between darkness and light, health and disease, safety and danger. The boys turn westwards, away from the sea, and flee back to the sanctuary of the city.

If the turn westwards is a trope which recurs, then, throughout *Dubliners*, it is also a trope of turning back from the Irish Sea, and this is especially evident in 'The Dead'. The Irish Sea is referenced explicitly just once in the story, it could be argued, when Gabriel asks Freddy Malins' mother 'whether she had had a good crossing' from her daughter's house in Glasgow.[25] The question of what constitutes a 'good crossing', culturally and politically, preoccupies the whole story, however, even if it hides in the seemingly insignificant details. The incongruity of the Conroys' 'goloshes', for example, a continental fashion, which as a word reminds Gretta of another cultural import, 'Christy Minstrels', serves to mark Gabriel out from the beginning as having failed to 'cross' cultures convincingly. 'O, on the continent, murmured Aunt Julia, nodding her head slowly', clearly signalling her bewilderment at Gabriel's latest importation. Gabriel has decided to take a room in the Gresham for the night, instead of travelling back out to their home in Monkstown, because of the 'east wind blowing in after we passed Merrion' the year before, which gave Gretta 'a dreadful cold'.[26] This seems an incidental detail, but it is the coldness of that east wind coming in from the Irish Sea which drives our attention out west, too. It is Miss Ivors, of course, who begins to direct Gabriel's imagination westwards, by inviting him to join an excursion 'to the Aran Isles . . . splendid out in the Atlantic', but she does so first by taunting him that he is a 'West Briton'.[27] The taunt had a potency in nationalist circles as a repudiation of cultural unionism, and it is specifically because Gabriel has written a book review for the English newspaper the *Daily Express* that Miss Ivors feels justified in goading him. As Christopher Harvie observes, '"West Briton" was a play on "North Briton", a neologism coined around the time of the Scottish Act of Union in 1707.'[28] In Ireland, it gained currency in the nineteenth century, in similar conditions as a response to the 1801 Act of Union, and at the same time as the development of the Holyhead road, steamship services across the Irish Sea, and railway connections between its ports brought into being a fast, efficient corridor for commercial, political, and cultural traffic between Dublin and London. There was no need for a gun emplacement at Pigeon House in 1902 because, as Harvie shows, the rapid innovations in

transport technology in the nineteenth century had transformed the Irish Sea
into an 'inland waterway', 'bounded by Bristol, Dublin, Belfast, and Glasgow',
and including that great hub of trade, migration, and slavery, Liverpool.[29] It
was 'a region of short voyages and rich cargoes', a region which Harvie argues
was central to the expansion and global dominance of the British Empire in
the eighteenth and nineteenth centuries.[30]

   To be a 'West Briton', then, is to behave as if there is no sea between
Ireland and Britain. It is to deny the force of Miss Ivors' terrestrial sense of
'your own country', and 'your own land', to deny the insular integrity of a
land called Ireland, surrounded by the sea.[31] And this is the motivation for
Miss Ivors' equation of the journey westwards, to the Aran islands 'splendid
out in the Atlantic', with 'your own land', since only by confronting the
sharper, tumultuous coastline of the west can she restore a sense of boundedness. The splendidness of the islands against the backdrop of the Atlantic
contrasts the apparent invisibility of the Irish Sea, as if only an ocean can now
vouchsafe the integrity of islandness. Her point seems amplified by the reply
Freddy Malins' mother gives to Gabriel, that she has had a 'beautiful crossing' over the Irish Sea.[32] The very facility of the crossing, the hospitality of
the sea, so to speak, is the cause of its implicit concern to Molly Ivors. It is a
treacherous sea, which allows the geography of Britain to slip too easily into
the street names of Joyce's Dublin: the very first street name mentioned in
Dubliners is, after all, Great Britain Street, and others – Westmoreland Street,
Dorset Street, North Richmond Street, Ely Place – point us back across the
water, too. Yet, as much as the Irish Sea may be a figure of treachery, the turn
westwards is itself troublesome, and, here again, even as Joyce's story takes
us across the middle of Ireland, it is a journey which alights curiously on the
figure of 'dark mutinous Shannon waves'.[33] Richard Ellmann has observed
the unusual meteorology of the final passage, with snow 'general all over
Ireland', and hints at the symbolic function of the snow and the mutinous
waves as images of 'crowding and quiet pressure', in the case of the snow, and
of the '"Furey" quality of the west', in the case of the mutinous waves.[34] He
identifies too that the passage is borrowing similes from the *Iliad*, and Homer's
image of snowflakes 'falling by the inlets and shores of the foaming sea, but
are silently dissolved by the waves'.[35] This may account for the hyperbole of
the description of the Shannon at this point of crossing, a river which is not
tidal beyond Limerick, and which would generate waves of small proportions,
perhaps, in stormy conditions, but not sufficient to warrant the impression of
mutiny. Joyce is turning his rivers into seas here, as, in the east, he has turned
his seas into rivers, and the Shannon roars up in the imagination as a boundary
to mark out the west as a different country, a place apart, while the east slides
imperceptibly towards a borderless England. As Kenner famously reminds

us, Joyce 'never relaxes his concern for what we cannot see': the turn away from the Irish Sea, the pathos of every encounter with the Irish Sea, mutedly marked as it may be, is as significant a trope in *Dubliners* as the corresponding and consequent move towards the west. The symbolic rendering of the Irish Sea as invisible, or a mirror, on the one hand, and of the Shannon and the Atlantic as mutinous and tumultuous, on the other, should alert us to Joyce's suspicion of the hermeneutics of maritime space. As Sidney Feshbach observes, 'Joyce's characters have feelings about the sea, but they do not leave the land: they are grounded.'[36] On an island, the inability to face the sea has debilitating, if not grave, consequences.

'THE SORDID TIDE OF LIFE':

A PORTRAIT OF THE ARTIST AS A YOUNG MAN

As Virginia Woolf would write of her novel *To the Lighthouse*, the sea can be heard throughout *A Portrait of the Artist as a Young Man*, from the sailor's hornpipe which Stephen's mother plays for him when he is a small boy, to the closing maritime fantasy of the 'black arms of tall ships that stand against the moon, their tale of distant nations'.[37] The sea haunts the novel's key scenes: Parnell's death is remembered as the passage of a ship towards the harbour;[38] Stephen's association of Dublin with freedom is specifically connected to his exploration of its docks and quays;[39] the preacher's topographical depictions of hell repeatedly draw upon maritime and littoral images;[40] Stephen's dream of otherworldly beauty takes place upon the shore on Bull Island;[41] and his final imagination of flight from Dublin, like the swallows he sees above the city streets,[42] is of transcending the sea which he lists as one of his fears.[43] Moreover, the sea inhabits the figurative language of the novel, especially relating to Stephen's emotions, which are charted as tides and waves, as in the following passage:

> How foolish his aim had been! He had tried to build a breakwater of order and elegance against the sordid tide of life without him and to dam up, by rules of conduct and active interests and new filial relations, the powerful recurrence of the tides within him. Useless. From without as from within the water had flowed over his barriers: their tides began once more to jostle fiercely above the crumbled mole.[44]

This passage precedes his seemingly passive entrance into the 'maze of narrow and dirty streets' of Dublin's red light district, and his seduction by the young woman who is herself forecast as 'some dark presence moving irresistibly upon him from the darkness, a presence subtle and murmurous as a flood'.[45] The function of tides and floods here as metaphors of powerful sexual and psychological drives is a familiar feature of literary representation. For Joyce, these maritime images appear simply to serve as symbols of the power-ful, natural forces, from 'without as from within', which are ranged against Stephen's attempts to obey the moral and sexual codes of the social order. The relationship between the sea and the land, and the daily drama which takes place on the shoreline, is figured as a contest between wild nature and human order. This seems entirely in keeping with what John Mack describes as 'the predominant Western view of the sea' as a 'quintessential wilderness', as 'a space not a place', and 'a space without ruins or other witness to the events which may have taken place on its surface'.[46] Yet even this figurative language of the sea, which is deployed frequently throughout the novel, correlates in interesting ways to the littoral geography of the city which Joyce depicts in the novel.

The history of Dublin is inseparable from its functions as a landing place, a harbour, and a port, from the ease with which the longboats of its Viking founders could beach on the shallow sands of Dublin Bay, to the pools in which medieval ships could drop anchor and transfer their goods to smaller ferries, and to the quays and docks at the mouth of the Liffey which form the modern port. But as Geoffrey Corry argues, since medieval times, the history of the port has been the constant 'battle to overcome the natural obstacles in the Bay':

> The most striking fact about Dublin Bay is that, when the tide goes fully out, an area of sand and mud flats is left 'high and dry', covering almost half the area of the Bay and extending from Dun Laoghaire right around the perimeter of the Bay to Sutton. In its most central part where the breadth of the sand measures up to four miles the force of the rivers Liffey, Dodder and Tolka have cut their own channel through this natural beach and divided it in half to form the North and South Bulls (so called from the roaring of the surf at high tide). Just where the river comes in contact with the incoming tide, a sand bar has formed which joins the sands of the North and South Bulls under water. This was not a deposit of silt brought down by the river, but merely a continuation of the beach between one Bull and the other, which the river had not the power to move.[47]

Before the construction of the north and south walls into the bay at the begin-ning of the eighteenth century, larger ships frequently had to unload their cargoes beyond Ringsend, and the bay was characterised by 'a complexity of channels both tortuous and dangerous', cut into the sands by the flow of the three rivers.[48] The Great South Wall, which was completed in 1795, extended five miles from the city into the bay, and it served to prevent the sand from the South Bull being washed into the approach channel to the port, as well as combining tidal flows with the ebb-flow of the river beyond the Poolbeg Lighthouse to scour part of the bar at the mouth of the channel. The success of the South Wall led the city corporation to commission the North Bull Wall in 1820, to extend the North Wall from Clontarf Head out to Poolbeg, a task which was completed within three years. The North Bull Wall concentrated the tidal and current flows to scour the whole of the bar, and to maintain a clear channel for navigation up to the city's quays. It did so by controlling the flow of both salt and fresh water within the bay: 'The final 2,000 ft of the wall was deliberately left, in part, at the height of the neap-tides, and in the end-section, at half-tide level, to permit the first half of the ebb-flow to escape over a wider exit than the channel itself.'[49] The control of these great flows of water resulted in 'a new era', according to Corry, in which Dublin port 'experienced a great leap forward both in the turnover of ships and money'.[50] The ever larger ships entering Dublin's port in the nineteenth century materialised the political connection to the British Empire embedded in the Act of Union (1801). Mastery of the bay was an essential infrastructural achievement in retaining Dublin's connections to the network of ports around the Irish Sea, most notably strengthening the route to London via Holyhead, especially after the development of steamships and railways, and, perhaps even more importantly, strengthening the city's global connections through Liverpool, which, as Ian Baucom has recently argued, with its long history of involvement in slavery and speculative, 'spectral' capitalism, was a key hub of Atlantic modernity.[51]

Stephen Dedalus encounters this connected and modernised Dublin when he wanders into the docks and quays on a walk which follows from Stephen's desire 'to meet in the real world the unsubstantial image which his soul so constantly beheld'.[52] 'Dublin was a new and complex sensation' for Stephen, as with his family's downward social move from Blackrock to Dublin, he experiences more freedom to explore the 'gloomy foggy city' at will.[53] The port represents the 'real world', the world made real to Stephen, and once he has 'timidly' circled around his neighbouring square and streets, and made 'a skeleton map of the city in his mind', he strides out 'boldly' along 'one of its central lines until he reached the customhouse'. The depiction of Stephen's 'circling' and the mental construction of a 'skeleton map' is important in prefiguring the boldness of a move into the port area, just as the figure of a city's 'central lines' suggests the idea of pre-determined routes or flows, along which Stephen is conveyed:

> He passed unchallenged among the docks and along the quays wondering at the multitude of corks that lay bobbing on the surface of the water

in a thick yellow scum, at the crowds of quay porters and the rumbling carts and the illdressed bearded policeman. The vastness and strangeness of the life suggested to him by the bales of merchandise stocked along the walls or swung aloft out of the holds of steamers wakened again in him the unrest which had sent him wandering in the evening from garden to garden in search of Mercedes. And amid this new bustling life he might have fancied himself in another Marseilles but that he missed the bright sky and the sunwarmed trellises of the wineshops.[54]

Stephen's experience of the docks is shaped partly by his imaginative absorption in the adventure narrative of Alexandre Dumas's *The Count of Monte Cristo*, and especially the Marseilles in which the novel's sailor-hero, Edmond Dantés, is falsely accused of treason and imprisoned on the eve of his marriage to the beautiful Catalan Mercédès. That Dublin might be mistaken for Marseilles, but for the climate and the wine, is not mere whimsy, but a reminder that ports are points of connection with distant places, in the material ways in which, as Stephen watches, 'bales of merchandise' from elsewhere are being unloaded onto Dublin's quays, as well as the imaginative ways in which adventure narratives move the action from port to port, island to island, and sea to sea, embodying what Margaret Cohen describes as 'a centrifugal movement outward to the edges of the known world and beyond'.[55] The climate might remind Stephen that he is not in Marseilles, but the cork stoppers floating on the river may serve as signs of the wine trade, and, in any case, as products of an industrial process of cork farming and manufacturing in the Mediterranean which grew with the maritime shipment of bottled goods in the nineteenth century, they are metonymic of global ocean trade.[56] Ringsend was home in Joyce's time to bottling plants, as it is home now to container yards. Just as the waves and tides in *A Portrait of the Artist* are both material and symbolic, so too these floating corks are both the physical detritus of port life and, a short time later in the narrative, symbolic of Stephen's emotions: 'His heart danced upon her movements like a cork upon a tide.'[57] The appearance of corks upon a tide as a metaphor so soon after Stephen's encounter of the 'multitude of corks' in the river suggests a correlation between the material and the symbolic, between the physical geography of Stephen's surroundings and its affective and psychic associations.

Joyce's novel may appear to depict Stephen as the frustrated exile, forever imagining escape, and constantly seeking to take physical and imaginative flight from his 'sordid' anchorage in Dublin. Yet, it is also continually binding Stephen's dreams to the materialities of place. In his aunt's kitchen, for example, he daydreams to the sound of her casual monologue, 'following the ways of adventure that lay open in the coals, arches and vaults and winding galleries and jagged caverns'.[58] The poverty of his life as a student is experienced as intellectual as well as material deprivation, with the physical sensation of itching from lice causing him to think of his thoughts as vermin also.[59] The imaginative association of places with books, which in his early adolescence, as we've seen, finds him questing around Dublin as if it is the Marseilles of *The Count of Monte Cristo*, is depicted in a more self-ironic manner later in the novel:

> His morning walk across the city had begun, and he foreknew that as he passed the sloblands of Fairview he would think of the cloistral silverveined prose of Newman, that as he walked along the North Strand Road, glancing idly at the windows of the provision shops, he would recall the dark humour of Guido Cavalcanti and smile, that as he went by Baird's stonecutting works in Talbot Place the spirit of Ibsen would blow through him like a keen wind, a spirit of wayward boyish beauty, and that passing a grimy marinedealer's shop beyond the Liffey he would repeat the song by Ben Jonson which begins:
> *I was not wearier where I lay.*[60]

Each of these associations of literature with place are mildly comic, of course, in their apparent proposition that there might be something reminiscent of sloblands in Newman's prose, or something grimy and marine about Elizabethan song. Cavalcanti is renowned for his Florentine love poems which dwell on the frustrations of reconciling the intellect and the senses, which is perhaps not an unlikely thought for Stephen to have passing the shops on the North Strand Road. As Kristian Smidt argues, Dublin port is recurrently the scene of Norwegian figures for Joyce, so perhaps the 'keen wind' from the docks which blows through him as he ventures down Talbot Place towards the Custom House reminds him of Ibsen for this reason.[61] We might think of these associations as imaginative transformations, with the sloblands of Fairview becoming the 'cloistral silverveined prose' of Newman in the same way as the grey-skied, gloomy seaport of Dublin becomes the sun-warmed Mediterranean harbour of Marseilles. But if they are transformations, Joyce implies, however absurdly or comically, a material basis for them in the places along the route which Stephen habitually takes to cross the city.

It is this context, of the constant intermeshing of the material and the literary or symbolic, which is crucial to understanding how Joyce deploys the dynamic littoral geography of Dublin within the novel, and it is most evident in the famous scene of Stephen's vision of the bird-girl in chapter four, which takes place on Bull Island. Stephen walks out along the North Bull Wall to Bull Island after he has decided to reject the priesthood, and instead to go to university. As he crosses the thin and frail wooden bridge which connects

Dollymount to the Bull Wall a group of Christian brothers pass him by, reminding him of what he has rejected. He is humbled by the model of love for fellow humanity which characterises their vocation, and chides himself for the shallowness of his own devotion. The narrative seems to change direction abruptly at this point, when Stephen 'drew forth a phrase from his treasure and spoke it softly to himself: "A day of dappled seaborne clouds"'.[62] This is a strange treasury indeed, for as Richard Brown observes, it is a phrase adapted from the work of Scottish geologist Hugh Miller, *The Testimony of the Rocks*, a book which finds geological evidence to support the creationist theory of Genesis, and which argues that species differentiation is not explained by the Lamarckian theory of evolution but by divine design.[63] Miller was a stonemason by trade, and a geologist by careful observation, largely along the shorelines of his home in Cromarty, and on occasional visits to the Orkney islands. Although his writings were perhaps eclipsed intellectually by the influence of Darwinism, he was an enormously popular and important writer, as Michael Shortland remarks, and there have been recent attempts to rank him 'alongside such contemporaries (and admirers) as Thomas Carlyle, John Ruskin and Charles Dickens'.[64] The phrase in Miller is 'a day of dappled breeze-born clouds', which Stephen mis-remembers and, as Brown points out, changes to a version which is 'meteorologically unsound' (although poetically, perhaps, Stephen is merely aligning the westward direction of the clouds with his view of the incoming waves, and the image of 'seaborne clouds' is later echoed in Stephen's sense of the synchronous movement of the clouds above him with the rivulets and seatangle below).[65] In Miller's text, the phrase comes in a long, eloquent passage in which he imagines the response of the 'great fallen spirit' watching the divine creator making the earth into a 'home of higher and yet higher forms of existence':

> And how, as generation after generation passed away, and ever and anon the ocean rolled where the land had been, or the land rose to possess the ancient seats of the ocean, – how, when looking back upon myriads of ages, and when calling up in memory what once had been, the features of earth seemed scarce more fixed to his view than the features of the sky in a day of dappled breeze-borne clouds, . . . the truth had at length burst upon him, that reasoning, accountable man was fast coming to the birth.[66]

Miller presents the argument in *The Testimony of the Rocks* that 'man . . . is what none of his predecessors on the earth ever were – a "fellow-worker" with the Creator'.[67] It is an argument which has a negative implication also, and in the same chapter, it may have been of interest to Joyce that Miller cites the physical degradation of the Irish, as well as other 'degraded races', as evidence of 'man as man himself has made him, – not man as he came from the hand of the Creator'.[68] The allusion to Miller in *A Portrait of the Artist* seems fleeting, and partial, but as Brown suggests, there is a 'semantic knot' bound up in the allusion which demands to be unpicked. Brown finds in this knot a story of poetic transference and the dependence of literary texts upon others for creativity and sophistication.[69] However, the specific location of Stephen's walk suggests that there is another semantic web at play here, one which has greater significance for Stephen's conversion to the role of 'artificer'.

Bull Island is a nineteenth-century development, adjoining the North Bull Wall, and stretching north-eastwards towards Howth. It is effectively a large sand bar which became an island as a result of the manipulation of currents and tidal flows by the North and South Walls of the port, and the natural colonisation of the raised sand and silt deposits by grassland. By the end of the century, it had become a substantial piece of land, three miles long, with coastguard houses and golf greens, with its long easterly beach and the North Bull Wall itself popularly used for sea bathing.[70] The engineering of the water flows within the bay, as well as land reclamation, meant that other banks and islands in the bay, such as the White and Shelly Banks off the South Wall, and Clontarf Island in the North Bay, had been eroded or vanished, so that Bull Island also became a key sanctuary for seabirds.[71] It is the bathers who first come to Stephen's attention on the island, as he heads out along the Bull Wall, and he is taunted by the voices of his schoolmates before he is affronted by the sight of their 'corpsewhite' naked bodies. The image of the sea as sordid suffuses the scene, from the very moment when Stephen crosses the wooden bridge on to the island: 'how his flesh dreaded the cold infra-human odour of the sea'.[72] As Joseph Kestner argues, Joyce's depiction of naked male homosociality on the shoreline 'has significant antecedents' in contemporary iconography of ephebic youth, not least in Whitman and Pater, but also in a broader artistic tradition of invoking the elements of Greek ephebic initiation: 'naked adolescence, vigorous athleticism, Apollonian solarity, dynamic limi-nality'.[73] The shoreline as a space of male bonding, then, and of uninhibited nakedness is the first marker for Stephen of the otherworldly character of the island, and one in which his homophobia and hydrophobia are closely linked. It is also, as Kestner observes, where Stephen's vision of the bird-girl begins, for the imagery of birds and flight begins to pervade his imagination from the moment his name is called by the boys.[74] 'Now, at the name of the fabulous artificer, he seemed to hear the noise of dim waves and to see a winged form flying above the waves and slowly climbing the air. What did it mean?'[75]

Stephen has not yet fallen asleep on the beach, nor yet set his enchanted eyes upon the girl 'whom magic had changed into the likeness of a strange and beautiful seabird', but already we are in a transformative landscape, in which

Stephen is apparently hearing and seeing 'winged forms' conjured into existence by words. Moreover, he appears to be changing into a bird himself: 'His
throat ached with a desire to cry aloud, the cry of a hawk or eagle on high, to
cry piercingly of his deliverance to the winds.'[76] As Anthony Roche argues of
this scene, 'The question insistently posed by the text is not what Stephen, in
his epiphany on the beach, is undergoing but in what domain his experience
is situated.'[77] Roche situates this experience firmly and persuasively within
the domain of the Celtic Otherworld, the island vision, showing Joyce's allusions to Yeats and Synge, and signalling the conventions of the *aisling* tradition which Joyce's chapter adopts. Yet the specific, environmental context
of Stephen's vision on an island forged into existence by modern maritime
engineering passes unremarked.

The figurative language of tides and floods which Joyce uses in *A Portrait of
the Artist*, as we saw earlier, is tied closely to the history of maritime engineering within Dublin port. The 'crumbled mole' over which the tides pour is
an accurate image of the most easterly stretch of the North Bull Wall, which
was constructed in such a way as to allow the spring tide to flow back into the
channel. The breakwaters, dams, and barriers are part of the elaborate scheme
of funnelling water into and away from the port, and allow the port to function as a waypoint for trade, migration, and communication. It is this infrastructural economy of water management which has shaped Bull Island into
existence, and it seems therefore an ironic setting for Tír na nÓg. Yet, it is not
simply an otherworldy, fantastical vision which overcomes Stephen on the
island, but a material, naturalist vision, too. As he wanders along the strand, he
observes the 'seawrack on the shallow side of the breakwater', and seaweed,
'Emerald and black and russet and olive'. The landscape Joyce describes is 'of
wild air and brackish waters and the seaharvest of shells and tangle and veiled
grey sunlight'. The apparent transformation of the girl standing on the shore
is fantastical:

> Her long slender bare legs were delicate as a crane's and pure save where
> an emerald trail of seaweed had fashioned itself as a sign upon the flesh.
> Her thighs, fuller and softhued as ivory, were bared almost to the hips
> where the white fringes of her drawers were like featherings of soft
> white down.[78]

However, as Stephen is described in a similarly transformed state, 'his throat
throbbing with song', the vision is one of Stephen and the girl imagined
as birds together. As evening is descending at this point, and Bull Island
renowned as a feeding and standing ground for over one hundred species of
birds, this vision might be taken as another example of Joyce's intermeshing
of the material and the symbolic, however.[79]

Stephen's epiphany, signalled most clearly in his cry of 'Heavenly God! . . . in an outburst of profane joy', is not simply a response to the presence of the girl, the return of his gaze 'without shame or wantonness', or the vision of her as a bird or even angel, but directly follows the sight and sound of her 'stirring the water with her foot hither and thither'.[80] The stirring of the waters, and the 'first faint noise of the gently moving water', integral to the image system of the novel, connects this moment of recognition between Stephen and the girl with the generative flows and ebbs of water which gives life to the city of which they are a part. This is the moment which represents Stephen's turn to the sea, as he strides out then, 'far out over the sands, singing wildly to the sea, crying to greet the advent of the life that had cried to him'.[81] The meeting of the sea and the sands is recognised as a place of generation, the feeding and breeding grounds of seabirds, the shifting ground where, as Miller described, 'the ocean rolled where the land had been, or the land rose to possess the ancient seats of the ocean'.[82] As Rachel Carson wrote in her preface to *The Edge of the Sea*, 'When we go down to the low-tide line, we enter a world that is as old as the earth itself – the primeval meeting place of the elements of earth and water, a place of compromise and conflict and eternal change.'[83] On Bull Island, however, this story of creation, change, and regeneration was dramatically recent. As Roche indicates, the beach scene concludes with a sentence in which the last verb, 'islanding', is remarkable for 'Joyce's dynamic conversion of a static noun into a present participle', which has a 'proliferating imaginative possibility for his own prose'.[84] But not just for his own prose. The image is that of 'the tide . . . flowing in fast to the land with a low whisper of her waves, islanding a few last figures in distant pools'. The present participle 'islanding' may mean isolation in this context, but the generative metaphors used throughout the scene of the shoreline, and the specific geography and history of the location, suggest a creative process broader than Stephen's artistic ambitions alone.

Moreover, the allusion to Miller, and the reverberations throughout the scene of an attempt to reconcile theological and geological explanations of existence and creativity, suggest that the role of Dedalus the artificer lies not merely in the mechanical innovations of prose, as a displaced form of priestly vocation, but in the broader naturalist and humanist sense in which Stephen can now look to 'desire to press in my arms the loveliness which has not yet come into the world'.[85] Bull Island is the material and symbolic location in which Stephen can embrace this new-found sense of how loveliness comes into the world, and glimpse a narrative of the relationship between the sea and the land which is alternative to the mercantile and imperial associations of the port. The 'white arms of roads . . . and the black arms of tall ships' may be his 'kinsmen . . . making ready to go, shaking the wings of their exultant and terrible youth', but Stephen's desire for flight, out to 'the ends of the earth', is one modelled upon the seabirds he has envisioned on the shoreline, and the swallows above his head, which 'have come back from the south'.[86]

The 'Shipping News' for 16 June 1904 records a steady flow of marine traffic to and from the port of Dublin.[87] The port handled the coming and going of twenty-eight ships that day, almost all of them passenger and cargo steamers. The 'threemaster' vessel which Stephen Dedalus turns to notice from Sandymount Strand, 'her sails brailed up on the crosstrees', 'silently moving, a silent ship', was not among them.[88] The 'Shipping News' does, however, log a routine and provincial view of Dublin in the early twentieth century. There was just one 'Foreign Arrival', the SS *City of Stockholm*, a Dublin-registered ship, which had come from Rotterdam 'with a general cargo', but even it had sailed via Belfast. The 'Foreign Departures' are equally unimpressive: the SS *Reindeer*, registered to London, sailed for Swansea, 'light' or without cargo, while the SS *City of Brussels*, another Dublin-registered vessel, sailed for Belfast with 'part cargo'. The bulk of Dublin's port traffic is recorded as 'Coastwise Arrivals and Departures', and here we find the routine voyages which mark out the provincial status of Dublin. Five ships, named the *Hibernia*, *Cambria*, *North Wall*, *Irene*, and *Snowdon*, belonging to the London and North Western Railway company, plied the route that day between Dublin and Holyhead, competing with the more prestigious mailboat service, which Stephen observes departing from Kingstown. A further three ships, the *Wicklow*, *Cork*, and *Adela*, came and went between Liverpool and Dublin. Another three ships, the *Duke of Gordon*, the *Olive*, and the *Dublin*, ferried passengers and cargoes to and from Glasgow. The SS *Belfast* sailed from and returned to the city of its name, and the *Argo* arrived from Bristol. And beyond that, ships of varying sizes and capacities hauled people and freight to and from a host of other ports on the western seaboard of Cumbria, Lancashire, and North Wales, and the names of those ports map out a less familiar geography of trade across the Irish Sea: Manchester, Silloth, Duddon, Harrington, Workington, Llandulas, Morecambe, and Whitehaven. In the same week, ships also travelled between Dublin and Runcorn, Ayr, Garston, Maryport, Preston, Portmadoc, Waterford, Douglas, Carrickfergus, Irvine, Cardiff, Wicklow, Bridgwater, Ardrossan, Neath Abbey, Laxey, and Port Talbot. There are few foreign sailings; the traffic which made Dublin a busy port connected the city instead to the rim settlements of the Irish Sea, from Ayrshire down to Somerset, and across the sea to the Solway, Cumberland, Lancashire, Wales, and the Isle of Man.

Yet there is little trace of this traffic in the Dublin which Joyce depicts. When Bloom fantasises about grand schemes to make him rich, one scheme to connect the Dublin Cattle Market to the terminal stations or branches of the railway companies and steamship companies which linked Dublin port to various parts of Britain, and further afield, is a clear signal of the importance of such traffic across and around the Irish Sea.[89] However, this is the only occasion in the novel on which there is mention of Glasgow, Lancashire, and Morecambe. There are only two passing references to Holyhead in *Ulysses*, a handful to Liverpool and to the Isle of Man, and none to Cumberland or any of its ports. More broadly, and more importantly, there are few allusions to Wales or the Welsh, to Scotland or the Scots, as distinctive places or peoples, and they are more often absorbed into a general and vague sense of Englishness or Britishness. Indeed, the word 'Wales' only appears in the novel in the form of several references to the 'Prince of Wales', and this is indicative of a more general tendency in *Ulysses*, notable from the opening treatment of Haines, to yoke the diverse elements of Britishness together with the imperial and monarchical state. Nels Pearson has commented upon this tendency, which he analyses as Joyce's refraction of the cultural and psychological effects of colonialism, when he argues that *Ulysses* diagnoses the problem of late colonial citizens who are 'easily caught between the habit of recognizing (or misrecognizing) the local and the daily in terms of competing national abstractions and the inclination to romanticize, obfuscate, or demonize existing extranational and subnational phenomena'.[90] Pearson is keen to bring together the contending strands in Joyce criticism, the internationalist Joyce championed most thoroughly by Richard Ellmann, and the nationalist Joyce espoused by Emer Nolan, Vince Cheng, Seamus Deane, and Declan Kiberd, to argue for a Joyce who mused on the coastline as a metaphor for the difficulties of founding a nation which could be internationalist in outlook. In Pearson's view, however, 'when it comes to the difficulties of developing a sustainable transnational consciousness', the characters in *Ulysses* 'struggle to apprehend the problem, to the extent that their own thoughts are liable to reveal its symptoms'.[91]

This is particularly notable in the case of Joyce's depiction of English characters, and many aspects of English culture and history, which Andrew Gibson argues amounts to a kind of Anglophobia, albeit a kind which took 'far subtler, more arrogantly insouciant, and much more cunning forms' than the anti-English prejudices of the Irish-Ireland movement associated with D. P. Moran.[92] It is not even particularly subtle, however, in the case of the first English character presented in the novel, Haines, who is depicted as an alien intruder from the outset, denied a first name, and, as he gazes out over the bay with eyes 'pale as the sea the wind had freshened', is characterised

by the narrator as 'the seas' ruler'.[93] Even though Haines is a committed
Hibernophile, speaks Irish, and studies folklore, and offers Stephen the classic
liberal apology for colonialism ('It seems history is to blame'), he raves in his
dreams 'about shooting a black panther', and professes to be 'a Britisher',
fearful that his nation will 'fall into the hands of German jews'.[94] He is
rather crudely emblematic of imperial power, of xenophobic nationalism, of
Britannia ruling the waves. As the maritime references in the case of Haines
indicate, in *Ulysses* the sea is recurrently associated with political power, and
with the material and symbolic forms of imperial domination.

As Claire Connolly argues, the opening 'Telemachus' section of *Ulysses*
repeatedly draws our focus out to sea, demanding attention to the sea as
a device for scaling the national in relation to the world beyond.[95] Buck
Mulligan is the first character to do this, while shaving upon the parapet,
enjoining Stephen to 'Come and look' at the sea: '*Thalatta! Thalatta!* She is
our great sweet mother.'[96] Stephen obeys, and looks down upon the water,
and then 'on the mailboat clearing the harbour mouth of Kingstown'.[97] The
mailboat is further out, just the smokeplume visible, when Haines looks out
at the sea a few moments later,[98] but the routine passage of the mailboat is
the subject of Bloom's attention as he wanders on Sandymount Strand in
the evening, when he has reason to think of a Dublin councillor en route
across the sea – 'Mailboat. Near Holyhead by now', and also 'Liverpool boat
long gone. Not even the smoke'.[99] These allusions to the mailboat, to cattle
ships, and to the *Erin's King*, a pleasure steamer which took passengers on
cruises from Dublin's Custom House Quay to Lambay, Dalkey, Ireland's Eye,
Howth, the Kish lightship, and Kingstown, keep Dublin Bay and the Irish Sea
in view on a recurrent basis throughout the novel. Yet it is a routine facet of
the novel that looking out at the bay invokes the notion of the sea as a border.

Shipping, in particular, is central to how national aspirations are imagined
and contested, as the citizen's speech in 'Cyclops' about a projected Irish navy
makes clear:

> Our harbours that are empty will be full again, Queenstown, Kinsale,
> Galway, Blacksod Bay, Ventry in the kingdom of Kerry, Killybegs,
> the third largest harbour in the wide world with a fleet of masts of
> the Galway Lynches and the Cavan O'Reillys and the O'Kennedys of
> Dublin when the earl of Desmond could make a treaty with the emperor
> Charles the Fifth himself. And will again, says he, when the first Irish
> battleship is seen breasting the waves with our own flag to the fore, none
> of your Henry Tudor's harps, no, the oldest flag afloat, the flag of the
> province of Desmond and Thomond, three crowns on a blue field, the
> three sons of Milesius.[100]

The citizen's concerns about 'empty harbours', as metonyms of the vanquished nation, are shared by others, it seems, for later in the novel in 'Eumaeus', during Bloom and Stephen's encounter with the sailor and the 'waifs and strays' in the cabman's shelter by the Custom House, we are told that 'All meantime were loudly lamenting the falling off in Irish shipping, coastwise and foreign as well, which was all part and parcel of the same thing . . . Right enough the harbours were there only no ships ever called.'[101] From the cabman's shelter, albeit in the dead of night, this sentiment would be difficult to sustain, as they are adjacent to the quays beside the most easterly bridge of the city, and as the 'Shipping News' reported above indicates, Dublin port was far from empty. Yet, as the citizen's vision suggests, it is not Dublin port, or indeed any of the Irish Sea ports, which are the subject of lament, but the Atlantic coastal harbours of the south and west. These harbours of legendary size upon the Atlantic coast, imagined by the citizen in much the same way that Joyce wrote about Galway in an article for *Il Piccolo della Sera* in Trieste, are weighted symbolically with the unfulfilled potential of Ireland as a colonised nation.[102] However, this symbolic loading of the west necessarily involves spurning the east coast, and perhaps especially the city of Dublin, implying that the ports and shores of the east are somehow themselves complicit in the compromise of national sovereignty. The citizen's nationalism must promise to deliver plenitude where colonialism has resulted in deprivation and scarcity, yet his preferred image of the nation restored to glory is of a battleship, which, in 1904, was already the symbol of an escalating global contest for maritime supremacy. The present circumstances of Irish shipping, meanwhile, are depicted in spectral terms – to the empty harbours and absent battleships invoked by the citizen, we can add the 'silent ship' which Stephen sees from the strand,[103] the 'phantom ship' which Bloom imagines also from the strand,[104] and the recurrent thoughts of both Stephen and Bloom about shipwrecks and the corpses of sailors. In *Ulysses*, then, the sea is constantly freighted with symbolic significance, both as the basis for political power in the form of commercial and military navigation, and as the spectral and sublime space of death and wreckage.

It is in this context, of the discourse of a future Irish nation which, in turning its back upon Britain, also turns its back upon the city which, as Robert Lloyd Praeger argued, 'has been and still remains the key to traffic between the two islands, and the natural hub of Ireland',[105] that I think Joyce's focus in two chapters ('Proteus' and 'Nausicaa') upon his two central characters visiting the shoreline of the east coast is worthy of greater attention from materialist perspectives. If the Atlantic coastline proved fertile terrain for ideas of Irish nationhood in the revival period, and especially in associating geographical remoteness with cultural and linguistic purity, then the Irish Sea coastline, with its saltmarshes, its long expanses of tidal sands, and its enclosure within the outstretched limbs of its larger island neighbour, seems to resist the notion of a border. As he wanders along Sandymount Strand, however, Stephen's first thoughts are drawn precisely to the notion of borders, to 'the nearing tide', to the 'Limits of the diaphane', to thoughts of a gate, a door, a cliff, to the limits of sight and blindness, sound and silence, solid and liquid.[106] As Ernesto Livorni argues, the opening passages of 'Proteus' are concerned with the same problem as Stephen considers in *A Portrait* when he tells Lynch that 'The first phase of apprehension is a bounding line drawn about the object to be apprehended', and the problem of apprehending a 'bounding line' is, of course, particularly acute along the tideline of the shifting sands of Dublin Bay.[107] As the coastline he walks along demonstrates, with its Martello towers, lighthouses, piers, and walls, shores are primary lines of geopolitical division, and can be co-opted to define the land within as an 'object to be apprehended', as an island (whether it be an 'Isle of saints', or an 'isle of dreadful thirst').[108] However, Stephen's thoughts also range across the many ways in which the shoreline is a site of connection, traversal, and obfuscation, and lead towards an archipelagic conception of the 'myriadislanded' nature of the object to be apprehended.[109]

Joyce's historical and mythological references in 'Proteus' bear out this conception, specifically in drawing attention to the archipelagic origins of Dublin:

> Galleys of the Lochlanns ran here to beach, in quest of prey, their blood-beaked prows riding low on a molten pewter surf. Dane vikings, torcs of tomahawks aglitter on their breasts when Malachi wore the collar of gold. A school of turlehide whales stranded in hot noon, spouting, hobbling in the shallows. Then from the starving cagework city a horde of jerkined dwarfs, my people, with flayers' knives, running, scaling, hacking in green blubbery whalemeat. Famine, plague and slaughters. Their blood is in me, their lusts my waves.[110]

The Lochlanns, or Norwegian invaders, founded the city in the eighth century as part of an archipelagic empire which controlled settlements right around the Irish Sea, with the Danes following shortly after from bases in the Hebrides and the Isle of Man.[111] The allusion to the 'turlehide whales' beached upon the shores which saved the people of Dublin from famine in the thirteenth century illustrates the continued dependence of the city upon the sea, and its affinity with those other ocean-rim peoples sustained by the bounties of the sea. The phrase recalling when 'Malachi wore the collar of gold' is borrowed from Thomas Moore's poem 'Let Erin Remember the Days of Old', and invites nationalist sentiment, except that here Joyce omits to mention that

Malachi defeated the Danes twice, and wore the collar of gold as a trophy of resistance. Instead, the passage emphasises permeability, not resistance. Of particular note in this passage, however, is the emphasis which it places upon a myth of origins from the sea itself, the founding invasion coming out of the waves, and this is a recurrent theme of the chapter. It recurs, for example, in the reference to that other foundational mythical figure of Irish Sea origins, Mananaan Mac Lir, literally 'son of the sea', from which the Isle of Man takes its name, and which Stephen sees coming in the waves: 'The whitemaned seahorses, champing, brightwindbridled, the steeds of Mananaan'.[112] It recurs, too, in Stephen's immediate association of the shoreline with creation and birth: in the midwives he observes coming down to the strand, in the story of Genesis, Adam and Eve, and 'Creation from nothing', in thoughts of his own genesis from his parents and his 'people', in the play upon 'Algy'/algae and the sea as 'our mighty mother', which references the story of evolution as one of descent from simple, marine organisms.[113]

Just as Stephen's aesthetic theories in *Portrait* revolve around questions of race and biology, so too, in 'Proteus', his theories of apprehension and form repeatedly dwell upon questions of evolution, species differentiation, and biological origins.[114] 'Proteus' has attracted a great deal of critical attention for its demonstration of philosophical theories of consciousness and aesthetics, yet its shoreline location seems in such treatments to be explained as a metaphorical landscape, with the sea, sand, waves, and tides providing abstract manifestations of Stephen's thoughts on metamorphoses and rhythm. Stephen announces his intention to attend to the material meanings of his shoreline location from the outset, however: 'Signatures of all things I am here to read, seaspawn and seawrack, the nearing tide, that rusty boot.'[115] As Gregory Castle argues, the import of this statement is not 'the hegemonic power of the sign and signification', but rather that Stephen's attempts to understand the history from which he strives to awake 'are situated in a context that suggests a profound connection between historical understanding and the cycles of nature'.[116] The beach condenses into one strip the natural cycles of tides, waves, generation, decomposition, erosion, and accretion with the historical cycles of migration, invasion, settlement, and demise. The shoreline is not just a metaphor of protean change, therefore, but a material embodiment of such change. Moreover, it supercedes the temporal dimensions of human scales of historical understanding in its exposure of the *longue durée* of geological time, and hence, as Stephen walks blindly upon the sands, stones, and shells, to the sounds of 'Crush, crack, crick, crick', he ponders the question, 'Am I walking into eternity along Sandymount strand?'[117]

Walking along Sandymount Strand, then, prompts Stephen to consider the nature of material existence itself, and the temporal scales of human agency measured against the cycles of water and rock, as well as other species. 'Proteus' establishes the connection early between what Robert Macfarlane calls the 'ways of walking that were also ways of thinking'.[118] Those ways of walking and thinking fold time in on itself, so that Stephen perceives the contact between different times, and different places, layered into the sand and shells:

> The grainy sand had gone from under his feet. His boots trod again a damp crackling mast, razorshells, squeaking pebbles, that on the unnumbered pebbles beats, wood sieved by the shipworm, lost Armada. Unwholesome sandflats waited to suck his treading soles, breathing upward sewage breath.[119]

The shoreline is littered with the detritus of the earth, with every 'breath' of the tide a sign of life and decay, and the remains of human efforts to 'rule the waves' lost amid the 'unnumbered pebbles'. This same shoreline waits to claim Stephen's body, too, sucking now at his soles, just as the sea has reclaimed the body of the man found 'bobbing landward', his corpse already a feeding ground for minnows.[120] When Stephen imagines the man 'Hauled stark over the gunwale', Joyce uses the same image as for the sandflats: 'he breathes upward the stench of his green grave'.[121] The recurrent image signals the association of 'sea air', conventionally linked in the nineteenth century with health and vitality, with human decomposition, either death or sewage. But that this gives life to the sea, feeding the generation of the same algae which in turn, in dying, produce the characteristic smell of 'sea air', is consonant with Joyce's image of the beach as a liminal space of life and death.

   The connection between life forms evident in this passage is present throughout the chapter. Already thinking of 'shells' as the slang term for money (and his copy of J. G. Wood's *Common Objects of the Sea-Shore* told him of money shells), fresh from his fraught discussion of money management with Deasy, Stephen thinks of the Ringsend fishermen as 'Human shells', and watches the 'Cocklepickers', a man and woman wading in the shallows, their dog close at hand.[122] The proximity of species piles up in a series of allusions, particularly around the dog, who first is like a 'bounding hare', 'chasing the shadow of a lowskimming gull'; his bark at the waves is associated with 'herds of seamorse', and the waves 'serpented towards his feet'.[123] He is then 'bearish' in fawning to the cocklepickers, his tongue likened to a wolf's, and his run like a 'calf's gallop'. The dog then encounters the carcass of another dog, 'brother', after which he 'claws' at the sand for something buried, 'his grandmother', 'soon ceasing, a pard, a panther, got in spousebreach, vulturing the dead'. The 'pard' plays upon Shakespeare's use of the Latin term for panther,[124] while also picking up a late nineteenth-century American contraction of 'partner', so that affiliation is suggested between the species. All of this takes place, of course, upon the South Bull, reputedly named because of the bull-like sound of the receding waves. Stephen is himself connected to the dog: both urinate on the sands, and both are brought to face the image of the dead of their own species. Joyce is demonstrating the very premise of Darwin's theory of evolution, in showing 'the nature of the affinities which connect together whole groups of organisms'.[125] Darwin begins his study of these affinities, of course, by showing the resemblances between the embryos of a human and a dog, and this is especially of note when we recall that Joyce described Stephen in a letter to Frank Budgen as 'the embryo'.[126] As Sandra Tropp has argued of Stephen's theories of aesthetics in *A Portrait of the Artist*, Joyce made use of Darwin and other scientists of physiology as surely as he did of Aristotle and Aquinas,[127] and if, as Paul Bowers has shown, Darwinian narrative suffuses Joyce's writing in 'Oxen of the Sun' and *Finnegans Wake*, it is equally pervasive in 'Proteus'.[128] It is not the uses to which Joyce puts Darwinian ideas in the service of theories of aesthetics, consciousness, nature, or language which concern me here, however, but the significance of those ideas in Stephen's experience of, and conception of, the shoreline as a material and political space.

In reading the shore as a material space (and Stephen even assures himself at the outset of its materiality: 'There all the time without you'), Stephen becomes preoccupied with its generative and degenerative associations, and with the evolutionary cycles embedded within its forms. The sea spawns life, and recycles dead matter. The overlaying of the Edenic myth of the first man and woman upon the cocklepickers seems even to relocate Eden out of the garden and on to the beach. Stephen too becomes part of this vision of 'primitive' humanity. When his boots crunch down on the shells and pebbles of the tideline, the sounds of 'Crush, crack, crick, crick' register, as if for the first time, the solidity of the beach, 'a stride at a time'.[129] Stephen attends to the noise and rhythm of his walking as if he has just learned to walk, as if he has been spawned indeed by the sea. The sounds might be read in interestingly ambivalent ways. On the one hand, 'crush, crack, crick' may be a human imitation of the sounds made by the geological processes which have shaped the earth, including the glacial movements responsible for some of the most curious and characteristic deposits of marine detritus along the Irish Sea.[130] On the other hand, the sounds indicate a destructive and conflictual relationship with nature. The historical examples of 'crick-crack' given by the *Oxford English Dictionary*, for instance, are almost all connected with the sounds of hunting or whipping animals, including Dinah Craik's poem about a hare hunted by 'Those creatures, who walk upright, and / make crick-cracks as they go'.[131] This would serve to connect Stephen to the 'point, live dog', as the pointer is a hunting dog, although, of course, Stephen behaves more like the hare, and 'shakes at a cur's yelping'.[132] A further layer to this evolutionary history which Stephen traces on the sands is that the pointer dog is an example of human manipulation of evolution, in breeding dogs to perform specific functions for human benefit, and therefore shows the interdependence of human and biotic evolution. The image of the hunter-gatherer, then, close to the 'community of descent' which Darwin theorised, underlies the scene, with Sandymount Strand fathomed as a prehistoric past of human foraging and hunting along the shoreline.

In discerning aquatic sources for human evolution, Stephen is also concerned, of course, to map the Darwinian explanation of language on to the neat literary genealogy proposed by Genesis. If, indeed, 'In the beginning was the word', what aquatic shape did such a word take? Stephen considers this question from materialist perspectives: 'These heavy sands are language tide and wind have silted here.'[133] This line has been cited frequently as a metaphor for language, and indeed Joyce is interested in the convergences of linguistic and physical processes, but this interpretation seems to avoid the more obvious syntactical arrangement, which places language as a metaphor for the sands. The sands are, after all, among the 'Signatures of all things I am here to read'. The waves too have their own 'fourworded wavespeech: seesoo, hrss, rsseeiss, ooos'.[134] As Sidney Feshbach demonstrates, there are ways of explicating the non-lexical sounds of 'wavespeech' to make them consonant with Stephen's immediate associations: 'Vehement breath of waters amid seasnakes, rearing horses, rocks.'[135] Yet each of these associations are, in turn, like the reputed origins of the names for Dublin's North and South Bulls, attempts to translate the language of the sea into other recognisable forms. Feshbach's point that the sounds are semantically productive, that the 'hrss' of the sea might take us through 'rearing horses' and back to the 'white-maned seahorses . . . of Mananaan', for example, simply illustrates that Joyce was interested in the ways in which the signatures of language evolution may also be read in the sounds and cycles of nature. The shoreline abounds with evidence of the minute scale of the human (and divine) word compared to the 'wavespeech' of the sea, and the testimony of the rocks and sand, a point which Joyce cannot refrain from stressing when Stephen scribbles imitative lines of verse on scrap paper on 'a table of rock', and wonders, 'Who ever anywhere will read these written words?'[136] It is the desolate, but necessary, lesson of his naturalist expedition to the seashore, to read the end of humanity, and the infinitesimal scale of human creativity, in the 'Human shells' of the Ringsend fishermen, the 'coche ensablé' (a barge sunken in silt) metaphor of prose writing, the 'stoneheaps of dead builders' buried in the construction of the South Wall (the boulders of which remind Stephen of 'mammoth skulls'), and the 'brown eyes saltblue' of the drowned man.[137] Against these scales of natural and geological evolution, the citizen's vision of Ireland as a battleship 'breasting the waves', or Stephen's own image of Haines as 'the sea's ruler', are obviously comic, although within their own measure, they are clearly not without force.

The shift in scale evident in Joyce's shoreline episode engenders a 'seachange' in spatial conception, away from the too obvious pitfalls which *Ulysses* demonstrates again and again of a terrestrial- and territorial-bound imagination. Locked out of the tower, newly nomadic, Stephen must now think in mobile and connective terms about the shoreline, not as a border, but as a site of intersection and relation. From the sands of Sandymount, he can think of Newhaven, Paris, and beyond, 'Across the sands of all the world'.[138] As the many languages used in the chapter illustrate, and the concept indeed of the world as 'myriadislanded', Stephen's view of this connected world is neither one of unity, the monoglot Eden, nor one of absolute insularity, policed by battleships. Instead, it is a differential, variegated, contested, and interdependent world, an archipelagic world, learned from what Gillian Beer recognises as Darwin's political affirmation 'that diversity, difference, nonconformity, otherness, are creative forms', and learned too from the awareness of differential spatial scales which Stephen steps out on the South Bull.[139]

For Bloom and Gerty MacDowell in 'Nausicaa', the shoreline is similarly of a different order from terrestrial experience. Sidney Feshbach argues that the chapter divides in half, that in Gerty's half 'sentimental cliché makes a mush of the few references to the sea', and that 'in Bloom's half, the sea is merely there'.[140] The two are connected, however, by the associations of the shoreline with sentimental fictions. The chapter opens, indeed, by framing a view of the sea within romantic and anthropomorphic tropes:

> The summer evening had begun to fold the world in its mysterious embrace. Far away in the west the sun was setting and the last glow of all too fleeting day lingered lovingly on sea and strand, on the proud promontory of dear old Howth guarding as ever the waters of the bay.[141]

Whereas 'Proteus' follows Stephen's attempt to read the material signatures of the sea and the shore, 'Nausicaa' is self-consciously set within a sentimental register, in which the sea and the bay are seen entirely in metaphoric terms, precisely the terms (the sea as 'our great, sweet mother') which Stephen has necessarily rejected. The chapter is dominated by aesthetic tropes borrowed from visual art, from popular theatre, and from maritime fiction. This is especially explicit when Gerty looks out to sea and thinks of the view as 'like the paintings that man used to do on the pavement with all the coloured chalks'.[142] Vicki Mahaffey has argued that these tropes highlight the ways in which Bloom's voyeurism relies upon a willed illusion, that of wanting to see Gerty as a 'show', a fantasy, which necessitates an elision of reality.[143] In the case of Gerty, Bloom is not aware of her physical handicap, and is relieved that he 'didn't know it when she was on show'.[144] The 'show' metaphor is extended when Bloom again considers that it would have spoiled his excitement to 'See her as she is': 'Must have the stage setting, the rouge, costume, position, music.'[145] The chapter suggests that the same applies to the sea. Bloom and Gerty are, after all, not walking (like naturalists) along the shoreline, but seated (like a theatre audience) on the rocks near the sea wall, an artificial barrier which serves to frame the shoreline as a beach for leisure and as an aesthetic object.

Sandymount Strand was developed when the completion of the sea wall in 1791 enabled the city to expand out to its eastern shores, and in the nineteenth century it became an affluent suburb, with houses built along the strand with 'sea views'.[146] The Church of St Mary, Star of the Sea, from which Gerty can hear the sounds of evening mass, was rebuilt in Sandymount in 1858, when the previous church of that name in Ringsend was too small to accommodate its expanding congregation. The move is perhaps of some significance for the theme of the chapter, since the church originally served a fishing and shipping community, but, removed to Sandymount, its patronage of seafarers was, in an affluent suburb, almost wholly symbolic. By the 1880s, with tram services running from O'Connell Street out to Sandymount, and a new promenade pier and baths beyond the Martello tower, the strand had become the nearest and most popular beach for Dubliners to enjoy. It was, according to an *Irish Times* celebration of the seaside suburb in 1875, 'healthful' and 'bracing', with the promenade 'as picturesque . . . as the cliffs at Brighton, or the terraces at Hastings', with perhaps even a superior view to either of those famous seaside resorts, 'such as the crescent coast line from our suburb to the pier at Kingstown'.[147] It was associated with romance, pleasure, and vitality, a time and space apart from the working city, and it must therefore too have its 'stage setting, the rouge, costume, position, music'. In other words, Bloom comes to Sandymount predisposed to connect artificiality with pleasure, to see the sea, and its 'seaside girls', as they really are not. Kasia Boddy links Bloom, in this respect, to a host of other '*fin-de-siècle* shoreline eroticists' in the work of Proust, Mann, and Eliot, who 'look at girls and boys against the backdrop of the sea . . . to see them as symbols, as mermaids, birds, classical sculptures, rare jewels or flowers'.[148] Boddy locates Joyce's beach scenes as part of a modernist reaction to the popularisation (and vulgarisation) of the shoreline, of its transformation as a space associated in the Romantic period with lone, sublime experience, to a crowded and condensed extension of modern industries of leisure and entertainment.

Edmund Gosse's lament for the passing of shoreline wilderness into the
playground of the masses is Boddy's key register of this transformation, with
Gosse's father's naturalist and scientific wonder at discoveries along deserted
beaches juxtaposed with the 'profaned, and emptied, and vulgarised' intrusions of modern-day seaside tourists.[149] Gosse's account describes the supposedly untouched shorelines of fifty years before in self-consciously Edenic
terms:

> if the Garden of Eden had been situate in Devonshire, Adam and Eve . . .
> would have seen the identical sights that we now saw, – the great prawns
> gliding like transparent launches, *anthea* waving in the twilights its thick
> white waxen tentacles, and the fronds of the dulse faintly streaming on
> the water, like huge red banners in some reverted atmosphere.[150]

As Gosse acknowledges, popular accounts of seashore rambles such as those
published by his father whetted public appetites for trips to the coast, and
served to foster the very 'intrusions' and 'violations' by 'An army of "collec-
tors"' which father and son came to bemoan.[151] Ellmann records Gosse as one
of the sources which would have influenced Joyce's interest in the figure of
the religious defector, and Thornton lists Philip Gosse's famous attempt to
align the findings of geology with the Bible, *Omphalos* (1857), as an obvious
reference point for 'Proteus'.[152] The relationship between father and son
seems pertinent to the juxtaposed narratives of the sea in Joyce's novel. Joyce
would surely have found much amusement, given the opening line which he
would later write to *Finnegans Wake*, in the idea of Adam and Eve among the
shellfish on a Devonshire beach, and it is difficult to avoid the possibility that
the cocklepickers in 'Proteus' are an ironic allusion to Gosse's coastal Eden,
just as Stephen's attention to the 'Signatures of all things that I must read'
might alert readers to the controversy of how to read the signs of the earth's
past raised by Philip Gosse's much derided idea that God included fossils, tree
rings, and Adam's navel in his original creation to imitate the signs of age.

It is tempting to read 'Nausicaa', with its emphasis from the outset on the
artificiality of the sea as it is presented to us in cosmetically enhanced shorelines like Sandymount, and its association of the seaside with a fall from Edenic
grace, as an antithesis to Stephen's materialist walk among the objects of the
shore. Yet Philip Gosse's reading of the geology of the shore was precisely that
of a faked world, a theatre of illusions, and so 'Nausicaa', with its recurrent
allusions to fake signs of youth, beauty, and vitality, returns to the same questions about origins, material signs, and illusions as preoccupy Stephen on his
walk. If 'Proteus' depicts Stephen on a quest to read the signs of the sea and
the shore as they really are, 'Nausicaa' ponders the effects of reading the signs
of the same world as they really are not. Fake signals of the maritime world

abound, from the sailors' hats and 'man-o'-war top' worn by the children, to the 'phantom ship' which Bloom sees in 'nightclouds' on the horizon.[153] Bloom's appearance to Gerty as an exotic foreigner from overseas (the same appearance which has attracted Molly to him) is deftly juxtaposed with his recollection, when thinking of sailors, of his one sea voyage, a 'Filthy trip' on board 'Erin's King', on a 'pleasure cruise' out to Kish lightship along with 'Drunkards out to shake up their livers. Puking overboard to feed the herrings.'[154] He is far from being an exotic traveller.

In 'Nausicaa', Joyce exposes the sea and the shoreline as social constructions of a territorial imagination, the inventions of a society increasingly estranged from the material realities of sea life. Bloom's reflections on maritime life owe much to the conventions of maritime fiction, to the novels and stories of Joseph Conrad, many of which were readily to hand on Joyce's shelves in Trieste, along with Max Pemberton's *Sea Wolves* and Filson Young's *The Sands of Pleasure*.[155] These thoughts take Bloom imaginatively to 'the ends of the earth somewhere', to the terrors of storms, shipwrecks, and sharks, and the clichéd exoticism of a 'Wife in every port'.[156] Yet the sole voyage he recalls brought him to the lightship he can see from the shore and back. The gap between the romance and the reality, between the story and the deed, highlights his alienation from the history and geography of his own city, and from the very real maritime connections and crossings which explain his own ancestry, marriage, and identity. Thus, Joyce situates Bloom at the end of the chapter unable to read the words on a piece of paper he picks up from the strand (perhaps the words Stephen has written, wondering about their posterity), and unable to complete the sentence he begins to draw with his stick on the sand, 'I. AM. A . . .'. The beach is itself unreadable for its signs of life: 'Hopeless thing sand. Nothing grows in it. All fades.'[157] Bloom, it seems, is deaf to the sounds of the 'wavespeech'. The chapter ends with the sound (heard from the clock on the mantelpiece of the priest's house) of a cuckoo, a bird famously associated with parasitism. The suggestion that Bloom is a parasite, of course, raises controversial associations with anti-semitic stereotypes. Yet, read in relation to the chapter's concern with the transformed and alienated relationship between Dubliners and their coastline, Bloom is not the only one implicated in the jibe. A city estranged from its own coastal origins, and which repudiates its connections to its sustaining natural environment (in which the sea is a 'view' which adds to property values), may justly be regarded as parasitic.

This, finally, takes us to the coastal patterning of *Finnegans Wake*, which begins and ends with the sea, and which delights in a triumphant return to the sea as an originary father-figure. *Finnegans Wake* is, famously, Joyce's 'water book', written in 'the languo of flows'.[158] It is primarily regarded, however, as a river book. As Marian Eide observes, the river is a key structural element of the text:

> The river Liffey, an embodiment of the character Anna Livia Plurabelle, provides an image for flexibility and fluctuation both in the writing of *Finnegans Wake* and in the perceptual habits necessary to interpret this text. In other words, fluidity is a sign in the text, but it is also a sign of the text. The river signifies a perceptual system, which, informed by the mechanics of fluids, creates an assemblage operating between water and embankments, fluids and solids, writing and interpretation, the reader and the text.[159]

Yet, perhaps an obvious point to make about the river as it is depicted in the text is that it is not so much the river system (as we might expect it to be from the text's opening and closing emphasis upon recirculation), as it is the tidal river, from the bay up to Chapelizod, which is the focus of the novel, roughly the terrain upon which the eponymous Finnegan, 'erse solid man', falls on the first page, with his head at Howth and his toes at Phoenix Park. The story of the river's source in Kippure, and of its course as 'the wiggly livvly', is told,[160] but it is the drama of the flow between the city's banks and out to sea which preoccupies the text more fully. The figure of recirculation at the beginning of the novel is arguably one of tidal processes, then: 'riverrun, past Eve and Adam's, from swerve of shore to bend of bay, brings us by a commodious vicus of recirculation back to Howth Castle and Environs'.[161] What is meant by 'Environs', in this context, is unclear, since it may be, as it has often been read, Joyce's fanciful way of figuring Dublin with the polysemous acronym HCE, which recurs throughout the text, but, more likely, given the topographical precision which characterises his work, it draws our attention to the extent of the bay as defined by Howth Head. At this point, Dublin Bay meets the Irish Sea, between the Baily and Kish lighthouses, a watery boundary for the city. Later in the novel, one of the narrators of the Norwegian Captain episode tells us of the 'prowed invisors' (the Vikings) whose 'infroraids' founded the city, their arrival, like those of others, marked at this watery border: 'Kish met. Bound to. And for landlord, noting, nodding, a coast to moor was cause to mear.'[162] 'Mear' undoubtedly resonates with 'mer', the sea, but as a verb it means 'to mark out a boundary', and its etymological traces from Old English relate particularly to property dealings in Ireland, with a scattering of dialectal usage in other borderline territories such as Northumbria, Westmorland, Cheshire, Shropshire, and Somerset (*OED*). On the most easterly piece of land defined by this river system, then, Howth Head, a castle has been built to define a border, to mark the boundary of property. Thus, as the narrator says, 'a coast to moor was cause to mear'. Joyce begins *Finnegans Wake* with the image of a natural system which gives rise or cause to territorial and proprietorial borders, which appear to be 'Kish met', or kismet, fated to be.

In the next line, however, against this association of the sea as a border, Joyce turns our attention to the archipelagic connections made possible by the sea: 'Sir Tristram, violer d'amores, fr'over the short sea, had passencore rearrived from North Armorica on this side the scraggy isthmus of Europe Minor to wielderfight his penisolate war.'[163] As can be expected of *Finnegans Wake*, the sentence contains a series of polysemous cultural and geographical allusions, which nonetheless concentrate upon a Celtic archipelago centred around the Irish Sea and the Atlantic seaboard of Western Europe. 'North Armorica' is an intriguing compound, since it contains the allusion to North America as McHugh annotates,[164] but also a Celtic network of coastlands and islands stretching from Brittany (Armorica) to Cornwall, Wales, and Ireland.[165] 'North' Armorica itself may be Joyce's playful allusion to Cornwall, from which the Breton language and peoples are reputedly derived (as well as the more general Brythonic connection with Wales), and indeed the name, Armorica, derives from Breton for 'by the sea', specifying not a particular locality or community, but rather a coastal relation. The legend of Tristram, too, references this archipelago, as the hero serves his uncle, King Mark of Cornwall, and falls in love with his uncle's bride-to-be, Iseult, daughter of the Queen of Ireland, whom he has been sent to accompany from Ireland, and he dies in Brittany. He is thus both an instrument (viola d'amour) and a violator ('violer') of love. The reference to his (re)arrival in Dublin makes a joke too that he is a passenger ('passencore' – not yet) who will come 'fr'over the short sea', as if stepping off the steamship from Holyhead. Thus Dublin is defined topographically by its tidal flows, by what the tides bring in and out, and by its maritime access to its coastal neighbours around the Irish Sea and the north-east Atlantic. It is 'this timecoloured place where we live in our paroqial firmament one tide on another, with a bumrush in the hull of a wherry'.[166]

Like *Ulysses*, *Finnegans Wake* frequently invites us to look out to sea, beyond the 'Cape of Good Howthe', to the 'irised sea', and out to the 'atalantic's breastswells'.[167] It embraces the languages of the sea in various forms, most notably the nautical language which preoccupies the Norwegian Captain episode, and the littoral language of tides, banks, and bars which pervades the novel. It also imagines what lies across the sea, figuring the connections made from shore to shore:

> When it's summwer calding and she can hear the pianutunar beyant the bayondes in Combria sleepytalking to the Wiltsh muntons, titting out through her droemer window for the flyend of a touchman over the

wishtas of English Strand, when Kilbarrack bell pings saksalaisance that Concessas with Sinbads may (pong!)[168]

In this passage from the Norwegian Captain's episode, the ship's agent is describing the tailor's daughter, who can apparently hear the pianotuner (or thunder), a sign of summer (or somewhere) calling, from 'beyond the beyond', a colloquial phrase meaning far away, and peeks out of her window looking to see her dream lover, the flying Dutchman, a sailor, over the vistas of an English strand. As McHugh notes, 'bayondes' is also a conflation of 'bay' and 'waves' (French *onde*), so that we are invited to imagine the sound coming over the waves and the bay from 'Combria' (conjoining Cumbria and Cambria, i.e. Wales) and the 'Wiltsh muntons' (the spelling of which combines Welsh and Wiltshire). This grafting of one place on to another is one of the most recurrent features of Joyce's treatment of place-names in the *Wake*, such as 'Brayhowth', 'Brighten-pon-the-Baltic', 'Daneygaul', 'Brettaine', 'Livpoomark', and of course the numerous plays upon 'Dublin' such as 'Durbalanars'.[169] In each case, Joyce figures a maritime connection, a way in which the sea collapses distance and turns identity into relation. It is perhaps especially notable, however, that Joyce figures the Irish Sea not in terms of visibility, but in terms of audibility:

> You could hear them swearing threaties on the Cymylaya Mountains, man. And giving it out to the Ould Fathach and louth-mouthing after the Holy Mealy with an enfysis to bring down the rain of Tarar.[170]

The distance between Dublin and Wales is just far enough to prevent visibility from shore to shore, but Joyce suggests in the above passages that they are within hearing distance, which is to propose instead an audible geography.

This is, perhaps above all, what *Finnegans Wake* is 'about', the audible geography of language, the audibility of other places and other peoples within the speech of any locality. As Laurent Milesi argues, 'If, according to Levinas, "language is hospitality," then the *Wake*'s linguistic-familial nucleus welcomes the other within according to the combinatory laws of hybridity and miscegenation which turn the work's geolinguistics into a spatial ethics.'[171] The 'geolinguistics' of *Finnegans Wake* famously spans the globe, taking into its stride elements of a wide range of European languages, including the Celtic languages fringed around Ireland's shores, fragments of Chinese, Arabic, and Japanese, some soundings in African and Melanesian languages, invented languages, and smatterings of pidgin, argot, and Creole, and putting them to work within an already globalised and globalising English. If *Ulysses* was about imagining one place through the lens of another, however, *Finnegans Wake* was about the impossibility of imagining one place without trying to see its relations to all others, and in this respect, the tidal comings and goings which shaped the history and community that is Dublin are Joyce's figures of global connections.[172] The sea, in other words, is that figure of globality which is also the material space in and through which peoples, languages, produce, and artefacts transact with others ('oceans of kissening').[173] In the terms established throughout the *Wake*, this is what it means to be a 'seaborn isle'.[174]

When compared to the hydrophasia which marks *Dubliners*, the concluding narrative of *Finnegans Wake* is especially notable for its loving rush into the sea: 'Sea, sea! Here, weir, reach, island, bridge. Where you meet I.'[175] From rain to river to sea, Joyce animates an ecosystem to tell the story of place, the crossing of the river into the sea imagined as a lonely daughter rushing into the arms of her 'cold mad feary father': 'Carry me along, taddy, like you done through the toy fair!'[176] The familial drama of return and embrace, enacted continuously before the eyes and ears of Dubliners in the river and the bay, is a constant breaching of the myth of territorial insularity, a 'mememormee' of the flows of people, commerce, and words which connect the 'yrish archipelago' to the world.[177]

NOTES

1. H. J. Mackinder, *Britain and the British Seas*. London: William Heinemann, 1902, 20.
2. James Joyce, *Ulysses*. Oxford: Oxford World's Classics, 1993, 5–6.
3. V. G. Childe, *Prehistoric Communities of the British Isles*. London: Chambers, 1940, 6.
4. Jacques Rancière, *On the Shores of Politics*, trans. Liz Heron. London: Verso, 2007, 1.
5. Ibid. 2.
6. James Joyce, *Dubliners*. Oxford: Oxford World's Classics, 2000, 148–9, 176. Although the reasons for Joyce's exploration of the turn westwards in *Dubliners* have been widely debated in the critical record, Frank Shovlin's *Journey Westwards: Joyce,* Dubliners, *and the Literary Revival* (Liverpool: Liverpool University Press, 2012) is a thorough and stimulating re-assessment of the depth of Joyce's knowledge of and allusions to the West of Ireland.
7. Joyce, *Dubliners*, 176.
8. One notable exception is Brewster Ghiselin in 'The Unity of *Dubliners*', in Peter K. Garrett (ed.), *Twentieth Century Interpretations of Dubliners*. Englewood Cliffs, NJ: Prentice-Hall Inc., 1968, 57–85. Ghiselin observes the 'frustration of Dubliners unable to escape eastward, out of the seaport and overseas, to a more living world' (60), and interprets the symbolism of the sea and the east in *Dubliners* as part of a Christian iconography. For Ghiselin, the eastward sea represents 'baptismal water', and sacramental orientation towards Eden, or the

Resurrection, and therefore a vitality opposed to the symbolism of death in the west.

9. Joyce, *Dubliners*, 141.
10. Ibid. 121.
11. Ibid. 84.
12. Ibid. 46.
13. Ibid. 14.
14. Ibid. 34.
15. George Moore, *Parnell and his Island*, ed. Carla King. Dublin: University College Dublin Press, 2004, 1.
16. Joyce, *Dubliners*, 30.
17. Hugh Kenner, 'Molly's Masterstroke', *James Joyce Quarterly*, 10 (Fall 1972), 20–1 (19–28). Shawn St. Jean provides a useful overview of the influence of, and responses to, Kenner's reading in 'Readerly Paranoia and Joyce's Adolescence Stories', *James Joyce Quarterly*, 35.4/36.1 (Summer/Fall 1998), 665–82.
18. Joyce, *Dubliners*, 27.
19. Ibid. 28–9.
20. Ibid. 28.
21. Moore, *Parnell and his Island*, 1.
22. Joyce, *Dubliners*, 14.
23. Marilyn Reizbaum, 'Urban Legends', *Eire-Ireland*, 45.1&2 (Spring/Summer 2010), 243, 248 (242–65).
24. 'Dismantling the Pigeon House Fort', *Weekly Irish Times*, 15 March 1902, 20.
25. Joyce, *Dubliners*, 149.
26. Ibid. 141.
27. Ibid. 148.
28. Christopher Harvie, *A Floating Commonwealth: Politics, Culture, and Technology on Britain's Atlantic Coast, 1860–1930*. Oxford: Oxford University Press, 2008, 14.
29. Ibid. 66.
30. Ibid. 57–85.
31. Joyce, *Dubliners*, 149.
32. Ibid. 150.
33. Ibid. 176.
34. Richard Ellmann, 'The Backgrounds of "The Dead"', *The Kenyon Review*, 20.4 (Autumn 1958), 523 (507–28).
35. Ibid. 523.
36. Sidney Feshbach, 'Literal/Littoral/Littorananima: The Figure of the Shore in the Works of James Joyce', in A. T. Tymieniecka (ed.), *Analecta Husserliana*, 19 (1985), 325–42.
37. James Joyce, *A Portrait of the Artist as a Young Man*. Oxford: Oxford World's Classics, 2000, 5, 213.
38. Ibid. 22.

39. Ibid. 55.
40. Ibid. 102, 111.
41. Ibid. 140–5.
42. Ibid. 190.
43. Ibid. 205.
44. Ibid. 82.
45. Ibid. 83–4.
46. John Mack, *The Sea: A Cultural History*. London: Reaktion, 2011, 16–17.
47. Geoffrey Corry, 'The Dublin Bar: The Obstacle to the Improvement of the Port of Dublin', *Dublin Historical Record*, 23.4 (July 1970), 138 (137–52).
48. Desmond F. Moore, 'The Port of Dublin', *Dublin Historical Record*, 16.4 (August 1961), 132 (131–44).
49. Donal T. Flood, 'The Birth of Bull Island', *Dublin Historical Record*, 28.4 (September 1975), 152 (142–53).
50. Corry, 'The Dublin Bar', 150.
51. Ian Baucom, *Specters of the Atlantic: Finance Capital, Slavery, and the Philosophy of History*. Durham, NC: Duke University Press, 2005, 3–34.
52. Joyce, *A Portrait of the Artist*, 54.
53. Ibid. 55.
54. Ibid. 55.
55. Margaret Cohen, *The Novel and the Sea*. Princeton: Princeton University Press, 2010, 11.
56. Arthur L. Faubel, *Cork and the American Cork Industry*. New York: The Cork Institute of America, 1941. See also Olive Jones and Catherine Sullivan, *The Parks Canada Glass Glossary*. Studies in Archaeology, Architecture and History. Ottawa: Ministry of Supply and Services, 1989, 149–50.
57. Joyce, *A Portrait of the Artist*, 58.
58. Ibid. 56.
59. Ibid. 197.
60. Ibid. 147–8.
61. Kristian Smidt, '"I'm Not Half Norawain for Nothing": Joyce and Norway', *James Joyce Quarterly*, 26.3 (Spring 1989), 333–50.
62. Joyce, *A Portrait of the Artist*, 140.
63. Richard Brown, *James Joyce and Sexuality*. Cambridge: Cambridge University Press, 1985, 158.
64. Michael Shortland (ed.), *Hugh Miller and the Controversies of Victorian Science*. Oxford: Clarendon Press, 1996, 3.
65. Joyce, *A Portrait of the Artist*, 144.
66. Hugh Miller, *The Testimony of the Rocks, or Geology in its Bearings: On the Two Theologies, Natural and Revealed*. Edinburgh: Thomas Constable and Co., Shepherd and Elliot, 1857, 260–2.
67. Ibid. 220.
68. Ibid. 256–7.
69. Brown, *James Joyce and Sexuality*, 158.

70. See H. A. Gilligan, *A History of the Port of Dublin*. Dublin: Gill and Macmillan, 1988, 93–4.

71. See P. G. Kennedy, 'Bird Life on the North Bull', *The Irish Naturalists' Journal*, 5.7 (January 1935), 165–8, and Alexander Williams, 'Bird Life in Dublin Bay: The Passing of Clontarf Island', *The Irish Naturalist*, 17.9 (September 1908), 165–70.

72. Joyce, *A Portrait of the Artist*, 140–1.

73. Joseph A. Kestner, 'Youth by the Sea: The Ephebe in "A Portrait of the Artist as a Young Man" and "Ulysses"', *James Joyce Quarterly*, 31.3 (Spring 1994), 245 (233–76).

74. Ibid. 246.

75. Joyce, *A Portrait of the Artist*, 143.

76. Ibid. 143.

77. Anthony Roche, '"The Strange Light of Some New World": Stephen's Vision in "A Portrait"', *James Joyce Quarterly*, 25.3 (Spring 1988), 324 (323–32).

78. Joyce, *A Portrait of the Artist*, 144.

79. Kennedy, 'Bird Life on the North Bull', 167.

80. Joyce, *A Portrait of the Artist*, 144.

81. Ibid. 145.

82. Miller, *The Testimony of the Rocks*, 261.

83. Rachel Carson, *The Edge of the Sea*. Boston: Mariner, 1998, xiii.

84. Roche, '"The Strange Light of Some New World"', 323, 330.

85. Joyce, *A Portrait of the Artist*, 212.

86. Ibid. 190, 213.

87. 'The Shipping News', *Freeman's Journal*, 17 June 1904, 5.

88. Joyce, *Ulysses*, 50. Gifford and others identify this three-master sailing ship as the *Rosevean*, bringing bricks from Bridgwater, which Elijah passes along the North Wall in 'Wandering Rocks' (240), and which is mentioned by the sailor in 'Eumaeus' as having arrived at eleven o'clock that morning (580), but this vessel arrived in Dublin on 15 June 1904, and is not recorded as having sailed on 16 June.

89. Ibid. 671.

90. Nels Pearson, '"May I Trespass on your Valuable Space?": *Ulysses* on the Coast', *Modern Fiction Studies*, 57.4 (Winter 2011), 635 (627–49).

91. Ibid. 637.

92. Andrew Gibson, *Joyce's Revenge: History, Politics, and Aesthetics in* Ulysses. Oxford: Oxford University Press, 2002, 4.

93. Joyce, *Ulysses*, 4, 18.

94. Ibid. 20, 4, 21.

95. Claire Connolly, 'Via Holyhead: Material and Metaphoric Meanings between Ireland and Wales', in John Brannigan (ed.), *The Literatures and Cultures of the Irish Sea*. UCDscholarcast: Series 7, 2013: <www.ucd.ie/scholarcast/scholar-cast35.html> (last accessed 25 April 2014).

96. Joyce, *Ulysses*, 5.

97. Ibid. 5.
98. Ibid. 18.
99. Ibid. 363–4.
100. Ibid. 314.
101. Ibid. 594.
102. James Joyce, 'The Mirage of the Fisherman of Aran: England's Safety Valve in Case of War', *James Joyce: The Critical Writings*, ed. Ellsworth Mason and Richard Ellmann. Ithaca, NY: Cornell University Press, 1989, 234–7.
103. Joyce, *Ulysses*, 50.
104. Ibid. 359.
105. Robert Lloyd Praeger, *The Way That I Went: An Irishman in Ireland*. Cork: Collins Press, 1997, 247.
106. Joyce, *Ulysses*, 37.
107. Joyce, *A Portrait of the Artist*, 178. Ernesto Livorni, '"Ineluctable Modality of the Visible": Diaphane in the "Proteus" Episode', *James Joyce Quarterly*, 36.2 (Winter 1999), 128 (127–69).
108. Joyce, *Ulysses*, 40–1.
109. Ibid. 47.
110. Ibid. 45.
111. Norman Davies, *The Isles: A History*. London: Macmillan, 2000, 214–15.
112. Joyce, *Ulysses*, 38.
113. Ibid. 38.
114. Joyce, *A Portrait of the Artist*, 175.
115. Joyce, *Ulysses*, 37.
116. Gregory Castle, '"I Am Almosting It": History, Nature, and the Will to Power in "Proteus"', *James Joyce Quarterly*, 29.2 (Winter 1992), 282, 286 (281–96).
117. Joyce, *Ulysses*, 37.
118. Robert Macfarlane, *The Old Ways: A Journey on Foot*. London: Penguin, 2012, 23.
119. Joyce, *Ulysses*, 41.
120. Ibid. 49.
121. Ibid. 49.
122. Ibid. 41, 46. See J. G. Wood's *Common Objects of the Sea-Shore*. London: Routledge, 1912, which was in Joyce's possession in Trieste.
123. Joyce, *Ulysses*, 46.
124. See *As You Like It*, II, vii, 150.
125. Charles Darwin, *The Descent of Man, and Selection in Relation to Sex*, vol. 1. London: John Murray, 1871, 2.
126. See Darwin, *The Descent of Man*, 14–16, and James Joyce, *Letters of James Joyce*, vol. 1, ed. Stuart Gilbert. London: Faber, 1957, 139.
127. Sandra Tropp, '"The Esthetic Instinct in Action": Charles Darwin and Mental Science in *A Portrait of the Artist as a Young Man*', *James Joyce Quarterly*, 45.2 (Winter 2008), 221–44.

128. Paul Bowers, '"Variability in Every Tongue": Joyce and the Darwinian Narrative', *James Joyce Quarterly*, 36.4 (Summer 1999), 869–88.
129. Joyce, *Ulysses*, 37.
130. See Praeger, *The Way That I Went*, 254–60.
131. D. M. M. Craik, *Our Year: A Child's Book, in Prose and Verse*. New York and Philadelphia: Frederick Leypoint, 1866, 163.
132. Joyce, *Ulysses*, 45.
133. Ibid. 44.
134. Ibid. 49.
135. Sidney Feshbach, 'Stephen's Wavespeech', *James Joyce Quarterly*, 44.3 (Spring 2007), 557–8.
136. Joyce, *Ulysses*, 47–8.
137. Ibid. 41, 42, 44, 49.
138. Ibid. 47.
139. Gillian Beer, 'Has Nature a Future?', in Elinor S. Shaffer (ed.), *The Third Culture: Literature and Science*. Berlin: De Gruyter, 1998, 26 (15–27).
140. Feshbach, 'Literal/Littoral/Littorananima', 334.
141. Joyce, *Ulysses*, 331.
142. Ibid. 341.
143. Vicki Mahaffey, 'Bloom and the Ba: Voyeurism and Elision in "Nausicaa"', *European Joyce Studies*, 22 (2013), 113–18.
144. Joyce, *Ulysses*, 351.
145. Ibid. 353.
146. M. O. Hussey, 'Sandymount and the Herberts', *Dublin Historical Record*, 24.3 (June 1971), 76–84.
147. 'Our Seaside Suburb', *Irish Times*, 2 September 1875, 5.
148. Kasia Boddy, 'The Modern Beach', *Critical Quarterly*, 49.4 (2007), 21–39.
149. Edmund Gosse, *Father and Son*. London: Penguin, 1982, 98.
150. Ibid. 97–8.
151. Ibid. 98.
152. See Richard Ellmann, *James Joyce: New and Revised Edition*. Oxford: Oxford University Press, 1982, 148n, and Weldon Thornton, 'An Allusion List for James Joyce's "Ulysses": Part III "Proteus"', *James Joyce Quarterly*, 1.3 (Spring 1964), 26 (25–41).
153. Joyce, *Ulysses*, 331, 332, 359.
154. Ibid. 362.
155. See Richard Ellmann, *The Consciousness of Joyce*. London: Faber, 1977, 97–134.
156. Joyce, *Ulysses*, 361.
157. Ibid. 364.
158. James Joyce, *Finnegans Wake*. Oxford: Oxford World's Classics, 2012, 621.
159. Marian Eide, 'The Language of Flows: Fluidity, Virology, and "Finnegans Wake"', *James Joyce Quarterly*, 34.4 (Summer 1997), 474 (473–88).
160. Joyce, *Finnegans Wake*, 204.
161. Ibid. 3.

162. Ibid. 316.
163. Ibid. 3.
164. Roland McHugh, *Annotations to Finnegans Wake*, 3rd edn. Baltimore: Johns Hopkins University Press, 2006, 3.
165. See Carl Waldman and Catherine Walsh, *Encyclopedia of European Peoples*. New York: Infobase, 2006, 75: 'At least since the Bronze Age Armorica, the region that would later become Brittany, was part of the Atlantic coastal network along which trade goods and cultural ideas flowed from the Mediterranean and coastal Spain to Armorica and on to Britain and Ireland and from the Netherlands on to Scandinavia.'
166. Joyce, *Finnegans Wake*, 29.
167. Ibid. 312, 318, 336.
168. Ibid. 327.
169. Ibid. 448, 320, 237, 292, 533, 594.
170. Ibid. 329.
171. Laurent Milesi, 'The *Habitus* of Language(s) in *Finnegans Wake*', in Valérie Bénéjam and John Bishop (eds), *Making Space in the Works of James Joyce*. London: Routledge, 2011, 150 (145–54).
172. Thomas Hofheinz's summary of the drama of the meeting of sea and land is useful here: see Hofheinz, '"Group Drinkards Maaks Grope Thinkards": Narrative in the "Norwegian Captain" Episode of "Finnegans Wake"', *James Joyce Quarterly*, 29.3 (Spring 1992), 651 (643–58).
173. Joyce, *Finnegans Wake*, 384.
174. Ibid. 387.
175. Ibid. 626.
176. Ibid. 628.
177. Ibid. 628, 605.

3

Virginia Woolf and the Geographical Subject

Less known to her the track athwart
Froom Mead or Yell'ham Wood
Than how to make some Austral port
In seas of surly mood.
                    Thomas Hardy, from 'Geographical Knowledge' (1905)[1]

Thomas Hardy's poem 'Geographical Knowledge' illustrates one of the central paradoxes of modernity, as described by Fredric Jameson, that 'the truth of experience no longer coincides with the place in which it takes place'.[2] The poem is about the postmistress of Lower Bockhampton, near Dorchester, in the 1870s, Christiana Coward, whose son is a sailor who knows 'All seas and many lands'.[3] Touchingly more attentive to the travels of her son than the needs of her postal community, Mrs Coward displays a ready knowledge and geographical awareness of Calcutta, Boston, and Gibraltar, and the maritime routes connecting places around the globe, but falters on the whereabouts of places and tracks within ten miles of her home. It seems, to use Ursula Heise's terms, that Mrs Coward has a good sense of planet, but little sense of place, that she is, in her own distinctive and tender ways, exemplary of the globalising experience of capitalism and empire which entail 'the emergence of new forms of culture that are no longer anchored in place'.[4] Hardy's poem cannot conceal the tone of lament for the loss of local knowledge which this experience comprises: the names of the localities unknown to Mrs Coward punctuate the poem's global geography, as markers of once meaningful places soon to be lost in the widening expanse of imperial cartography.
    As Heise argues, a similar sense of lament for the loss of local knowledge

against the encroachments of global modernity has played a powerful and emotive role in contemporary environmentalist discourse, amounting to a claim that 'The basis for genuine ecological understanding . . . lies in the local'.[5] The task of literature in shaping and recuperating that 'ecological understanding' of the local has been keenly debated in the environmental humanities over the past two decades. In a seminal essay published in *ISLE* (*Interdisciplinary Studies in Literature and Environment*), Robert Kern argued that 'all texts are at least potentially environmental . . . in the sense that all texts are literally or imaginatively situated in a place, and in the sense that their authors, consciously or not, inscribe within them a certain relation to their place'.[6] Kern's affirmation of the potential of literature for environmental thought was responding to Lawrence Buell's observation that twentieth-century under-standings of representations of nature in literature have typically stressed 'the formal or symbolic or ideological properties of those representations', and written off 'the literal reality of place or environment in their reading'.[7] For Buell, this has made modern literary professors and students frequently 'anti-environmentalists in their professional practice', whatever their personal and political commitments.[8]

The roots of that professional practice lie in the emergence of the academic discipline of 'English' in the early twentieth century, and its formative rela-tionship with the coterminous literary and aesthetic movements known to us as modernism. Modernist writing poses a particular challenge for ecocritical readings of place and locality, however, not just because of its privileging of a symbolist aesthetic, but because of its insistence, as Andrew Thacker argues, that 'multiple forms of space and geography . . . cannot, it seems, be kept apart', citing 'Peter Walsh's juxtaposition of private thoughts, metropolitan streets and British imperialism in India' in Virginia Woolf's *Mrs Dalloway* as an example.[9] Bonnie Kime Scott argues that it is not just place which has gener-ated difficulty for scholars of modernist writing, but nature and environment more generally. This has been manifest in critical studies of Virginia Woolf, she argues, in which 'we have been reading for an urban, technical, and popularly cultural Woolf', and that even 'proponents of the new modernist studies', notable for their recuperation of materialist modernisms, 'seem little more interested than their predecessors in modernist uses of nature'.[10] Scott's book on Woolf and nature, *In the Hollow of the Wave*, is one of the key contri-butions in recent years to the 'greening of modernism', and specifically to an ecocritical turn in Woolf studies. This turn has been marked quite decisively, one might even say voluminously, by the almost coterminous publication of Christina Alt's *Virginia Woolf and the Study of Nature* (2010), the papers from the Twentieth Annual International Conference on Virginia Woolf (2010) published in two separate proceedings as *Virginia Woolf and the Natural World* and a special issue of the *Virginia Woolf Miscellany* on 'Woolf and Nature', and another special issue of the *Virginia Woolf Miscellany* on 'Eco-Woolf' (2012).[11] Quite suddenly, it seems, Woolf's work can be read in the service of an environmental ethics of place and nature which was unimaginable and, perhaps more pertinently, undesirable for previous generations of critics who, with few exceptions, saw her work as exemplary of a cosmopolitan, urban modernism.

Yet Woolf's writings present a challenge to what Heise calls the 'Place-oriented discourses' of contemporary ecocriticism and environmentalism which 'deploy notions of "dwelling," "(re)inhabitation," "land ethic," "bioregionalism," or, more rarely, "land erotic" as their anchoring concepts'.[12] The challenge is that Woolf seems precisely not to be 'anchored' to the land in much of her work, and indeed recurrently fuses, transposes, and mythologises one place into others. This was noted by E. M. Forster's much quoted remark about her first novel, *The Voyage Out*, which features a long sea voyage (upon which Woolf never herself embarked) to South America (which she never visited): 'It is a strange, tragic, inspired book whose scene is a South America not found on any map and reached by a boat which would not float on any sea, an America whose spiritual boundaries touch Xanadu and Atlantis.'[13] In the novels which defined her reputation as a high modernist in the 1920s, it is the symbolic abstraction from place which appears most problematic for an environmental ethics of rootedness or '(re)inhabitation'. Even in *Mrs Dalloway* (1925), in which the geography of London plays a vital material and affective role, characters never seem to inhabit the actual places in which they are depicted, and the novel makes this clear from the opening passages, in which Clarissa's feet are in Westminster but her mind is in Bourton, through to the depiction of Septimus Smith's traumatic visions of London transformed into the apocalyptic battlefields of Flanders. Woolf's geographical disorientation is most acute, however, in the case of *To the Lighthouse* (1927), which is ostensibly set on the Isle of Skye in the Inner Hebrides, but, as Jan Morris puts it, 'it is really a protracted and accurate evocation of St Ives Bay in Cornwall, with the Godrevy lighthouse in the distance'.[14]

'NO PLACE IN PARTICULAR':
TO THE LIGHTHOUSE, SKYE, AND THE NATURAL SCIENCES

For biographers, and critics interested in biographical readings of Woolf's work, it makes perfect sense, therefore, to read *To the Lighthouse* with the geography of St Ives and the Atlantic coast of Cornwall in mind. As David Bradshaw observes, Woolf 'had neither visited Skye (she first set foot on the island in 1938), nor the Hebrides, nor even Scotland when she began to write this novel in 1925',[15] and even in 1933, six years after the novel was published, she wrote to Ethel Smyth: 'I wish I knew the geography of the British Isles. I dont at once visualise Hebrides, Skye, and the rest.'[16] The result is a strange geography, which, as a review in the *Glasgow Herald* put it, 'has an absurd lack of resemblance to the west coast of Scotland'.[17] The setting of a large country house situated close enough to a fishing 'village' or 'town' for Mrs Ramsay to walk there comfortably, from which a bay and a lighthouse can be seen, as indeed can passing steamships, simply doesn't map on to any possible location in Skye. If the town is based upon the only 'town' in Skye, Portree (as Bradshaw identifies it), the geography is all wrong: there is no lighthouse visible in the distance, no sand dunes in 'soft low pleats', and the houses do not 'fall away' on both sides down to the quay.[18] The novel is strangely detailed about some aspects of the material means of getting to Skye, as Mrs Ramsay tells Mr Bankes, for example, to catch the 10.30 train from London Euston station,[19] which would take Mr Bankes to Glasgow and on to Mallaig, but there is no mention of the infrequency of steamship connections to the island (around the time Woolf was writing, there were just two steamers each week to Skye from Mallaig).[20] Indeed, there is no mention of any of the characters having to cross the sea to get to the island, let alone difficulty in doing so, which is especially odd given the novel's preoccupation with whether or not it will be possible for the Ramsays to sail to the lighthouse. So too, when Mrs Ramsay considers their remoteness from London, she first exaggerates that they are three thousand miles, but then, 'if she must be accurate, three hundred miles',[21] whereas a glance at a scaled map of Britain would show that Skye is more than double that distance. It is a more accurate distance, however, from London to St Ives.

The inaccuracies of Woolf's depiction of Skye were made plainly obvious to her by some of her early readers and acquaintances. She wrote in a letter to her sister, Vanessa:

> Lord Olivier writes that my horticulture and natural history is in every instance wrong: there are no rooks, elms, or dahlias in the Hebrides; my sparrows are wrong; so are my carnations: and it is impossible for women to die of childbirth in the 3rd month – He infers that Prue had had a slip (which is common in the Hebrides) and was 9 months gone. This is the sort of thing that painters know nothing of.[22]

Olivier was a Fabian who occupied several important posts in the British colonial administration in the early twentieth century, most notably as the Labour government's Secretary of State for India in the 1920s. He was also a Hogarth Press author, and in 1927, contributing to an impressive list of anti-imperialist books published by Hogarth, he published his *The Anatomy of African Misery*, a book which condemned the racist laws of the South African government. His observations upon Woolf's inaccuracies are perhaps the basis for comments she made in a letter to Daphne Sanger, in which Woolf wrote that

> I don't myself much mind about peoples' ages and topography – not, that is to say, in a book like mine where the writer is trying to do something else. I should mind in Jane Austen, because I think she leads you to expect that kind of accuracy. Still I will try next time to be either quite inaccurate or quite accurate.[23]

The latter resolution is revealing, however light-hearted its intention, for Woolf's understanding that 'accuracy' is an affect in literary writing, and not just a matter of proficiency or knowledge. Certainly Mrs Ramsay's exaggeration and then 'accurate' correction of the distance from London to Skye seems to foreground the very question of accuracy of spatial representation. Woolf's defence against the charge of inaccuracy, then, is not just her artistic indifference to the native habitats of bird and plants, or indeed the geography of the British Isles, but it is also to turn our attention to the constitution and premises of 'accuracy'.

This is a familiar theme in critical discussions of the novel's representation of art. Lily Briscoe's painting makes 'no attempt at a likeness' of the scenes before her, and seems remote and incomprehensible to Mr Bankes who has in his drawing room a large painting 'of the cherry trees in blossom on the banks of the Kennet'.[24] Mr Bankes's painting gives him pleasure for two reasons: that it reminds him of the honeymoon he spent on the banks of the Kennet, and that the painting is now 'valued at a higher price than he had given for it'. Lily's painting, on the other hand, is apparently not recognisable for its subjects, but consists of forms, shapes, masses, and lines, and the geometric relations between them. Mr Bankes's appreciation of art depends upon its exactitude, upon its realistic approximation of what one sees, whereas Woolf foregrounds the relationship between Lily's art and her inexact perceptions of the natural world. From Lily's perspective, 'some bird chirped in the garden', and the clouds uncover 'the little space of sky which sleeps beside the moon'.[25] Lily's inexactitude, in other words, seems to approximate to what Lord Olivier was chastising in Woolf, a lack of knowledge about natural history and science, leading to a lamentable lack of resemblance to the subject depicted. At stake in such questions of accuracy, of course, are the very gendered structures of power and representation which are at the heart of Woolf's writings. This is particularly the case, it could be argued, in relation to depictions of landscape, in which 'accuracy' is dependent upon aligning one's perspective with existing geopolitical and patriarchal knowledge. The epistemological critique of resemblance as the primary criterion of artistic achievement is one common to many modernist writers and artists, most notably Woolf's friend Roger Fry, of whom she wrote a biography in her final years. The thematisation of inaccuracy in relation to this critique, however, is of particular concern to Woolf in this novel, who seems to risk too much in setting her novel, exactly, almost recklessly, upon an island which she had never visited and did not know.

The question of accuracy, of science and art, is at stake in the novel from the first line: '"Yes, of course, if it's fine tomorrow," said Mrs Ramsay.'[26] Mrs Ramsay makes a promise to her son James based on speculation about the weather, speculation which is immediately and repeatedly disputed by her husband, and later by his acolyte, Charles Tansley: '"But ... it won't be fine."' The word 'fine', as it is used by both Mrs and Mr Ramsay, is one of the handful of terms used by the Meteorological Office in describing and forecasting the weather which, as the *Oxford English Dictionary* defines it, means 'bright', 'comparatively free from cloud', or at least 'free from rain'. The common reference to the word 'fine', which of course is also used in common parlance as a subjective adjective, would tend to suggest that the daily weather forecast printed in *The Times* newspaper is the likely source of Mr Ramsay's certainty (although, given the remoteness of the island, it is less clear that the timely arrival of the newspaper would permit this). Commencing in 1861, with some interruptions following controversial errors in forecasting, *The Times* printed daily reports of weather observations, which became increasingly detailed in their forecasts. By the time the first part of the novel is set, in 1908 or 1909, most reports occupied a column length of the newspaper, and included a crude isobar map of the British Isles and Western Europe, as well as temperature, barometric, and hygrometric readings, and a brief regional forecast for the weather on the day the newspaper was published which consisted of wind direction, wind strength, expected condition ('fine', 'fair', 'rain', 'mist', 'fog', or, perhaps more often, 'changeable'), and a rough approximation of temperature (for example, 'moderate', 'lower', 'normal'). It should be clear, however, even from the language used in the forecast, not to mention their highly limited range (the day of publication), that weather forecasting was a matter of fairly crude calculations which produced cautious predictions. Had Mr Ramsay a copy of *The Times* to hand, it may have given him the information with which to make an educated guess about the likely course of the following day's weather, but not the certainty of 'fact' which he upholds testily against his wife's seemingly flighty speculations.

Without the newspaper forecast, the means by which Mr Ramsay and Charles Tansley 'tell' the weather are wind direction and atmospheric pressure. To support his elder mentor's insistent prediction that 'it won't be fine', Tansley holds 'his bony fingers spread so that the wind blew through them', and declares, 'It's due west.'[27] A short time later, when Mr Ramsay again declares 'irascibly' that there is no possibility of going to the lighthouse, Mrs Ramsay asks, 'How did he know?'[28] But, thinks Mr Ramsay, it cannot be fine, 'Not with the barometer falling and the wind due west.' Yet the signs by which the two men read the impending weather are far from easy to decode, and in fact depend upon a much greater array of information than that visible on the barometer or tangible from the wind. They depend upon a typology of weather produced over long periods of observation and recording.[29] As Mark Monmonier shows, storm forecasting was 'very much a process of early recognition, informed guessing, and careful tracking'.[30] The professional meteorologist could make 'an educated prediction' of the path of a storm, 'but because weather is quirky, the forecaster remained alert for a sudden acceleration or shift in direction'. Or, to put it in Mrs Ramsay's words, because 'The wind often changed'.[31] The only way of arriving at more 'precise, reliable predictions', Monmonier argues, was to 'exploit atmospheric history as a forecasting model', and this 'required a comprehensive catalog of storms and weather maps'.[32] Weather forecasting did not occur with the invention of the barometer, but was 'a triumphant collaboration of science, technology, bureaucracy, and cartography':

> Science provided the instruments for measuring temperature and pressure as well as broad but useful theories of atmospheric behavior. Technology furnished the electric telegraph, which allowed the rapid collection of perishable data from widely separated weather observers and the equally efficient dissemination of forecasts. Bureaucracy afforded the institutional framework for hiring, training, paying, and supervising several hundred weather observers as well as for building and maintaining a vast network of weather stations. And cartography contributed the base maps and graphic codes with which nineteenth-century meteorologists organized their data, visualized the atmosphere, and made educated guesses about the next day's weather.[33]

Even with this elaborate, extensive, and sophisticated network of observers and scientists, forecasts could still be inaccurate, and could still falter as a result of insufficient data, or the difficulty of finding comparative historical models of atmospheric behaviour. As Peter Lynch argues, in the early twentieth century 'weather forecasting was very imprecise and unreliable . . . [The] forecaster used crude techniques of extrapolation, knowledge of climatology and guesswork based on intuition; forecasting was more an art than a science.'[34] Yet, if Mr Ramsay has any reason to be certain of his weather prediction for the following day, it is surely because of this bureaucratic and technological state apparatus of meteorological forecasting, which had emerged in the mid-nineteenth century as a result of naval and military requirements.

The pioneer of the meteorological service for the British Isles was Captain Robert FitzRoy, a naval officer, who was commissioned to organise the first 'met office' after the disastrous loss of a Royal Navy ship in a storm near Balaclava on 14 November 1854, just three weeks after the cavalry charge at Balaclava which inspired Tennyson's poem 'Charge of the Light Brigade', from which Mr Ramsay repeatedly quotes the line 'Someone had blundered'. These two events of the Crimean War are intimately related by error: the cavalry charge was the result of topographical imprecision about the location of the enemy position to be attacked, and the shipwreck of the HMS *Prince* just a few weeks later was the result of a failure to warn the ship of an impending storm which, FitzRoy believed, was entirely predictable. The sciences of topography and meteorology emerged decisively in subsequent years, so that when Mr Ramsay offers, by way of appeasing his wife's doubts about his meteorological knowledge, to 'step over and ask the Coastguards if she liked', he was gesturing towards that imperial system of scientific knowledge, communications technology, and military-industrial power which had ringed the British Isles in the latter half of the nineteenth century with coastguard stations, lighthouses, weather observatories, and telegraph offices. These were the safeguards against 'inaccuracy', navigational and meteorological, which would protect the commercial and political interests of the heart of the Empire. These were the guarantors of Mr Ramsay's promise of certainty.

There was no guarantee of safety in the seas of the Hebrides, however, as Woolf's readers in the 1920s would have recalled all too well. A particularly tragic event in the recent history of the islands had been the sinking of the troopship the Admiralty Yacht *Iolaire*, which was carrying almost three hundred sailors and soldiers back to their home in Lewis in the Western Hebrides on New Year's Day of 1919. The ship was approaching the harbour at Stornoway under fair conditions with good visibility when it ran aground on rocks near the shore, and as it sank various attempts to bring the passengers and crew to safety foundered, resulting in the loss of over two hundred lives. It is perhaps this event, one of the worst maritime disasters in British waters in the twentieth century, and a cruel tragedy particularly for a small island, which informs Woolf's depiction of the town and its harbour in Skye: 'The lights of the town and of the harbour and of the boats seemed like a phantom net floating there to mark something which had been sunk.'[35] Thoughts of shipwreck haunt the novel, from Mrs Ramsay's thoughts of a drowned sailor and 'beaten mariners', and Mr Ramsay's fantasy of himself as a ship's captain in a 'broiling sea', in the first part of the novel, through the images of a 'silent apparition of an ashen-coloured ship' in the ghostly middle section, and on to Mr Ramsay's recited lines from Cowper's 'The Castaway' ('we perished', 'each alone'), Macalister's story of the sinkings and drownings of a recent storm, and Cam's dark contemplations as she looks down into the depths of the sea: 'About here, she thought, dabbling her fingers in the water, a ship had sunk.'[36] So persistent are these images of the shipwreck and drowned sailors that one could argue they constitute an image system in which the lighthouse and the coastguard are turned from beacons of salvation into frail tokens of hope against the ineluctable powers of the seas and the weather.

Yet the central figure of the lighthouse encapsulates an alternative image system also, one which represents not just a human attempt to overcome the awesome power of the sea, like the weather forecast, but connects the Hebridean islands with alternative, folkloric sources of knowledge which signify human fragility. The lighthouse beam and its reflections are also seen by Mrs Ramsay as 'ghost lights', portents of her own death. The lighthouse beam is seen as a 'steady light, the pitiless, the remorseless, which was so much her, yet so little her, which had her at its beck and call'.[37] Later, she sees a spectral 'ripple of reflected lights', which give her a feeling 'of peace, of rest'.[38] In 'Time Passes', the slowly decaying house is depicted as invaded by 'certain airs' which are directed by 'some random light . . . from some uncovered star, or wandering ship, or the Lighthouse even', 'sliding lights' which seem to presage the deaths of Mrs Ramsay, Andrew, and Prue.[39] In the ghostly scene in the third part of the novel, in which the wind slackens to stillness, leaving the Ramsays' boat adrift, a 'green light' engenders in Cam 'a change [which] came over one's entire mind and one's body shone half transparent enveloped in a green cloak'.[40] The sudden change may be connected to an unexplored meaning of the word 'fine', which is its nautical meaning, a 'fine breeze', sufficient to propel a sail boat. The stillness and unbearable closeness into which the boat-trippers are compelled seems connected to a ghostly haunting by Mrs Ramsay, who has the last word, perhaps, on whether or not the day is 'fine'. The belief in ghost lights was not exclusive by any means to the Hebrides and Scottish Highlands, but in a lengthy article of stories and recollections from the west of Scotland, R. C. Maclagan makes clear that it is 'deep-seated' in the islands as well as in other Celtic peripheries of the British Isles.[41] In the Hebrides, Maclagan shows, the appearance of ghost lights, variously called 'solus bais' (death light), 'solus taisg' (spectre light), or 'manadh bais' (death warning or manifestation), has been associated with shipwrecks, coastal deaths, and the deaths of wealthy or important island people. The evidence he cites includes cases where the 'ghost lights' seen from the coast turn out to be lighthouses, but were nevertheless associated for the islanders with a warning.[42] In *To the Lighthouse*, the clear association of the lighthouse with spectral lights and portents of death indicates not only that Woolf was aware of the persistence of such pre-Christian 'superstitions' in the Hebrides, but that these beliefs co-exist and contend with the modern scientific discourses which sought to gain mastery over nature with precisely such instruments as the lighthouse and the telegraph. More specifically, however, Woolf's 'ghost lights' connect her back, in perhaps surprising ways, to the ethnographic interest in the association of the peripheral archipelagic geographies of the British Isles with folkloric and pagan survivals which characterised the Celtic Revival. For Woolf, it seems, there is clearly more than one way to read the sky, and while Tansley stretches his bony hand to feel the direction of the wind, and thus apparently to know tomorrow's weather, Mrs Ramsay gazes at the 'sliding lights' which tell a much longer, and bleaker forecast.

In the 1920s, as Woolf was contemplating and writing *To the Lighthouse*, the weather was the subject of intense scientific and cultural interest. The Meteorological Office, newly transferred after the First World War to the Air Ministry, published a series of extensive volumes intended to advance basic research on weather prediction, often for general maritime use. These included Napier Shaw's four-volume *Manual of Meteorology* (1926), a Royal Navy commissioned volume on *The Weather of British Coasts* (1918), *The Seaman's Handbook of Meteorology* (1918), *The Weather Map: An Introduction to Modern Meteorology* (1918), and the *Meteorological Glossary* (1918). Weather forecasts were also disseminated more quickly and widely when the Air Ministry in 1924, and then the BBC in 1925, commenced daily radio broadcasts of the shipping forecast, which communicated a general synopsis for the British Isles and its sea regions, as well as detailed regional forecasts of wind speed, wind direction, and weather conditions, including gale warnings. The science of weather forecasting itself, however, was also in the process of revolutionary change, in terms of both atmospheric physics and mathematical computation. Although it took many years for his research to result in more accurate forecasting, the Norwegian physicist Vilhelm Bjerknes reported his discoveries in 1919–20 of thermodynamic and hydrodynamic processes within the atmosphere which became popularly known as 'warm fronts' and 'cold fronts', features which played a large part in determining whether or not the weather would be 'fine'.[43] The founding figure of modern computational methods of weather prediction, meanwhile, was Lewis Fry Richardson, whose book *Weather Prediction by Numerical Process* (1922) advanced the mathematical basis for weather forecasting today, but whose practical demonstrations were hampered by the inadequacy of his data.[44] The work of Bjerknes, in particular, was widely reported at the time, and perhaps appealed to a more general readership because of its dramatisation of atmospheric processes as spiralling 'fronts' contending against each other from emergence through to occlusion.[45] The 'new meteorology', as it was called, drew heavily upon the previously unexplored spaces of weather data collection – the upper atmosphere and over the seas – which were only possible with early twentieth-century developments in aerial flight technology and ship-borne radio telegraphy.[46] The effect of these new developments in meteorological science was to cast into historical obscurity the weather typologies and barometrical determinism of weather forecasting of prior decades, and for Woolf's first readers, therefore, Mr Ramsay's dogged certainty that 'it won't be fine' is more a quaint assertion of faith than accurate prediction. Mrs Ramsay, of course, comes to accept that faith, to aver that it will rain tomorrow, as indeed Mr Ramsay also concedes, as a matter of social grace, to his wife's doubts, but by then Woolf has made clear that the dispute between them is not about fact and fiction, or about science and superstition, but about the social role of the weather.

As Paula Maggio argues, 'weather is an integral part of the action' in Virginia Woolf's novels, and the relationship between weather and fiction is the subject of some discussion in her essays.[47] There are no elaborate or detailed descriptions of the weather, as if the weather was an informative background to the action of the characters, nor would we expect this, given Woolf's critique of the fictional style of Edwardian novelists.[48] Instead the weather functions integrally within her work to highlight what Maggio calls 'the symbiotic connection between the human world and the natural world'.[49] In particular, for Woolf the weather, and, more generally, climate, is related in very specific ways to place, as a determinant of human environment and culture, and in her fiction and essays she demonstrates a keen understanding of climate change and the interdependence of climate and different forms of social organisation. This begins in her first novel, *The Voyage Out*, in which the vast wild forests, stony red earth, and bright blue seas of South America are associated with madness, fever, and weariness.[50] It is perhaps most comically expressed in chapter five of *Orlando*, when nineteenth-century England is characterised (indeed determined) by a great cloud which hung 'over the whole of the British Isles', raining down perpetually, and changing 'the constitution of England' in every aspect, the character of its homes, the colours of its landscapes, the habits and diets of its people, and, most notably, producing fertility everywhere – the men grow beards and write intolerably long books, the women bear more and more children, the houses are covered in ivy.[51] On the other hand, Isa Oliver in *Between the Acts* thinks a great deal about a prehistoric England as a primitive wilderness with a tropical climate, and with no sea separating it from the European mainland.[52] In her recurrent preoccupation with the ways in which the 'naturally aqueous . . . atmosphere' of England has shaped its history, and all aspects of its social and cultural life, Woolf was entirely in keeping with prevailing theories about the role of climate in determining the differential geopolitics of human civilisation. It was a view which, in some of its contemporaneous forms, explained the dominance or superiority of certain civilisations as profoundly shaped by climatic conditions.

Ellsworth Huntingdon's work is most clearly associated with this theory, and in his book *Civilization and Climate* he advanced the hypothesis that 'a particular kind of climate is necessary to the development of high civilization'.[53] He studied the effects of certain climatic conditions on productivity, health, and vitality, and plotted the 'ideal conditions' geographically against a survey which invited respondents to identify the areas of the globe they most associated with the highest achievements and virtues in human civilisation. The result (perhaps predictably) was a map in which these 'ideal conditions' corresponded exactly to the parts of Europe and North America which dominated the early twentieth-century world, with few exceptions. In fact, Huntingdon could be even more precise than this. He identified four places in the world which satisfied the conditions of lying chiefly within a mean temperature range from 38° (Fahrenheit) to 60°: England, the Pacific coast of the northern United States, New Zealand, and Patagonia. In relation to England, he differentiates it in particular from neighbouring regions:

> At London the thermometer averages 38° in January and 63° in July, while at Liverpool the figures are 39° and 60°. If an average of 50° at all seasons were ideal, southwestern Ireland with a range from 45° to 59° and the Hebrides from 42° to 55° would be more ideal than London.[54]

Neither south-west Ireland nor the Hebrides turns out to be ideal, however, because they suffer from 'an excess of moisture' which 'lessens man's energy'. The key to the ideal climate, in Huntingdon's view, lay in the relationship between moderation and variability, which produced the optimum conditions for working, with sufficient stimulation from moderately variable weather. Storminess was a positive attribute, within moderation, as it produced variations. Either side of these conditions lay regions which were too cold or too hot, too wet or too dry, and uniform weather induced depression, while excessively variable weather induced nervousness. These climatic conditions were not permanent, of course, and Huntingdon charted the historical correspondence of shifting climates and shifting 'centers of civilization' to argue for his model of ideal climate.[55] The climatic equation for England's success as a civilisation therefore was that 'the mean temperature of the seasons and the degree of storminess are both highly favorable, while the seasonal changes are only moderate'.[56] The variations were the key as people benefited mentally and physically from 'the stimulus of changes', and hence, Huntingdon argued, one could improve the climatic factors influencing the potential for achievement by seasonal migration: 'Today the seacoast in many regions, for example on the Atlantic shore of America from New York to Boston, is bordered by an almost continuous line of houses. At first people went to these only in the summer. Now many go for week-ends at almost all seasons.'[57] This, he acknowledged, was confined at present to the more affluent classes, but within fifty years would be a more prevalent means of optimising climatic variations to improve the conditions for 'high civilization'.

Woolf's explanations of the relationship between English weather and English literature in her essays do not make explicit any such claim to superiority; instead, they make clear the relationship between variable or wet weather and English forms of sociability and culture. For Woolf, the variability of the weather has its social uses, namely in establishing intimacy in conversation. Indeed, conversation about the weather is the analogy Woolf uses in 'Mr Bennett and Mrs Brown' for the manner in which a writer must 'get in touch with his reader by putting before him something which he recognises, which therefore stimulates his imagination, and makes him willing to co-operate in the far more difficult business of intimacy'.[58] Woolf would have had in mind Samuel Johnson's famous remark that 'It is commonly observed, that when two Englishmen meet, their first talk is of the weather; they are in haste to tell each other, what each must already know, that it is hot or cold, bright or cloudy, windy or calm.'[59] Thus, Woolf begins *To the Lighthouse* by using the analogous conversation about the weather as the means of getting in touch with the reader. But, instead of a sociable description of the weather as it is, which would be plainly visible and consensual to both speakers, the turbulent disagreement between Mr and Mrs Ramsay turns upon predicting the weather, thus signalling the more general theme in the novel of uncertain futures. So much of the novel is directed towards the question of what will be, of predictions about future careers or marriages, of insurances against future disasters, or improvements to incline one towards better futures, and these are constantly indexed to the variable, unpredictable weather. As Johnson wrote in the same essay, 'in our island every man goes to sleep, unable to guess whether he shall behold in the morning a bright or cloudy atmosphere, whether his rest shall be lulled by a shower, or broken by a tempest'. Woolf associates this variability with the coast, with the sights and sounds of the sea which, as Mrs Ramsay ponders, is 'for the most part a measured and soothing tattoo to her thoughts', like 'some old cradle song', but 'at other times suddenly and unexpectedly . . . like a ghostly roll of drums remorselessly beat the measure of life, made one think of the destruction of the island and its engulfment in the sea'.[60] From the cradle to the grave, in other words, the variable conditions of the weather and the sea set the tempo and rhythm of island life.

The weather forecast, and its extension into the shipping forecast broadcasts in 1924, makes visible and audible the coastal geography of that variability. The weather map issued by the Meteorological Office dramatises the rising and falling of isobars in geometric contour lines which lie like another country over the British Isles, Western Europe, Iceland, and Scandinavia. So too the prognosis for the sea regions of the shipping forecast draws our attention outwards to the coastal borders of the British Isles, connected by storms and winds to neighbouring shores. Initially, the shipping forecast divided the British Isles into thirteen sea regions: Shetland, Tay, Forties, Humber, Dogger, Thames, Wight, Channel, Severn, Shannon, Mersey, Clyde, Hebrides. Seven of the thirteen were named after river estuaries, three after islands, and three after seas. The daily broadcasts brought to listeners this rhythmic pattern of the weather and the sea, a coastal drama of gale warnings, falling pressure, veering winds, and, always, 'rain later'. It was a forecast designed for mariners, but has long had aesthetic and cultural appeal beyond its practical function.[61] This aesthetic appeal of coastal and maritime living is one which Woolf makes central to her novel. The lighthouse is, from the outset, primarily an aesthetic and symbolic object, a stimulus to the imagination, from James's excitement at the prospect of sailing to it as a child to the inspiration it gives Lily to finish her painting with 'a line there, in the centre'.[62] The children bring the sea into the house, in the form of crabs, seaweed, shells, reeds, and stones, which Mrs Ramsay understands also as the raw materials of their creativity.[63] The novel uses the coast as the site of the picturesque, the romantic, and the dramatic: it is what the painters come to paint, where the lovers first embrace, but also where dangerous cliffs and dangerous waves might steal away the lives of children at play.

For Mr Ramsay, too, the sea is a source of wonder and entertainment, for as he listens to the fisherman, Macalister, telling his story of ships in a storm, Mr Ramsay 'relished the thought of the storm and the dark night and the fishermen striving there':

> He liked that men should labour and sweat on the windy beach at night, pitting muscle and brain against the waves and the wind; he liked men to work like that, and women to keep house, and sit down beside sleeping children indoors, while men were drowned, out there in the storm. So James could tell, so Cam could tell (they looked at him, they looked at each other), from his toss and his vigilance and the ring in his voice, and the little tinge of Scottish accent which came into his voice, making him seem like a peasant himself, as he questioned Macalister about the eleven ships that had been driven into the bay in a storm. Three had sunk.[64]

The voyeuristic pleasure which Mr Ramsay derives from the fisherman's story of ships sinking and men drowning, at least as seen by his children, brings into the foreground important questions about the relationship between the Ramsays and the island. Mr Ramsay's 'little tinge of Scottish accent' may hint at a Scottish family background which has been anglicised and educated to a trace, or, as Cam and James believe, represents a desire to 'seem like a peasant', to play at being a peasant. That Mr Ramsay likes to hear such stories of men drowning at sea, and women waiting quietly by their children's beds, gestures towards the wider cultural currency of such stories throughout the nineteenth century and into the twentieth, in the novels of Melville, Cooper, Marryat, Hugo, Kipling, and Conrad. Woolf was well aware of this tradition, and wrote of the 'double vision' which characterised Conrad's fictions of maritime heroes, in which 'To praise their silence one must possess a voice. To appreciate their endurance one must be sensitive to fatigue.'[65] A similar complex interplay of emotions and ethics is at work in Mr Ramsay, who modulates his voice and inclines his body to align himself with Macalister, thereby perhaps expressing a sense of affinity, and yet Mr Ramsay's pleasure in Macalister's stories is based upon his privileged social distance from the physical labour and danger of maritime work.

It is this interplay of proximity and distance, both geographical and ethical, which is fundamental to understanding why and how Virginia Woolf sets her novel in Skye. Although her geography is all wrong, and her natural history, Woolf shows no such lack of knowledge about the social conditions which brought the Hebrides repeatedly to the attention of the wider British public in the early twentieth century. For all that *To the Lighthouse* is famous as a work of aesthetic symbolism, it is also a novel of surprising insight into contemporary social conditions. The very title of the first part of the novel, 'The Window', alludes partly to Mrs Ramsay's seemingly quirky obsession with opening windows and closing doors, which reflects medical recommendations for the care of tuberculosis patients, and for the prevention of the spread of tuberculosis. The National Association for the Prevention of Tuberculosis reported in 1928 that 'the Hebridean islands of Lewis, Harris, Skye, and Mull' were 'regions in which the incidence of tuberculosis is relatively very heavy, and which are, by reason of their inaccessibility and scattered population, "backward" in matters of health'.[66] In both Skye and London, the novel tells us, Mrs Ramsay performs charitable work with the sick and the poor, and makes notes of 'wages and spendings, employment and unemployment', hoping to cease to be merely charitable, and become 'an investigator elucidating the social problem'.[67] This may be as whimsical a fancy as Mr Ramsay's image of himself as the leader of an expedition, or a primitive fisherman battling the elements, but Mrs Ramsay's ruminations upon the social problem appear to be well informed. Although it is clear that there is a great disparity between rich and poor in both Skye and London, the novel references the particular high rates of emigration, unemployment, and poverty in Skye which are exacerbated by the lack of a proper hospital, the frequent food shortages, and precarious dependence of the islanders upon a fishing industry vulnerable to profiteering as well as the weather.

It might be argued that Woolf distracts our attention from recognising that the salient topic of Mrs Ramsay's dinner table is the poor state of the island's fishing industry by diverting us instead towards the culinary triumph of the Boeuf en Daube, or Charles Tansley's urge to be included in the conversation of the men, or Lily's refusal to facilitate him. Yet the two are intimately and constantly connected. Gathered around a dining table which can seat twenty, Mrs Ramsay's guests enjoy French cuisine, of which William Bankes declares 'there is plenty for everybody'.[68] Meanwhile, as the snatches of discussion about fishing perforate through compliments about the soup, we learn that 'the fishing season was bad; that the men were emigrating. They were talking about wages and unemployment. The young man was abusing the government. William Bankes . . . heard him say something about "one of the most scandalous acts of the present government".'[69] Tansley's seemingly egotistical urge to join in the conversation about the fishing industry is, it seems, partly fuelled by the fact that his grandfather was a fisherman, and his father a chemist, so that, unlike others around the table, he knows something of the difficulties of social advancement. At the time this part of the novel is set, the Hebrides were certainly reputed as requiring a political solution, on account of bad fishing seasons, land sub-division, poor social conditions, and, an ominous sign, heavy dependence upon the potato crop.[70] The Royal Commission on the Poor Laws and the Relief of Distress, reporting in 1909, used a highly problematic racial comparison to make its point about conditions in the Hebrides: 'Many of the houses are more worthy of a Kaffir kraal than a section of Great Britain', and, further, stated that 'the condition of affairs here described seems scarcely credible in the twentieth century'.[71]

Woolf's early readers, however, were likely to associate this discussion of the fishing industry with more recent government failures to protect Hebridean fishermen from illegal trawling and from profiteering. A common complaint from Skye was that fishermen were restricted in the volume of fish that they could sell, and at a price of ½d per herring, for example (equivalent to the purchasing power of 6p in today's currency), and ¾d per mackerel (9p today), while the same fish was sold in London markets for eight or nine times that price.[72] Woolf does not tell us the price of fish, nor the routes to market, nor does she detail the effects which this form of economic exploitation has on the health, living conditions, and welfare of the people of Skye. She is no Arnold Bennett. Instead, Mrs Ramsay just happens to be reading James the Grimm brothers' 'fairy tale' of 'The Fisherman and his Wife', a story which has particular poignancy in relation to the poverty of local fishermen, the profiteering endemic in the fish market, and the stormy seas around the Hebrides. Woolf has her own distinctive and effective means of reminding her readers of the harsh lessons of capitalist economics. Such inequities of the

economic market around the British Isles contribute to the gulf between rich
and poor which Mrs Ramsay observes, and to the distress widely reported in
the islands in the early 1920s. Food shortages were reported in 1920 when
teachers made representations to government departments about the malnourishment of Skye children.[73] In December 1923, the Hebridean islands
were in the news again, under the headline 'Distress in the Western Isles:
20,000 Threatened with Starvation':

> The potato crop is a failure, the hay has been ruined by rain, heavy gales
> from the Atlantic have destroyed the harvest, and on account of the
> sodden state of the peat there is a shortage of fuel. There is no work of
> any kind beyond one or two small schemes of road resurfacing.[74]

It was all very well being able to predict whether or not 'it will be fine', but the
weather forecasts made little difference on an island deprived of the economic,
social, and medical resources to deal with seasonal climatic fluctuations.

In David Bradshaw's account of the reasons why Woolf set *To the Lighthouse*
on Skye, the island is associated through Walter Scott and Samuel Johnson
with Jacobite and Scottish nationalist sympathies, and serves as a cipher for
Woolf's critique of imperialism.[75] While this is a compelling reading, it
arguably overestimates Woolf's distance from the material meanings of the
island in attributing Woolf's evocations of Skye to literary associations alone,
rather than to the economic, political, and scientific contexts discussed above.
More importantly, however, the Skye of Woolf's novel occupies a peculiarly
ambivalent position in relation to empire. It is part of Britain, a British isle,
protected by the same coastal defence apparatus as St Ives and Brighton and
Newcastle, accessible from London by train (and an unmentioned steamer),
and home to people who can think of empire as elsewhere. Yet, it is also an
especially vulnerable, 'underdeveloped' part of Britain, associated in the minds
of Woolf's early readers with poverty, illness, starvation, and emigration, and
associated too with a precarious dependence upon subsistence farming and
fishing, and the vagaries of the weather. In this sense, Woolf's depictions of
Skye involve a constant interplay of its proximity to, and distance from, the
'centre', from a metropolitan elite for whom the island is refreshingly scenic,
its people romantically primitive, and its climate exhilaratingly dramatic.
Woolf's inaccurate rendering of the island, therefore, whether intentional or
not, produces for her readers the same 'cracked looking-glass' view which
Miss La Trobe deploys in *Between the Acts* to turn the question of representation back upon 'ourselves'.

The Skye of Woolf's novel is a fictive construct shadowing and exposing an
underlying geopolitics of social, cultural, and economic division and conflict
which had become particularly acute and particularly apparent in the 1920s. If

one implication of the passing of the generations between the first part of the novel and the third is the demise of British confidence and certainties about empire, then Woolf's determination to set her novel on a Scottish island should be read as an indication of her interest in consequent questions about the Britain which would remain after the dissolution of empire. The violent rise of Irish nationalism which resulted in the secession of the Irish Free State from the Union in 1922, along with the emergence of political parties dedicated to Scottish and Welsh nationalism in the early 1920s, made a reconfiguration of the meaning of Britishness and the British Isles inevitable. Such a reconfiguration, however, imposed itself to varying degrees depending precisely on one's location. Peter Walsh has no imperative to question the certainty of the 'Britishness' at the heart of the British Empire as he walks amidst the imperial architecture of central London, from which power radiates outwards to every corner of the globe like the leaden circles of time which Mrs Dalloway imagines booming out from Big Ben. Nor, it seems, more problematically, does this question arise for Woolf in relation to Cornwall. Yet Woolf's inaccurately rendered Skye insists upon the problem of borders, and specifically of a Britain defined as an island, as an insular whole. For Michael Gardiner, this anxiety about what constitutes Britishness when the Empire shrinks back to Britain's shores is constitutive of Anglo-modernism. 'Eliot belongs near the end of an Anglican, seafaring, imperialist aesthetics which had slid under Greater Britain,' writes Gardiner, reading *The Waste Land* as a poem explicitly concerned with 'the loss of control over water'.[76] *To the Lighthouse* is responding to the same crisis in British political and economic identity, but through its attention to coastal peripheries and the question of what constitutes islandness, Woolf's novel is exploratory, even anticipatory, of a changed landscape.

Woolf's setting figures a receding Britain structured by inequalities, a Britain in which confidence in determining the future through empire, science, and commerce has given way to a profound recognition of the limits of human agency. As Gillian Beer argues, the lighthouse marks 'the furthest reach and limit of human concerns, an attempt to create a margin of safety before the sea's power becomes supreme'.[77] If Skye itself denotes a limit space of Britishness, a peripheral outpost, it also signifies the meeting of land and sea, human and non-human, subject and object, culture and nature, life and death. Crucial to the novel, Beer argues, is Woolf's recurrent preoccupation with posterity, with what survives us, as individuals, as nations, as species. For Beer, 'there is a constant unrest about the search after a permanence which places humanity at the centre', most clearly visible in Woolf's deployment of the shipwreck and the empty house as material manifestations of a post-human future.[78] Beer compellingly sees Woolf, *avant la lettre*, as a writer addressing ecological themes.

Yet it should also be recognised that these concerns are not separated in the novel from questions of place and nation. Mr Ramsay's contemplation of his legacy finds him worrying that 'The very stone one kicks with one's boot will outlast Shakespeare', the national icon.[79] More generally, subjectivity and consciousness are inseparable from place in the novel, and topography is insistently used as an analogy of thought, whether this is Mr Ramsay 'thinking up and down and in and out of the old familiar lanes and commons' of his childhood, or Lily's thoughts 'rising and falling with the sea' before her eyes.[80] These associations between human consciousness and place frequently turn apocalyptic, especially around images of the shoreline: Mr Ramsay is compared to a 'desolate seabird', for example, alone on a 'little ledge facing the dark of human ignorance', while 'the sea eats away the ground we stand on'.[81] Later in the novel, when Cam looks back towards the island, the distance they have travelled in the boat has given the shoreline 'a changed look, the composed look, of something receding in which one has no longer any part'.[82] She struggles to identify their home, 'gazing at the shore whose points were all unknown to her'.[83] The land fails to be readable to her from the sea, which compels a different spatial perspective, one in which she slowly sees that the island has 'a place in the universe':

> It was like that, then, the island, thought Cam, once more drawing her fingers through the waves. She had never seen it from out at sea before. It lay like that on the sea, did it, with a dent in the middle and two sharp crags, and the sea swept in there, and spread away for miles and miles on either side of the island. It was very small; shaped something like a leaf stood on end.[84]

Yet this fragile sense of the island as place is only possible for Cam from the distance afforded by the sea, just as James too comes to see the lighthouse differently, to recognise that 'Nothing was simply one thing',[85] and in a series of connected passages, this seems to lead directly to Lily Briscoe's thoughts back on the coast about spatial scales: 'so much depends, she thought, upon distance: whether people are near us or far from us'.[86]

Lily has in fact been thinking about the relationship between proximity and love throughout the novel, perhaps most memorably in the passage in which she is 'Sitting on the floor with her arms round Mrs Ramsay's knees', wondering if physical intimacy brings about emotional knowledge.[87] But in the final part of the novel, this question about intimacy and knowledge is reframed in topographical terms, about the place and its associations through memory, in ways which Ursula Heise might recognise as bearing down upon the prevailing assumption behind many environmentalist movements 'that sociocultural, ethical, and affective allegiances arise spontaneously and "naturally" at the local level'.[88] Lily is only able to complete her vision, which depicts Mrs Ramsay and her son James as geometric shapes within a formal composition of spatial relations between shapes, just as James and Cam come to new understandings of their own places in the world, by putting place into relation with other places. Nor is their affection for place determined by any sense of rootedness or origination: it is, in Edward Casey's words, based on 'an elective affinity between memory and place'.[89] The local is not some insular point of origin, in other words, but rather is defined precisely by the model by which Cam, James, and Lily come to see it, as a place seen in relation to other places, and bounded within a web of interconnected locations. This is an entirely different model of topographical relation than the radiating circles and zonal blocks of *Mrs Dalloway*, of course: Woolf's spatial model in *To the Lighthouse* is archipelagic. Woolf had not visited and did not know Skye or the Hebrides when she wrote the novel, but *To the Lighthouse* is nonetheless preoccupied with an archipelagic view of the British Isles in the course of their becoming post-Empire, and post-British. It is an attempt to think through the place in the world of a stormy, fragile, and deeply divided archipelago, receding to nature, peripheral to the centres of global modernity, and desperately in need of new visions of its relations with others.

'ENGLAND AM I . . .': EUGENICS, DEVOLUTION, AND VIRGINIA WOOLF'S *BETWEEN THE ACTS*

One of the most popular accounts of England of the interwar years, H. V. Morton's *In Search of England* (1927), which had sold over a million copies by 1939, urged the increasingly urbanised English to travel the country's villages and rural heartlands, to reconnect to their 'common racial heritage', and thus take 'a step nearer that ideal national life'.[90] At the heart of Morton's account are eugenic anxieties about degeneration – about the 'racial anaemia' of the urban English, and about a loss of vitality to the 'character and physique' of the race – and these anxieties are inseparable from imperial notions of England as the 'mother' of an empire. Morton conceived of his journey 'in search of England' while recovering from illness in Palestine, and, as Wren Sidhe argues, rigorously delineates in his work between those inhabitants of England who he suggests are racially English, and those who are 'impure' and 'inferior': Jews, Irish, and Chinamen.[91] The English race, Morton argues, is rooted in the English soil, and he concludes his narrative in a churchyard among the gravestones, where he says, 'I took up a handful of earth and felt it crumble and run through my fingers, thinking that as long as one English field lies against another there is something left in the world for a man to love.'[92]

The prevalence of eugenic and racial ideas and concerns in Morton's narrative is not especially distinctive. In the month in which Virginia Woolf's 1941 novel *Between the Acts* is set, June 1939, *The Times* newspaper provided numerous examples of the same concerns about racial health, about birth rate and population decline, and about the preservation of the rural as a haven of racial identity and tradition. Such concerns were expressed in news articles, editorials, and letters to the editor, some of which came from prominent scholars in the field of eugenics such as Reginald Ruggles Gates and Alexander Carr-Saunders.[93] Anxieties about the physical health of the 'race' were exacerbated by the anticipated war against Germany, and tended to focus on the fitness of conscriptable men. However, the preoccupation with the health and preservation of rural England, and with the sustainability of the English population as a result of a falling birth rate, was clearly more general and persistent, and signalled the tensions arising from the ever more apparent weaknesses and failures of the British Empire (weaknesses evident, perhaps, since the Boer War). Arguably the eugenic inflection of debates about these issues was characteristic of the interwar period.

Virginia Woolf's interest in eugenics, and the influence of Darwinian and Galtonian theories of heredity and breeding on her work, have been the subject of considerable debate in recent years, most notably in Donald Childs's *Modernism and Eugenics* (2001). Childs's book does not refer to Woolf's last novel, *Between the Acts*; this is perhaps a strange omission, given the novel's preoccupation with ancestry, racial stock, and the future of the English as a 'race', although Childs explains that his aim is not to be comprehensive but illustrative of Woolf's eugenic preoccupations.[94] Nonetheless, *Between the Acts* exhibits eugenic concerns throughout. Giles and Isa Oliver regard William Dodge, the homosexual artist who visits their house with Mrs Manresa, as a 'half-breed' and 'a poor specimen' respectively, and Giles's violent reaction to Dodge suggests that he may subscribe to negative eugenic 'solutions' to the question of breeding.[95] The 'village idiot' is also the focus of such questions about breeding,[96] with several characters willing his disappearance,[97] and repeatedly distinguishing him from 'we who are civilized'.[98] Eugenics debates are also figured through the image of an empty cot ('the cradle of our race', in Mrs Swithin's description) in the nursery of Pointz Hall,[99] and in Giles's father Bartholomew's contemplation of whether Mrs Manresa would make a more suitable breeding mate for his son than Isa,[100] who has borne him a son whom Bartholomew brands a 'cry-baby'.[101]

Beside allusions to both negative and positive forms of eugenics, *Between the Acts* is concerned with ethnography more generally. Mrs Swithin is repeatedly drawn back to the book she is reading, H. G. Wells's *The Outline of History*, the popular Darwinian account of human history first published in 1920, and to thoughts of Wells's depiction of primeval England as a post-glacial swamp, inhabited by 'the iguanadon, the mammoth, and the mastodon; from whom presumably, she thought . . . we descend'.[102] Narratives of descent abound in the novel, and take many different forms: family ancestry, racial or national history, human evolution, and so, too, the evolution of animal and plant life. More significantly, the novel alludes, albeit sometimes obliquely, to the anthropological and archaeological methods upon which such accounts as Wells's *Outline* depended to establish their narratives of racial history.[103] Bartholomew refers to the 'skull shape' of his sister, Mrs Swithin, as proof of their kinship, while 'flesh and blood', the more conventional figure of kinship, is understood as a 'mist'.[104] Although the novel later jokes about skull collecting as a Victorian hobby,[105] craniology remained the key tool of physical anthropologists in constructing racial history, and in Woolf's lifetime its chief exponent, Cambridge professor Alfred Cort Haddon, was known as 'the head hunter'.[106] Giles is figured as a particular racial type, and, it is implied, a fit mate for breeding, through the straight lines of his face, his blue eyes, and fierce, untamed expression.[107] The face is also used as an index in establishing that Miss La Trobe is not 'pure English', but a foreigner, with 'Those deep-set eyes; that very square jaw' reminding Mrs Bingham '– not that she had been to Russia – of the Tartars'.[108] In these examples, the two most important methods in the armoury of contemporary physical anthropologists – cranial and facial indices – are deployed to register the ancestral and racial provenance of the characters. Such allusions to eugenic and ethnographic ideas are inseparable, however, from the rural setting of the novel, the repeatedly figured 'view' of the landscape, which, as in Morton's text, is symbolically loaded as 'the very heart of England'.[109]

As Mark Hussey has shown, *Between the Acts* is steeped in contemporary debates about rural preservation, and the symbolic significance of the countryside as the 'face' of English national character.[110] The novel alludes to this context from the outset, with discussion of the village water supply. The Women's Institute had lobbied the Ministry of Health for improvements to rural water supplies, which in 1939 were estimated to remain inadequate for one-eighth of the rural population.[111] The village is thus an index of the uneven development of the technologies of modernity: there is no piped water supply, and the village is contemplating a new location for that rather antiquated method of waste management, the cesspool. Yet this is the age of the aeroplane, as Woolf's 'Mr Oliver, of the Indian Civil Service, retired' recognises:

> From an aeroplane, he said, you could still see, plainly marked, the scars made by the Britons; by the Romans; by the Elizabethan manor house; and by the plough, when they ploughed the hill to grow wheat in the Napoleonic wars.[112]

The aeroplane enables the villagers to become newly conscious of the land-scape as a cultural palimpsest. However, what it reveals is not merely a sense of continuity or longevity, but disturbance, in ways similar to George Sturt's depiction of rural English life in *Change in the Village* (1912).[113] Against the pastoral discourse of the rural as a retreat from modernity, Woolf shows the 'countryside' as scarred by historical change, marked at every turn by war, invasion, and persecution. The continuity between the present and the past is a continuity of disturbance. The immediate context for the Women's Institute lobbying for better water supplies for rural areas was the anticipation of mass evacuation of children to the country during the impending war. Woolf reg-isters in the opening of her novel the contending discourses of rural life and rural preservation in England, that the rural is materially impoverished and underdeveloped, while also central to the national imagination. 'The nation's best children should come from the country,' declared Lady Denman, chair of the National Federation of Women's Institutes, yet in terms of water supply, housing, education, and maternity care, much of England's rural society was inadequately equipped to fulfil this ideal.[114] Such aspirations to equip rural vil-lages with the infrastructure to foster the 'nation's best children' are important reminders that eugenics, the science of racial health, was intimately connected to other health sciences, connections which are of course abundantly evident in the ways in which the language of 'pollution', 'impurity', 'cleansing', 'steri-lisation' and so on cross so easily between medical and political discourses. Woolf's village lacks an adequate water supply, but her opening references to the 'cesspool' and 'the gutter' bear the weight of moral and political discourses about the 'health' of rural society which are of national significance.[115]

The seemingly inevitable involvement of the British state in the war in Europe increased Woolf's sense of a more local attachment to her Sussex home in Rodmell, and the countryside around it, as Hermione Lee observes in her biography, yet there was still some ambivalence in her feelings about this rural version of an imagined England: 'She partly liked this "queer" "con-traction of life to the village radius", and partly found it alarmingly constrict-ing.'[116] It was the city, specifically London, Woolf explained to Ethel Smyth, which formed the core of her sense of patriotism, although she admits to some feelings of identification with an English rural idyll:

> You never shared my passion for that great city. Yet it's what, in some odd corner of my dreaming mind, represents Chaucer, Shakespeare, Dickens. It's my only patriotism, save one vision, in Warwickshire one spring when we were driving back from Ireland and I saw a stal-lion being led, under the may and the beeches, along a grass ride; and I thought that is England.[117]

It is a curious vision of England, a glimpse from a motor car of Warwickshire preferred to her lived experience of a Sussex village. It is also a vision of contrasts, 'the may' abundant with folkloric associations going back to ancient Celtic cultures, while the 'grass ride' is a carefully engineered facet of wealthy estates, many of which would form the basis for the country parks of postwar Britain.[118] The journey from Ireland, where she and Leonard had stayed on holiday with Elizabeth Bowen in 1934, prompted her to write in her diary that 'Horses rule England, as salmon rule Ireland', but 'that' England represented an increasingly estranged idea of the country, perhaps understandably given that Woolf observed this from her car.[119] The horses, like the salmon, the grass rides, and the protected woods, belonged to a rural landscape which was being made available to leisured visitors, a constructed 'view' of rural society which had little to do with cesspools, higher instances of infant mortality, and poor housing conditions. It is the tension between these two versions of rural England which forms an essential part of Woolf's village pageant in *Between the Acts*, as if Woolf is adapting the question which recurs in the conclusion of *To the Lighthouse* to read: 'So that was England, was it?'

Woolf is deliberately vague about the geographic location of *Between the Acts*. The indications provided in the novel are misleading and perhaps even contradictory. Many of the place-names are invented, although some are real, and in the main they tend towards locations in the south-east of England, around Sussex and Kent. Hermione Lee suggests that Pointz Hall is modelled upon Rodmell.[120] However, on the first page of the novel, Mrs Haines is told that 'nightingales didn't come so far north', suggesting a northern location, as nightingales are found in the south and south-east of England, as far north as the Wash.[121] Later, the narrator tells us that 'the train took over three hours to reach this remote village in the very heart of England', presumably from London, and admittedly by express and branch lines, making it difficult to establish any sense of precise distance.[122] Most confusing of all, however, is the uncertainty of the distance from the sea, and this is of particular significance in a novel concerned with the question of what happens when 'England' construes a contracted vision of itself as an island. Mrs Swithin wonders if they are one hundred or perhaps one hundred and fifty miles from the sea (impossible, since no part of England is further than seventy miles from the sea), to which Bartholomew responds with impressive precision that they are 'thirty-five miles only' from the sea, although there is no reason to accept this measurement as any less subjective than Mrs Swithin's exaggerated sense of remoteness.[123] To map the novel according to these indicators, in a manner akin to Franco Moretti's tracing of the England of Jane Austen's novels, might place us somewhere in Derbyshire, or possibly even Warwickshire, even though it seems more like Sussex.[124] Woolf's point, elaborately and deceptively signposted, is that Pointz Hall is the symbolic heart of pastoral discourses of inter-war Englishness, the idealised location of a racial and national imagination of 'home', which Mrs Swithin is eager to see as safely insular from the threatening sea when in fact it is precariously exposed. Perhaps of equal significance is the way in which the bizarre equivocation of Woolf's characters about their remoteness from the sea advertises a distinct change in the geography of Woolf's own fiction, which had embraced fractal coastlines and pulsing waves, most notably in *To the Lighthouse* (1927) and *The Waves* (1931), but here self-consciously withdraws to a location which is not merely remote from the sea but to which, as the opening paragraph makes clear, even piped water has not found access. The effect is of a willed, almost pathological hydrophasia, bound up, of course, in the recurrent and troubling figure of the disappearance of the sea as a barrier between England and Europe: '"Once there was no sea," said Mrs Swithin. "No sea at all between us and the continent."'[125]

The relationship between the sea and English nationalism is, as David Bradshaw argues, the subject of Woolf's critique in *Between the Acts*. Bradshaw quotes from Sir Henry Newbolt's patriotic celebration of the role of the sea in English national life to explain 'why neither the sea nor the seaside figure prominently in modernist literature beyond the writings of Conrad, Joyce and Woolf'.[126] The 'island history' which forms the fragmented narratives of the pageant is not only, as Bradshaw argues, threatened by the imminent menace of German invasion and bombing, but also depends upon nationalist figurations of the sea as, to use Newbolt's terms, an Englishman's 'boundary' and 'safeguard', as well as the 'highroad of his food supply and his foreign travel'.[127] The Empire depended famously upon 'ruling the waves', upon overseas commerce and naval supremacy, which made England's ports the loci of global trade and cultural contact, even as pastoral discourses of English insularity preserved the imagination of an unchanged core. Tropes of insularity and mastery dominate such imperialist representations of the sea, whereas Woolf, arguably throughout her oeuvre, constantly draws attention to the sea as a figure of porosity, dissolution, maternity, otherness, and fantasy. The seclusion of Pointz Hall from the sea, and the imagined absence of the sea from the channel between England and the European continent, raise the very question about what constitutes a sea-less England, an England seemingly in retreat to its remote hinterlands, and afraid of getting wet there. The house itself was built 'in the hollow, facing north . . . to escape from nature', itself then emblematic of an insularity doomed to fail.[128] In the winter of 1939, Woolf was reading Freud and Darwin, and, as Lee shows, thoughts of the struggle for life, the contest between creation and extinction, and reversion to primitivism worked their way into *Between the Acts*.[129] Darwin's *Journal of Researches*, in particular, in narrating the extensive sea voyage upon which he observed the evidence of evolution, geographical distribution of species, and extinction, would have informed Woolf's sense of the sea and shorelines as generative spaces.

There are hints of such evolutionary thought throughout *Between the Acts*, in the association of Mrs Manresa with exotic 'spice islands' and 'fresh air', for example, as euphemisms for an implied racial difference which promises to renew or replenish the local, stagnant gene pool.[130] The early reference to a new cesspool may have such eugenic associations also. Inland, rural England may be the nation's 'heart', but with its graveyards populated by the same few names it is also, Woolf suggests, marked by degeneration. If the countryside is not 'a view', not capable of sustaining pastoral discourses of national vitality, then it is 'land merely, no land in particular',[131] and the recurrent allusions to evolutionary discourses make clear that the land will be there 'when we're not'.[132] The only hope in the novel for regeneration is associated with water, when Lucy Swithin stands over a lily pool, and sees in the contours of the leaves the shapes of 'Europe . . . India, Africa, America'.[133] In insular fashion, and in keeping with the novel's depiction of anxieties about proximity to the sea, and about the consequences for England, and the British state, of the demise of the Empire, the pond becomes symbolic of the world: 'Above, the air rushed; beneath was water. She stood between two fluidities, caressing her cross.'[134] Her faith is rewarded by the sight of her favourite carp, glimpsed so rarely near the surface, prompting her to imagine a debate with her brother about evolution, in which she maintains a belief in the role of beauty and faith, against his bleak insistence on the determining drives of sex and greed.[135] Beauty is 'the sea on which we float', she thinks, and, of course, her name is symbolic of superstitious faith in the coming of rain, but even this fleeting glimpse of evolutionary redemption in the lily pool ends unpromisingly, with Mrs Swithin having 'nothing to give [the fish] – not a crumb of bread', and the fish disperse, seeming then to validate the grim view attributed to her brother that the fish thrive on greed alone.[136] 'Beauty' and 'faith' are thus implied to be the temporary and provincial conceits of a humanity which is not necessary to the natural world, just as earlier in the novel Lucy recognises the transience of modern conceptions of both Englishness and Britishness when she reads in Wells's *Outline* of the geologically recent phenomenon of a sea separating 'England' from the European continent. The symbolic location of the novel ties its preoccupations with eugenics and ethnology not only to a general intellectual interest in evolutionary debates and questions of human heredity, but to specific anxieties about the provenance and significance of a racialised understanding of Englishness. As Robert Young argues in *The Idea of English Ethnicity* (2008), nineteenth-century ethnology gradually moved from definitions of racial identity fixed to birth, 'blood-lines', and place, towards what Young sees as an expansive and potentially liberal association with 'language, looks, and culture'.[137] While this made Englishness a 'translatable identity' for the needs of the Empire and the diaspora, however, it also made Englishness a 'curious emptiness', delocalised and boundless.[138] It is this paradoxical figure of an Englishness which presumes to be both descriptive (of a landscape, a geography, a race, a nation) and adaptive (of an empire, a language, a culture) which accounts for the constantly shifting object of the collective pronoun in the novel. 'We' both includes and excludes, in different iterations, the village idiot, the 'half-breed' William Dodge, the colonial Mrs Manresa, the presumed foreign Miss La Trobe, as well as the working-class villagers and the household staff of Pointz Hall. The characters of *Between the Acts* are, as in Morton's travelogue, clearly 'in search of England', an England which seems impossible to delineate and define.

Despite the ethnographic obsessions of the characters, any attempt in the novel to establish a fixed sense of racial identity fails. The graveyards to which local families point as evidence of their ancestry prove a certain longevity, but compared to Mrs Swithin's thoughts of primeval beasts, swamps, and an 'England' which was not divided from Europe by a channel, such ancestry appears temporary and contingent. Indeed, the novel works hard to establish that any attempt to define human resemblances can extend to resemblances between the human and the animal: in the opening pages, Mrs Haines is 'goosefaced', while Isa and Mr Haines are swans, and such examples of theriomorphism are paired with examples of anthropomorphism – a cow coughs, a bird chuckles.[139] The resemblances drawn between Bartholomew and his Afghan hound remind us of this point throughout the novel. In the pageant, the cows and swallows inadvertently fill in the gaps between scenes, and, it is suggested by the Reverend Streatfield, they are part of Miss La Trobe's moral about the inseparability of the human and the natural: 'Dare we ... limit life to ourselves?' asks Streatfield, a question with as much significance for the differential allocation of human-ness across racial categories as for human and animal similarities.[140] This is to recognise that Woolf's allusions to ethnographic and eugenics debates, and the legacies of Darwinism more generally, can be shown to work against racial discourses.

Increasingly in the 1920s and 1930s, the scientists of race – whether in physical anthropology, sociology, archaeology, or other disciplines – were recognising the redundancy of race as a meaningful or applicable term. Alfred Cort Haddon, for example, in his book *The Races of Man* (1924), acknowledged 'race' to be 'an artificial concept', which was difficult to apply to those 'groups of mankind that exhibit so many intermediate characters ... due to racial mixture through long periods of time', or 'that may be undifferentiated stocks'.[141] Britain was one such case, he argued, comprised of 'a general

mingling of peoples . . . which renders the task of disentangling them a peculiarly difficult one'.[142] Haddon's later study, *We Europeans*, co-written with
Julian Huxley and Alexander Carr-Saunders, begins with an attack on the
'pseudo-science' associated with 'race', and the various errors and confusions
involved in the use of the term.[143] It concludes with a passionate appeal against
'racialism', arguing that the danger of 'race' as a term is that it draws upon
a sense of scientific validity, and yet has 'no precise or definable meaning'
in science.[144] Published first in 1935, with a Penguin edition in 1939, *We
Europeans* preferred the term 'ethnicity' to 'race', and clearly attempted to
distinguish its survey of biological and ethnic characteristics from the adoption of 'race' and 'racism' in 'the literature of more violent nationalism'.[145]
Both of these studies were popular publications, the findings and arguments
of which also found expression in daily newspapers.[146] Woolf's novel, too,
tends to associate the exclusionary tendencies of racial discourse with those
characters associated with violence, Giles and his father in particular, whereas
other characters – Isa, especially – are shown to be interested in, and open
to, the 'other' voices which might be heard beyond the limits of the racial or
national. As David Bradshaw suggests, in response to Donald Childs, 'surely,
it is Woolf's *rejection* of "imperial" ideologies (whether those of the state or
the masculinist scientific community of her day) which brings a characteristic
edge to her fiction'.[147] Woolf's novel is, I would argue, contiguous and inter-
fused with what Elazar Barkan has characterised, in a study of the same name,
as 'the retreat of scientific racism' in the interwar period.[148]

In *Between the Acts*, it is precisely this rejection of imperial ideologies and
the pseudo-science of race through which the problem of a devolved, post-
imperial Englishness is articulated. What is Englishness if it is not about race,
or nationality, or empire? Any attempt to establish a sense of identity or tradition for England beyond the terms of empire and race falters. English literature
might foster a sense of history and belonging beyond the appeal of race, and
might promote alternative values and voices, as indeed is the implication of
F. R. Leavis and Denys Thompson's argument in *Culture and Environment*
(1933) that an English literary education is a substitute for the lost folk culture
of the 'organic community',[149] but in Woolf's novel the characters' fondness
for quoting from Shakespeare, or Keats, or Swinburne, frequently turns out
to be misquotation. Such comic misquotation might be read as a riposte to
Leavis, Henry Newbolt, and even her own father, Leslie Stephen, for that
late Victorian and Edwardian obsession with forming canons upon which a
renewed sense of national identity and allegiance might be based. The pageant
also seems to parody any notion of a unifying cultural history, with Queen
Elizabeth none too distinct in the play from the shopkeeper, 'licensed to sell
tobacco',[150] who plays her part, the eighteenth century reduced to a bawdy

satire, and the Victorians caricatured in ways which make them unrecognisable and unlovable to those like Mrs Lynn Jones who remember the age fondly. So too, in the pageant, whenever the play demands the actors to say something about what England is, or about the connective threads of English history, words are forgotten, or the wind blows hard to make their voices inaudible, or an interval makes the audience conscious of discontinuities. This occurs from the very beginning when the prologue forgets what she should say after 'England am I . . .',[151] and again when Hilda, the carpenter's daughter, has to be prompted to say 'O, England's grown a girl now'.[152] In the final interval, the very thought of what the pageant will reveal about 'ourselves' in 'present time'[153] unsettles the audience, and causes them anxiety about the object of the play. The meaning of the final scene, in which the actors hold up mirrors to the audience to show 'ourselves', has been the subject of much debate in critical interpretations of the novel. Gillian Beer argues that the audience cannot see 'anything more than shallow images of themselves';[154] Madeline Moore argues that the audience see nothing of themselves in the mirrors at all;[155] Galia Benziman reads the mirrors psychoanalytically through Lacan and Winnicott as a device through which the fragmentary, individualised identities of the audience are refracted into a 'collective self-image that may supply the English nation with a sense of shared origin and belonging'.[156] Jed Esty's interpretation of *Between the Acts* emphasises this same appeal within the novel, exemplified in the mirror scene of the pageant, to 'a ritualized nativism that reintegrates artist and audience into a common culture'.[157] Marina MacKay notably goes further than this in highlighting wartime fears of invasion as the immediate context for Woolf's revisionary account of Englishness, seeing the novel as more closely allied to 'the familiar history of Their Finest Hour' than is usually acknowledged.[158]

Yet if, as Esty argues, *Between the Acts* is a 'controlled experiment in devolution', in attempting to give expression to some new sense of what Englishness might mean beyond empire and race, then it is an experiment which repeatedly and consistently fails.[159] As much as the impending war brings a renewed consciousness of the territorial and maritime borders of 'England', particularly of the channel which separates England from continental Europe, the pageant strays repeatedly back into the imperial domains from which Englishness gained its dominant political and cultural meanings. Both the pageant and pastoral forms used in the novel to bear the weight of an implied nativism, which many critics have suggested is Woolf's 'dissenting version of the island story', are comprised of leftover scraps of state or imperial ideologies, like the garlands left over from the 1937 Coronation.[160] Seen in this way, the pageant and the pastoral seem more like Eliot's 'fragments I have shored against my ruins' in *The Waste Land* (1922), more symbolic of dissolution, than the experimental seeds of a regenerated England.[161] Dissolution seems a kind of resigned response to the association of any kind of community with empire and race. The Victorian policeman tells the audience that 'wherever one or two, me and you, come together', there too must be the eye of the Empire, to which the only reply seems to be dispersal. 'Dispersed are we; who have come together,'[162] the gramophone repeats, beckoning the audience to remember the 'joy, sweet joy, in company',[163] yet that company is constantly tainted by the semiotics of racial and imperial history. No summation of the play is possible, so they must resort to the ritualised closure of the 'national' anthem, 'God Save the King', an anthem which pretends to resolve into one figurehead the competing regional and national tensions within the British State.[164]

So the audience disperses, leaving us first with the family, and then in the final scene alone with Isa and Giles, the strained marriage, contemplating the primeval origins of life, the fight and the embrace from which 'life might be born'.[165] As a metaphor for new communal beginnings, this seems even bleaker than Orwell's famous characterisation of England as 'a family with the wrong members in control', and with 'all its cupboards bursting with skeletons'.[166] One could take the metaphor of dispersal, the refrain of 'Dispersed are we', in the direction suggested by Jessica Berman, towards an 'oppositional cosmopolitan politics', an evacuation of a native or official sense of English community, and an understanding of community as an endlessly connective attempt to imagine the collective as a 'lived-in otherness' (as Mrs Swithin tells William Dodge, 'we live in others').[167] Berman's argument that Woolf's experiments with community in *Between the Acts* can be traced far earlier in her work is a useful corrective, I would argue, to a tendency to characterise Woolf's final novel as exceptionally political, or as a retreat from cosmopolitan modernism. And yet the novel can only point towards such 'lived-in otherness', bound as it is to the genre of pastoral, and to familial and nativist metaphors. Ultimately, the significance of the novel in relation to a devolved, post-imperial Englishness is to suggest a series of questions about its inherited traditions and cultural resources, about what happens when 'palaces tumble down',[168] for example, or what history might be like 'without the army',[169] or how would it be if there was no sea between England and the continent.[170] Englishness would not then constitute an inherited set of qualities or values, but would rather take the form of an historical and moral responsibility, a 'burden', as Isa suggests, 'laid on me in the cradle; murmured by waves; breathed by restless elm trees; crooned by singing women; what we must remember; what we would forget'.[171] It is that sense of responsibility, of a vow to imagine Englishness beyond empire, beyond race, which characterises Woolf's ambition in *Between the Acts*, and which is that novel's principal legacy for a post-devolutionary imagination of an independent England.

NOTES

1. Thomas Hardy, 'Geographical Knowledge', *The Complete Poems*, ed. James Gibson. Basingstoke: Palgrave, 2001, 287–8.

2. Fredric Jameson, 'Cognitive Mapping', in Cary Nelson and Lawrence Grossberg (eds), *Marxism and the Interpretation of Culture*. Urbana, IL: University of Illinois Press, 1988, 349 (347–60).

3. Martin Ray, 'Thomas Hardy's "Geographical Knowledge"', *Notes and Queries*, 53.3 (September 2006), 343–4.

4. Ursula K. Heise, *Sense of Place and Sense of Planet: The Environmental Imagination of the Global*. Oxford: Oxford University Press, 2008, 10.

5. Ibid. 28.

6. Robert Kern, 'Ecocriticism: What Is It Good For?', *ISLE: Interdisciplinary Studies in Literature and Environment*, 7.1 (2000), 10 (9–32).

7. Ibid. 9.

8. Lawrence Buell, *The Environmental Imagination: Thoreau, Nature Writing, and the Formation of American Culture*. Cambridge, MA: Harvard University Press, 1995, 85.

9. Andrew Thacker, *Moving through Modernity: Space and Geography in Modernism*. Manchester: Manchester University Press, 2003, 7.

10. Bonnie Kime Scott, *In the Hollow of the Wave: Virginia Woolf and Modernist Uses of Nature*. Charlottesville, VA: University of Virginia Press, 2012, 2.

11. See Christina Alt, *Virginia Woolf and the Study of Nature*. Cambridge: Cambridge University Press, 2010; Kristin Czarnecki and Carrie Rohman (eds), *Virginia Woolf and the Natural World: Selected Papers from the Twentieth Annual International Conference on Virginia Woolf*. Clemson, SC: Clemson University Digital Press, 2011; Kristin Czarnecki (ed.), 'Woolf and Nature': Special Issue, *Virginia Woolf Miscellany*, 78 (Fall/Winter 2010); and Diana Swanson (ed.), 'Eco-Woolf': Special Issue, *Virginia Woolf Miscellany*, 81 (Spring 2012).

12. Heise, *Sense of Place and Sense of Planet*, 29.

13. Quoted in Karen R. Lawrence, *Penelope Voyages: Women and Travel in the British Literary Tradition*. Ithaca, NY: Cornell University Press, 1994, 158.

14. Jan Morris (ed.), *Travels with Virginia Woolf*. London: Hogarth Press, 1993, 3.

15. Virginia Woolf, *To the Lighthouse*, ed. and intro. David Bradshaw. Oxford: Oxford World's Classics, 2006, xxvii.

16. Virginia Woolf, *The Letters of Virginia Woolf, Vol. 5: 1932–1935*, ed. Nigel Nicolson. New York: Harcourt Brace Jovanovich, 1979, 218.

17. Quoted in Bradshaw, 'Introduction', *To the Lighthouse*, xxviii.

18. Woolf, *To the Lighthouse*, 14.

19. Ibid. 27.

20. 'Motor Roads in Skye', *The Times*, 27 February 1922, 6.

21. Woolf, *To the Lighthouse*, 25.

22. Virginia Woolf, *A Change of Perspective – The Letters of Virginia Woolf, Vol. 3: 1923–1928*, ed. Nigel Nicolson. London: Hogarth, 1977, 379.

23. Ibid. 398–9.
24. Woolf, *To the Lighthouse*, 45.
25. Ibid. 43.
26. Ibid. 7.
27. Ibid. 8.
28. Ibid. 29.
29. Such typologies of weather were available in a number of volumes which might have been consulted by Woolf, and would seem to confirm Mr Ramsay's suspicions that the weather 'won't be fine'. For example, *The Seaman's Handbook of Meteorology* (London: HMSO, 1918) reads the falling barometric pressure and westerly wind as part of a weather pattern which is likely to result in rain and increasing winds, although, as the depression passes, conditions change to squally with bright intervals (101–2). Hence, depending on the movement of the low pressure area, either Mr or Mrs Ramsay may be proved correct by this pattern.
30. Mark Monmonier, *Air Apparent: How Meteorologists Learned to Map, Predict, and Dramatize Weather*. Chicago: University of Chicago Press, 1999, 10.
31. Woolf, *To the Lighthouse*, 29.
32. Monmonier, *Air Apparent*, 15.
33. Ibid. 7.
34. Peter Lynch, *The Emergence of Numerical Weather Prediction: Richardson's Dream*. Cambridge: Cambridge University Press, 2006, 4.
35. Woolf, *To the Lighthouse*, 57.
36. Ibid. 31, 69, 96, 109, 135, 136, 156.
37. Ibid. 54.
38. Ibid. 85.
39. Ibid. 104.
40. Ibid. 150.
41. R. C. Maclagan, 'Ghost Lights of the West Highlands', *Folklore*, 8.3 (September 1897), 203–56.
42. Ibid. 217–18.
43. See Monmonier, *Air Apparent*, 57–80.
44. See Lynch, *The Emergence of Numerical Weather Prediction, passim*.
45. 'Meteorology of To-day', *The Times*, 21 August 1922, 13.
46. 'New Meteorology', *The Times*, 29 August 1925, 6.
47. Paula Maggio, 'Digging for Buried Treasure: Theories about Weather and Fiction in Virginia Woolf's Essays', *Virginia Woolf Miscellany*, 78 (Fall/Winter 2010), 25 (23–6).
48. See 'Mr Bennett and Mrs Brown' and 'Character in Fiction', *Selected Essays*. Oxford: Oxford World's Classics, 2008, 32–6, 37–54.
49. Maggio, 'Digging for Buried Treasure', 24.
50. Virginia Woolf, *The Voyage Out*. Oxford: Oxford World's Classics, 1992, 321, 350.
51. Virginia Woolf, *Orlando*. Oxford: Oxford World's Classics, 2008, 217–18.

52. Virginia Woolf, *Between the Acts*. Oxford: Oxford World's Classics, 1992, 27.

53. Ellsworth Huntingdon, *Civilization and Climate*. New Haven: Yale University Press, 1915, 271.

54. Ibid. 129–31.

55. That sense of shifting centres of civilisation was associated in the early 1920s with Howard Carter's discoveries in Egypt of the preserved burial chambers of Tutankhamun, reports of which were heavily inflected by the sense that one great civilisation (the British Empire) was unearthing the remains of another, ancient civilisation (Egypt). The terms would be repeated, with a different inflection, after the Second World War when Harold Macmillan told John F. Kennedy that Britain would play Greece to America's Rome.

56. Huntingdon, *Civilization and Climate*, 133.

57. Ibid. 293.

58. Woolf, 'Character in Fiction', 48.

59. Samuel Johnson, 'Discourses on the Weather', *The Idler*, 11 (24 June 1758), n.p.

60. Woolf, *To the Lighthouse*, 16–17.

61. See John Brannigan, 'Dreaming of the Islands: The Poetry of the Shipping Forecast', in John Brannigan (ed.), *Reconceiving the British Isles*. UCDscholarcast: Series 4, 2010: <http://www.ucd.ie/scholarcast/scholarcast25.html> (last accessed 25 April 2014).

62. Woolf, *To the Lighthouse*, 7, 170.

63. Ibid. 25.

64. Ibid. 136.

65. Virginia Woolf, 'Joseph Conrad', *The Essays of Virginia Woolf, Vol. 4: 1925– 1928*, ed. Andrew McNeillie. London: Hogarth, 1994, 229 (227–33).

66. 'National Association for the Prevention of Tuberculosis', *The British Medical Journal*, 2.3527 (11 August 1928), 264–5.

67. Woolf, *To the Lighthouse*, 11.

68. Ibid. 86.

69. Ibid. 77.

70. 'The Hebrides', *The Times*, 14 April 1906, 10.

71. Reported in *The British Medical Journal*, 2.2551 (20 November 1909), 1476–7.

72. 'Profiteering in Fish', *The Times*, 23 August 1919, 6, and also 30 August 1919, 6.

73. 'Plight of Isle of Skye', *The Times*, 9 April 1920, 7.

74. 'Distress in the Western Isles', *The Times*, 13 December 1923, 9.

75. Bradshaw, 'Introduction', *To the Lighthouse*, xxvii–xxxiv.

76. Michael Gardiner, *The Cultural Roots of British Devolution*. Edinburgh: Edinburgh University Press, 2004, 31–2.

77. Gillian Beer, *Virginia Woolf: The Common Ground*. Edinburgh: Edinburgh University Press, 1996, 43.

78. Ibid. 41.

79. Woolf, *To the Lighthouse*, 32.

80. Ibid. 38, 124.

81. Ibid. 38.
82. Ibid. 137.
83. Ibid. 139.
84. Ibid. 154.
85. Ibid. 152.
86. Ibid. 156.
87. Ibid. 44.
88. Heise, *Sense of Place and Sense of Planet*, 34.
89. Edward S. Casey, *Remembering: A Phenomenological Study*. Bloomington: Indiana University Press, 1987, 214.
90. H. V. Morton, *In Search of England*. London: Methuen, 1932, vii. See Wren Sidhe, 'H. V. Morton's Pilgrimages to Englishness', *Literature and History*, 12.1 (2003), 57–71; David Matless, *Landscape and Englishness*. London: Reaktion, 1998, 64–6; Michael Bartholomew, 'H. V. Morton's English Utopia', in Christopher Lawrence and Anna-K. Mayer (eds), *Regenerating England: Science, Medicine and Culture in Inter-War Britain*. Amsterdam: Rodopi, 2000, 25–44; and Michael Bartholomew, *In Search of H. V. Morton*. London: Methuen, 2004.
91. Sidhe, 'H. V. Morton's Pilgrimages to Englishness', 59, 66, 69.
92. Morton, *In Search of England*, 280.
93. See *The Times*, 20 June 1939, 10, and 28 June 1939, 10, respectively.
94. Donald J. Childs, *Modernism and Eugenics: Woolf, Eliot, Yeats, and the Culture of Degeneration*. Cambridge: Cambridge University Press, 2001, 24.
95. Woolf, *Between the Acts*, 45–6.
96. Ibid. 79.
97. Ibid. 100.
98. Ibid. 174.
99. Ibid. 66.
100. Ibid. 17.
101. Ibid. 107.
102. Ibid. 8.
103. See Wells's use of craniology in *The Outline of History* to suggest that humanity had always been divided into two races, a superior, lighter-skinned northern race, and an inferior, darker-skinned southern race. H. G. Wells, *The Outline of History*. London: Cassell, 1951, 86–7.
104. Woolf, *Between the Acts*, 23.
105. Ibid. 150.
106. See A. Hingston Quiggin, *Haddon the Head Hunter*. Cambridge: Cambridge University Press, 1942.
107. Woolf, *Between the Acts*, 43–4.
108. Ibid. 53.
109. Ibid. 15.
110. Mark Hussey, *'I'd make it penal': The Rural Preservation Movement in Virginia Woolf's* Between the Acts. Bloomsbury Heritage Series. London: Cecil Woolf, 2011.

111. 'Call for Rural Reforms', *The Times*, 8 June 1939, 13.
112. Woolf, *Between the Acts*, 3–4.
113. See George Bourne, *Change in the Village*. Harmondsworth: Penguin, 1984.
114. 'Call for Rural Reforms', *The Times*, 8 June 1939, 13.
115. Woolf, *Between the Acts*, 3.
116. Hermione Lee, *Virginia Woolf*. London: Vintage, 1997, 745–7.
117. Virginia Woolf, *The Letters of Virginia Woolf, Vol. 6: 1936–1941*, ed. Nigel Nicolson and Joanne Trautmann. New York: Harcourt Brace Jovanovich, 1980, 460.
118. The folkloric associations of the may and beeches would certainly lend themselves to Woolf's patriotic feelings about the landscape in this passage, although not without interesting implications about the kind of England which is being celebrated. The best guide to the rich history and placelore surrounding both species is Richard Mabey's *Flora Britannica*. London: Sinclair-Stevenson, 1996, 71–84 and 209–15.
119. Virginia Woolf, *The Diary of Virginia Woolf, Vol. 4: 1931–1935*, ed. Anne Olivier Bell. Harmondsworth: Penguin, 1983, 218.
120. Lee, *Virginia Woolf*, 429.
121. Woolf, *Between the Acts*, 3.
122. Ibid. 15.
123. Ibid. 27.
124. Franco Moretti, *Atlas of the European Novel 1800–1900*. London: Verso, 1998, 11–73.
125. Woolf, *Between the Acts*, 27.
126. David Bradshaw, '"The Purest Ecstasy": Virginia Woolf and the Sea', in Lara Feigel and Alexandra Harris (eds), *Modernism on Sea: Art and Culture at the British Seaside*. Oxford: Peter Lang, 2011, 114 (101–15).
127. Ibid. 113–14.
128. Woolf, *Between the Acts*, 7.
129. Lee, *Virginia Woolf*, 722–4.
130. Woolf, *Between the Acts*, 37.
131. Ibid. 189.
132. Ibid. 49.
133. Ibid. 184.
134. Ibid. 184.
135. Ibid. 185.
136. Ibid. 185.
137. Robert Young, *The Idea of English Ethnicity*. Oxford: Blackwell, 2008, 2.
138. Ibid. 236.
139. Woolf, *Between the Acts*, 3–5.
140. Ibid. 173.
141. A. C. Haddon, *The Races of Man and Their Distribution*. Cambridge: Cambridge University Press, 1924, 139.
142. Ibid. 77.

143. Julian Huxley, A. C. Haddon, and A. M. Carr-Saunders, *We Europeans: A Survey of 'Racial' Problems*. Harmondsworth: Penguin, 1939, 7.

144. Ibid. 216–36.

145. Ibid. 21.

146. See, for example, 'The Problem of Race', *The Times*, 28 March 1936, 17.

147. David Bradshaw, 'Eugenics: "They Should Certainly Be Killed"', in David Bradshaw (ed.), *A Concise Companion to Modernism*. Oxford: Blackwell, 2003, 52 (34–55).

148. See Elazar Barkan, *The Retreat of Scientific Racism: Changing Concepts of Race in Britain and the United States between the World Wars*. Cambridge: Cambridge University Press, 1992.

149. F. R. Leavis and Denys Thompson, *Culture and Environment: The Training of Critical Awareness*. London: Chatto and Windus, 1933, 1.

150. Woolf, *Between the Acts*, 84.

151. Ibid. 70.

152. Ibid. 73.

153. Ibid. 161.

154. Beer, *Virginia Woolf: The Common Ground*, 24.

155. Madeline Moore, *The Short Season Between Two Silences: The Mystical and the Political in the Novels of Virginia Woolf*. Boston: George Allen and Unwin, 1984, 170.

156. Galia Benziman, '"Dispersed are we": Mirroring and National Identity in Virginia Woolf's *Between the Acts*', *Journal of Narrative Theory*, 36.1 (2006), 69 (53–71).

157. Jed Esty, *A Shrinking Island: Modernism and National Culture in England*. Princeton: Princeton University Press, 2004, 104.

158. Marina MacKay, *Modernism and World War II*. Cambridge: Cambridge University Press, 2007, 43.

159. Esty, *A Shrinking Island*, 96. Esty's title, 'A Shrinking Island: Modernism and National Culture in England', and the argument he develops that imperial contraction meant a refocusing in English literature on the meanings of Englishness, elide the ways in which the devolutionary implications of the end of the Empire for Scotland and Wales repeatedly complicate the figures of the supposed 'islandness' of England. Scotland and Wales are mentioned six times in Esty's book, each time conjoined as if they were, in Esty's words, 'in tow' (38).

160. Woolf, *Between the Acts*, 24. Woolf must have been aware of the ways in which pageants, although appearing in the guise of folk and village culture, were closely bound up with triumphal imperial and monarchist sentiments. One such example, 'Kenilworth Castle Pageant', mastered by the grandson of Louis Parker, the architect of modern English pageantry, is reported in *The Times*, 17 June 1939, 10.

161. T. S. Eliot, *Collected Poems 1909–1962*. London: Faber, 1974, 69.

162. Woolf, *Between the Acts*, 176.

163. Ibid. 177.

164. Ibid. 175.
165. Ibid. 197.
166. George Orwell, *Inside the Whale and Other Essays*. London: Penguin, 1957, 78.
167. Jessica Berman, *Modernist Fiction, Cosmopolitanism, and the Politics of Community*. Cambridge: Cambridge University Press, 2001, 156, and Woolf, *Between the Acts*, 64.
168. Woolf, *Between the Acts*, 125.
169. Ibid. 141.
170. Ibid. 27.
171. Ibid. 139.

4

Literary Topographies of a Northern Archipelago

The island, that's all the earth I know.

Samuel Beckett, *The Unnamable*

In June 1939, *The Times* reported the disappearance of the Cocos Islands in the Indian Ocean, when a flying boat called the *Guba*, which was seeking to establish a route from Britain to Australia that did not involve crossing the Mediterranean, failed to find the islands.[1] The islands were found again the following day, when the *Guba* reported less cloud cover, but the momentary disappearance sparked an editorial and a string of letters in the following days about the peculiar tendencies of islands. 'Continents at least stay, for practical purposes, where they are', declared the *Times* editorial, 'no matter with what commotions man may distract their surfaces; but there is no counting on islands.'[2] The editorial goes on to recount renowned instances of mythological and imaginary islands, and to remark upon some of the many literary uses of island settings, such as Stevenson's *Treasure Island* (1883), J. M. Barrie's *Mary Rose* (1920), and Charles Morgan's popular but now largely forgotten play *The Flashing Stream* (1938). The editorial also mentions the case of Thompson Island in the South Atlantic, which recent maritime expeditions had repeatedly failed to find. Thompson Island was declared non-existent in 1943, yet as recently as 1928 the British government had sold export licences to Norwegian whalers to trade in whale oil and guano from the island, and later that year they consented to a diplomatic agreement which ceded British sovereignty of the island over to Norway. An essay in *The Geographical Journal* of 1928 included the sketches and maps produced by Captain Norris from his voyage of the region in 1825 which had laid the foundation of British territorial claims over Thompson and Bouvet Islands, and argued that 'There seemed no ground for questioning its existence, though there was some degree of uncertainty in its position'.[3] In the same year, a retired naval commander, Rupert Gould, in a chapter of his book devoted to 'doubtful islands', held fast to the belief that there were unexplored areas around the South Atlantic seas in which Thompson Island may yet be found.[4] 'Thompson Island had better realize it has been warned', scolded the *Times* editorial in June 1939, 'no island can expect to be recognized as existing unless it turns up now and then.'[5]

The response to these vanishing islands in the 1920s and 1930s illustrates an important paradox in the cultural significance of islands. On the one hand, as Godfrey Baldacchino argues, 'islands have occupied such a powerful place in modern Western imagination', from Ithaca and Atlantis, to Avalon and Tír na nÓg, 'that they lend themselves to sophisticated fantasy and mythology'.[6] On the other hand, islands have long been useful as laboratories in the study of biological and cultural processes, from Charles Darwin's use of the Galapagos islands in *The Origin of Species* (1859), and Alfred Russel Wallace's contemporaneous biogeographical work in the Malay archipelago, through to the birth of modern anthropology with the island-based studies of Alfred Cort Haddon, Margaret Mead, and Bronislaw Malinowski in the early twentieth century. Islands are therefore both 'hard-edged' microcosms of continental or mainland life, and alternative spaces, utopian or dystopian, in the imperial and national imagination, from Thomas More's *Utopia* (1516) to George Orwell's *Nineteen Eighty-Four* (1949). The problem in all of this, as Pete Hay argues, is the absence of the physicality and the phenomenology of islands themselves, an absence for which Hay holds the metaphorical and abstracting tendencies of literary and cultural studies responsible, and makes a case for their omission from island studies altogether, like Plato's case for the banishment of poets from the polis.[7] Yet, Hay's wish for a way of seeing islands 'in themselves', outside of the means of cultural representation, is itself, of course, a mythical abstraction, an illusion upon which every island fantasy depends.

It might be argued that the literature of the 1930s, especially as reputed in the work of the Auden generation, represented precisely this turn away from the metaphorical and abstracting tendencies of high modernism, to forms of documentary realism, or even what we might call a 'revisionary' modernism, which were capable of precisely such material and phenomenological perspectives. Whereas Joyce's version of Ithaca, Woolf's famously displaced vision of the Hebrides, or Yeats's escapist fantasy of Innisfree might be argued to give Hay's case against literature some support, what Jed Esty describes as 'the anthropological turn' in the late modernism of the 1930s made possible a renewed sense of the cultural particularity and ethnolinguistic distinctiveness of specific places or regions.[8] Indeed, Kristin Bluemel suggests that the generation of writers she calls 'intermodernist' were explicitly concerned to recuperate the validity of the 'provincial, countryside or regional landscape as site of origins or identity', in contrast to the metropolitanising tendencies of modernism.[9] The extent to which this 'demetropolitanization', to use Esty's unlovely word, manifested itself not just in an 'insular turn' towards national or regional cultures, but in a rather more literal 'insular turn' towards islands, is a notable feature of the writings of the late 1920s and the 1930s throughout the British and Irish Isles.

   Yet, in contrast to nationalist appropriations of islands as cultural and racial repositories of pre-modern 'purity', and imperialist figures of islands as symbolic origins, the literature of islands in the 1930s, I would suggest, is inherently connective, relational, and material.[10] One of the best-known examples of the period's fascination with islands is a collaboration between an English and an Irish poet, W. H. Auden and Louis MacNeice's *Letters from Iceland* (1937), a playful mockery of the contemporary penchant for literary reportage from peripheral regions. MacNeice followed this with *I Crossed the Minch* (1938), a book purporting to record the poet's tour around the Western Isles of Scotland, but which is extraordinarily deconstructive of the travel genre, and of any apparent Celtic connections which justified MacNeice's decision to visit. As Edna Longley argues, this was also 'the decade of two influential island poems: Louis MacNeice's "The Hebrides" and Hugh MacDiarmid's "Island Funeral"', as well as MacDiarmid's part manifesto, part travelogue, *The Islands of Scotland* (1939).[11] It was the decade in which Compton Mackenzie made his home in Barra, identifying himself conspicuously with Scottish nationalism, although his islomanic tendencies from his earlier sojourns in the Mediterranean had already been satirised in D. H. Lawrence's story 'The Man Who Loved Islands' (1927). The period is known for the proliferation of island literature in Gaelic, most notably from the Blasket Islands, off the south-west coast of Ireland, and among which the most celebrated works are Tomás Ó Criomhthain's *An tOileánach* (*The Islandman*) (1929), Muiris Ó Súileabháin's *Fiche Blian ag Fás* (*Twenty Years A-Growing*) (1933), and Peig Sayers' autobiography *Peig* (1936).[12] Of these, Ó Criomhthain's work was encouraged, edited, and translated by a Yorkshireman, Robin Flower, who fell in love with the Blaskets in the course of his research on medieval Irish manuscripts, whilst Ó Súileabháin's book was influenced, edited, and translated by a Londoner, George Thomson, a classical scholar and committed Marxist, who saw island life as a close approximation of Homeric Greece. It was also, rather strangely, introduced by E. M. Forster, who described *Twenty Years A-Growing* as 'an account of neolithic civilization from the inside', where 'it has itself become vocal, and addressed modernity'.[13] Forster specifically cites John Millington Synge as an exemplar of the modernist appropriation of islands as spaces 'outside' of modernity, and suggests an argument which Jill Frank makes meticulously in her study *Islands and the Modernists* (2006).[14]

This flurry of archipelagic literature, then, is characterised by the circulation of people and ideas between the islands, and is certainly marked by the perception that the islands on the western edge, be they the Blaskets, the Arans, or the Hebrides, represent peripheral extremes of mainland society. As was evident in one of the urtexts of the genre, Synge's *The Aran Islands* (1907), the islands represented the extremes of a sense of rootedness, even timelessness, but they also represented the extremes of social change, particularly in the case of rapid depopulation and emigration. Pete Hay suggests one of the key reasons for social and cultural obsession with islands:

> Perhaps *the* most contested faultline within island studies is whether islands are characterised by vulnerability or resilience; whether they are victims of change, economically dependent, and at the mercy of unscrupulous neo-colonial manipulation, or whether they are uniquely resourceful in the face of such threats.[15]

This, I would argue, was a question of particular urgency throughout the British and Irish Isles in the 1920s and 1930s, when the very notion of the 'wholeness' of 'Britain', 'England', or the 'United Kingdom' was undermined politically and culturally by the emergent sovereignty of the Irish Free State (1922) and its constitutional claim to the 'whole island of Ireland' (1937), by the Scottish Renaissance of the 1920s, by the formation of Plaid Cymru (1925) and the Scottish National Party (1934), and by the palpable decline of British imperial power across the globe.[16] George Orwell argued that if the Empire disintegrated, England would be reduced to 'a cold and unimportant island where we all have to work very hard and live mainly on herrings and potatoes'.[17] Although he would spend some of his final years living on Jura, subsisting on such a diet, Orwell's point was that England, or more properly Britain, as an island, could not sustain its prosperity from its own natural resources. In reply to Orwell's prospect of a Britain returned to its own shores, Hugh MacDiarmid, living then on Whalsay in the Shetlands, in *The Islands of Scotland* looked forward to such a fate, and held fast to the belief that 'all that is still greatest in literature and art and philosophy was created . . . in places as lonely and bare as these islands are'.[18] What did 'islandness' mean to such writers in the 1930s? Did it entail insularity, a word which connotes both security and isolation? Did it appeal to this generation of late modernist writers as an idea of remoteness, primitivism, and subsistence free of the ideological and ethical compromises of metropolitan prosperity? Did 'islandness' promise to restore a material sense of location, of place, to ideas of regional, or even national, identity through the association of islands with rootedness? Or did 'islandness' promise not just a corrective but an alternative to the dominant conceptions of identity and belonging of the past? The aim of this chapter is to examine this 'islomania' of the 1930s for its potential to imagine post-imperial and post-metropolitan forms of community and citizenship.

BETWEEN THE ISLANDS: MICHAEL MCLAVERTY,
LATE MODERNISM, AND THE INSULAR TURN

Michael McLaverty's fictional representations of Rathlin are exemplary of what might be characterised tentatively as an emergent archipelagic consciousness in the literature of the British and Irish Isles in the interwar period. McLaverty's island is both a 'laboratory for the study of cultural process', in the words of J. D. Evans, particularly of then current cultural concerns about island sustainability, degeneration, and cultural purity, and, at the same time, a distinctive habitat, a locality, interconnected with, and interdependent upon, other configurations of social and cultural belonging.[19] McLaverty spent long periods of his childhood on Rathlin Island, located between the North Antrim coast and the Mull of Kintyre, and it is a setting to which he returns again and again in his fictional writings. It is the location for some of his best-known stories, such as 'The Wild Duck's Nest' (1934, 1947), 'The Prophet' (1936), and 'Stone' (1939), as well as the first part of his first novel, *Call My Brother Back* (1939), and the whole of *Truth in the Night* (1951). For Sophia Hillan King, it is most clearly associated with McLaverty's emergent phase as a writer in the 1930s, where the island is a 'superficially idyllic setting', associated with childhood joy and innocence, but ultimately also with loss and decay.[20] That sense of loss is biographical, Hillan King argues, reflecting McLaverty's own sense of longing for the island which was partly his childhood home, but it is also more philosophical. McLaverty's island writings are characterised, Hillan King writes, by a 'note of regret, almost of grief at the passing of a kind of prelapsarian purity', fuelled by a sense of Rathlin's distinctiveness from the modernity of the mainland, and by an equally keen awareness of the decline of the island population and the demise of its cultural peculiarities.[21] Concerns about population decline abound in the early stories and in *Call My Brother Back*. At the end of the first chapter of *Call My Brother Back*, the child protagonist, Colm, learns that in his great-grandfather's time 'There were three schools in the island . . . and now there's only one with forty wee childer in it', and, more pointedly, his father pronounces that 'The people's not the same as they used to be; there's a softness in them'. Another islander summarises the problem: 'All the young are goin' away, the ould people are dyin' and there's nobody marryin'.'[22] This, in crude form at least, is a more or less accurate representation of McLaverty's characterisations of island life, preoccupied with the leaving of the young, the dying of the old, and the difficulty of finding marital partners. More particularly here, the 'wee-ness' of the 'childer', and the 'softness' of the people, implies that the depopulation of the island is not simply caused by famine and emigration, that is, not simply the result of economic and political factors, but is also the consequence of inherent, degenerative factors within the people themselves.

Such echoes of eugenic concerns about degeneration, heredity, and sustainability are by no means rare, of course, in the literature of late modernism, and in Irish writings of the period are most clearly associated with the late Yeats of *Purgatory* (1939) and *On the Boiler* (1939). The affinity of literary and anthropological interests in the early twentieth century has been a significant point of exploration in the new modernist studies,[23] and in recent studies of the Irish Revival.[24] Rathlin Island was not subject to the same degree of scientific and cultural interest as the Arans, Blaskets, or Hebrides, all of which were the bases for a flurry of ethnographic, linguistic, and literary publications in the first half of the twentieth century.[25] As an island between islands, compared to islands on the periphery, or 'islands beyond islands', perhaps Rathlin was not sufficiently remote, or not sufficiently liminal, to lend itself to the cultural and scientific imagination. It was, however, the subject of one of the first physical anthropological surveys of racial types to be completed in Ireland. Michael A. MacConaill, a graduate of the Department of Anatomy in Queen's University Belfast, made a study of male islanders in July 1923, the results of which he published in the *Proceedings of the Belfast Natural History and Philosophical Society*. MacConaill surveyed twenty men, photographing them as well as taking twenty measurements and several observations on physical attributes such as weight, height, cephalic index, nasomental, bizygomatic, and bigonial facial measurements, hair form and colour, and eye colour. These were the indices of racial identity for the trained physical anthropologist, and, in a manner interestingly replicated in the recent mapping of the Irish human genome, they are only meaningful in relation to the subject's self-reported ancestry.[26] All of MacConaill's subjects except one were born on the island, and their fathers were born on the island, although seven of the twenty had mothers who were born in the neighbouring counties of Antrim and Derry. This in itself is an interesting finding, although MacConaill doesn't comment upon it, of the statistical prevalence of marriage between island men and non-island women but not, it seems, the other way round. The more likely emigration of women from the island probably accounts for this tendency. MacConaill's measurements confirm his impression of the racial commonality of the men of Rathlin:

> The people are distinctly fair-skinned . . . The skin is smooth and rather matt in texture. The eyes are light in colour . . . The form of the hair

is slightly waved; in only three of the men could it be classed as straight
. . . The face is long . . . with high cheek bones . . . and a well developed
lower jaw . . . The nose is prominent with well developed alae.[27]

The common technique of physical anthropologists of the time was to aggregate the measurements of their study to arrive at such a description as if of one
individual who serves as racial archetype for the group. The results confirm
for MacConaill that the men of Rathlin belong to 'a well-defined race-group,
the Gall-Ghaedhil or Norse-Irish', and that they share kinship with the southern parts of the west of Scotland. They remain distinct as islanders, however,
despite their intercourse with Antrim and south-west Scotland. MacConaill
quotes from a 1786 description of the islanders by the Rev. William Hamilton
that 'want of intercourse with strangers has preserved many peculiarities',
which MacConaill writes is 'true today', while also observing the dwindling
of the population as a result of famine and emigration, and the dwindling too
of the Gaelic language in the island.[28] For MacConaill, then, Rathlin is of
interest because of the qualities most commonly associated with island ecologies: the 'isolation' and 'boundedness' which R. J. Berry argues gives them
their peculiar genetic and cultural traits, and the fragility of their biological
systems, which places them constantly at risk of extinction.[29] As such, then,
for anthropologists as well as some prominent late modernist writers, islands
were exemplary sites of both eugenic and ecological anxieties, distinctively
local, and yet bound up with intrinsically internationalist perspectives on the
human race and its planetary habits.[30]

McLaverty's writings are exemplary of this anthropological turn in late
modernism, and for their preoccupation with the relationship between material space and subjective perspectives. McLaverty's first published story, 'The
Green Field' (1932), is set on a fictional version of Rathlin, called Innisdall,
and the story works hard in its opening paragraphs to fix an image of the coastal
geometries of the island in relation to the sea and the mainland. Three times
in the opening ten lines of the story, the narrator describes Maura Murphy's
view from the island school in which she teaches, of 'the sea and the mainland', 'the blue sea and the grey land', and 'the sea and the dark mountains
of the mainland', before the story uses island metaphors for parts of the island
landscape: patches of corn are described as 'green islets in a grey sea', and the
eponymous green field is described as an 'oasis'.[31] The story concerns the
farmer-fisherman who owns the green field, Frank King, who looks to Maura
for companionship and love, but whose hopes are dashed when she asks him
to sell her the field so that she can marry a teacher from the mainland and
settle on the island. There is clearly an ethnological concern underlying the
story, about the sustainability of island life, as it is evident that Maura is Frank's

only hope of a marriage partner. Frank's forty-year-old unmarried sister, with whom he bickers, particularly about strangers to the island, is symbolic of the unrelieved and 'inexpressible loneliness' which he faces without Maura.[32] The green field, an obvious symbol of fertility amidst the greyness of rock and sea-scape, is itself lost to the island in Frank's consent for Maura to live on it, since it will pass from useful agricultural land to the aesthetically pleasing choice of a home for Maura and her husband, whose labour is intellectual rather than manual. The story is not mature work: it wears its symbolism too heavily, and makes too much of the pathetic fallacy, in which the weather matches the mood of the characters. However, it does make clear the interdependence of human with other life forms on the island, and the slow encroachment of mainland customs and economies upon island ecologies. The transition of the island from a worked, material landscape to an aesthetic landscape is also figured in the story, with no sense of resentment, but in pairing the proximate words 'loveliness' and 'loneliness' in his descriptions of the characters' feelings about the island, McLaverty shows that there are casualties in this transition.[33]

The fragility of island ecologies, human and non-human, is also the concern of 'The Wild Duck's Nest', published originally in 1934, and revised in 1947. In it, a young boy named Colm discovers the nest of a wild duck, handles the egg before replacing it, and then is tortured by the thought that the duck will forsake the egg. In the original version, McLaverty concludes on a dark note: Colm returns to the nest to allay his fears, but in doing so he disturbs the duck, who in flapping away from Colm drops the egg, which smashes against the rocks below.[34] Colm's anxiety is that in handling the egg he has 'sinned', but McLaverty's focus is not just on the boy's moral dilemma. Rather, it is on the fragile co-existence and interdependence of human and non-human life forms. McLaverty is charting the anxious, delicate relation-ship between human and animal worlds: Colm is located within a physical landscape described with a naturalist's precision, with a 'western limestone headland', a lake fringed with 'bulrushes, wild irises and sedge', and where the differences between a wild duck and a tame duck, and between the eggs of a duck and a gull, are matters of intimate knowledge. It is clear in the story that the wild duck is a rare sighting, and its nest is an untidily built, fragile assembly of rushes, straw, and feathers on a tidy islet of grass in a lake. Here, then, are the precarious beginnings of life on the island, an image not simply symbolic of, but fully implicated in, Colm's own island childhood.

In 'The Prophet' (1936), another young boy growing up on the island, Brendan, longs to have the gift, for which his grandfather was renowned, of 'telling the weather'. His grandfather's rheumatism is implied as the likely source of his gift, yet Brendan wishes it to be a hereditary intuition. Brendan fails to intuit the weather, however, and attempts to read the signs of changing weather in the landscape and sky around the island: 'the Mull of Kintyre was smothered in fog; and turning round he saw a tonsure of mist on Knocklayde. He smiled at the prospect of more rain.'[35] Partly the story is concerned with inexperience, and a child's longing for authority and wisdom, and partly too the story is about weather forecasting as an especially valuable island skill, and therefore one prized by a young boy keen to follow in the traditions of his family. His grandfather's gift is symbolic of a sense of harmony with the ecology and climate of the island, whereas Brendan's attempts to read the signs of nature fail. However, a darker side to island society is also suggested by the story, since his grandfather's prophecies earned him a reputation as a 'quare ould fella' and 'an old witch', and Brendan's attempts to tell the weather are received with the same sense of scorn.[36] McLaverty's Rathlin is not depicted as a site of alternative superstitions and myths, glorious in its differences from the mainland, but rather as a society pressed harder by material circumstances into insularity and suspicion.

In several of McLaverty's stories, the weather figures significantly in high-lighting the fragility of human and non-human life on the island, and in levelling differences within island society. This is especially evident in 'Stone' (1939), in which Jamesy Heaney, 'the last of the Heaneys left on the island', tired of local taunts about his childlessness, sets his mind foolishly upon buying the tallest headstone possible for his own grave so that his name will outlive that of his neighbours, but his hopes for posterity are dashed when he witnesses the power of a storm to smash graveyard stones to pieces.[37] The storm also devastates his shed, tears up his tree, and wreaks havoc with his thatched roof. The obvious reading suggests the vulnerability of human society to the power of nature, and McLaverty's Rathlin fictions abound with reminders of the powers of sea and wind to destroy human life and habitation, powers which may indeed be read allegorically for the effects of modernity upon a community associated with long traditions of subsistence fishing and farming. Set against this, the story nonetheless suggests a common resilience among the islanders in their diverse attempts to impose meaning upon the 'rocky desert' which the island would be without them.[38] For the men who taunt Jamesy, 'family' and 'stock' are the only meaningful signs of human endurance, while for Jamesy 'stone' is the language of posterity. Yet, at the heart of the story is a question about the nature of this relationship between human signification, or meaning-making, and the materiality of place. In the era of empires, reichs, and nations, McLaverty's fictions reflect on the ways in which material place, the specific sense of locality shaped by sea, land, and climate, defines and makes the identities of the people who inhabit it, not the other way around. Jamesy is left at the end of the story with the cold realisation that the island has made its mark upon him, but that his claims upon the island are as tenuous as 'the withered heather clinging for life to the barren rocks' which he sees on his way to the graveyard.[39]

Although all of the short stories set on Rathlin include specific geographic details, in terms of its topography, climate, and habitation, none of them locate the island in relation to the world beyond. In the short stories, the island is conceived as a world, complete in its sense of itself as a society, if not sufficient economically. In McLaverty's first novel, *Call My Brother Back* (1939), however, it is clear that the island is both connected with, and dependent upon, a wider network of places and communities. The swans are understood to have come from Scotland. Fish and potatoes are sold in Ballycastle, where the islanders buy meat, clothes, and shoes, and obtain medical services. The young hero of the novel, Colm, can only become a teacher in Belfast, where he already has an older sister and brother; otherwise, his future, the novel implies, consists of dwindling expectations of a land hard to work, and from which it is harder to make a living. Wider geographies are suggested too, by the steamship wrecked on the island shoreline, from the holds of which the islanders salvage much needed shoes, clothes, furniture, and other supplies, and by Colm's Uncle Robert, tattooed and worldly wise, who has stokered ships to India. The sea is understood as a means of passage, communication, and connection, rather than as an insulating boundary, in *Call My Brother Back*.[40]

The difference between the geography of the short stories and the geography of the novel might simply be accounted for in formal terms: novels, we might generalise, lend themselves to more capacious spatial frameworks than short stories, and may even need the broader canvas against which to unfold their more expansive plots and distribute their more numerous characters. However, this would place too much stress upon the form dictating the geography. A comparison of the short stories with *Call My Brother Back* makes clear a key distinction between them: the short stories succeed in representing the island only as an island. It appears to be any island, or indeed even a metaphorical island, as McLaverty's first published story, 'The Green Field', suggests in its title, and in adopting islandness as a metaphor. The novel is far more successful in articulating the particularity of the island, but it does so within an expanded geography, in which the island may be seen from outside, and as a locality in relation to other localities, as well as within wider regional, national, and international contexts. The geography shapes the form, or, as Franco Moretti argues, '*each space determines, or at least encourages, its own kind of story*'.[41]

This is most obvious in the contrast between the first part of the novel, set on Rathlin, and the second part, set in Belfast. Indeed, it is Colm's older brother, Alec, who later dies a violent death in Belfast as an IRA gunman, who articulates the particular sense of 'between-ness' which characterises the island, when he tells Colm: 'Times I wonder whether we're Irish at all sitting here between Ireland and Scotland; nobody's darling and nobody wantin' us.'[42] The novel frequently alludes to the Scottish coastline and hills which can be seen from Rathlin, as well as Knocklayde mountain and Ballycastle in Antrim, allusions which continually serve to figure the island's 'between-ness' also. McLaverty may even suggest a critique of the insularity of his earlier work in the ways in which the 'island-bound' narrative of the first part of the novel sees the island as a kind of womb-figure: Colm is depicted on two occasions in foetal positions, and the island is associated as the maternal body in several images, such as 'the shoulder of the island', 'rock-face', the 'lap' of a hill, and, perhaps most pointedly, in the description of the shore 'where black rocks nippled by limpets breasted the sea'.[43] In contrast, in the second part of the novel, in which he has moved to Belfast, Colm sees the island as a material space, a space of objects along a shoreline:

> He put his hand in his pocket for a pencil and his fingers touched a green marble pebble which Jamesy had given him the day he left the island. He took it out and looked at it in the palm of his hand. It was polished from rubbing against the things in his pocket; he turned it over admiring its tiny vein of white and its freckles of brown; and as he looked at it a shore took shape in his mind: grey stones in a curve, and down by the edge of the tide the pebbles rattling as the waves came slashing in, farther back dry sticks eaten by sea lice, a frayed piece of rope, whitened limpet shells that crackled under the feet, and a bicycle tyre with rusted rims . . .[44]

This is not the aesthetically idealised landscape of 'The Green Field', nor the immutable rock of 'The Prophet'; instead, Colm is drawn to what Rachel Carson called 'the marginal world' of the shoreline, a topography ever-changing, and ever-connective, in which 'one creature is linked with another, and each with its surroundings'.[45] The pebble which Colm carries in his pocket bears quite different connotations, therefore, from the fabled tradition of carrying native soil, and indeed from the figure of epistemological and ontological obscurity which preoccupies Robert Frost in his more famous literary articulation of the pebble in 'For Once, Then, Something'.[46]

It is only in Belfast that the significance of Rathlin's particularity as an island between islands becomes apparent. The violence and alienation associated with Belfast are inseparable from the symbolism of its street names, 'Oxford Street, Victoria Street, Cromac Street, Durham Street, Townshend Street, Carlisle Circus', the markers of a failed colonial geography.[47] When Colm is drawn towards memories of Rathlin, as he frequently is, it is as an island between Knocklayde and Kintyre, an island comprised of sea, wind, and a restless shoreline. Even its names, which he recalls as 'words full of music', 'Lagavristeevore, Killaney, Crocnacreeva, Carnasheeran, Crocaharna', are hybrid, adapted names.[48] Colm's acceptance, and even celebration, of this topography of between-ness is evidently also opposed to his brother's advocacy of violent nationalism, with its inability to conceive of the island as a place in which other places merge and mingle. In contrast to Esty's notion of late modernism as restoring cultural integrity as 'a second-order universalism', McLaverty's insular fictions come to dispense with the 'romance of wholeness', or the 'ambiguous embrace of national identity', and instead describe islands in connective, hybrid, and liminal terms.[49] In a typically late modernist turn, McLaverty's writings highlight the materiality and phenomenology of the islands as physical and social spaces, at the same time as they insist upon a complex figurative economy in which islands are relational, transformative nodes.

If, as Pete Hay argues, islands are 'special places, paradigmatic places, topographies of meaning in which the qualities that construct place are dramatically distilled', then they warrant particular study in an age popularly characterised as one in which the specificities of place are eroded by the homogenising processes of globalisation.[50] All of the island writings of the 1930s express anxiety about the erosion of island particularity as a result of commerce and migration, including McLaverty's fictions. Nostalgia for an implied, pre-modern insularity is certainly a persistent feature of such writings. Yet, it is clearly not the only sentiment, nor even the dominant sentiment, in McLaverty's writings. If McLaverty began by depicting islands as singular, bounded places, defined by anthropological and materialist concerns about the sustainability of island ecologies, human and non-human, he showed in his novel at the end of the decade that the vulnerability of the island to contact with other places was also its strength, that its 'between-ness' made it more, not less, exemplary as a model of archipelagic identities and relations.

'IN THE COLD-LIPPED ATLANTIC': PEADAR O'DONNELL'S ISLAND COMMUNITIES

The first book which Peadar O'Donnell saw as a child, and which was read to him by his father, was an illustrated version of *Robinson Crusoe*.[51] O'Donnell was born and brought up in the Rosses of West Donegal, within sight of the islands of Innisfree, Inniskeeragh, and Rutland in the mouth of Dungloe Bay. Defoe's story of the lonely struggle for existence on remote islands, now widely regarded as a parable of capitalist individualism and colonial exploitation, could hardly be a more significant contrast to O'Donnell's emphatically communitarian versions of island life in *Islanders* (1927) and *Wrack* (1933).

Yet, although the island fascination which inspired Defoe's novel undoubtedly makes it an antecedent of the islomania of 1930s writers, there were more
immediate literary and social contexts which informed O'Donnell's writings
about the islands off the coast of Donegal. *Wrack*, for example, was publicised
as 'even closer to fact and as intimately true in atmosphere' as Synge's *Riders
to the Sea*.[52] The character of Ruth in *Islanders* is drawn to the Rosses, to live
close to the islands, out of 'a desire born of the Abbey Theatre, and fostered by
short trips to Kerry and Connemara', and this, in large part, incites her romantic interest in the novel's hero, Charlie Doogan, as 'my big, wild man of the
sea'.[53] In the same novel, the willingness of the islanders to hide a murderer
from the mainland, and the ease with which an island woman falls in love with
him, echoes closely the alternative morality of island life which had famously
attracted Yeats and Synge in their depictions of the Aran islands.[54]

O'Donnell's biographer, Peter Hegarty, traces the genesis of *Islanders*
to the basement of Mountjoy Jail, where O'Donnell was held captive as a
Republican prisoner of the newly formed Irish Free State, and the dreary
isolation of his cell led him to fond recollections of fishing among the islands
off the Rosses, an image of the islands as outside of, and indifferent to, the
vicious internecine events of the Irish Civil War which became an important
part of the novel's depiction of insular life.[55] The Civil War context, and
its deep impact upon the politics of the Irish state for later generations, is
important, not least because a key motivation for Republican opposition to
the Anglo-Irish Treaty was the partition of the island of Ireland, and the passionate commitment to an idea of Ireland as 'a whole island'. The Republican
leader of the time, Eamon de Valera, would later, in the 1937 Constitution
of Ireland, assert the national claim to sovereignty over 'the whole island of
Ireland, its islands and the territorial seas',[56] a claim which even those advising
him at the time counselled against as a form of 'Hibernia Irredenta', and which
was removed in 1998 by a referendum of the Irish electorate on the Belfast
Peace Agreement.[57] O'Donnell depicts the islanders of Inniscara as blithely
uninterested in the national struggle for such a 'whole island', unaware of the
names of glorified nationalist leaders such as Wolfe Tone or John Mitchel, but
nevertheless, the 'wholeness' and communality of the island depicted in the
novel promise to act as forceful indices of an alternative to mainland society.
Indeed, it is Ruth's Abbey Theatre-inspired vision of the islanders in mythic
terms which the novel allows, albeit perhaps cursorily, to win out against the
more cynical depictions of material deprivation and encroaching modernity.

Both *Islanders* and *Wrack* provide carefully detailed depictions of the hardships of island life, and pose a tension between those islanders who value the
'small, knowable community' for its integrity and sociability, and those who,
like Mary Jim in *Wrack*, are suffocated by the constant struggle against the sea:

> MARY JIM: I hate the sea. I hate to look at it. I hate [to] walk in it . . .
> If it was living couldn't it give us some share of life? What have we to
> get as it is? Carrigeen, sloak, dilsk; everything that's dead and clammy
> . . . [If] only I could run and run till there was no sea.[58]

At the end of the play, the sea has claimed the lives of some of the island's
best fishermen, drowned in a storm despite their ship being captained by Peter
Dan, 'the greatest helmsman between the Foreland and the mouth of the
Shannon',[59] thus perhaps endorsing Mary Jim's dread of the power and hardships imposed by the sea, echoed in one of the final lines of the play by the
widowed Fanny, who curses the island and 'the hungry belly of the sea'.[60] Yet
Wrack is also a parable about the dangers of individualism, since the tragedy at
sea is partly caused by the helmsman's desperate determination to win a catch
from the sea, no matter what the consequences. Earlier in the play, Hughie
rebukes the women for talking critically of the sea, and blames fishermen for
their own tragic deaths in stormy seas, for 'it would be a queer island man that
couldn't tell when the sea would be like that'.[61] 'Natural' is the term most
frequently used as praise in the play: Peter Dan is credited for his skills as a
helmsman for being 'as natural to the sea as its own waves',[62] Hughie lauds the
sea as 'the most natural thing in the world',[63] and, perhaps most significantly,
when Brigid, Hughie's wife, is aroused sexually by the memory of his heroic
return from a sea rescue, she tells him 'There's a lot of nature in the world,
my boyo', to which he responds by advancing swiftly to her, lifting her chin
presumably to kiss, before they are then interrupted.[64] It is a scene which is
notable for its potential to be performed in a manner which makes explicit
the association between proximity to 'nature' and sexual frankness, especially
remarkable as it is Brigid who displays arousal first.

   In *Islanders*, too, sexual arousal is implied between Ruth and Charlie, with
the female character again most clearly signalled as leading the sexual advance.
She first meets him when he flings open the door of her house after rowing
from the island to fetch her brother, the doctor, to attend to his sister in
childbirth:

> 'My God! The Danes have landed – a Viking,' she added with vigour,
> commenting on the man who had entered. He was tall; he was drenched;
> he was excited; his face was pale, rugged, granite-like. His hair was black
> and short, scattered irregularly, as heavy rain flattens hair. He was bare-
> footed; he wore a sleeveless vest. It was Charlie Doogan.[65]

Charlie is figured here as an archetype of primitive masculinity; O'Donnell's
prose conveys his rawness, energy, and simplicity. It is matched by Ruth's
'vigour', however, and from this moment it is clear that Ruth is not just the

theatre-going romantic from the city, but, importantly, a physical match for Charlie. This is confirmed in the next scene, when Ruth accompanies Charlie and the doctor to the island, and when landing ashore is made difficult in stormy conditions, she leaps into the sea to swim alongside him, upon which an islander remarks, 'By the Lord, she's stuff.'[66] In contrast to some of the island women, especially Charlie's mother, who have been weakened by hunger, poverty, and physical toil, Ruth is the epitome of vigorous health. Moreover, her confidence in making clear her sexual attraction to Charlie contrasts with the relative passivity of the island women, perhaps especially Charlie's first intended mate, Susan. The novel explains Ruth's sexual confidence, perhaps, in relation to her class position, and her urban background, and hence it might be argued that she is always figured as an outsider. However, this does not detract from the forceful implication that Charlie and Ruth are idealised mates, figured in eugenic terms as exemplars of racial health. This is perhaps made most evident in the scene in which Charlie beats the lighthouse keeper in a boat race intended to display masculine prowess, when his mother worries about him weakening because 'he's not fed for it', to which her neighbour proudly replies, 'But he's bred for it.'[67] The juxtaposition of these countervailing discourses of material poverty and racial strength is a significant trope in island writings of the early twentieth century, of course, especially along the Atlantic rim.

The theme of breeding arguably pervades the novel, since the racial health of the island is constantly in focus. It is clear from early in the novel that the island economy depends upon its strongest, fittest members migrating to the farming communities of Lagan in east Donegal for work, or further to Scotland for grain and potato harvesting, or from there even to America, the richest source of remittances.[68] The poverty and 'over-population' of the islands and coastlands of west Donegal was marked out for concern by geographer Thomas Walter Freeman, in an essay published in 1941 on 'The Congested Districts of Western Ireland', as an area of 'thickly settled coast-lands', with 'potatoes and oats growing in black-soiled fields protected by high walls against the incursions of sheep and goats. Here and there a ruined cottage bespeaks the abandonment of the struggle.' For Freeman, 'the population could not be supported without the resources of seasonal migration and the remittances of the filial-minded in America and elsewhere'.[69] Charlie is self-evidently the most likely character to emigrate, a possibility made imminent when his mother faints from malnourishment, which is itself arguably, like Freeman's image of the deserted cottage, a synecdoche of the famine which constantly threatens the existence of remote, peasant communities. The novel prevaricates about whether island life is debilitating (Charlie is indirectly attributed the thought, for example, that it is 'a sapless life, without joy, without hope'),[70] or the cradle of strength and vitality (Ruth asks of Charlie, rhetorically, 'Is it sitting like this on the rocks makes you great, I wonder?').[71] In Ruth's version, the island is a last bastion of a distinctive, vital mode of peasant existence, which has still the capacity to breed men whom she depicts in Nietzschean terms as great, wild, and big, able to overcome the elements and their rivals through willpower. But the difficulties of wresting an existence from the sea and the sparse land stifle the opportunities for growth on the island, which is too much dependent upon the fortunes cast up by the sea in the form of herring shoals, or taken away by storms. The result is that, as one islander remarks, 'The island's only a nursery for foreign parts', with its most able members destined to leave in order to earn the income which keeps the island from starvation.[72]

O'Donnell's materialist representation of the economic realities of island life constantly strain against the mythic conceptions of primitivism and racial vitality. For Ruth, the island may be a repository of a form of antiquated peasant existence which she has hitherto only known on the stage of the Abbey Theatre. However, the novel also intimates the thoroughly modern economic structures in which island society is intermeshed. Charlie's sisters find employment through a hiring fair which links a mobile labour force to the vicissitudes of market demand; his imminent migration to Scotland, and perhaps to America, is itself indicative of a networked circuit of labour movement which is bound to an industrial scale of food production and distribution; the cash windfall which Charlie and other islanders make from their herring catches may be understood by their families as divine providence, but the alchemic process of turning herring into cash happens only because of the capacity of a modern railway infrastructure to deliver the fish to urban markets. As O'Donnell makes clear, the daily lives of the islanders may resemble feudal society, but every facet of their existence is precariously dependent upon market capitalism as a system of trade, employment, and infrastructure. There are signs, of course, of their resentment of its deep inequities: Charlie goes to the mainland to avenge the death of his sister caused by a callous employer, the islanders complain of the exploitative prices charged by mainland traders, and, interestingly, given the novel's racial allusions, the hiring farmers are compared to 'the Jew that was sellin' the pictures'.[73] Charlie must also resort to poaching to feed his family. The latter example, in particular, is implicated as part of the alternative morality of the island, for, as Grattan Freyer writes, Charlie's defence of poaching that 'it was rightly come by' is 'in strict conformity with Catholic social teaching that theft by a starving man is no theft'.[74] Freyer means by this that 'it is no revolutionary act', although when set against the materialist ways in which O'Donnell depicts the island's dependence upon capitalist modes of exchange, labour, and property relations, it is hard to see how it is not at least an act of defiance. However defiant they may be, and how valiantly they may rage against hardship to win the struggle for existence on their own wet rocks in the Atlantic, O'Donnell's islanders are nevertheless fully integrated into the uneven processes of capitalist modernity, their 'wildness' merely the determinations of capitalist cultural exoticisations of its own remote reaches.

Islanders concludes with an implied, which is to say imaginary, happy ending. Since Ruth, as an urban, middle-class, educated woman, would not fit into the mythic culturescape of remote insularity, and since Charlie cannot leave the island without sounding the symbolic death knell of the island community, O'Donnell has them part company, each resolved that their union is impossible. Instead, the novel implies a future union between Charlie and Sarah, and both enabled to stay on the island. The storms have passed, literally and metaphorically, and O'Donnell's descriptions of the island indulge in some pathetic fallacy: 'It was a healthy kind of night, with a warm southern breeze, and a flood-tide, the sea shimmering in a jellied haze.'[75] The island is allowed to return to its insularity, with the prospect of an indigenous marriage, and the bringing of life and warmth on the flood-tide and the southern breeze. It is a convenient fiction of insularity, with the island restored to health and self-sufficiency, and to the illusion of being a place apart, mysterious to, and oblivious of, the wider world. It is the closest O'Donnell comes to depicting his own desert island, in the manner of a Robinson Crusoe, but the novel has already exposed it as a lie.

STONY LIMITS:

HUGH MACDIARMID AND THE RETURN OF

THE CELTIC ARCHIPELAGO

After Yeats, there is no other writer in the British Isles to take so seriously the idea of a Celtic Revival as Hugh MacDiarmid. In his polemical autobiography, *Lucky Poet*, MacDiarmid professed to 'work for the establishment of Workers' Republics in Scotland, Ireland, Wales and Cornwall, and indeed, make a sort of Celtic Union of Socialist Soviet Republics in the British Isles'.[76] Perhaps this was not quite what Yeats had in mind politically, but MacDiarmid did echo the sense of racial unity, and 'shared a vision of leadership by aesthetic example', in the words of Patrick Crotty,[77] which informed Yeats's conception of the Celtic archipelago. He even quoted approvingly from contemporary German celebrations of the racial virtues of Celtic peoples, in particular Rudolf Bringmann's claim that 'the Normans were culturally inferior to the Gaels'.[78] MacDiarmid modelled his efforts to form and lead a Scottish literary renaissance partly upon the work of Yeats, Synge, and Joyce, and read critical work such as Daniel Corkery's *Hidden Ireland* (1924) and Aodh de Blacam's *Gaelic Literature Surveyed* (1929), as well as important books on Celtic civilisation such as *The British Edda* by L. A. Waddell (1930), *The Greatness and Decline of the Celts* by Henri Hubert (1934), and *Six Thousand Years of Gaelic Grandeur Unearthed* by L. Albert Hermann (1936).[79] Among his most self-conscious influences, MacDiarmid in particular praised the work of Charles Doughty, the author of an extraordinary Edwardian example of epic poetry, *The Dawn in Britain* (1906), which gives poetic form in early English to antiquarian myths of Celtic Britain, and the Eurasian origins of its peoples.[80] In *The Islands of Scotland* (1939), a book which MacDiarmid dedicated to 'all my friends on the Faroes, the Shetlands, the Orkneys, the Hebrides, the Isle of Man, and in Wales and Cornwall and Ireland', some of these studies are cited to give support to MacDiarmid's radically archipelagic claim that 'the original impetus to civilisation was an ur-Gaelic initiative, and it is impossible to write about the Scottish islands today without remembering that, recognising civilisation's urgent need today to refresh and replenish itself at its original sources'.[81] Such a view of the *longue durée* of European civilisation, MacDiarmid contends, would mean that 'the very basis of our conceptions of British history and culture would be torpedoed and very different conceptions take their place'.[82]

MacDiarmid's renowned commitment to Scottish nationalism was, importantly, grounded not simply in the political immediacies of post-First World War, and post-Irish independence, contexts, but in a deeper sense of historical division which was underpinned by racial theories and myths. For MacDiarmid, both Irish and Scottish cultural and political nationalism were *revival* movements because they returned to a course of racial history interrupted by foreign invasion or usurpation, and thus much of MacDiarmid's writing dwells upon the idea of searching for routes of return, which would themselves be, in a typically modernist fashion, sources of rejuvenation. Yet, it is also characteristic of MacDiarmid to see racial histories in peculiarly convoluted terms, as in his *Poems of the East-West Synthesis*, in which he claimed, after L. Albert Hermann's arguments concerning Gaelic racial ancestry, that, like Stalin, 'We are Georgians all. / We Gaels'.[83] It was a curious attempt, perhaps self-conscious in its convenience, to link Gaelic nationalism to Russian communism, thus to racialise communism and communise nationalism, and relied upon an astonishingly associative logic which connected the contemporary fate of Scotland with revolutionary Russia, with independent Ireland, and with vague and sometimes tenuous histories of ancient migratory movements across Europe, encompassing most Eastern and Northern European peoples, with the notable exception of the English, for whom MacDiarmid reserved an especially emphatic sense of exclusion.

MacDiarmid moved to the Shetland Islands in 1933 partly in flight from an increasingly impoverished and precarious existence in England, and although he accepted the invitation of an island doctor, David Orr, believing that he would stay for a few months, he and his family lived on Whalsay for eight years, during which time he produced some of his most important poems.[84] MacDiarmid had been brought up in the Lowlands of Dumfriesshire, just twenty miles north of Carlisle; he was schooled in Edinburgh, worked as a reporter on the Welsh-English border, served in the medical corps in Salonica, Italy, and France, and visited Ireland as an honoured guest for the Tailteann Games in 1928, before moving to London in the late 1920s, where his first marriage failed, and he met his second wife, Valda Trevlyn, from Cornwall. Thus Whalsay island extended his already considerable geographical and cultural experience of the British Isles and Europe, but, with just nine hundred inhabitants, and no running water, sewerage, or lighting, it was a challenging environment, and one which he would come to identify as emblematic of the margins from which Scotland, and the Celtic archipelago more expansively, could be revived.

His first, and one of his most productive, experiences on the island was to join a herring expedition with a local fishing crew.[85] In his 'Shetland Lyrics', which return to the synthetic Scots of the earlier works which had first brought him to public attention, *Sangschaw* (1925), *Penny Wheep* (1926) and *A Drunk Man Looks at the Thistle* (1926), MacDiarmid returns too to lyrical reflections upon the elemental concerns of non-metropolitan lives. The simplicity of herring fishing, albeit against stark economic and elemental challenges, strikes the poet most compellingly in his opening lyrical poem, 'With the Herring Fishers': 'O it's ane o' the bonniest sichts in the warld / To watch the herrin' come walkin' on board / In the wee sma' 'oors o' a simmer's morning' / As if o' their ain accord.'[86] The unity of the sailors with the herring they fish, perhaps not a reflection of their own feelings, is nevertheless one which impresses MacDiarmid sufficiently to take it further in the next poem, 'Deep-Sea Fishing', where he writes of the fishermen: 'I kent their animal forms / And primitive minds, like fish frae the sea, / Cam' faur mair naturally oot o' the bland / Omnipotence o' God than a fribble like me.'[87] The sentiment is perhaps itself bland, that the sailors with their 'primitive minds' are closer to nature and closer to God than the poet who struggles to shear himself away from a concern with aesthetics and semantics, yet there is an optimism about the sense that the use of synthetic Scots can bring the experiences of an educated Lowlands poet into the same ken as Whalsay fishermen. The self-deprecation of the term 'fribble' intimates, in a manner reminiscent of Synge, a feeling of wonder at the superiority of the so-called 'primitive minds' of the islanders, at a way of living which seems harmonious with the natural world, even as MacDiarmid is acutely conscious of the demise of herring fishing as a viable means of subsistence in Shetland.

The Scots of the 'Shetland Lyrics' is less flamboyant, less consciously estranging, than the lyrics of *Sangschaw*. It is a language MacDiarmid is attempting to open up to accommodate his new experiences, rather than a vehicle to convey a sense of where he comes from. At sea with the Shetlanders, MacDiarmid contemplates the fishermen's myths of 'Jeannie MacQueen', and the flights of fancy of imagining himself a 'bonxie' (a great skua) or a sea eagle, which 'Gets in resonance wi' the sun / And ootshines't like a turnin' wing', or the gulls of 'Mirror Fugue', which 'Seem to equal the croods / O' the white waves by joinin' / Hands wi' the cloods'.[88] There is, as Louisa Gairn has argued more generally of MacDiarmid's Shetland poetry, an ecological theme running through these poems,[89] informed by a naturalist's interest in the rich ecosystem of the islands, but there is also, with equal persistence, a psychological theme, about the desire for a kind of mental cleansing which is rehearsed in the poems through an immersion in the imagined alternative psychology of birds and fishermen. 'I delight in this naethingness,' declares the poet in 'De Profundis', while in 'To a Sea Eagle' he is happy to be 'left in the void'. In the 'Shetland Lyrics', MacDiarmid dallies with the notion of a return to a primitive state of mind, and ponders what would happen if 'an ardent spirit / Should submerge a' it's learned'.[90]

In later works, MacDiarmid quoted approvingly from the writings of Trigant Burrow, an American social psychologist, especially from his *The Biology of Human Conflict* (1937), in which he argued that modernity entailed a 'dissociative process' of increasingly substituting language for 'physiological experience', and therefore, as MacDiarmid quotes, 'man has lost touch with the hard and fast milieu of actual objects and correspondingly with the biological solidarity of his own organism'.[91] It is an argument which MacDiarmid relates immediately to the ethnographic observation, made by 'a spokesman of An Cumann Gaidhealach', that 'there is nothing surprising in the fact that the healthiest parts of Scottish Gaeldom – physically, psychologically, economically and otherwise – are precisely those in which Gaelic is still purest and most generally used, and English intrudes least'.[92] The strength of the Gaelic language denotes, for MacDiarmid, geographical areas which have remained remote from the encroachments of a debilitating (English) modernity, by implication a degenerative influence upon racial health. Whereas Burrow observes the neurotic symptoms of psychological dissociation as 'common to the modern race',[93] MacDiarmid delineates a geography in which the islands of Scotland may be the outliers of such neuroses, the repositories of an aboriginal state of mental health, symbolised by the close union of the fishermen with their catch. Interestingly, however, MacDiarmid's deductions from such an equation of geographic remoteness, minority language survival, and racial health are not biological, but linguistic. Hence, in contrast to the argument notoriously advanced by Edwin Muir that 'Scotland can only create a national literature by writing in English', which was itself dependent upon Muir's own theory of a 'dissociation of sensibility' caused by the fact that 'Scotsmen feel in one language and think in another', MacDiarmid espoused and indeed practised the revival of Scotland's minority languages, in the hope that they would express the lives and loves bound in the histories and intricacies of those languages.[94] MacDiarmid can be said to have single-handedly revived literary use of Scots, and, in Seamus Heaney's view, he inspired Sorley MacLean 'to become the redemptive genius of modern poetry in Gaelic',[95] although his call for 'a recovery of the old Norn tongue' amongst Shetlanders was perhaps unlikely to produce much effect.[96] Nonetheless, in contrast to Muir, who believed that such languages were exhausted, for MacDiarmid the use of Scots, especially the synthetic Scots fashioned in his poetry, was of interest for its inherent potential for newness, for the effects which it could have on modern readers.

Margery Palmer McCulloch makes this argument from the outset in her study, *Scottish Modernism and its Contexts, 1918–1959*, that writers such as MacDiarmid, Muir, and Catherine Carswell 'were engaged in a *modern* project', and 'were seeking to reach out from an aesthetically and politically revitalised Scotland to interact with the international scene'.[97] In MacDiarmid's case in the 1930s, the possibilities of a revitalised Scotland lay not in its cities, nor in its exiles abroad, but in its 'exclaves', its remote and peripheral islands, highlands, and borders, from which its neglected languages still encoded distinctive mythologies, communal rituals, and patterns of living which were both residual from distant pasts and, importantly, anticipatory of different futures. There was nothing essentialist, nor romanticist, about such a vision. *The Islands of Scotland* offered a materialist analysis of the means by which the islands could be the sources of greater prosperity and equity in Scotland, just as its vision of Scotland was of an archipelago of differences which, united politically, could 'realise the high alternative value of a thorough realisation of all of them'.[98] In his essays upon the diverse islands of Scotland, it is clear that for MacDiarmid what is paradoxically intrinsic or inherent in such spaces is the historical actuality and necessity of their looking outwards. The Shetlands look out to Scandinavia and the Faroes, while a Gaelic archipelago extends from the Hebrides around the north and west coasts of Ireland. It is the 'unapprehended possibilities' of such archipelagic thoughts which lead MacDiarmid to 'speculate upon the very different course not only Scottish, and English, but world history would have taken if the whole of the mainland of Scotland had been severed from England and broken up into the component islands of a numerous archipelago'.[99]

Yet, despite the fact that MacDiarmid's vision of the islands is materialist, communist, modern, pluralist, and internationalist in outlook, it seems surprisingly attracted to diverse ultra-nationalist, ethnological, and eugenicist sources. MacDiarmid quotes approvingly from Lord Lymington, a pro-Nazi English ruralist, and author of *Famine in England* (1938), from Raymond Cattell, controversial for his eugenicist arguments for selective breeding in *The Fight for Our National Intelligence* (1937), and from German academics of racial history such as Hermann, Bringmann, and Ernst Ludwig Fischer, whose arguments accorded closely with the racial theories popular in Nazism. MacDiarmid also draws upon a sense of racial inherence when he complains about English government policies in the Hebrides which are 'as appropriate if the stock were negroes as to the actual Gaelic stock', a comment which implicitly aligns Gaelic Hebrideans with the privileges of whiteness, and, oddly, chides imperialism for race blindness.[100] Where possible, MacDiarmid draws upon ethnological accounts of the islanders, commenting upon physical size and shape, intelligence, and disposition, but he laments that 'few contributions have yet been made to British ethnology, at least in respect of the Shetlanders, the Orcadians, and the Hebrideans'.[101] The anthropological focus of much of MacDiarmid's prose descriptions of the Scottish islands is characteristic of the more general 'anthropological turn' which Jed Esty has argued is a defining feature of late modernism, of course,[102] but in MacDiarmid, although it is shaped by eugenic and racial discourses, it also takes on a distinctly environmental character.[103] He writes, for example, that 'the differences between the Orcadians and the Shetlanders can clearly be referred to the physical differences of the islands in the two archipelagos, and to the general differences in work illustrated by the statement that the "Orcadian is a farmer with a boat, the Shetlander a fisherman with a croft"'.[104] However insubstantive such generalisations may be, MacDiarmid seeks to explain inter-insular differences, within what appear to him to be racially similar peoples, by reference to geology and environment.

This is, arguably, the driving force of the argument laid out in MacDiarmid's poem 'Island Funeral', first published in *The Islands of Scotland*.[105] The poem begins amidst the grey stones of its island setting, repeating the word 'grey' eleven times in its opening seven verses, and words such as 'stones', 'walls', 'rock', 'slab', and 'boulders', within the same verses, to compel the impression of an island formed of rock, and dominated by the ubiquity of its forms. Even the sand flung up from the dug grave is 'dark grey', and the 'sea and sky / Are colourless as the grey stones'. The funeral procession is described as 'a little snake' which 'winds ... between the walls of irregular grey stones', and later 'like a stream flowing into a loch', metaphors which encode human ritual within natural forms, and as diminutive forms compared to the 'grey world' of sea, sky, and stone visible all around them. 'This burial is just an act of nature,' the poem states, a closing in of the grey sand and stones against which the islanders have struggled to wrest a living. The dominance of the landscape in the poem amplifies the poem's detachment from people: the men are 'like figures cut from cardboard', the women 'wear black shawls, / And black or crimson skirts', writes the poet, as if observing a painting. The poet is positioned towards the back of the funeral procession, and therefore figured as a participant, but not emotionally connected to the unnamed person who the poet supposes 'had been a "grand woman"'. MacDiarmid writes of the islanders as if they were already dead, describing his admiration for their furnishings, 'tongue-and-groove cleats, / The lipped drawer, and the diameters of finials', one of their proverbs, 'Every force evolves a form', and the 'clear old Gaelic sound' which he likens to 'a phrase from Beiderbecke's cornet', and which he strains to hear in 'the din of our modern world'. These are the scraps of Hebridean culture which are the material manifestations of the 'Minds or souls with the properties I love / – The minds or souls of these old islanders', the fragments which will exist after the 'last funeral' on the island. Yet that celebration of island culture is premised upon detachment, either in the figure of the lonely and aloof poet who loves 'to go into these little houses / And see and touch the pieces of furniture', or in the barely audible survival of the Gaelic sound 'in Edinburgh or Glasgow or London'. These are ghostly figures, as the islanders depicted in the poem are themselves ghostly, mere shadows which fleet across the surface of a world of objects, which grow out of and return to the grey stone of the island. It is a poem which attracts little attention even among MacDiarmid scholars, perhaps because of its mawkish sentimentality for Gaelic culture, perhaps because its sentiments are expressed plainly and trenchantly in English verses which admit not a single word of Gaelic, nor (with the exception of the word 'Gaelic' itself) even an anglicised form of Gaelic. It is a poem which, obstinate in its confinement to English, enacts the entombment of the very Gaelic culture it professes to admire. For the poet of *A Drunk Man Looks at the Thistle,* who famously disagreed bitterly with Edwin Muir's provocative argument about the redundancy of the Scots and Gaelic languages, 'Island Funeral' seems either a spectacular admission of defeat, or an ironic performance of the very argument Muir had made three years earlier.

It has been widely noted that at the very time MacDiarmid was challenging Muir's arguments vociferously, he was himself abandoning the use of Scots, and writing in English. His most important poem from his Whalsay period, however, and the one which touches most directly on the possibilities of an archipelagic consciousness, is 'On a Raised Beach', a poem written in English, but which experiments freely and creatively with the possibilities of defamiliarising the language. The displaced shoreline setting of the poem (a raised beach, as Michael Whitworth points out, locates the poem on 'the margins of an ancient sea')[106] brings the poet to an immediate and profound sense of contested origins, geological, biological, and mythical. 'All is lithogenesis – or lochia, / Carpolite fruit of the forbidden tree,' declare the opening lines of the poem, announcing a stanza which is remarkable, even in MacDiarmid's work, for its raid upon the *Chambers* dictionary.[107] In an attempt to describe stone, that most fundamental of objects, MacDiarmid reaches for a language of texture, colour, and geology: 'Celadon and corbeau, bistre and beige, / Glaucous, hoar, enfouldered, cyathiform'. This is clearly a 'poetry of fact', as MacDiarmid intended, and aligns him with the other so-called 'documentary' poets of the Auden generation, but it is also a tactile language, a language sensual in its conflation of stone and flesh: 'I study you glout and gloss . . . and like a blind man run / My fingers over you, arris by arris, burr by burr, / Slickensides, truité, rugas, foveoles'. These are words which fuse biology and geology, breathing life into stones, just as the stanza also recalls the black stone in the 'Caaba' in Mecca, and the 'Christophanic rock' moved in the Christian story of the Resurrection, sacred myths of stones. The raised beach brings the poet to a confrontation with such myths of creation, the fossilised evidence around him presenting an alternative, evolutionary, and geological story of earth's beginnings into consciousness. 'What artist poses the Earth écorché thus, / Pillar of creation engouled in me?' asks the poet, as the raised beach conjures images of human organs exposed, or the liminal points at which bodily organs are both inside and outside. The raised beach is thus figured as the place where the sea has disgorged up the debris of the earth's geological origins, the fundaments from which the earth derives its 'haecceity', its uniqueness as a 'thing-in-itself', to use the Heideggerian term.

As Scott Lyall points out, MacDiarmid's interest in the language of the geology of the Shetlands was inspired by the geological survey of the islands which was conducted by G. V. Wilson and his team in 1933, and especially by his close friendship with one of the team, Thomas Robertson.[108] It is not difficult to appreciate its appeal. As the title of MacDiarmid's collection, *Stony Limits*, implies, the poet was already impressed with the remoteness, isolation, and apparent barrenness of the geologically exposed landscape he chose to inhabit in Whalsay, but the exposure of rock also revealed stories of the very formation of the earth, and the evolutionary stages of its life forms. Wilson's accounts of the survey and field trips to the Shetlands highlight the prevalence of 'a highly diversified series of metamorphic rocks' which make up the islands, and which consist of the fabulously termed 'injected siliceous and hornblendic garnetiferous schists and gneisses', with 'occasional limy beds', 'shimmer aggregate', 'purple pebbly arkoses', and 'coarse felspathic grit'.[109] It is not just the poetic strangeness of such language which might have appealed to MacDiarmid, but the drama of creation and evolution which is told in the geological literature of the time. In H. H. Read's account of the metamorphic rocks in Valla Field in Unst, for example, a narrative is constructed from stages of metamorphism, characterised first by 'the production of staurolite, kyanite, garnet and biotite in true pelitic rocks', followed by the 'injection of granitic materials', unstable minerals, the 'intrusion' of 'spessartitic sills and dykes', and then 'a large dislocation, adjacent to which politic blocks affected by the earlier metamorphisms were changed into chlorite-sericite-schists'.[110] Living on islands which are frequently transposed southwards on maps of the British Isles, in a small settlement on Whalsay called 'Sodom' in an unfortunately anglicised corruption of the Norse name 'sud heim' (meaning southerly home), and in which the poet frequently felt cut off from the rest of the world, MacDiarmid could hardly not be impressed by the language of dislocation, intrusion, and metamorphism which geologists used to tell the story of the Shetlands.

It is notable, however, that a comparison of the language of the geological reports with MacDiarmid's poem finds the poet drawn not towards the vocabulary of geological composition and formation, but to the words which might be used to describe the sight and feel of stone. His concern in 'On a Raised Beach' is not the cold, pre-human, or post-apocalyptic vision of a stone world empty of conscious life, but precisely the interaction between the animate and inanimate: 'I must begin with these stones as the world began,' he writes, a philosophical proposition, perhaps, that consciousness must come to terms with the haecccity of stone. This is why both Lyall and Gairn find this poem a fruitful source for considering MacDiarmid as an ecological poet: 'On a Raised Beach' attempts to interrogate and re-imagine the relationship between human beings and the physical environment. It re-calibrates the status of humanity on a planet clearly borrowed to sustain merely temporary forms of life, and exposes as presumptions the poses of human superiority: 'The red blood which makes the beauty of a maiden's cheek / Is as red under a gorilla's pigmented and hairy face. / Varied forms and functions though life may seem to have shown / They all come down to the likeness of stone.'[111] Among the fossilised remains of extinguished forms of life strewn up on the stormline of a beach, the poet is compelled to historicise human life on evolutionary and genetic scales which make futile the 'imaginings of men', especially those which spurn their 'roots' in 'the common earth'. Lyall rightly suggests that the poem emphasises an eco-Marxism, an appreciation of the earth as a common base upon which all human life is sustained, and which ought then to be the source for the social organisation of a common humanity.[112] MacDiarmid rejects any faith which cannot accommodate this phenomenological understanding of the foundations of life, and the poem's profession of ecological awareness becomes almost sloganistic: 'What happens to us / is irrelevant to the world's geology / But what happens to the world's geology / Is not irrelevant to us.'[113]

The philosophical consideration of the 'haecceity' of stone, and the relationship of human existence, and indeed aesthetics, to the phenomenology of the earth, invites comparison, of course, with another thinker who has been influential upon contemporary ecological thought, Martin Heidegger. Heidegger gave the first version of his essay 'The Origin of the Work of Art', in which he moves from the 'thingness' of stone to the question of how humans dwell upon the earth, and draw the earth into art, as a lecture in Freiburg in 1935.[114] 'A stone is worldless,' writes Heidegger, meaning that it is outside the realm of dwelling and meaning, whereas 'The peasant woman . . . has a world because she dwells in the overtness of beings, of the things that are'.[115] Heidegger considers the relationship between the earth, which is 'self-dependent', objective, spontaneous, and the world, which is 'ever non-objective', as one of constant striving in relation to each other. The earth is only appreciable as earth because of its difference from the human-made, representational domain of worldliness. Likewise, the world cannot appear as the made and imagined realm it is without the bare, resistant 'thingness' of the earth. Conceptually, then, the earth and the world are co-dependent, yet not symmetrical. When Heidegger considers the properties of stone, his conclusions resonate with MacDiarmid's poem:

> A stone presses downward and manifests its heaviness. But while this heaviness exerts an opposing pressure on us it denies us any penetration into it. If we attempt such a penetration by breaking open the rock, it still does not display in its fragments anything inward that has been disclosed . . . It shows itself only when it remains undisclosed and unexplained.[116]

Heidegger does not believe that either art or science can apprehend the 'thingness' of stone, or disclose anything inward, and against its indefatigable facticity, the abstractions and theorising of human discourse seem inadequate, and detached. It could be argued that MacDiarmid's poem enacts this very point, announcing the necessity of getting 'into this stone world', and striving to describe the look and feel of stone, and yet in its very striving acknowledging the impossibility of artistic apprehension. MacDiarmid's thoughts on stone and dwelling, and the role of art in presencing, all seem strangely and implausibly proximate to Heidegger's late essays, in one form or another, yet it should be recalled that Heidegger's essays are readings of a German Romantic tradition, whose foremost exemplars such as Rilke were important sources for MacDiarmid's own thoughts on the relationship between consciousness and the environment. Heidegger's thinking on the relationship between earth and world functions as a call for a re-inhabitation, a new dwelling, upon and with the earth, and a unity of 'work-being' which is most acute in the 'intimacy of striving' between earth and world.[117] In this call, of course, there is a strong sense of the appeal of primitivism which is so widely evident in modernist art and literature, but so too a call for a future form of dwelling which is ecologically in harmony with our physical surroundings.

MacDiarmid's poem strives towards intimacy with the physical environment. It does so through tactile and visual descriptions of stone, and tries again through 'the old Norn words – hraun / Duss, rønis, queedaruns, kollyarum; / They hvarf from me in all directions / Over the hurdifell – klett, millya, hellya, hellyina bretta, / Hellyina wheeda, hellyina grø, bakka, ayre,- / And lay my world in kolgref'.[118] The Norn words which he retrieves from obscurity describe a landscape of stone, both of geological formations, and of the cairns which are the only reminders of human habitation, symbols which the poem goes on to use of the triumph of stone in sealing 'us fast in our graves'. The cairns, and the very words the poet uses to describe them ('queedaruns', 'kollyarum', 'rønis'), testify to the transience of humanity, but they also testify to the intimacy between language and the landscape. 'This is no heap of broken images,' writes MacDiarmid, protesting against T. S. Eliot's famous poetic disdain of rocky waste lands, but an ecology which needs to be reckoned in the human imagination. It is in recognising the humility and frailty of human existence on earth that MacDiarmid moves to one of his closing metaphors for this relationship: 'Not so much of all literature survives / As any wisp of scriota that thrives / On a rock'.[119] Here again, MacDiarmid flaunts an awareness of scientific discourse when he alludes to 'de Bary's and Schwendener's discovery / Of the dual nature of lichens', but it is the bare stone, not the symbiosis between the animate lichens and inanimate rock, which brings the poet the consciousness of 'The beginning and the end of the world, / My own self, and as before I never saw / The empty hand of my brother man, / The humanity no culture has reached'.[120] In contemplating the bare alterity of stone, its imperviousness to human habitation, and the alternative creationist narrative of lithogenesis, MacDiarmid is able to comprehend the failures of so-called civilisation, and to glimpse the basis upon which a new ecology of existence might be imagined.[121]

The shoreline, perhaps inevitably, tends to be a highly symbolic setting in poetry, and there are undoubted echoes of Matthew Arnold's 'On Dover Beach' and Tennyson's 'Crossing the Bar', to take just two examples, in MacDiarmid's raised beach poem. There are, as MacDiarmid's poem reflects, sound scientific and biological foundations for understanding the seashore as a microcosmic space. As C. M. Yonge points out in the New Naturalist volume *The Sea Shore*, 'The zonation of life which spreads over thousands of ascending feet on land is, on a rocky shore, telescoped within a few score yards.'[122] For environmental writers, also, the shoreline has a deep fascination, as Rachel Carson argues, as 'the place of our dim ancestral beginnings' and 'the primeval meeting place of the elements of earth and water, a place of compromise and conflict and eternal change'.[123] The drama of the contest between sea and land, and the distinctive biota of shoreline environments, is further heightened in the bounded, isolated geographies of islands, and the geological history exposed on raised beaches especially. In MacDiarmid's poetry, it is clear that islands are microcosmic of tensions between human life and the physical environment, just as Alan Bold argues that the poet was conscious, in contrasting his own frugal, sometimes impoverished existence on Whalsay with the residence of the local laird, that the island was 'a microcosm of an unjust society'.[124] It is the evident inequities of social organisation on the island which spur the poet to consider the possibilities of new beginnings, of the roots of new forms of dwelling upon the earth.

   Like Heidegger secluded in his Black Forest home, however, these thoughts become mired in solipsism, in dwelling alone, in an island society of one.[125] In his essay 'Life in the Shetland Islands', for example, MacDiarmid begins by describing how, shortly after his arrival on Whalsay, he felt compelled to retreat further for a few days to the uninhabited island of Linga, where he could pretend to live the life of a Robinson Crusoe, albeit on an island considerably less temperate, and less bountiful, and, importantly, within sight of the inhabitants of Whalsay.[126] In 'On a Raised Beach', too, MacDiarmid comes to admire the detachment of the stone, and feels in his compulsion to 'shed the encumbrances that muffle / Contact with elemental things' that he is conscious only of being 'kindred' to 'the beginning and ending of the world, / The unsearchable masterpiece, the music of the spheres, / Alpha and Omega, the Omnific Word'.[127] This is followed by the renunciations of 'all that all other men / Think', and the refusal to 'surrender to the crowd'. His poem 'In the Shetland Islands', published first in *The Islands of Scotland*, is a manifesto for such a hermit life, the 'pleasure of my own company' on an island where he is 'no further from the "centre of things" . . . than in London, New York, or Tokio'.[128] He denounces the idea that island life is 'an insulation from life', and avers, with an aristocratic sense of intellectual superiority, that 'To be exclusively concerned with the highest forms of life / Is not to be less alive than "normal" people'. Out in the 'stony limits' of this archipelago, MacDiarmid figures no sense of lived community, no sense of affinity with either the islanders or the distant masses, and so the imagination of the 'unapprehended possibilities' of a common humanity seem perversely lonely. Yet it is from that sparse and stony imagination of island life, from the Germanic philosophical contemplation of alienation and overcoming, from the fantasy of a Robinson Crusoe in the Shetlands, that MacDiarmid begins to lay out the possibilities of a connective, utopian archipelago, the vision with which he concludes *The Islands of Scotland*:

> There are invisible bridges from every one of the Scottish islands, I think, that cross as far as the mind of man can go and reach across whatever space lies between us and anything that has ever been or ever will be apprehensible by the minds of men, – bridges to even greater ends, I think, than Mr Henry Beston was thinking of when . . . he said that good writing on Nature is 'a bridge of the soul's health over an abyss'.[129]

'WITHIN THESE BREAKWATERS':
W. H. AUDEN'S ICELANDIC IMAGINATION

'I know more about Northern mythology than Greek,' wrote W. H. Auden,[130] and it is a distinguishing feature of his relationship to modernism, according to Paul Beekman Taylor, that 'While Eliot and Pound looked back to classics to free their art from contemporary contexts, Auden sought the archaic in Norse tradition'.[131] The roots of that search were personal and familial: Auden's father had read Icelandic sagas and folk tales to him as a child, and Auden himself identified his surname etymologically with the Norse god Odin. The linguistic and cultural significance of Norse tales and names to English was deepened for Auden at Oxford, where he 'was drawn to the exoticism of Old English', and inspired by J. R. R. Tolkien's recitation of a long passage of *Beowulf*.[132] Chris Jones has shown how deeply Auden mined his knowledge of Icelandic and Old English sources in his early poetry, especially the verse play *Paid on Both Sides* (1928), which animates the modern setting of an English public school with the language and themes of ancient saga forms, while at the same time debunking the heroic function of ancient poetry as merely an incitement to violence.[133] The extent to which Auden's fascination with Norse folk poetry was also connected to a wider sense of Germanic culture has been discussed in considerable depth in the critical record,[134] and Auden himself observes, on meeting Hermann Goering's brother in Iceland, that 'The Nazis have a theory that Iceland is the cradle of the Germanic culture'.[135] He even teases in 'Letter to Lord Byron' that his ancestral name should make him 'the living wonder' to German Nazis, as 'really pure', and 'The Nordic type, the too too truly Aryan'.[136] Yet, although it might be argued that Auden's interest in Norse and Anglo-Saxon poetries was partly motivated by a search for shared linguistic histories and myths in Northern Europe, it is also clear that Iceland represented an escape, or at least respite, from what Auden saw as the common doom of European civilisation. He associated Iceland with exile, not least because of the recurrence of exilic themes in Norse mythology, and wrote that he could think of no other peoples 'among whom I should prefer to be exiled'.[137]

Auden's identification of islands with exile and refuge is, arguably, one of the most persistent themes in his life, as well as his work, from his early family holidays on the Isle of Wight, to later holidays with friends on Rügen Island in the Baltic in 1931, and in the same year a trip with a lover to the Shetlands, the three months he spent on Iceland with MacNeice in 1936, the 'queen's paradise' he encountered on Fire Island, just off Long Island, in 1946, and through to his frequent spring and summer holidays in Ischia, off Naples.[138] As Auden was well aware, islands figured predominantly as romantic, symbolic locations in the literary imagination, associated, as he depicts metonymically in 'Paysage Moralisé' (1933), with an impossible pastoral ideal.[139] In the moral landscape charted in the poem, islands are fugitive destinations, the homes of gods or castaways, and are presented as myths or utopias rather than lived environments:

> Each in his own little bed conceived of islands
> Where every day was dancing in the valleys
> And all the green trees blossomed on the mountains,
> Where love was innocent, being far from cities.[140]

'Paysage Moralisé' is an important poem in Auden's oeuvre because it exposes the symbolic economy of landscape, that islands, cities, valleys, and mountains function in mobile and connective ways to each other within that economy. As its title suggests, the poem depicts a psychic landscape, its features unnamed, its time unspecified. It has analogues in Nietzsche's topographical markers in *Thus Spake Zarathustra*, as well as figurative uses of landscape in symbolist poetry, most notably for Auden in Eliot's *The Waste Land*. In Auden's poem, the cities are starving, however, the harvests rotting, and islands figure as a mythic dream of utopia, a possible source of salvation, which would only diminish when the 'sorrow' of the people melts. Then 'water / Would gush, flush, green these mountains and these valleys, / And we rebuild our cities, not dream of islands'.[141] As Lucy McDiarmid argues, Auden shares with Yeats and Eliot a post-Romantic vision of the role of the poet as one who provides his society with its 'self-consciousness' of 'common bonds', and who simultaneously finds his own salvation in the material community affirmed in his poetry.[142] As such, Auden argued in the conclusion to *The Enchafèd Flood*, his study of the sea in Romanticism, that the post-Romantic poet was 'not the nomad wanderer through the desert or over the ocean, but the less exciting figure of the builder, who renews the ruined walls of the city'.[143] It is a vision which suggests an appropriative and acquisitive relationship towards islands, which would always be peripheral sources of replenishment and entertainment to the greater needs of civilisation.

Auden's travels in Iceland in 1936, and his collaboration with MacNeice in the publication of *Letters from Iceland*, have been figured in precisely these terms, as a diversion, 'a piece of fun'. 'It was not an experience that changed him,' writes his biographer Humphrey Carpenter, especially as his Iceland trip coincided with news that the war in Spain had begun, which 'immediately brought him back to the "real" world again'.[144] Similarly, the book itself has often been read, or even dismissed, as an entertaining holiday from the serious business of poetry, and both Marsha Bryant and Tim Youngs have commented on the unjust marginalisation of *Letters from Iceland* in Auden criticism.[145] Bryant makes the case for seeing *Letters from Iceland* as a late modernist collage which critiques the anthropological conventions of documentary representation, while Youngs insists upon reading it as a travel text which is relentlessly self-conscious and revisionist of the genre. 'Perhaps', Youngs argues, it is the book's 'air of casualness', constantly promoted by Auden and MacNeice, 'that fosters readings of *Letters* as an unplanned mélange', but this is to deny the ways in which 'Nazism and nationalism impinge increasingly on the book's consciousness': '*Letters* may be fun', writes Youngs, 'but it is deadly serious.'[146] The last line of the book, after all, written by MacNeice in the 'Epilogue', proposes to drink to Auden's health 'before / The gun-butt raps upon the door'.[147] Auden, too, declares in his 'Letter to Lord Byron' on his return from Iceland that 'I'm home to Europe where I may be shot'.[148] There was no escape from the urgency and gravity of the European political crisis, but both Auden and MacNeice figure the Iceland trip in terms of a temporal and geographical remove, a deferral of the inevitable descent into violence. MacNeice figures Iceland as the hermit retreat from the 'noise, the radio or the city', where we are 'Always on the move and so do not remember / The necessity of the silence of the islands, / The glacier floating in the distance out of existence'.[149] But for him and Auden, the exilic holiday to Iceland is a pretence. 'Here we can practise forgetfulness,' MacNeice writes, but from the book's many allusions to the looming crisis 'in the world below', such 'forgetfulness' is clearly a strained effort.[150] In 'Journey to Iceland', Auden declares that 'Islands are places apart where Europe is absent', but follows this immediately with doubt: 'Are they? The world still is, the present, the lie, / And the narrow bridge over a torrent / Or the small farm under a crag / Are natural settings for the jealousies of a province.'[151] On an island which Auden calls 'Sagaland', the bitter blood feuds of the mythic past are obvious analogues for the gathering forces of violence and tyranny across Europe, and so Iceland might appear to be 'apart' from Europe, and 'before' the onset of war, but is recurrently afforded what Paul Beekman Taylor calls a 'unique centricity' to the oblique narrative of European crisis which shadows *Letters from Iceland*.[152]

Beekman Taylor argues, in common with Humphrey Carpenter, that the three months Auden spent in Iceland were not a retreat from Europe, but rather a step out to an island dislocated from, and therefore enabling 'a privileged and protected perspective over', the crisis-bound civilisation of the West.[153] The model, Beekman Taylor suggests, might well have been 'the rim of [Asgard], the domain of the Norse gods from which the worlds of men and giants can be surveyed'.[154] The journey to Iceland recounted in the eponymous poem, therefore, is a mythic journey, and however much the traveller comes in search of 'natural marvels', 'the glitter / Of glaciers', or the sites of local folk legends, it remains only 'the fabulous / Country impartially far'.[155] Its remoteness ensures that it will always be 'fabulous', that is, a land merely of fables, and never capable of becoming real, or a home, for Auden's traveller. It is, in Auden's mind, a fit landscape for exile, for placing oneself judiciously and critically apart from one's home. Thus, the very form of *Letters from Iceland*, with its collage of documentary photographs, letters, poems dedicated to friends, and mock travel reportage, directs the reader constantly back to the 'homes' of its authors. In Auden's case, this is the 'England, my England' he addresses in the fifth and final 'Letter to Lord Byron':

> England, my England – you have been my tutrix –
>   The Mater, on occasions, of the free,
> Or, if you'd rather, Dura Virum Nutrix,
>   Whatever happens I am born of Thee;
>   And Englishmen, all foreigners agree,
> Taking them by and large, and as a nation,
> All suffer from an Oedipus fixation.[156]

This stanza represents Auden's declaration of homecoming, but it is hardly an endorsement of his home, depicted in the three matriarchal poses of 'tutrix', 'Mater', and 'Nutrix', figures which suggest the English public school, rather than familial bonds.[157] His profession of filial love is qualified in disarmingly casual ways: England is only 'on occasions' the mother of the free; the phrase 'Whatever happens' places everything in doubt except the bare fact that 'I am born of Thee'; and finally, love of England is equated, at least in the eyes of foreigners, with the neurotic consequences of psychological and sexual attachment between the infant and its mother, an 'Oedipus fixation'. In the poem which Auden felt gave shape to *Letters from Iceland*, Byron's exilic, rebellious, and comic spirit is preferred to the earthy provincialism of Richard Jefferies, Thomas Hardy, and Edward Thomas, and gives Auden the 'authority / For finding Wordsworth a most bleak old bore'. It is a preference which seems to signify Auden's positioning of himself as deracinated artist, and for whom, therefore, the 'travel' genre is a highly significant mode of representing landscapes, societies, or nations from a mobile perspective.

For the late modernist generation of writers, of course, as Paul Fussell argues, travel 'abroad', and writing about it, was almost *de rigueur*.[158] Yet, if there is a pattern to such travel, it is undoubtedly southwards, and mainly to the Mediterranean. In the 1920s and 1930s, a literary map of British writing would have to extend to Robert Graves in Majorca, Norman Douglas and Compton Mackenzie in Capri, Lawrence Durrell in Corfu, D. H. Lawrence and Basil Bunting in Italy, Somerset Maugham in the French Riviera, and, indeed, much further afield, to the many writers who travelled to, and lived in, Asia and America. Auden followed this pattern later, of course, but the turn northwards, to Iceland, is an interesting spatial and symbolic deviation from the pattern which Fussell emphasises. Fussell situates the movement of the interwar writers as a reaction against the enforced insularity of England during the First World War, citing E. M. Forster's remark in 1915 that England felt 'most insistently an island, and there are times when one longs to sprawl over continents'.[159] The 'south' was associated with sex and sun, and it is no coincidence that some of the period's most controversial books concerning sexuality and sexual morality, such as Douglas's *South Wind* (1917), Lawrence's *Lady Chatterley's Lover* (1928), and Compton Mackenzie's *Extraordinary Women* (1928), were either set in, or published in, Italy. Forster's contrast of island confinement and continental sprawl is perhaps not quite prophetic, as many of the writers mentioned above came to live on Mediterranean islands, but nonetheless, the comparison emphasised different spatial sensibilities, with the more expansive geography of the 'south' associated with a more liberal and expansive sense of sexuality and morality also. As Fussell makes clear, the depiction of the 'south' in British writing of the period is constantly measured against the perceived deficiencies of life in Britain, particularly focusing on the tropes of weather, food, and sex.[160] It might be argued, therefore, that *Letters from Iceland* is the result of an experiment in travelling northwards, to investigate how an alternative topographical frame might be constructed of Britain from the perspective of its most northerly inhabited neighbour.

The sources from which Auden quotes most extensively in his parodic miscellany of extracts, entitled 'Sheaves from Sagaland', and 'addressed to John Betjeman', reveal his concern with this question of perspective. Reading through the books listed in Auden's bibliography, it is readily apparent that each successive author sets out to correct the exaggerations and fabulations of others, from Niels Horrebow's *Natural History* (1750), which was commissioned to 'make void the severe and false accusations against this island' of John Andersson's *Natural History* (1746),[161] to Richard Burton's *Ultima*

Thule (1875), which admonishes his predecessors for 'prodigiously exaggerated' descriptions, and reports that where George Mackenzie, in *Travels in Iceland* (1812), 'gallops between Reykjavik and Thingvellir along the edge of a "dreadful precipice" . . . I saw only the humblest ravine'.[162] Auden draws upon these sources playfully, beginning with the opening quotation, from Pliny Miles's *Nordurfari, or Rambles in Iceland* (1854), to establish that 'Iceland is real'.[163] In the section on 'The Natives', Auden juxtaposes chapter headings imitating the pseudo-scientific discourse of Horrebow's naturalist account of the island with quotations from various authors concerning the physical and cultural characteristics of the Icelanders which seem mock-serious, such as Burton's anthropological accounts of islanders' eyes as 'dure and cold as a pebble', and their 'temperament' as 'nervoso-lymphatic and at best nervoso-sanguineous'.[164] The very form of 'Sheaves from Sagaland' replicates a characteristic of many of its sources, which is to quote extensively from scientific texts as a way of establishing an impression of cultural authority. Auden's sources are the work of botanists, mineralogists, and anthropologists, as well as leisured travellers; *Letters from Iceland* is parodic not just of the travel genre, but of the cultural positioning of scientific discourses about other geographies and peoples. Outside of quotation, or parody, Auden tends to recoil from romantic exaggeration, and the folly of racist typology. 'I consider Iceland, / Apart from Reykjavik, a very nice land,' he jokes in 'Letter to Lord Byron',[165] and in his letter to Kristian Andreirsson, in response to a request for his impressions of Iceland, he says of nature that everything worth saying is already well known and available in tourist guides, and of the character of the people that 'This is a silly thing to write about'.[166]

In contrast to the mythologies of Viking sagas, and the romanticism of 'Ultima Thule', then, Auden offers instead an account of tolerable food, pragmatic guides, traversable roads, dull architecture, hospitable but ordinary people, and a landscape which is interesting but hardly the stuff of the Wordsworthian sublime. Even its most admirable traits in Auden's view – that it is the closest to a classless society he has known, that it has not succumbed to extreme forms of nationalism, nor the worst aspects of modernisation – are not celebrated or examined in any detail. In his 'Letter to Lord Byron', he admits that the book's understatement, and avoidance of 'glib generalisations', may give readers and critics the impression of being duped, or mocked; that the book may function 'under false pretences', and therefore be 'a flop'.[167] It is the awareness of the pretence which Auden seeks to effect, the failure of a mode of authoritative representation which will return the reader's attention to the source of authority. 'The poet's eye is not one from which nothing is hid,' writes Auden, and his photographs also expose that there is no such thing as 'the impersonal eye of the camera'.[168] In his letter to Kristian

Andreirsson, Auden concludes by joking of his intended 'revenge' of making Andreirsson write his impressions of England, and it is this notion of a reciprocal view of England which recurs in the final sections of the book, in the return to England, 'Up the long estuary of mud and sedges', and the return to England's position in relation to Europe.[169] It is here, in England, that Auden and MacNeice contemplate 'the guilt of human action', and the 'gun-butt raps upon the door'.[170] The view from one island ('that island never found', as MacNeice puts it)[171] gives rise to the concluding view from another, of the impossibility of standing outside of the bloody and treacherous course of history, of the seemingly endless saga of human violence and cruelty. Against the Nazi claim that Iceland is 'das Land',[172] it is the unexceptionalism of the island which Auden and MacNeice are most at pains to bare before their readers.

According to Edward Mendelson, in the 1930s the island 'supplanted the border as Auden's geographical sign of entrapment and enclosure'.[173] It might be more accurate, however, to say that it was the island as a figure of borders and thresholds which preoccupied Auden during this period, and that 'entrapment and enclosure' were not the only meanings he attributed to islands. 'Look, stranger, at this island now' (1935), a poem which provided the title for his second poetry collection (both its English title, *Look, Stranger!*, and Auden's preferred title, which was used for the American edition, *On This Island*), figures a series of natural borders: 'at the small field's ending', 'Where the chalk wall falls to the foam', 'the tide, / And the shingle', and the final image of the harbour.[174] Perhaps the most interesting border figured, however, is the opening sensory images of the poem, of the 'leaping light' of sunrise, and the 'swaying sound of the sea' which wander 'through the channels of the ear'. The topographical image of human perception of the sea, of the sounds of the sea entering the ear 'like a river', figures a hymenal point of connection between the human and the natural, between subject and object. The 'leaping light', itself an anthropomorphic image, is said to be 'for your delight', and the light 'discovers' the island, which again transposes the relationship between subjective perception and objective occurrence. The description of the ships seen from the island as both 'floating seeds' and 'on urgent voluntary errands', as if of their own volition, encapsulates this interplay between the human and the natural.

The poem enjoins the reader, addressed as 'stranger', to adopt a passive, receptive mode: 'Look', 'stand stable here / And silent be', and 'pause'. Static natural phenomena, however, are described with verbs denoting activity and mobility: 'the chalk wall falls to the foam', 'its tall ledges / Oppose' the tide, and 'the shingle scrambles after the suck- / ing surf'. As humans become part of the static landscape, and the landscape on the shoreline becomes one associated with motion, Auden seems intent on showing the interplay between subjectivity and space, or indeed the spatiality of subjectivity. The poem ends with an image of 'the full view' of the coastal scene which 'may enter / And move in memory as now these clouds do, / That pass the harbour mirror / And all the summer through the water saunter'. The harbour 'mirror' may be read as a romanticist metaphor for the narcissism of all human projections upon the landscape, but given that Auden figures the body in topographical terms, as well as anthropomorphising the landscape, the image seems a more complex metaphor for the ways in which subjectivity is framed and embedded within place. The deictic features of the poem to indicate the figured landscape – 'this island', 'here', 'Here', 'Far off', 'these clouds', as well as the temporal deictic word 'now', used twice – enact, or perform, this sense of subjectivity tied to, and inseparable from, the places which surround it, and in which it is inevitably embodied.

'Look, stranger, at this island now' has often been read as a poem about England. David Gervais reads it, oddly, as a detached view of England from above, a 'bird's eye view', despite the fact that the poet commands the 'stranger' to 'Stand stable here', and to pause 'Here at the small field's ending'.[175] John Fuller describes its critical reputation in terms of a sense of 'rediscovered Englishness' and the threats of war and coercion contained in the 'delicately prophetic suggestions' of the final stanza.[176] Yet this reading rests too heavily upon juxtaposing the 'voluntary' errands of the ships with the wartime role which such ships would be conscripted to perform when Britain was isolated by the Nazi occupation of France, a sense of insularity which Auden can hardly be expected to have prophesied in 1935 with any exactitude. John Boly also reads the poem's island location as England, and reads its insularity as the 'archetype of a private world', yet this relies upon identifying the location as Dover because of the poem's allusion to chalk cliffs.[177] Edward Mendelson's reading of the poem is a useful corrective to the ease with which 'this island now' is equated with England, specifically in asserting that Auden's location here is 'not England at all, but the holiday island of his art'.[178] Given that the poem was written and published immediately after Auden's poem for Isherwood, known by its first line as 'August for the people and their favourite islands', which recalls Auden and Isherwood's holidays upon the Isle of Wight and Rügen Island, islands associated with 'dreams of freedom', love, and sanctuary from 'the dangerous flood of history',[179] it seems reasonable to presume that 'this island' is not necessarily England, and that 'chalk wall' refers more intimately (for Auden) to the chalk cliffs of the Isle of Wight. Indeed, the geological reference to the 'chalk' composition of the coastline is the only allusion in the poem which might place a limit on where we locate what is otherwise a symbolic landscape. The Isle of Wight is, of course, part of England, and often associated with the idea of an England in microcosm, or even a 'theme park' miniature of England, but geographically at least it is a distinctive and separate island. The opening allusion to 'this island', therefore, may be both more local and more intimate than the detached view of England which has frequently been attributed to the poem. But the misreading of one island for another, or of one part of the archipelago for a single entity called 'England', as Auden might have appreciated, is not without its own particular kind of truth. It is revealing, I would suggest, of the powerful mythology of English insularity, based itself upon the elision of a distinction between England and Britain, that those brief synecdochic phrases – 'this island now' and 'Where the chalk wall falls to the foam' – are sufficient to secure a reading of the poem as referring to England, epitomised for Gervais in the image of John Betjeman reciting the poem for a television documentary from a helicopter above the white cliffs of Dover.[180]

If the 'chalk wall' of the Isle of Wight has been misread as the cliffs of Dover, this is perhaps also because Auden did write about Dover in his poem of that title, where the 'historical cliffs' are indeed synecdochic of comforting and homely ideas of England. 'Dover' (1937) similarly figures the shoreline as a threshold, with its 'sea-front' an elegant show before the 'impersonal water' of the sea, a show which derives from 'a vague and dirty root', 'inland'.[181] It is the 'front' of England, therefore, the border which stands out to define the meaning of the centre, and yet 'Nothing is made in this town'. Instead, the town thrives on knowing 'what the soldiers want / And who the travellers are'. Dover is depicted as the gateway to England, the lighthouses standing 'Like twin stone dogs opposed on a gentleman's gate', symbolic sentinels guarding the 'made privacy of this bay'. Dover, and the shoreline of the English Channel more generally, has particular symbolic significance in cultural representations of Englishness, as Aubrey de Selincourt shows in *The Channel Shore* (1953), as 'the chief nursery of British seamanship' and 'the richest in memory, the most celebrated in story and song and the most beloved'.[182] Moreover, de Selincourt argues that it is the consciousness of the island geography of Britain which is the cause of investing the shoreline and the 'English Channel' with national symbolism, and he uses a domestic metaphor similar to Auden's to convey the sense of a protective and proprietorial border marked out by the sea and coastline: 'A coast without a harbour is like a house without a door.'[183] Auden's Dover is freighted with historical associations, overlooked by the ruined Roman pharos, the 'dominant Norman castle', and the old town's 'keep and its Georgian houses', and filled now with the soldiers in pubs, 'The Lion, the Rose or the Crown', depicted not prophetically awaiting war, but instead killing time, 'Their pauper civilian future'. The passage from historical to modern England is tracked through these architectural traces, and the well-worn roads, like 'a tunnel through the downs', are the signs of the dense historicity of Dover as a place of transit.

For all that history, however, and all the national symbolism invested over centuries in the protective, defensive imagery of the island coastline of Britain, Auden is interested in the shift of perspective, the altered topography, which comes from changing the geographical frame. If in his work on Iceland he is constantly alert to the contending maps of an island which can be figured as outside, on the periphery of, and central to European 'civilisation', of its various kinds, the poem about Dover highlights a similar awareness of how England might be the subject of contending geographies. The idea that geographical conceptions are both subjective and contingent is conveyed through the recurrent figure of the 'constructed bay' and 'made privacy of this bay', which manufactures the illusion of a safe, knowable haven, against the projected otherness beyond: 'Within these breakwaters English is spoken; without / Is the immense improbable atlas'. Here, the 'breakwaters' conjures the image of what they are holding off – the vast, raging seas which threaten destruction – in order to figure the fragility and locality of where 'English is spoken'. It is an image which, arguably, cleaves off the Empire as an indistinguishable part of 'the immense improbable atlas', a purely textual, imaginary form in the minds of those enclosed within the harbour, and one incapable of apprehension. Held protectively within the arms of the harbour, then, is the small enclave, the safe haven, of a community defined as a speaking community, the very model of a small knowable island.

Dover is depicted, then, not just as a beacon of the imperilled border of England, but as England itself, as the whole island encapsulated within harbour walls. It is a poem which, not surprisingly, Jed Esty draws upon in *A Shrinking Island*, as it neatly exemplifies the very process Esty describes of interwar England as 'a culture that is becoming minor', and becoming 'a knowable and a provincial unit, the antithetical ground to cosmopolitan possibility'.[184] The figure of a 'minor' England is one that Auden uses towards the end of the poem, when he shifts perspective to the view from 'The aeroplanes' which 'fly in the new European air, / On the edge of that air that makes England of minor importance'.[185] The repetition of the word 'air' emphasises the elemental shift away from the coastal geographies of land and water which have defined the maritime discourses of English nationalism. There is a simple point here about the obsolescence of the natural cliffs and the made harbours as figures of defence and definition in an age which will be characterised by air travel and air war. That the 'European air' is 'new' also introduces a temporal scale, indicating that process of *becoming* minor which Esty historicises as the overarching narrative of English decline. Yet Auden introduces another shift in temporal and spatial scale immediately after these lines: 'And the tides warn bronzing bathers of a cooling star, / With half its history done'. The poem moves back to another frame, zooming out to a planetary and geological scale in which the cooling sun at some future point will spell the end of all human habitation, in which the borders marked by those terms, 'England', 'Europe', 'Empire', will themselves be meaningless. The final note of the poem is not provincialism but contingency: 'Some are temporary heroes: / Some of these people are happy'. Auden's sense of contingency is not one of absolute relativism, or of a cosmopolitan abandonment of scale, however, but is instead one of a renewed sense of the interrelationships and interdependencies between places and between temporal and spatial scales. The work of his early career, of what Mendelson has influentially cast as 'the English Auden', abounds with experiments in this scaling of human history and geography, in juxtaposing historical and topographical frames. In the 1930s, this took the form of struggling to imagine a powerfully archipelagic revision of the geographies and histories of the islands to the north-west of Europe, in which there was no one utopian, omphalic island 'home', or centre, but rather a constant, mobile interplay between the thresholds, passages, and scales through which islands could be, however contingently, represented.

'FELT ROUTES':
LOUIS MACNEICE AND THE NORTH-EAST ATLANTIC ARCHIPELAGO

In 'Ode', the final poem in his collection *Poems* (1935), Louis MacNeice writes of the necessity to 'become the migrating bird following felt routes . . . And without soaring or swerving win by ignoring / The endlessly curving sea and so come to one's home'.[186] Much has been written about MacNeice's search for 'home', his fraught and critical relationship with Ulster, Ireland, and England, and about the difficulty of his 'place' within either Irish or English literary traditions. John Kerrigan has suggested, however, that MacNeice might be seen more productively as a 'self-consciously archipelagic' poet:

> the Anglo-Irish polarity that structured MacNeice's reception during the Troubles is starting to seem restrictive. It can only enhance his standing that so many more of his qualities are visible if he is thought about in the context of what the Good Friday Agreement calls 'the totality of relationships among the peoples of these islands'.[187]

Placing him in such a context, or ascribing to his work the epithet 'archipelagic', is not merely a laudatory gesture, however, but a recognition of the significance of cultural precursors in the work of thinking through the complex negotiation of devolution, and the local ecologies of the British and Irish islands. MacNeice's work, particularly in the 1930s, is constantly struggling with the very restrictions which Kerrigan has observed in his later critical reception. It is imbued, of course, with neo-Yeatsian snarls at commercialism, and liberal jibes at the puritanism and atavism of the societies in which he grew up and lived, but these tendencies are equally weighted with the impulse towards, and longings for, the 'felt routes' of alternative northern and Atlantic geographies, new poetries of what Andrew McNeillie calls the 'unnameable archipelago',[188] which is, like MacNeice's conception of the world in 'Snow', 'Incorrigibly plural'.[189] In his joint venture to Iceland with W. H. Auden (*Letters from Iceland*, 1937), and his ironic travelogue of the Hebrides (*I Crossed the Minch*, 1938), and many of his poems published in the 1930s, there is no untrammelled island utopia, but instead a sensing of the need for new vocabularies of habitation, new geographies of connection and living between the islands.

'Ode' begins with two figures of disillusioned utopia, the town of Bournville in the English Midlands which, for all its vaunted aspirations as a social model, pollutes the air with a smell 'coarse with chocolate', and the poet's 'frivolous nostalgia' for 'the Atlantic', which is likened to 'celluloid abstractions', a metaphor perhaps conscious of those abstractions of rugged Atlantic coast life which Robert Flaherty had produced in his film *Man of Aran* (1934). In 1928, writing on a cruise to Norway, MacNeice had written to his friend Anthony Blunt that he 'Might go to Aran Islands like Synge. & eat lobsters and salmon all the time',[190] but although the romantic appeal of the West of Ireland is a recurrent theme in MacNeice's work, it is frequently undermined by a hard-won scepticism of the mythology of the West. So between the industrial dream of a model and mechanical social order, and the agrarian dream of a remote, peasant culture, MacNeice's 'Ode' attempts to ply a new route. Written as an expression of MacNeice's hopes for his son to grow up unencumbered by such useless illusions of utopia, and with some noted resemblances to Yeats's 'A Prayer for my Daughter', the poem is drawn repeatedly back to 'the shore of the regular and rounded sea' as a site in which it is possible to imagine 'one's peace while the yellow waves are roaring'. At its bleakest implications, it is a poem written on the birth of his son that looks forward to a peaceful death for his son, that sees the passing of generations as the only meaningful marker of human existence on earth: 'I remember all the houses where parents / Have reared their children to be parents'. In part, this is all he can hope for, since the store of sensory memory to which he turns for consolation – the sounds which awaken in him a sense of 'summer's athletic ease', for example – are also possibly an 'augury of war'. There are no absolutes he can pass on to his son, no god or science on which his son can depend, so instead the poet and his son 'Must become the migrating bird following felt routes'. It is an interesting metaphor, not least because the motivational factors of bird migration – breeding and feeding – are tied by analogy in the poem to generational anxieties about human migration, but also because in the 1930s, when MacNeice wrote 'Ode', the science for understanding the 'felt routes' of bird migration was underdeveloped. The practice of ring-tagging birds, which had been widely practised only since the beginning of the twentieth century, told ornithologists the range of bird migration, but not how birds navigated precise routes, often across oceans and continents. Whether it was by instinctual sense of direction, astrological and solar navigation, visual memory, or some kind of genetic memory, bird migration scholars such as Landsborough Thomson and Charles Patten were uncertain, and so MacNeice's poetic emphasis upon the 'felt' navigational routes of birds is rather apt.[191] In being both remarkable and habitual, the migration of birds serves MacNeice as an appropriate metaphor for human existence, neither nomadic nor sedentary, following routes long charted by others, but nonetheless singular, and extraordinary.

The 'felt routes' of MacNeice's own migrations took him from his birth-place in Belfast, with holidays to the much romanticised West of Ireland origins of his parents, along the shore to Carrickfergus, and across the Irish Sea to schools in Sherborne in Dorset and Marlborough in Wiltshire, university in Oxford, and lecturing jobs in Birmingham, London, and briefly in New York, and later jobs for the British Council and extensively for the BBC took him to Greece, India, Egypt, Ceylon, Ghana, and South Africa from his home in England, with Ireland an infrequent destination for visits and holidays in his adult life. The pattern is one dictated by work, and only partly by feelings, with the exception, of course, of MacNeice's profound sense of the impossibility of 'living' in Ireland, or indeed of 'feeling oneself' in England, as he wrote to his friend E. R. Dodds.[192] His BBC commissions took him on a sometimes riotous, often drunken tour of the closing days of Empire, the lights of one powerful notion of Britishness dimming darker with every tour, and as Alan Gillis argues, the reputation of his late poetry is really as 'a laureate of homelessness and alienation'.[193] But the dead ends of Empire, and the suffocating nationalism of the new Irish state, were already evident in his poetry of the 1930s. The 'felt routes', to which 'Ode' directs MacNeice as well as his son, are not the well-worn paths of his later biography, but rather the uncharted waters of an alternative geography of connection and belonging which began to take shape in his early work. Yet it is difficult to discern the shape, since, as Terence Brown has argued, traffic, travel, and tourism become key metaphors and motifs throughout his work, and develop finally into 'a metaphoric uniformity – the journey . . . towards death'.[194]

To discern a new direction for his migrations, a new shape for his belonging, MacNeice first embarks upon a rigorous criticism and abandonment of the various claims upon his identity. 'Valediction' is as clear a declaration of independence from everything which the newly formed states of Ireland and Ulster symbolised as could be written. The poem directs the reader through a series of injunctions to 'see Sackville Street', 'See Belfast', 'Park your car in Kilkenny, buy a souvenir', and 'swank your fill, / But take the Holyhead boat before you pay the bill'.[195] Ireland, both north and south, is depicted as cold, fake, murderous, and drably sentimental, a place which romanticises its own origins and shrouds its petty miseries in 'Sham Celtic crosses' or 'leaps to a fife band'. Yet MacNeice recognises too the powerful hold of the island on him: 'I cannot be / Anyone else than what this land engendered me', even though he vows also to 'exorcise my blood / . . . I will acquire an attitude not yours / And become as one of your holiday visitors'. Strikingly, MacNeice uses the two most popular and charged metaphors for racial and national belonging here – blood and land – to signal his own difficult entanglements in what he depicts as a mythology of Irishness. And the verbs – engender, exorcise – make it clear that the desired transformation from subject, or son, to the carefree attitude of the holiday visitor who can treat the land as scenic confection or casual playground will be painful and uncertain. The renunciation is an act of denial, a denial of pleasure as well as pain: 'I must go east and stay, not looking behind'. The poem announces none of the possible promise of going east, nothing of futurity other than the calculated return of the casual visitor, but instead dwells on his extrication from 'your drums and your dolled-up virgins and your ignorant dead', from the litany of violence, ritual, and myth which seem to the poet indefatigable.

In the poem 'Birmingham', MacNeice continues this process of demythologising the places of his belonging, for English cities present no antidote to the rural mysticism of Ireland, or the grimy veneers of Ulster. Birmingham is depicted in Eliotic terms as the unreal city, comprised of facades and tricks; whatever beauty it has is 'jerry-built', and exploitative of 'sweated labour'. After the 'Saturday thrills', the summer entertainments, or the respite of lunch hour, the factory chimneys still 'call . . . sleep-stupid faces through the daily gate'. The conspicuous modernity of MacNeice's England renders it no less sham, and ultimately no less dreary in its delusions, than the romanticised scenes of Irish and Ulster atavism. A survey of MacNeice's early poetic renderings of his various residences in Ireland and England might conclude with his own blunt, proto-Larkinesque line from 'An Eclogue for Christmas' that 'One place is as bad as another'.[196] Yet this would miss the point that what MacNeice is doing in his early poetry is not an expression of existential alienation or archetypal modernist rootlessness, but a clearing of the accumulated mythologies and ideologies of place in the British and Irish Isles. This is accomplished through a relentless uprooting and scouring of place: 'Train to

Dublin' refuses the destination, and gives the reader instead a series of images as ephemeral as 'the shadow of the smoke of this train upon the grass';[197] 'Belfast' comprises geological and maritime images of the city's people, formed of 'basalt' and 'mica', 'And the salt carrion water brings him wealth', a city built upon commerce and murder, with no sense in the poem of how it might be called a home;[198] both 'Valediction' and 'Upon this Beach', in very different ways, advocate the life of the 'tripper', consciously opposed to the life of the settler;[199] and, perhaps most emphatically, MacNeice's poem about his childhood home town, 'Carrickfergus', recalls the sounds, smells, and sights of that town, but ends in Dorset, recalling the 'steamer . . . that took me to England – / Sweat and khaki in the Carlisle train'.[200] Migration is a persistent theme and trope in MacNeice's poetry, but it is always a migration from ideas of place, as much as it is migration from places themselves. As Peter McDonald argues, one reason why MacNeice has struggled to gain full recognition in either Irish or English literary canons is the constant destabilisation of the very categories of 'Ireland' and 'England' implicit in his work.[201]

MacNeice's most famous poem, *Autumn Journal* (1939), similarly works to demythologise national narratives of belonging, juxtaposing them with local and planetary scales of geographic meaning. Place is defined in MacNeice's poem only through movement, through a traversal of place. Indeed, place-names of distinctive localities appear most noticeably in lists of the towns along a railway line – 'West Meon, Tisted, Farnham, Woking, Weybridge'[202] – or along a road – 'Bewdley, Cleobury Mortimer, Ludlow'[203] – where their significance as 'places' is erased by their function merely as names glimpsed at speed by the traveller passing by. If there is a conscious acknowledgement of Edward Thomas's 'Adlestrop' here, the poem also makes clearer than Thomas the accelerated process of transformation which renders places into mere names on a map, the barest signals of routes taken. *Autumn Journal* is, of course, a record of transformation, of the intense period of anticipation prior to the outbreak of the Second World War, and is a poem preoccupied with the differing scales of time – daily, seasonal, and historical – and of place – local, national, and planetary – in which human life is meaningful. It is particularly concerned, however, to dislodge myths of insularity associated with contemporaneous Irish and English nationalist discourses. It famously admonishes Irish isolationism, which would shape the policy of Irish neutrality during the war: 'There is no immunity in this island either'.[204] Against de Valera's protectionist policies of promoting Irish self-sufficiency, MacNeice counters with the acerbic analogy of 'A cart that is drawn by somebody else's horse / And carrying goods to somebody else's market'.[205] In similar ways to the poem 'Valediction', MacNeice is scathing in his critique of romantic Ireland, but Ireland is not the only target of his attack on insularity. The words

'insulates', 'insulated', and 'insulate', used across the poem, connect three separate references to myths of protection from the encroachments of the world
outside the islands. The first instance appears in the opening lines of the poem,
in coastal Hampshire, where 'close-clipped yew / Insulates the lives of retired
generals and admirals', but presumably, with the impending signs of war,
not for long.[206] Section XII of the poem uses the word 'insulated' also in the
sense of a desperate last illusion of peace before the onset of war, when 'the
legions wait at the gates'.[207] The third instance of the word balances the myth
of insular Ireland with the equally false sense of a protected England: 'There
is straw to lay in the streets; call the hunchback, / The gentleman farmer, the
village idiot, the Shropshire Lad, / To insulate us if they can with coma /
Before we all go mad.'[208] The poem draws us forward and back, shrewdly
across the British and Irish Isles, between the myths of insularity which define
nationalist narratives of exceptionalism, be they agrarian idylls of frugal self-
sufficiency and world-oblivious localism, or pastoral dreams of a 'merrie' rural
retreat from modernity. MacNeice returns forcefully to this point at the end of
Autumn Journal when he poses the question about what should fill our dreams:
'Of Tir nan Og or South Sea islands, / Of a land where all the milk is cream /
And all the girls are willing?'[209] Or instead, MacNeice asks, shall we not dream
of 'a possible land / Not of sleep-walkers, not of angry puppets, / But where
both heart and brain can understand / The movements of our fellows'?[210]
Against the myopic nationalisms of England and Ireland, then, with their
dreams of island utopias, or rather island hideaways, MacNeice poses instead
an alternative geography, a geography in which the 'hungry faces' of Spain[211]
are connected to the 'generals and admirals' on the Hampshire coast, in which
we are all 'Following the curve of a planet'.[212] *Autumn Journal* critiques Irish
and English nationalisms, then, not just by showing their reliance on the same
myths of rural and island insularity, but also by showing their interdependence upon global scales of transformation and belonging. And, just as in the
'felt routes' of 'Ode', it is the *movement* of people, not their rootedness, which
demands understanding, as if indeed human scales of belonging can only be
understood in terms of motion, migration, and traversal.

   It is precisely along these lines that we might consider MacNeice's travel
narratives of the period – *Letters from Iceland* and *I Crossed the Minch* – as sharing
the same preoccupations as his poetry. The term 'travel narratives', of course,
does not adequately describe these books, which are idiosyncratic compendia
of prose and poetry, letters and journals, fictional personae and travel reportage. The very assemblage form of both books suggests a radical indeterminacy
of approach, or an underlying irony to their very pretence to be travel records.
Auden and MacNeice collaborated on *Letters from Iceland*, which goes, almost
comically and certainly briefly, through the motions of pretending to be a

travel book, with a section 'For Tourists' advising on customs and expectations, and another 'addressed to John Betjeman' which compiles quotations
from diverse sources on every aspect of Icelandic geography, culture, and
history. Similarly, *I Crossed the Minch* contains a 'Potted History', and journal
accounts of MacNeice's tour of the Hebrides, but MacNeice begins with the
admission that he set out for the islands without knowing that the inhabitants predominantly speak Gaelic, thus limiting his ability to 'become intimate
with the lives of the people', and thereby turn authoritative guide for his
prospective readers.[213] In the case of both books, there is an important question of tone raised by their glib assemblage of the conventional ingredients of
the travel narrative, which certainly in English writing has long and involved
associations with cultural imperialism. MacNeice's acknowledgement of his
ignorance of the language of the Hebridean islanders might be regarded as
cavalier, and perhaps characteristic of the presumptuous disposition of colonial
travel narratives, which may claim authority to depict others without having
gained intimacy or acceptance. Likewise, Auden and MacNeice in *Letters from
Iceland*, although they acknowledge from the outset that a 'travel book owes so
little to the writers, and so much to the people they meet', proceed to provide
accounts of their travels and of the island which adopt an attitude which
might certainly be read as condescension. In both cases, however, the tone is
inseparable from the general frivolity evident in the juxtaposition of fictional
personae, poetry, letters, and drab journal records of diet and weather. A travel
narrative which informs the reader that 'The sitting-rooms of Icelandic farms
are all rather alike', or that 'One waterfall is extraordinarily like another',
may be regarded, perhaps, as treating its subject matter with some scepticism, even irony.[214] To be fair, also, even the titles of both works make no
claim to authority on their respective subject locations, and MacNeice's *I
Crossed the Minch*, in particular, begs to be considered a mock-heroic title.
There is an argument to be made, then, that *Letters from Iceland* and *I Crossed
the Minch*, if they seem to belong to the genre of travel writing, are in some
regards deconstructive of that genre, playfully ironic with its conventions,
and frankly dismissive of its claims to cultural knowledge. Yet, in the context
of MacNeice's already established poetic interest in islands and insularity, the
decision to travel to, and write about, Iceland and the Hebrides, to turn to a
northern hopscotch tour of islands, raises serious questions about an underlying archipelagic theme in his work.

Much of *I Crossed the Minch* is shaped by a scaling of the Hebrides against
the measure of MacNeice's experiences and perceptions of other places, so
that he draws comparisons between the Hebrides and Ireland, Ulster, Achill,
Connemara, London, Birmingham, Cumberland, Iceland, and Norway.
'The lava-fields of Iceland cured me of the idea that a landscape cannot be

too bleak,' he writes, comparing the stones of Iceland with the stones of Connemara, which in turn are compared to his hopes of finding 'the right ratio of life and barrenness' in the landscape of the Hebrides.[215] Throughout the book, MacNeice makes clear that the distinctiveness of the islands could only ever be defined in relation to its archipelagic neighbours. Ireland, in particular, is a recurrent figure of comparison: 'the islanders, like the Southern Irish, show a disregard for time and penny-in-the-slot efficiency'.[216] So, too, MacNeice's depiction of the islands must be differentiated from an already established genre of travel writing about them, a genre to which he happily, perhaps opportunistically, contributes, but of which he is deeply sceptical: 'you should never believe what people in England tell you about other countries,' he writes, and that warning undergirds the constant measuring of MacNeice's observations of the islands against the sentimental expectations he has acquired from travel writings about the islands.[217] *I Crossed the Minch* is a narrative of deflated hopes and misplaced expectations, conveying even in its formal dedication to MacNeice's 'native informant', Hector MacIver, that it is a book likely to disappoint his island hosts, being the 'book of an outsider who has treated frivolously what he could not assess on its merits'.[218] Yet, however appropriate it is to see *I Crossed the Minch* as a 'potboiler', written for financial gain, the conscious, even strategic frivolity of the book's deflationary approach to the distinctiveness and value of the islands requires some explanation. MacNeice explains that his purpose in going to the Hebrides was to find his own sense of Celticism reflected and amplified in the islanders, 'a sentimental and futile hope', as it turns out, and a hope, moreover, about which his earlier poetry had already shown healthy scepticism. The idea of some vague sense of racial affinity which might mysteriously crystallise in MacNeice on sustained and close contact with some actual Gaels is dismissed in the same sentence in which it is raised. If there is an archipelagic sense of affinity and connection to be constructed in the relations between the Hebrides and other parts of the north-east Atlantic, MacNeice swiftly dismisses the racial discourse underpinning such a notion in its Yeatsian version. So, too, the idea of a common coastal consciousness shared along the Atlantic seaboard simply doesn't accord with MacNeice's disappointed reaction to much of the coastal landscape of the islands. In Mull, for example, he complains that 'The grass seemed to run down to the sea. I do not like this. There should be no philandering between sea and land.'[219] In Claddach, he protests melodramatically at the 'mere vomit of a sea, flats of slime and seaweed, a dead lagoon of limbo' which lies between Claddach and Kirkibost Island.[220] It compares unfavourably with his romanticised vision from his childhood of the Atlantic seen for the first time in the West of Ireland as 'a regular leap of white like the flash of an animal's teeth'.[221] MacNeice is clinical, perhaps even scathingly unsentimental, in casting a cold eye on the romanticisation of the landscape and people of the Hebrides, and, if the travel book as a generic type relies upon selling the idea of remote places to a largely metropolitan readership, MacNeice perversely and persistently discourages further travel. His apparently melancholic declaration on the opening page, 'I doubt if I shall visit the Western Islands again', turns out over the course of the book to be a more frank, and measured, summary of MacNeice's assessment of the real interest of the islands to the unconnected traveller.[222]

There is scant reference in *I Crossed the Minch* to other books about the Hebrides, although, as Tom Herron records,[223] it was a popular subject of travel books in the 1930s. MacNeice records meeting Barra's most famous resident, the writer Compton Mackenzie, who would become even more famous an island writer when he published *Whisky Galore* (1947), but he engages with Mackenzie as a celebrity rather than a writer.[224] However, in MacNeice's playful demythologising of Celticist and romanticist tendencies in island writings, it is difficult to accept that he was unaware of the exaggerated extent of such tendencies in books such as Seton Gordon's *Islands of the West* (1933). Gordon combined the keenly scientific approach of the expert naturalist with a deeply romantic sense of the Western Isles as a world still governed by Celtic spiritual beliefs in the power of the tides: 'True it is that when the Atlantic at the imperious bidding of the pale moon pours in a mighty irresistible stream north-east past Malin Head and Tory Island, past Barra, Mingulay and Mull of the Great Hills, the clustered shore clans of the Isles awake.'[225] MacNeice's book eschews both: he sheds little light on the particularities of natural or human habitation of the islands, and he responds to the drunken feeling of being at one with the Celtic lore of the islanders by rushing off to Stornoway 'to try and buy a copy of the *Listener*', which would at least give him the sense of being back in touch with his cherished metropolitan literati.[226] MacNeice prefers to constantly remind his readers, self-reflexively, that he is a thoroughly metropolitan being, and this might be read as an effective means of subverting the assumptions of the travel genre. Yet, what both Gordon and MacNeice share, albeit expressed in quite different ways, is a sense of the islands as belonging to an archipelagic geography which defies conventional state or national boundaries. Gordon traces the language, customs, and beliefs of the Hebrides through connections with Connemara, Tory, Inishbofin, and the Scilly Isles, mapping an arc of islands and fractal coastlines fringing the Atlantic which for the most part share in common the Gaelic language, and the persistence of Celtic myths and lore. The Irish newspapers reflected some sense of this archipelago when reporting on Hebridean affairs,[227] and there is some evidence of interest in the Hebrides among Irish readers.[228] MacNeice bears out something of this geography in the way in which the Hebrides conjure in his mind comparisons with Achill, Connemara, and Iceland, but it is devoid of romanticism. In returning to England, for example, MacNeice sees a 'flashy poster' in a railway station advertising 'Visit the Western Isles: A Wonderland of Colour', to which his trenchant response is that 'there was more colour in Birmingham'.[229]

Such anti-romantic expressions in *I Crossed the Minch* might be regarded as examples of what Tom Herron describes accurately as the 'tonal promiscuity' of the work, but MacNeice's 'promiscuity' masks a deeper search for a sense of connection, for some idea of place which might be called home, and, most pertinently here, his search seems repeatedly to take him to islands, and to ideas of islands, which might, magically, bear within them the seeds of an alternative way of life. The search was not his alone. Valentine Cunningham has written insightfully of the remarkable alignment of left-wing pastoralism of the 1930s with a training in classical scholarship, and perhaps even more strikingly how many of these same intellectuals had immediate familial connections with Northern Irish Protestantism, most notably E. R. Dodds, Cecil Day Lewis, George Thomson, and MacNeice himself.[230] Thomson is most notable among them for his explicit depiction of the lives of twentieth-century Blasket islanders as the cultural analogues of Homer's Greeks:

> The conversation of those ragged peasants, as soon as I learnt to follow it, electrified me. It was as though Homer had come alive. Its vitality was inexhaustible, yet it was rhythmical, alliterative, formal, artificial, always on the point of bursting into poetry . . . Returning to Homer, I read him in a new light. He was a people's poet.[231]

For Thomson, visiting the Blaskets enabled him to see, and to argue for, Homer as a prototypical poet of proletarian life, *avant la lettre*, but also, of course, this entailed seeing life on the Blaskets as an idyllic mode of pastoral existence. As a Marxist, Thomson could find some inspiration in the idea that pre-capitalist economic relations persisted in such 'outlying or secluded communities',[232] which he celebrated as 'a simple culture, but free from the rapacity and vulgarity that is destroying our own'.[233] Auden saw something of this vitality of 'folk-poetry', which he believed comparable to pre-industrial Europe, in the frontier and prospecting communities of America.[234] MacNeice was immersed in classical pastoral, however, like Thomson, and perhaps this is one notable source of his attraction to 'the Celtic or backward fringes' of the British Isles which he hoped remained the home of 'natural (some will call it primitive) culture'.[235] Yet, MacNeice distrusts the terms of this investment of proletarian romance and nobility in the supposed outliers of the British Isles, which has 'made a Mecca of the Blaskets',[236] and distrusts the association of the Hebrides with ideas of primitive dignity and self-sufficiency, not least because his allusions to dependence upon the dole and tinned food suggest 'an island invaded by the vices of the mainland'.[237] Those 'vices of the mainland' are walked in to the islands on the boots of 'trippers' just like MacNeice, of course, who is keenly aware of the responsibilities of the travel genre in which he writes both for the idealisation of remote places and the corresponding demise of their remoteness. MacNeice craves the idealisation of the Hebrides, and his happiest moments on the islands come when walking alone with a map, 'not meeting a person on the way',[238] or when, in the company of islanders, he can imagine that somehow this community embodies a 'Celtic timelessness'.[239] It is certainly the case that these moments are rare intrusions in a narrative which is predominantly characterised by scepticism and incredulity, and yet *I Crossed the Minch* cannot wholly abandon the hopes or fantastical notions upon which it was founded. Just as Thomson imagines the Blaskets as not only a remnant of pre-capitalist society, but also a harbinger of a future model of community, so too MacNeice is drawn towards the idea of the Hebrides as embodying similar potential:

> Their traditional language needs no artificial cultivation, their population is small enough to allow of a genuine community feeling, their social life is still homogeneous (though commercialisation may soon drive rifts through it), lastly the sea still separates them from their neighbours.[240]

At this point in the narrative, MacNeice quotes a line in Greek from Aeschylus's *Agamemnon*, spoken by Agamemnon's wife, Clytemnestra: 'There is the sea and who shall drain it dry?'[241] The line might be interpreted both as a statement of some arrogance, claiming power over the sea, which Clytemnestra acknowledges in her subsequent lines has been the source of great wealth for her household, and as a statement of futility, akin to the Irish mythological tale of Cuchulainn's fight with the waves, or the English legend of King Canute commanding the tides to stop. It has little significance for the point MacNeice is making, other than to suggest resonance between the seafaring communities of ancient Greece and those of the Hebrides. It is precisely the resonance which Compton Mackenzie remarks upon to MacNeice, that the landscape glimpsed through 'a little ship's window' in Mackenzie's Barra house 'was the nearest thing to Greece this end of Europe'.[242] Like Thomson, then, MacNeice glimpses ancient Greece in the familial, 'primitive' communities of the Gaelic-speaking Atlantic seaboard. The continuity proposed by such an analogy is registered in some of MacNeice's poems which figure the sea as timeless, most notably 'The Sea' from *Blind Fireworks* (1929) and 'Thalassa' (1964). Yet, the analogy is more interesting than a specious form of universalism: the classical parallel poses a challenge to the notions of blood kinship or racial continuity which underpin Celtic Revivalism, precisely by proposing instead similarities which are cultural and material, and more precisely which relate the cultural to the material. For MacNeice this is crucial, since his initial assumption of affinity with Gaelic islanders is misplaced: such affinity would be based on a mythology of race, whereas it is clear in *I Crossed the Minch* that the changing cultural patterns of life on the islands are directly connected to changing material circumstances. To affect affinity to a folk or peasant primitivism (for which MacNeice interestingly uses the image of 'Synge's hobnailed boots chasing girls' naked feet')[243] would, in such conditions, be an empty formalism: it would falsify the terms of his relationship to the islands, which, as he realises melancholically, can only be that of a 'tripper'.

Cunningham is too quick, however, to lump MacNeice's 'The Hebrides' and 'Leaving Barra' in with a species of 'travelmaniac' writing which he criticises as a 'literature living greedily off its authors' experiences of foreign places', too ready to accept MacNeice's own sense of complicity in tourist voyeurism and exploitation.[244] MacNeice mocks himself as a 'tripper', but his trips are really searches for connection, quests for affinity which even if they fail nevertheless ask questions about the relations between 'these islands'. For MacNeice, although he cannot belong to them, the homogeneity, longevity, and finitude of the Hebridean communities constitute ripe conditions for the survival of a kind of island nationalism, while he can see little possibility of this in Scotland, and for a socialist dreaming of 'a federation of differentiated communities',[245] nationalism, even if reactionary, might at least have its provisional uses in defining the terms of such differentiation. However, as MacNeice acknowledges of his more romantic moments on the islands, perhaps the comforts of nationalism are always about the illusion of insularity, a point which becomes particularly significant in his caustic address to Ireland in 'Neutrality' (1944), where the sea becomes a source of moral rebuke: 'to the west off your own shores the mackerel / Are fat – on the flesh of your kin'.[246] The Irish government's declared policy of neutrality in the Second World War was, for MacNeice, a coldly logical extension of the insularity which nationalism fostered. It confirmed and exaggerated the sense which is already evident in his poetic depictions of Ireland in the 1930s that the myth of islandness was less a product of romance than of cold indifference to those outside the bounds of the nation. Yet, as Clair Wills suggests in her account of MacNeice's prolonged stay in neutral Ireland at the beginning of the war, there is perhaps some censure of his own temptation to remain in Ireland masked in his later depiction of neutrality as cold-blooded escapism.[247] The insularity of islands was not wholly without appeal in a world descending into genocide and mutual mass destruction. 'You will find in this book no picture of island Utopias,' declares MacNeice in the introductory chapter of *I Crossed the Minch*, but while this is incontestable it does not capture the book's lingering sense of a man in search of island utopias.[248]

The reviewer for *The Times* distinguished the poetry included in *I Crossed the Minch* from its prose, praising the poetry for not containing any of the 'smartness or sophistication' which comes between the poet and the island-ers in the playful fictional interludes and ironic tone of much of the prose.[249] It might be argued that the 'smartness' and 'sophistication' is a register of MacNeice's uneasy relationship to the ready urbanite sentimentalism and misty Celtic romanticism about islands, and especially Atlantic fringe islands, which had become a cliché of Irish and British writings in the early twentieth century, and perhaps even long before. It might also be argued that the poetry included in *I Crossed the Minch* should be considered in intimate relation to, even in dialogue with, that 'smartness' and 'sophistication' of the prose. Yet, as the final section of *I Crossed the Minch*, the poem 'On Those Islands' (also published in the collection *The Earth Compels* (1938) as 'The Hebrides') does suggest a closer affinity between the poet and the islands, an affection which survives and outlives the smart, breezy dialogue of MacNeice's fictional per-sonae of 'Hetty and Maisie'. Terence Brown alludes to the poem as 'richly celebratory of Hebridean life', and Heather Clark sees in it 'several stock Revivalist motifs', perhaps even 'a dialogue with Yeats's "The Lake Isle of Innisfree"', whose speaker also dreams of surrendering to an island otherworld free from time and modernity', except that, as both Brown and Clark point out, the poem also recognises island life as fantasy only for someone like MacNeice who is not from the islands.[250] The poem dramatises this distance of the speaker from the intimacies of the island communities in its refrain, repeated twelve times, 'On those islands', with its deictic word indicating a spatial, and an implied emotional, detachment. MacNeice clusters together a series of images of the islands which conform to conventional expectations of remote, rural life: 'No one hurries', 'peasant', 'The houses straggle', 'fra-grant peat', 'No one repeats the password for it is known', 'ancestral rights', 'unspoiled by contact', 'their land though mainly stones', 'a lost breed', and many more.[251] These images of quiet and intimate peasant life jostle with the encroaching signs of modernity, some already familiar in Synge's *The Aran Islands*: 'The photos . . . of the successful sons / Who married wealth in Toronto or New York', 'the bus, not stopping, / Drops a parcel for the lonely household', the 'dole' and 'old-age pensions'. Cunningham emphasises how many of the movements figured in the poem appear to be negative.[252] It is more striking, however, how many of them are ambivalent. 'No one hurries' may be read, for example, as a sign of pastoral ease, or of systemic lethargy. 'No one repeats the password for it is known' may be read as a sign of communal familiarity, or of pathological insularity. Equally, 'the bus, not stopping, / Drops a parcel for the lonely household' could be an action which either compounds or relieves the loneliness of the household. The more one appreciates the ambivalence of such figures in the poem, the more evident it becomes that 'On Those Islands' is an exercise in studied (even affected) detachment, an attempt to depict islands and their peculiarities without romanticising their 'primitivism'. MacNeice concludes by alluding to the survival of neighbourliness and the preservation of familial and communal customs. The islands are places 'Where a few surnames cover a host of people / And the art of being a stranger with your neighbour / Has still to be imported', where people 'still can live as their fathers lived'.[253] In themselves, these lines are also ambivalent, and can be read as celebrations of island life only in juxtaposition with the figure of 'the tyrant time', absent from the islands, which signals 'people to doom / With semaphore ultimatums tick by tick'. On the islands, 'There is still peace', to which MacNeice immediately adds the caveat, 'though not for me and not / Perhaps for long'. MacNeice constructs here an elaborate depiction of the dependence of the islands upon the mainland, and vice versa: the 'peace', neighbourliness, and traditionalism of the islands belong to a figurative system in which they are meaningful only in relation to the 'tyranny' of modernity, only, that is, in relation to the very metropolitan norms to which they appear to contrast. It is impossible, in other words, to see them outside of that system of representation in which island life is constantly exoticised as peaceful, harmonious, and frugal. And yet, encoded into those representations of island life are the lingering ideals of knowable, human communities, in which each death is a communal death, and each life a noble bearing of communal values. MacNeice's poem might be read as a lament for the, perhaps inevitable, passing of this way of life, but the poem is at the same time a hymn to a possible future, a mapping of the forms of communal life which, in Raymond Williams's terms, are now residual, but which might become emergent.[254] Thus, MacNeice's imaginative preoccupation with the islands of the north-east Atlantic archipelago, critical and sceptical always, nevertheless find in them not the dying remnants of a primitive life beyond modernity, but instead models of how such thoroughly modern, globally connected, and penetrated spaces still manage to maintain, even if only for some time, forms of communal living strange to, and estranging of, metropolitan society. This explains the artful oscillation in MacNeice's island writings between intimacy and disavowal, proximity and distance, sincerity and irony, for ultimately it is only by preserving the strangeness of islands, their constant ambivalence as figures of totality and eccentricity, that MacNeice understands their usefulness as models of survival and re-inhabitation, beacons by which one might, like the migrating birds following their 'felt routes', eventually 'come to one's home'.

NOTES

1. 'Indian Ocean Flight Delayed', *The Times*, 6 June 1939, 13.
2. 'Islands Lost and Found', *The Times*, 9 June 1939, 17.
3. 'Bouvet Island', *The Geographical Journal*, 72.6 (December 1928), 537.
4. Rupert T. Gould, *Oddities: A Book of Unexplained Facts*. Glasgow: Glasgow University Press, 1928, 124–62.
5. 'Islands Lost and Found', *The Times*, 9 June 1939, 17.
6. Godfrey Baldacchino, 'Editorial: Islands – Objects of Representation', *Geografiska Annaler: Series B – Human Geography*, 87.4 (2005), 247–8.
7. Pete Hay, 'A Phenomenology of Islands', *Island Studies Journal*, 1.1 (2006), 26, 29 (19–42).
8. Jed Esty, *A Shrinking Island: Modernism and National Culture in England*. Princeton: Princeton University Press, 2004, 1–22.
9. Kristin Bluemel (ed.), *Intermodernism: Literary Culture in Mid-Twentieth-Century Britain*. Edinburgh: Edinburgh University Press, 2009, 1–14.
10. In this sense, the book is working broadly within archipelagic paradigms of critical study of the British and Irish Isles, as they have been defined and extended by J. G. A. Pocock, *The Discovery of Islands: Essays in British History*. Cambridge: Cambridge University Press, 2005; John Kerrigan, *Archipelagic English: Literature, History, and Politics 1603–1707*. Oxford: Oxford University Press, 2008; and Christopher Harvie, *A Floating Commonwealth: Politics, Culture, and Technology on Britain's Atlantic Coast, 1860–1930*. Oxford: Oxford University Press, 2008.
11. Edna Longley, 'Irish and Scottish "Island Poems"', in Robert McColl Millar (ed.), *Northern Lights, Northern Words. Selected Papers from the FRLSU Conference, Kirkwall 2009*. Aberdeen: Forum for Research on the Languages of Scotland and Ireland, 2010, 143–61.
12. See Tomás Ó Criomhthain, *An tOileánach: Scéal a Bheathadh Féin*. Baile Átha Cliath: Clólucht an Tálbóidigh, 1929 (published in translation as Tomás Ó Crohan, *The Islandman*, trans. Robin Flower. Dublin: Talbot Press, 1934); Muiris Ó Súileabháin, *Fiche Blian ag Fás*. Baile Átha Cliath: Clólucht an Tálbóidigh, 1933 (published in translation as Maurice O'Sullivan, *Twenty Years A-Growing: Rendered from the original Irish by Moya Llewelyn Davies and George Thomson*. Harmondsworth: Penguin, 1938); and Peig Sayers, *Peig: A Scéal Féin*. Baile Átha Cliath: Clólucht an Tálbóidigh, 1936 (published in translation as Peig Sayers, *Peig: The Autobiography of Peig Sayers of the Great Blasket Island*, trans. Bryan MacMahon. Dublin: Talbot Press, 1973).
13. E. M. Forster, 'Introductory Note', in Maurice O'Sullivan, *Twenty Years A-Growing*. Oxford: Oxford University Press, 1983, v–vi.
14. Jill Frank, *Islands and the Modernists: The Lure of Isolation in Art, Literature, and Science*. Jefferson, NC: McFarland and Co., 2006.
15. Hay, 'A Phenomenology of Islands', 21.
16. The point accords with analyses argued more fully by Michael Gardiner in *The*

      Cultural Roots of British Devolution. Edinburgh: Edinburgh University Press, 2004, and Raphael Samuel in 'Unravelling Britain', *Island Stories: Unravelling Britain* (vol. 2 of *Theatres of Memory*). London: Verso, 1998, 41–73.

17. George Orwell, *The Road to Wigan Pier* [1937]. Harmondsworth: Penguin, 1962, 140.

18. Hugh MacDiarmid, *The Islands of Scotland*. London: Batsford, 1939, x–xi.

19. J. D. Evans, 'Islands as Laboratories for the Study of Cultural Process', in A. C. Renfrew (ed.), *The Explanation of Culture Change: Models in Prehistory*. London: Duckworth, 1973, 517–20.

20. Sophia Hillan King, *The Silken Twine: A Study of the Works of Michael McLaverty*. Dublin: Poolbeg, 1992, 29–48.

21. Sophia Hillan King, 'The Note of Exile: Michael McLaverty's Rathlin Island', in Gerald Dawe and John Wilson Foster (eds), *The Poet's Place: Ulster Literature and Society, Essays in Honour of John Hewitt, 1907–1987*. Belfast: Institute of Irish Studies, 1991, 182–3 (181–92).

22. Michael McLaverty, *Call My Brother Back*. Belfast: Blackstaff, 2003, 10.

23. See, for examples, Michael Bell, *Literature, Modernism and Myth: Belief and Responsibility in the Twentieth Century*. Cambridge: Cambridge University Press, 1997; Michael North, *The Dialect of Modernism: Race, Language, and Twentieth-Century Literature*. Oxford: Oxford University Press, 1994; Jeremy MacClancy, 'Anthropology: "The Latest Form of Evening Entertainment"', in David Bradshaw (ed.), *A Concise Companion to Modernism*. Oxford: Blackwell, 2003, 75–94; Marc Manganaro, 'Modernist Studies and Anthropology: Reflections on the Past, Present, and Possible Futures', in Pamela L. Caughie (ed.), *Disciplining Modernism*. Basingstoke: Palgrave, 2010, 210–20; and Elazar Barkan and Ronald Bush (eds), *Prehistories of the Future: The Primitivist Project and the Culture of Modernism*. Stanford: Stanford University Press, 1995.

24. See, for examples, Mary Burke, 'Evolutionary Theory and the Search for Lost Innocence in the Writings of J. M. Synge', *Canadian Journal of Irish Studies*, 30.1 (Spring 2004), 48–54; Gregory Castle, *Modernism and the Celtic Revival*. Cambridge: Cambridge University Press, 2001; and Sinead Garrigan Mattar, *Primitivism, Science, and the Irish Revival*. Oxford: Oxford University Press, 2004.

25. For examples, in relation to Aran, see A. C. Haddon and C. R. Browne, 'The Ethnography of the Aran Islands, County Galway', *Proceedings of the Royal Irish Academy (1889–1901)*, vol. 2 (1891–1893), 768–830, and J. M. Synge, *The Aran Islands*. London: Penguin, 1992; in relation to the Blaskets, see the auto-ethnographical work of the Blasket writers cited above; and in relation to the Hebrides, and the Atlantic coastal regions more widely, see Seton Gordon, *Islands of the West*. London: Cassell, 1933.

26. Pin Tong et al., 'Sequencing and Analysis of an Irish Human Genome', *Genome Biology*, 11: R91 (2010), 1–14.

27. Michael A. MacConaill, 'The Men of Rachrai', *Proceedings and Reports of the Belfast Natural History and Philosophical Society, for the Session 1922–1923*. Belfast: The Northern Whig, 1924, 6 (4–7).

28. Ibid. 5–6.
29. R. J. Berry, *Islands*. New Naturalist Library. London: HarperCollins, 2009, 49.
30. A revival of such interest in islands and biological and genetic questions might also be traced in recent studies of genetic ancestry in Ireland, Britain, and the eastern Atlantic seaboard: see, for examples, Brian McEvoy et al., 'The *Longue Durée* of Genetic Ancestry: Multiple Genetic Marker Systems and Celtic Origins on the Atlantic Façade of Europe', *American Journal of Human Genetics*, 75 (2004), 693–701, and Colm T. O'Dushlaine et al., 'Population Structure and Genome-wide Patterns of Variation in Ireland and Britain', *European Journal of Human Genetics*, 18 (2010), 1248–54.
31. Michael McLaverty, 'The Green Field', *The Irish Monthly*, 60 (August 1932), 497 (497–504).
32. Ibid. 502.
33. Ibid. 502.
34. Michael McLaverty, 'The Wild Duck's Nest', *The Irish Monthly*, 62 (April 1934), 236–40.
35. Michael McLaverty, 'The Prophet', *The Irish Monthly*, 64 (February 1936), 95 (95–101).
36. Ibid. 100.
37. Michael McLaverty, 'Stone', *Collected Short Stories*. Belfast: Blackstaff, 2002, 32–42.
38. Ibid. 39.
39. Ibid. 42.
40. Here, it is worth noting the turn to maritime studies in recent literary criticism, including important publications such as Cesare Casarino, *Modernity at Sea: Melville, Marx, Conrad in Crisis*. Minneapolis: University of Minnesota Press, 2002; Hester Blum, *The View from the Masthead: Maritime Imagination and Antebellum American Sea Narratives*. Chapel Hill: University of North Carolina Press, 2008; Lara Feigel and Alexandra Harris (eds), *Modernism on Sea: Art and Culture at the British Seaside*. Oxford: Peter Lang, 2011; and Margaret Cohen, *The Novel and the Sea*. Princeton: Princeton University Press, 2010, as well as the special issue of the *PMLA* devoted to 'Oceanic Studies', 125.3 (May 2010).
41. Franco Moretti, *Atlas of the European Novel 1800–1900*. London: Verso, 1998, 70 (italics in original).
42. McLaverty, *Call My Brother Back*, 46.
43. Ibid. 1, 4, 24.
44. Ibid. 57.
45. Rachel Carson, *The Edge of the Sea*. Boston: Mariner, 1998, 1–2.
46. Robert Frost, 'For Once, Then, Something', *The Poetry of Robert Frost*, ed. Edward Connery Lathem. London: Vintage, 2001, 225.
47. McLaverty, *Call My Brother Back*, 65.
48. Ibid. 65.
49. Esty, *A Shrinking Island*, 8–9.
50. Hay, 'A Phenomenology of Islands', 31.

51. Peter Hegarty, *Peadar O'Donnell*. Cork: Mercier Press, 1999, 13.

52. Peadar O'Donnell, *Wrack: A Play in Six Scenes*. London: Jonathan Cape, 1933. Inside flap of dust jacket.

53. Peadar O'Donnell, *Islanders* [1927]. Cork: Mercier Press, 2005, 67, 122.

54. Ibid. 98.

55. Hegarty, *Peadar O'Donnell*, 9.

56. *Bunreacht na hÉireann/Constitution of Ireland*. Dublin: Government Publications, 1990, 4–5.

57. Gerard Hogan (ed.), *The Origins of the Irish Constitution, 1928–1941*. Dublin: Royal Irish Academy, 2012.

58. O'Donnell, *Wrack*, 19–20.

59. Ibid. 51.

60. Ibid. 95.

61. Ibid. 50.

62. Ibid. 51.

63. Ibid. 49.

64. Ibid. 52.

65. O'Donnell, *Islanders*, 68.

66. Ibid. 71.

67. Ibid. 85.

68. O'Donnell's depiction of the role of seasonal migration from the islands gives fictional insight into a process which has drawn the attention of historians for how seasonal movements to Scotland, in particular, enabled the people of west Donegal to subsist: see Cormac Ó Gráda, 'Seasonal Migration and Post-Famine Adjustment', *Studia Hibernica*, 13 (1973), 61 (48–76). See also Nellie Ó Cléirigh, 'Life in the Rosses, Co. Donegal, in the 1890s', *History Ireland*, 13.2 (March/April 2005), 8–9.

69. T. W. Freeman, 'The Congested Districts of Western Ireland', *Geographical Review*, 33.1 (January 1943), 8 (1–14).

70. O'Donnell, *Islanders*, 95.

71. Ibid. 122.

72. Ibid. 76.

73. Ibid. 40.

74. Grattan Freyer, *Peadar O'Donnell*. Lewisburg: Bucknell University Press, 1973, 41.

75. O'Donnell, *Islanders*, 125.

76. Hugh MacDiarmid, *Lucky Poet: A Self-Study in Literature and Political Ideas*. London: Methuen, 1943, 27.

77. Patrick Crotty, 'Swordsmen: W. B. Yeats and Hugh MacDiarmid', in Peter Mackay, Edna Longley, and Fran Brearton (eds), *Modern Irish and Scottish Poetry*. Cambridge: Cambridge University Press, 2011, 20–38.

78. Ibid. 27, and also *The Golden Treasury of Scottish Poetry*. London: Macmillan, 1940, xxii. MacDiarmid had clearly read a review of Bringmann's *Geschichte Irlands: Ein Kampf Um Die Volkische Freiheit* (1939) in the *Times Literary*

Supplement. Bringmann's book was one of several German historical works published during the Nazi period which, as one reviewer in *Irish Historical Studies* suggested, was more revealing of German interest in Ireland than as contributions to Irish historiography. See J. F. O'Doherty, 'Reviews', *Irish Historical Studies*, 2.6 (September 1940), 217–18. Joachim Fischer has also noted how markedly right-wing German interest in Ireland was in the mid-century period: 'Reviews', *Irish Studies Review*, 9.2 (2001), 266 (264–6).

79. See Alan Bold, *MacDiarmid*. London: Paladin, 1990, 398, and Kenneth Buthley, *Hugh MacDiarmid*. Edinburgh: Oliver and Boyd, 1964, 61, 99.

80. Charles M. Doughty, *The Dawn in Britain*. Six volumes. London: Duckworth, 1906. MacDiarmid comments upon Doughty in the essay 'Charles Doughty and the Need for Heroic Poetry', *Selected Prose*, ed. Alan Riach. Manchester: Carcanet, 1992, 125–36. For Doughty's influence upon modernism, see Herbert F. Tucker, 'Doughty's *The Dawn in Britain* and the Modernist Eclipse of the Victorian', *Romanticism and Victorianism on the Net*, 47 (August 2007): <http://www.erudit.org/revue/ravon/2007/v/n47/016705ar.html> (last accessed 6 May 2014).

81. MacDiarmid, *The Islands of Scotland*, ix.

82. Ibid. ix.

83. Hugh MacDiarmid, *Complete Poems 1920–1976*, vol. 1, ed. Michael Grieve and W. R. Aitken. London: Martin Brian and O'Keeffe, 1978, 677.

84. Bold, *MacDiarmid*, 326–36.

85. Ibid. 332–4.

86. MacDiarmid, *Complete Poems*, 437.

87. Ibid. 438.

88. Ibid. 440–1.

89. Louisa Gairn, 'MacDiarmid and Ecology', in Scott Lyall and Margery Palmer McCulloch (eds), *The Edinburgh Companion to Hugh MacDiarmid*. Edinburgh: Edinburgh University Press, 2011, 82–96.

90. MacDiarmid, *Complete Poems*, 440–1.

91. MacDiarmid, *The Islands of Scotland*, xi. See Trigant Burrow, *The Biology of Human Conflict: An Anatomy of Behavior, Individual and Social*. London: Macmillan, 1937.

92. MacDiarmid, *The Islands of Scotland*, xii.

93. Ibid. xii.

94. On this famous disagreement between Muir and MacDiarmid, see Bold, *MacDiarmid*, 389–92.

95. Seamus Heaney, 'A Torchlight Procession of One', *Parnassus: Poetry in Review*, 21.1–2 (1996), 11 (11–29). Patrick Crotty also notes MacDiarmid's influence on MacLean in 'Swordsmen: W. B. Yeats and Hugh MacDiarmid', 25.

96. MacDiarmid, *The Islands of Scotland*, 59.

97. Margery Palmer McCulloch, *Scottish Modernism and its Contexts, 1918–1959: Literature, National Identity and Cultural Exchange*. Edinburgh: Edinburgh University Press, 2009, 6.

98. MacDiarmid, *The Islands of Scotland*, 8.

99. Ibid. 8.

100. Ibid. 4.

101. Ibid. 92.

102. Esty, *A Shrinking Island*, 1–22.

103. See Paul Robichaud's essay on the 'participant' anthropology of MacDiarmid's writings, and for the wider significance of anthropology to Scottish modernism: 'MacDiarmid and Muir: Scottish Modernism and the Nation as Anthropological Site', *Journal of Modern Literature*, 28.4 (Summer 2005), 135–51.

104. MacDiarmid, *The Islands of Scotland*, 96–7.

105. The poem was published in MacDiarmid, *The Islands of Scotland*, 29–36, but for ease of reference, citations here are from MacDiarmid, *Complete Poems*, 575–83.

106. Michael Whitworth, 'Culture and Leisure in Hugh MacDiarmid's "On a Raised Beach"', *Scottish Studies Review*, 9.1 (Spring 2008), 139 (123–43).

107. MacDiarmid, *Complete Poems*, 422.

108. Scott Lyall, *Hugh MacDiarmid's Poetry and Politics of Place: Imagining a Scottish Republic*. Edinburgh: Edinburgh University Press, 2006, 121. See also Bold, *MacDiarmid*, 331, 337.

109. G. V. Wilson and J. Knox, 'The Geology of the Orkney and Shetland Islands', *Proceedings of the Geologists' Association*, 47 (1936), 270–82.

110. H. H. Read, 'The Metamorphic History of Unst, Shetland', *Proceedings of the Geologists' Association*, 47 (1936), 288 (283–93).

111. MacDiarmid, *Complete Poems*, 425.

112. Lyall, *Hugh MacDiarmid's Poetry and Politics of Place*, 122.

113. MacDiarmid, *Complete Poems*, 428.

114. Martin Heidegger, 'The Origin of the Work of Art', *Poetry, Language, Thought*, trans. Albert Hofstadter. New York: HarperCollins, 1971, 15–86.

115. Ibid. 43.

116. Ibid. 45.

117. Ibid. 46, 48.

118. MacDiarmid, *Complete Poems*, 427.

119. Ibid. 431–2.

120. Ibid. 432.

121. Michael Whitworth's argument that MacDiarmid's poem is participating in a contemporary debate about the relationship between leisure and culture, and the possibilities of rebuilding a unified culture, is compelling, but perhaps emphasises the role of stone as a metaphor for culture too readily over an appreciation of the poem's argument for the alterity of the earth to the culture-making world. See Whitworth, 'Culture and Leisure in Hugh MacDiarmid's "On a Raised Beach"', 123–43.

122. C. M. Yonge, *The Sea Shore* [1949]. The New Naturalist. London: Bloomsbury, 1990, 2.

123. Carson, *The Edge of the Sea*, xiii.

124. Bold, *MacDiarmid*, 327.

125. See Jonathan Bate's discussion of the complex relationship between Heidegger's philosophy of dwelling, particularly in the light of its influence upon contemporary ecocriticism, and the philosopher's renowned associations with Nazism, and his reclusive personal life in the Black Forest: *The Song of the Earth*. London: Picador, 2000, 251–83.

126. Hugh MacDiarmid, 'Life in the Shetland Islands', *Selected Prose*, ed. Alan Riach. Manchester: Carcanet, 1992, 85–97.

127. MacDiarmid, *Complete Poems*, 429.

128. MacDiarmid, *The Islands of Scotland*, xv–xvi, and also *Complete Poems*, 574–5.

129. MacDiarmid, *The Islands of Scotland*, 136.

130. W. H. Auden and Louis MacNeice, *Letters from Iceland* [1937]. London: Faber, 1967, 210.

131. Paul Beekman Taylor, 'Auden's Icelandic Myth of Exile', *Journal of Modern Literature*, 24.2 (Winter 2000–1), 215 (213–34).

132. Chris Jones, 'Auden and "The 'Barbaric' Poetry of the North": Unchaining One's Daimon', *The Review of English Studies*, 53.210 (2002), 167, 169 (167–85).

133. Ibid. 167–85.

134. See H. M. Waidson, 'Auden and German Literature', *Modern Language Review*, 70.2 (1975), 347–65; Breon Mitchell, 'W. H. Auden and Christopher Isherwood: The "German Influence"', *Oxford German Studies*, 1 (1966), 163–72; and Sigurds Dzenitis, *Die Rezeption Deutscher Literatur in England durch Wystan Hugh Auden und Christopher Isherwood*. Hamburg: Hartmut Lüdtke Verlag, 1972.

135. Auden and MacNeice, *Letters from Iceland*, 117.

136. W. H. Auden, *The English Auden: Poems, Essays and Dramatic Writings, 1927–1939*, ed. Edward Mendelson. London: Faber, 1986, 189.

137. Auden and MacNeice, *Letters from Iceland*, 211.

138. Humphrey Carpenter, *W. H. Auden: A Biography*. London: George Allen and Unwin, 1981, 20, 61–2, 122–3, 131, 195–202, 345, 360–88.

139. W. H. Auden, *Collected Poems*, ed. Edward Mendelson. London: Faber, 2007, 119–20.

140. Ibid. 119.

141. Ibid. 120.

142. Lucy McDiarmid, *Saving Civilization: Yeats, Eliot, and Auden Between the Wars*. Cambridge: Cambridge University Press, 1984, 7.

143. W. H. Auden, *The Enchafèd Flood: or The Romantic Iconography of the Sea*. London: Faber, 1951, 125.

144. Carpenter, *W. H. Auden*, 202.

145. See Marsha Bryant, 'Auden and the "Arctic Stare": Documentary as Public Collage in *Letters from Iceland*', *Journal of Modern Literature*, 17.4 (1991), 537 (537–65), and Tim Youngs, 'Auden's Travel Writings', in Stan Smith (ed.), *The Cambridge Companion to W. H. Auden*. Cambridge: Cambridge University Press, 2004, 68–9 (68–81).

146. Youngs, 'Auden's Travel Writings', 74, 76.
147. Auden and MacNeice, *Letters from Iceland*, 253.
148. Auden, *The English Auden*, 197.
149. Auden and MacNeice, *Letters from Iceland*, 30.
150. Ibid. 33.
151. Ibid. 24. There are several versions of this poem, with quite different versions of the lines quoted above. In *The English Auden* (203), for example, the corresponding lines read 'For Europe is absent. This is an island and therefore / Unreal'. In *Collected Poems* (151), the lines read 'Europe is absent: this is an island and should be / a refuge'. Both are dated July 1936 by Edward Mendelson. Similarly, there are three versions of the line which in its best version in *Letters to Iceland* reads 'And each port has a name for the sea' (23), but which in *The English Auden* (203) reads disappointingly 'and the ports have names for the sea', and in *Collected Poems* (150) 'every port has its name for the sea'. In any case, as Auden confesses in his letter to Isherwood which included the poem, the line should have read 'the poets have names for the sea' (*Letters from Iceland*, 25), but 'the mistake seems better than the original idea'.
152. Beekman Taylor, 'Auden's Icelandic Myth of Exile', 219.
153. Ibid. 219; see Carpenter, *W. H. Auden*, 196.
154. Beekman Taylor, 'Auden's Icelandic Myth of Exile', 219.
155. Auden and MacNeice, *Letters from Iceland*, 23–4.
156. Auden, *The English Auden*, 197.
157. 'Dura Virum Nutrix' (Stern Nurse of Men) was and is the motto of Sedburgh, a public school in Cumbria, which Auden idealised in his youth, having fallen in love with two of its former pupils. See Carpenter, *W. H. Auden*, 78–9.
158. Paul Fussell, *Abroad: British Literary Traveling Between the Wars*. Oxford: Oxford University Press, 1980, 11.
159. Ibid. 10.
160. Ibid. 15–23.
161. Niels Horrebow, *The Natural History of Iceland*. London: A. Linde et al., 1758, vii.
162. Richard F. Burton, *Ultima Thule; Or, A Summer in Iceland*. London: William P. Nimmo, 1875, xi.
163. Auden and MacNeice, *Letters from Iceland*, 58.
164. Ibid. 63.
165. Auden, *The English Auden*, 188.
166. Auden and MacNeice, *Letters from Iceland*, 210–11.
167. Auden, *The English Auden*, 173–4.
168. Ibid. 217, 219.
169. Auden and MacNeice, *Letters from Iceland*, 197.
170. Ibid. 250, 253.
171. Ibid. 252.
172. Ibid. 59.
173. Edward Mendelson, *Early Auden*. London: Faber, 1981, 333.

174. Auden, *The English Auden*, 157–8.
175. David Gervais, *Literary Englands: Versions of 'Englishness' in Modern Writing*. Cambridge: Cambridge University Press, 1993, 157.
176. John Fuller, *A Reader's Guide to W. H. Auden*. London: Thames and Hudson, 1970, 107.
177. John R. Boly, 'Auden and Modern Theory', in *The Cambridge Companion to W. H. Auden*, 142 (137–51).
178. Mendelson, *Early Auden*, 337.
179. Auden, *The English Auden*, 155–7.
180. Gervais, *Literary Englands*, 157.
181. Auden, *The English Auden*, 222–3.
182. Aubrey de Selincourt, *The Channel Shore*. London: Robert Hale, 1953, 3, 5.
183. Ibid. 2.
184. Esty, *A Shrinking Island*, 218–19.
185. Auden, *The English Auden*, 223.
186. Louis MacNeice, *Collected Poems*, ed. Peter McDonald. London: Faber, 2007, 32–7.
187. John Kerrigan, 'The Ticking Fear', *London Review of Books*, 30.3 (7 February 2008), 15–18.
188. Andrew McNeillie, 'Editorial', *Archipelago*, 1 (Summer 2007), vii (vii–viii).
189. MacNeice, *Collected Poems*, 24.
190. Louis MacNeice, *Letters of Louis MacNeice*, ed. Jonathan Allison. London: Faber, 2010, 192.
191. See A. Landsborough Thomson, *Bird Migration*. London: Witherby, 1936, and C. J. Patten, *The Story of the Birds*. Sheffield: Pawson and Brailsford, 1928.
192. MacNeice, *Letters*, 459.
193. Alan Gillis, '"Any Dark Saying": Louis MacNeice in the Nineteen Fifties', *Irish University Review*, 42.1 (Spring 2012), 106 (105–23).
194. Terence Brown, '"What am I doing here?" Travel and MacNeice', in Fran Brearton and Edna Longley (eds), *Incorrigibly Plural: Louis MacNeice and his Legacy*. Manchester: Carcanet, 2012, 83 (72–84).
195. MacNeice, *Collected Poems*, 7–10.
196. Ibid. 3.
197. Ibid. 17–18.
198. Ibid. 25.
199. Ibid. 7–10, 24.
200. Ibid. 55.
201. Peter McDonald, *Louis MacNeice: The Poet in his Contexts*. Oxford: Clarendon Press, 1991, 1–9.
202. MacNeice, *Collected Poems*, 102.
203. Ibid. 117.
204. Ibid. 139.
205. Ibid. 139.
206. Ibid. 101.

207. Ibid. 128.

208. Ibid. 145.

209. Ibid. 163.

210. Ibid. 163.

211. Ibid. 158.

212. Ibid. 102.

213. Louis MacNeice, *I Crossed the Minch* [1938], intro. Tom Herron. Edinburgh: Polygon, 2007, 7.

214. Auden and MacNeice, *Letters from Iceland*, 113, 135.

215. MacNeice, *I Crossed the Minch*, 33.

216. Ibid. 13.

217. Ibid. 70.

218. Ibid. 3.

219. Ibid. 115.

220. Ibid. 74.

221. Ibid. 26.

222. Ibid. 7.

223. Tom Herron, 'Introduction', in MacNeice, *I Crossed the Minch*, xi.

224. MacNeice, *I Crossed the Minch*, 97–104.

225. Gordon, *Islands of the West*, 7.

226. MacNeice, *I Crossed the Minch*, 8.

227. See, for example, a report on Compton Mackenzie's account of life in Barra, 'Living off the Map', broadcast on BBC radio on 7 October 1936, in 'A Happy Island', *Irish Times*, 13 October 1936, 6, which laments that the 'virility' of the Outer Hebrides as described by Mackenzie is not to be found on Ireland's Atlantic islands.

228. Boswell's *A Tour to the Hebrides* was among the most widely read books in Dublin in December 1936: see 'What Dublin is Reading', *Irish Times*, 5 December 1936, 7.

229. MacNeice, *I Crossed the Minch*, 106–7.

230. Valentine Cunningham, 'MacNeice and Thirties (Classical) Pastoralism', in Brearton and Longley (eds), *Incorrigibly Plural*, 85–100.

231. George Thomson, *Studies in Ancient Greek Society: The Prehistoric Aegean.* London: Lawrence and Wishart, 1949, 540.

232. George Thomson, *Island Home: The Blasket Heritage.* Dingle: Brandon, 1988, 80.

233. Ibid. 85.

234. W. H. Auden, 'Introduction', *The Oxford Book of Light Verse.* London: Clarendon Press, 1938, xix (vii–xx).

235. MacNeice, *I Crossed the Minch*, 7.

236. Ibid. 74–5.

237. Ibid. 8.

238. Ibid. 200.

239. Ibid. 209.

240. Ibid. 14.

241. Ibid. 14. The translation is from MacNeice's own translation of *Agamemnon*, which he published in 1936: see Louis MacNeice, *The Agamemnon of Aeschylus*. London: Faber, 1936, 45.

242. MacNeice, *I Crossed the Minch*, 101.

243. Ibid. 212.

244. Valentine Cunningham, *British Writers of the Thirties*. Oxford: Oxford University Press, 1988, 351.

245. MacNeice, *I Crossed the Minch*, 16.

246. MacNeice, *Collected Poems*, 224.

247. Clair Wills, *That Neutral Island: A Cultural History of Ireland During the Second World War*. London: Faber, 2007, 71–8.

248. MacNeice, *I Crossed the Minch*, 18.

249. 'A Poet in the Hebrides', *The Times*, 5 April 1938, 10.

250. See Terence Brown, *The Literature of Ireland: Culture and Criticism*. Cambridge: Cambridge University Press, 2010, 137, and Heather Clark, 'Leaving Barra, Leaving Inishmore: Islands in the Irish Protestant Imagination', *Canadian Journal of Irish Studies*, 35.2 (Fall 2009), 32 (30–5).

251. MacNeice, *Collected Poems*, 68–71.

252. Cunningham, *British Writers of the Thirties*, 358.

253. MacNeice, *Collected Poems*, 71.

254. Raymond Williams, *Marxism and Literature*. Oxford: Oxford University Press, 1977, 122–3.

5

Social Bonds and Gendered Borders in Late Modernism

> Therefore if you insist upon fighting to protect me, or 'our' country, let it be understood, soberly and rationally between us, that you are fighting to gratify a sex instinct which I cannot share; to procure benefits which I have not shared and probably will not share; but not to gratify my instincts, or to protect either myself or my country. For . . . in fact, as a woman, I have no country. As a woman I want no country. As a woman my country is the whole world.
>
> Virginia Woolf, Three Guineas[1]

Virginia Woolf puts these objections to the warmongering rhetoric of the 1930s in the voice of a fictional 'outsider', who resents the language of common bonds, protection, and national unity, on the grounds that women have not been equal parties to the benefits of society, and therefore should not be expected to share the same passion for the defence or continuation of that society. Rationally, for Woolf, women exist outside of the bonds of nationality, for such bonds are dictated and governed by men, in their own interest and according to their own 'sex instinct'. Emotionally, she recognises that these bonds are not so easily loosed, but, she argues, if

> some love of England dropped into a child's ears by the cawing of rooks in an elm tree, by the splash of waves on a beach, or by English voices murmuring nursery rhymes, this drop of pure, if irrational, emotion she will make serve her to give to England first what she desires of peace and freedom for the whole world.[2]

This passage from *Three Guineas* is illustrative of what Susan Stanford Friedman identifies as a key watershed running through Woolf studies, between those who see Woolf as ultimately an internationalist, writing 'for the whole world', and those who see her as ultimately provincial, in which it is always 'England first'.[3] Friedman resists this distinction by arguing that Woolf's handling of geopolitical scales is more complex, that 'Her work – materialist as it so often is – exhibits an early feminist formulation of a locational politics', in which 'geopolitical power relations begin at home in the patriarchal structure of the family', and extend through the local, the national, and the global.[4] Woolf's 'locational politics' in this passage from *Three Guineas* are, indeed, quite specific. Her 'outsiders' are specifically the 'daughters of educated men', whose romantic notions of Englishness have been 'imbibed . . . from the governess', and the 'country' at stake is England, and not the Britain or even British Empire over which her fictional male addressee has some dominion, and from which he takes his title of King's Counsel.[5] The England which inspires love in the child is also associated with very particular and emblematic images, the same images of the elm tree, the waves, and the cradle songs of the nursery which Woolf associates with the 'burden' of Englishness in *Between the Acts*.[6] These three images in particular represent different ideas of how regions might be defined, by their distinctive biota (elms have a special place in the English cultural imagination),[7] by their boundedness (in this case, by the sea), and by their language and culture. Woolf's question, which is of course, as Friedman argues, a powerful one for contemporary feminism, but also for other social groups for whom the social contract is inequitable and unfulfilled, is, how are the cultural bonds and spatial borders of identity experienced differently according to gender? And, by extension, how are they experienced differently according to class, race, ethnicity, nationality, sexuality, region, and the various intersections and transactions between these categories?

This question is of special significance too for an archipelagic approach to the literatures and cultures of the Irish and British Isles. It is particularly notable, of course, that the islomania of the 1930s was a distinctly male phenomenon, often with significant consequences for the figuration (or sometimes the non-figuration) of women. Indeed, the story of the literary habitation of islands from Thomas More's *Utopia* (1516) to William Golding's *Lord of the Flies* (1954) is overwhelmingly male, and often solitary, with few exceptions. To adapt James Clifford's question in *Routes* about the gender implications of a focus on travel, does a focus on islands, coasts, and the sea inevitably privilege male experiences?[8] In the case of sea narratives, this is often obviously the case. Ships have conventionally been, and largely remain, predominantly crewed by men. In fishing communities, this can result in stark spatial and symbolic divisions. As John Mack observes, 'North Sea trawlermen not only bar women from their ships, but will not go to sea if a woman has even touched the guardrail of their boat.'[9] The same trawlermen, according to Redmond O'Hanlon, live in houses often 'set against the sea', facing inwards, like defensive squares:

> no one who earns his living from the real chaos of the sea would want to look at it as he goes to sleep — no, these squares are defensive only in the mind; in here, it's peace, the female, sex, the wife, domesticity, the children, the deep rewards of life. Out there it's . . .[10]

In Neil Gunn's *Morning Tide* (1931), it is a sign of Grace's growing maturity that she understands the opposing attitudes of her parents towards the elemental power of the sea, 'from which her mother recoiled, on which her father adventured'.[11] In Gunn's fishing community in Caithness, the separation of women from men is 'fateful and eternal', with Grace's mother shown to be the 'centre' and 'life-warmth' of the home, while her father is 'praised not merely for fine seamanship, but for the seamanship that conquers come what will'.[12]

So too, in Eiluned Lewis's *The Captain's Wife* (1943), the titular character, Lettice Peters, is the centre of the home, managing daily and seasonal routines, which are interrupted by the periodic shore leaves of her husband, which always begin with a lavish outpouring of exotic gifts, 'jars of preserved ginger and Chinese chow-chow, guava cheeses from Brazil and barrels of dried apples from California', and 'chinchilla furs' for her and her daughter, Matty.[13] Lettice thinks of these exotic goods as 'welcome additions to her store cupboard', but Lewis is subtly implying here the gendered temporal rhythms of sea life, in which the landbound captain's wife must think in the long term of stores and conservation, whereas she knows that her husband 'cannot really afford the presents he heaped on the family with so lavish a hand'.[14] Matty also notices this gendered rhythm of behaviour in her aunt and uncle, in the contrast between the prim, feminine order of thrift and discipline of her aunt, and the extravagance, impetuosity, and high spirits of her sea-captain uncle, home on a few days' leave, which she will forever associate with the sealskin muff, lined with satin, which he buys for her in a department store in Liverpool.[15] For the men of the novel, appearing intermittently between the excitement and adventure of voyages around the world, the sea means opportunity, wealth, and novelty. Lewis makes it clear that Lettice and her daughter envy this life: Lettice remembers her early married life at sea with her husband as the happiest times of her life, while Matty wishes that she could grow up to be a boy, so that she could go to sea. Yet, for the women of the novel, the sea is a dividing space, wasteful and terrible, and Lewis draws our attention to the gendering of the sea itself when a ship is wrecked off the coast of her fictional setting, 'Idrisland', based upon St David's Head, in the tidal race known as 'The Bitches'.

In such fictional depictions, the sea is not a space outside of society, but an extended arena for the social divisions of labour which prevail upon land. Philip Steinberg argues that the ocean is a heterotopic space, located 'within a series of contradictions within capitalism's material processes and spatial properties', which both challenges and reproduces the 'dominant order of society'.[16] Yet, with the exception of a few examples of feminist science fiction in which the sea is a space of alternative conceptions of social organisation, it is not clear from Steinberg's account that the ocean is heterotopic in terms of gendered power structures. In Margaret Cohen's study of sea fiction, it is also the case that female protagonists are exceptional, and the capacities for sea novels to depict shipboard life as model republics is somewhat limited by the almost complete absence of women from them. Although Cohen argues that the message of 'democratic empowerment' encoded in sea fiction was 'translatable to other fraternities – and sororities', it is nonetheless the case, as she states, that 'Women are generally barred from acceding to craft's empowered agency', and the few examples she cites are cross-dressing female pirates from the eighteenth century.[17] In the twentieth century, life at sea remained predominantly male, and rather than producing alternative or potentially utopian models of social organisation, the equation of maritime work with masculinity served to intensify gendered hierarchies of labour. Such iconic films as John Grierson's *Drifters* (1929) and Robert Flaherty's *Man of Aran* (1934) promoted the idea that fishing in particular retained an association with a primitive, pre-modern struggle between men and nature, an image of masculinity as mastery, which was eagerly consumed (and presumably reproduced) by a generation of men who were mainly living in cities and working as cogs in an industrial and capitalist machine. The masculine labour of the sea, it could be argued, remains the dominant narrative of maritime museums, which, as Phyllis Leffler argues, have tended to be organised around 'ships, watercraft, ship models . . . maritime instruments [and] the heroism of naval leaders'.[18] As Valerie Burton argues, the gendering of maritime work itself is also particularly entrenched and persistent: 'Men and women work apart even in the most recently (re)organised of fisheries.'[19]

The coast, it could be argued, is an equally problematic gendered space in the twentieth century. Seaside resorts such as Blackpool, Brighton, and Scarborough advertised for visitors using posters depicting girls in risqué swimming costumes. The seaside was associated with 'dirty girls', as Peter Gurney shows in his study of the Mass Observation survey of Blackpool in 1937, which was based upon an image which reflected class divisions as much as gender divisions. The survey was conducted in Blackpool largely because, like other seaside resorts, it was reputed to be 'a place of sin and illicit sex', an idea reinforced by the publicity images of female bathers, the slot machine peep shows, and 'naughty' postcards.[20] Philip Larkin demonstrates an acute perception of the sexual politics of these gendered representations of the seaside, perhaps surprisingly, in his poem 'Sunny Prestatyn', in which the railway poster depicting a girl 'in tautened white satin', advertising 'Come to Sunny Prestatyn', is clearly understood as a sexualised and fetishised object. It is not long after the poster is 'slapped up', an appropriately resonant image of domestic violence, that it is defaced, with 'Huge tits and a fissured crotch . . . scored well in, and the space / Between her legs held scrawls / That set her fairly astride / A tuberous cock and balls'.[21] The scene of Larkin's poem is not itself, of course, the seaside, but a billboard poster which could be anywhere, and the focus therefore is on the symbolic place of the seaside in cultural representations. In itself, this reflects the same geographical relationship which John Betjeman indicates in his poem 'Beside the Seaside', when he writes that 'England leaves / Her centre for her tide-line'.[22] The seaside is peripheral geographically to the major centres of population in England, and, as can be seen in the Mass Observation survey of Blackpool, it was also assumed to be a space apart from normal social rules and inhibitions. The survey expected women to behave differently, to be more flirtatious, more sexually active, more 'available', than in their working and living environments.

Similarly, Betjeman begins his poem with a mass exodus from the towns to the coast in which it seems that the attractions of the seaside are classless: people differ only in how they get to the seaside, the rich in their Rovers, the middle classes in their Morris Eights, the poor by train and on foot. Yet, the chosen seaside destination itself is indicative of social class, as well as every facet of behaviour and dress: 'A single topic occupies our minds. / 'Tis hinted at or boldly emblazoned in / Our accents, clothes and ways of eating fish . . . That topic all-absorbing, as it was, / Is now and ever shall be, to us – CLASS.'[23] The seaside was not a place apart, in other words, but deeply encoded in the same gender and class structures of capitalist society elsewhere. J. B. Priestley came close to articulating this argument in *English Journey* (1933) in his disdainful depiction of Blackpool, which he described as 'a complete and essential product of industrial democracy', which was replacing 'the old hearty [English] vulgarity' with a 'machine-made' culture borrowed from America.[24] For Priestley, Blackpool extended the industrial processes of Lancashire into the leisured space of the seaside, so that what was fictionalised for visitors as paradise on the periphery was often merely a more intense projection of the same hegemonic relations which governed the workplace and the home. Moreover, the trip to the seaside was not a retreat from the industrial metropolis, but a foray into the juxtaposed locations of modernity, with, as Priestley described, 'Broadway hits', 'nigger minstrels', and Hollywood 'talkies' performing along the same sea-front as electric trams and illuminations, palm readers and hypnotists, bingo halls and sweet shops. For Doreen Massey, to focus on the spatial distribution of gender power relations necessarily entails a recognition of how 'localities can in a sense be present in one another, both inside and outside at the same time', a view 'which stresses the construction of specificity through interrelations rather than through the imposition of boundaries and the counterposition of one identity *against* an other'.[25] The coast may appear to present itself as a boundary, and the seaside may seem carnivalesque, where social and sexual regulation is suspended, but these fictions have definite functions within the construction of a normative political subjectivity. Hegemonic constructions of gender, race, nation, sexuality, and class are reinforced, perhaps even amplified, at the coastline.

It is clear from Priestley's account of Blackpool that the seaside has also had a long and troubled relationship with the politics of racial representation. Priestley bemoans, as another sign of 'industrial democracy', the 'weary negroid ditties' of the blackface minstrels who form a core part of seaside entertainment.[26] Indeed, it is important to keep in focus the significance of a discursive structure of lament and belatedness to representations of the seaside, especially in terms of race and nation. As Betjeman did before him, Larkin was right to see the summer exodus to the sea as 'half an annual pleasure, half a rite', one key function of which was to replay the past as if it was 'Still going on, all of it, still going on!'.[27] By the time Larkin wrote this in 1969, the seaside was both at the forefront of entertainment technologies and late capitalist consumption, and a capital site of nostalgia and lament for a supposed golden age of national unity.

The significance of the coast as a battleground in the Second World War is an important factor in nostalgic discourses of the seaside, and is one of the reasons why, as Les Back describes, seaside towns 'occupy a special location in the national imaginary'.[28] Back's work focuses, however, on the more recent ways in which seaside towns like Margate, Dover, and Hastings have become 'the new frontier for the defenders of exclusive national culture and "rights for whites"'.[29] For Daniel Burdsey, 'the English seaside is a highly racialized environment', for several reasons: the resident and tourist populations of seaside resorts in England tend to be 'overwhelmingly white'; this in turn makes the seaside more likely to function as a 'landscape of exclusion' for non-white ethnic minorities; and 'contemporary seaside amusements and entertainments promote exoticized, orientalist representations of the ethnic or racial Other', in ways which are different but in some respects continuous from the blackface minstrels which Priestley disdained.[30] The ritual summer exodus to the beach, therefore, might be seen in this racialised context not as an innocent leisure pursuit, but to some degree an act of national and potentially racial signification, performing a fantasy, however conscious or unconscious, of an imaginary past of social and racial homogeneity. The performance of such a ritual on the highly symbolic maritime borders of the nation raises difficult questions for the transformative aspirations of the archipelagic model, for in the ritual re-making of a 'white' England at the seaside, bolstered by orientalist fantasies in the amusements, and a plentiful supply of national flags and gol-liwog dolls in the sea-front shops, we face the residual yet potent mythologies of English imperialism.

The spaces in which the archipelagic conception of the Irish and British Isles which I have been tracing in this book is most visible, then – the coast, the sea, and islands – have clearly been systematically gendered, classed, sexualised, and racialised. Yet, in the twentieth century, the most dramatic development in literary history has been the massive extension of the liter-ary franchise, as it were, and the surge of great and populous traditions of women's writing, working-class writing, and writing from more diverse ethnic groups than have hitherto been celebrated in British and Irish litera-ture. This chapter examines a series of literary works which might be aligned with those traditions as they turn to the coast, to seas, and to islands, in the late modernist and postwar era, with a particular focus on women's writing and Caribbean writing to extend and problematise the critical frameworks of the archipelagic.

'(THERE HAD BEEN A WAR ON)': LATE MODERNISM AND THE LITTORAL IMAGINATION IN ELIZABETH TAYLOR'S *A VIEW OF THE HARBOUR*

Elizabeth Taylor's *A View of the Harbour* begins with trawlers putting out to sea, and ends with a yacht hoving into the harbour, so replicating the rhythm of those fictions of sea adventure and endeavour which Margaret Cohen has recently shown to be central to the evolution of the novel form itself.[31] Yet, despite depicting recurrent attempts to imagine the coastline as picturesque, adventurous, or romantic, Taylor's novel repeatedly figures its darkness, quea-siness, and noise. The novel inhabits a peripheral landscape shaped by interac-tion with the sea, and ruled by the temporalities of sea life. The rhythm which pulses through the lives of the characters who live in the fictional seaside town of Newby, closely modelled upon Scarborough, is measured by the waves and the tides, the coming and going of the fishing fleet, and the lighting of the lighthouse lamp. The seasonal rhythm of the coastline also gives the novel its peculiarly dark and unyielding outlook:

> Spring comes last of all to the seaside. The tight buds of those shrubs
> which seemed to kneel upon the cliff-side looked as if they never would
> unfurl. Out in the country, fields, hedgerows, woods exulted with
> green; birds sang. In London, barrows were stacked with rhubarb and
> daffodils. But at the harbour only the light changed and the days gradu-
> ally lengthened.[32]

The novel is remarking upon a meteorological and ecological phenomenon
here – it is true evidently that the density of water, and the cooling of air
over the seas, creates the conditions whereby the coastline remains slowest to
turn to spring – but Taylor's 'tight buds . . . [which] looked as if they never
would unfurl' are also, of course, sexually symbolic, after the manner of Eliot,
or even Lawrence. The popular idea of the seaside as the site of Bacchanalian
excess and carnivalesque revelry is acknowledged in the novel, figured most
knowingly perhaps in the reference to the Donald McGill postcard of 'a fat
woman bending down to make a sand-castle, red bloomers', with the caption
'"What would you do, chums?" printed underneath'.[33] Yet Taylor depicts
instead a small, provincial outpost, shunned apparently even by the turn of the
seasons, and threatened with decay and infertility. Almost all of the characters are tightly bound in their own wintry shells, frustrated in their desperate
search for romance, or resigned to the convenience of a loveless marriage.
The novel ends with an impending marriage, and the possibility that the
comically named Prudence, a bronchial sufferer who constantly goes out into
the cold night air of the harbour, might form a relationship with the young
poet, Geoffrey Lloyd, but neither prospect is depicted romantically, or even
hopefully.

The coastline was repeatedly figured in late nineteenth- and early
twentieth-century culture as a vital scene of rejuvenation, even simply as a
visual spectacle. As Lara Feigel and Alexandra Harris argue in their collection of essays, *Modernism on Sea*, the literary geography of English modernism
encompasses 'the cliffs and promenades of the English coast', as much as the
more obvious urban locations.[34] The symbolic significance of those seaside
locations recurs in Taylor's work, but with different inflections. When Lily
Wilson wishes to escape the salacious undertones of the librarian's 'Puritanical
conversation', for example, she climbs the hill which lies between Newby's
beach and harbour, to gain some sort of relief and pleasure from the view.
Yet, looking down upon the shoreline, she has to hold back her tears, and
'turned away from the sight of the place which only love had made tolerable'.[35] But then she opens her eyes again, and looks 'deliberately at the long
sands on either side of the pier and the waves creaming over in silence far
below'.[36] Her determination to look again is stoical, but it is clear nonetheless

that the shoreline bears no new possibilities for Lily, marks no new beginning, just as regaining her cherished view of the harbour does not prove to rejuvenate Mrs Bracey's failing health, but merely provides her with more sources of prurient gossip. The novel repeatedly alludes to the shoreline as a marginal space, defined by sea and sky as marking the limits of habitable land, yet this is no Romantic, or modernist, sublime space, of death, or nature, or terror. Instead, it is a kind of anti-sublime, a bathos, or comic depth, into which the pretensions of Taylor's characters are relentlessly, and mercilessly, ducked.

Taylor's novel is an anti-romance, drawn more purposefully towards grim and lonely endings, and it is poignant that the closing funeral of Mrs Bracey offers more hope than the novel's promised wedding. The implication of Taylor's passage on the late arrival of spring to the seaside might be to suggest that summer's fruits will still appear, but for many of the characters in the novel, it seems, a late flowering may be too late. Iris dreams fruitlessly of the chance of a film star appearing in the harbour bar; Maisie has missed her opportunity to find love with Eddie; Lily's reputation is ruined by the false gossip of Mrs Bracey; Beth Cazabon seems hopelessly detached from the real emotional dramas of her family and friends as she wrestles to complete her novel, including an affair between her husband and her best friend, Tory Foyle; and Tory attempts to escape from loneliness and scandal by marrying an old sailor, Bertram Hemingway, who himself looks upon the prospect joylessly, and with some trepidation. It is particularly striking in this novel, however, how closely the anti-romantic turns of plot and character are wedded to an anti-littoral aesthetic. The sea and the coastline seem perpetually to darken the mood, so that it might almost be described as a pathetic fallacy in which landscape, or in this case seascape, generates or determines the action of the novel. The coastline is described as 'colourless and windswept', as 'a rather odd locality', as 'dingy' and 'sordid', only becoming picturesque at a distance, and the sea is repeatedly figured as 'dark'.[37] The entertainments of the harbour town are also portrayed in gloomy terms: the waxwork museum displays 'the unfamiliar faces of forgotten murderers', the harbour bar is empty and grim, and the librarian is a prurient censor, who seems to be stalking Lily Wilson. *A View of the Harbour* is a seaside novel, written in the peak period of seaside holidays, but it resolutely demythologises the popular ideal of the seaside as a space of freedom, pleasure, and excess, the ideal upon which Graham Greene and Elizabeth Bowen had already drawn in *Brighton Rock* (1938) and *The Death of the Heart* (1938) respectively. As Nicola Beauman's biography suggests, Taylor's novel shares the same melancholic depiction of the seaside as Marcel Carné's film *Le Quai des Brumes* (1938), in which Nelly tells Jean 'every time dawn breaks we think something new will happen, something fresh. And then the sun sets and we just go to bed.'[38]

This anti-littoral aesthetic is, I want to argue, connected closely to the aftermath of modernism, indeed, to use a shipping metaphor, to what follows in the wake of modernism. The most obvious modernist intertext of Taylor's novel is Woolf's *To the Lighthouse*. The sea can be heard throughout Taylor's novel too, with the lighthouse a constantly remarked presence. Like Woolf's novel, the completion of a painting forms part of the plot structure, and the traumatic consequences of a major war are figured in parenthesis. Yet, in almost every respect, Taylor's novel is a bathetic revision of these elements of Woolf's novel. Bertram's painting, which begins with a line, ends in failure, and is in any case possibly the kind of seascape depiction which Woolf's novel disparages as 'green and grey, with lemon-coloured sailing-boats, and pink women on the beach'.[39] It could be argued that Bertram is modelled upon the Scarborough-based artist Frank Henry Mason, who had served in the Royal Navy and became a famous artist of marine and coastal subjects, especially for idyllic railway posters, usually painted in a 'light impressionist' style, except that Bertram is not depicted as a successful artist. Bertram conceives his painting as a companion piece, or really as competition, for a painting titled 'View of the Harbour' by a Mr Walker, which hangs in a dark corner of the harbour bar and which Bertram thinks is 'all painted in brown gravy', and imagines in contrast 'his own picture shimmering with light'.[40] But his painting fails to capture the time of day, 'the very thing [he] most hoped to do', and the 'strokes of colour' which should give the impression of light instead 'had the congealed appearance of sealing-wax'.[41] The painting is no vision, then, but simply a view, and Taylor further underscores the bathos of this moment by having Bertram present the painting to the bar owner, Mr Pallister, whose response is to remark that it is 'Interesting . . . what two people can make of the same view. We all see places a bit different to what the next man does.'[42] With such wisdom ringing in his ears, Bertram gets ready to leave the harbour, presumably to make way for 'the next man'.

Woolf's novel abounds in tragedy, love, and vision. *A View of the Harbour* is a novel about monotony, loneliness, and resignation, all the while seen through a relentlessly sardonic lens. Taylor is perhaps most sardonic about the figure of the novelist herself, Beth Cazabon, the name itself undermining her pretensions to writing great work, and signalling her detachment from the world around her. Beth is depicted ironically as a novelist of 'perception', as so involved emotionally and imaginatively in the lives and loves of her characters that she seems oblivious to her husband's affair with her best friend, so caught up in the story she writes of a dying child that, as her own daughter turns up for lunch, she 'could not bring herself to welcome this living one'.[43] She is a novelist whose work apparently is full of funerals, but who has never been to one.[44] Yet Beth is also a kind of Lily Briscoe figure, at least in her determination to write, and in the politics of that determination. Taylor brings Beth's feminism into focus when her aptly named best friend, Tory Foyle, takes her place for a day in the family home, and fulfils the domestic duties so well 'that it was almost a reproach'.[45] The implications of this scene are transferred on to Prudence's pet cats, where at mealtimes the female cat waits for the male cat to take his fill of food before she will eat, even when Beth tries to make the female 'betray her nature'.[46] Here Taylor makes clear the context in which Beth's writing, and her frequently figured oblivion to her husband and children, is socially coded as unnatural, and entails a complex interplay of guilt, pleasure, and necessity. Compared to Lily Briscoe's refusal to marry, which is her own declaration of *non serviam*, the everyday manifestations of Beth's determination to write are portrayed comically and bathetically, and, of course, closely mirror, in self-deprecating fashion, the compromises constantly negotiated by Taylor herself. In this sense, Beth is also a kind of Mrs Ramsay figure, again comically, when for example she responds to a compliment by Tory's son, Edward, by saying, with a laugh, 'I was beginning to feel I was nothing in myself'.[47] The laugh here is arguably characteristic of late modernism's distinction from modernism, as Sara Crangle has explored in an essay on 'Ivy Compton-Burnett and Risibility'.[48]

N. H. Reeve argues in relation to allusions to Woolf's novel in *A Wreath of Roses* (1949) that 'Taylor's use of Woolf seems to exhibit some classic symptoms of the struggle with the strong predecessor, an uncertain wavering between homage and parody'.[49] Both homage and parody are key characteristics of Taylor's use of Woolf, but in *A View of the Harbour* the allusions to Woolf are more consistent, and less agonistic, than in *A Wreath of Roses*. As Reeve goes on to show, indeed, what distinguishes Taylor from Woolf is the refusal of 'the apocalyptic imagining' of modernism in Taylor's work. The best example of this in *A View of the Harbour* is the figuration of the war. Woolf's parenthetical references to the First World War are transformative and momentous: no relationship remains unchanged between the first and third sections of the novel, and a decisive break with the past has occurred. Taylor's allusions to the Second World War are equally parenthetical. Parts of aircraft and wreckage are dredged up from the seabed in trawler nets, with 'crabs, plaice, sole, cod'.[50] The possibility that the harbour café might serve tinned salmon, and not freshly caught fish, still lingers, and salmon pink is a recurrent colour motif in Taylor's palette. The deserted bar still bears a 'soiled card' announcing 'We Do Not Recognise The Possibility of Defeat', a wonderfully ambivalent statement which can be read as either stoicism or solipsism. Mrs Wilson wonders on first sight if Bertram Hemingway is a spy, 'forgetting that the war was over'.[51] The novel dwells on neither the significance of the war, nor the significance of its ending, and it is this refusal of significance, of momentousness, which Taylor shares, albeit in a different mode of writing, with Beckett in *Waiting for Godot*, or Dylan Thomas in 'A Refusal to Mourn the Death, by Fire, of a Child in London'.

The earliest reference to the war in the novel, however, is the most interesting in terms of Taylor's tone. As Bertram Hemingway looks at the view of the harbour and the sea-front, contemplating his tea, we are told that 'The scene was empty again, except for men gathering up coils of rusty barbed-wire (there had been a war on) from the foreshore'.[52] The symbolism of rusty barbed-wire on the seashore itself is obvious in relation to the mode of picturesque representation which Bertram has been contemplating. In fact, Bertram has presumably had to be ruthlessly selective in constructing his 'view' of the harbour to avoid the unpicturesque remnants of wartime defences. But the parenthetical phrase 'there had been a war on' somehow undermines the potential gravity of this allusion to war. In parenthesis, it reads of course as if it was spoken as an 'aside', a digressive reminder to the reader, in case the reader was unaware of that little thing called war. And it is 'a war', not 'the war', the pervasive contraction with which we are most familiar in national discourse, as in 'Don't mention the war'. That it is 'a war' makes it preposterously unclear which war, and when, as if it did not matter. Moreover, the inclusion of the word 'on' to make the phrase 'there had been a war on' is arguably suggestive of an occasional event, such as a fair or a church fete, the mess from which has now to be cleared up. War had been 'on', now it is off, but lurking in that dismissive, digressive, parenthetical phrase, with its apparently redundant adverb, is the implication of the always imminent possibility of war's recurrence. The tone is startlingly light, almost blithe, refusing the mythology and the momentousness of 'the war', but the implication is resoundingly bleak.

There is bathos, therefore, in the tone of Taylor's novel too, in this case taking the parenthesising of war which Woolf had used to such powerful effect in *To the Lighthouse* (and which forms the basis and title of David Jones's late modernist epic poem of 1937, *In Parenthesis*), and adapting it to undermine the egregious significance of war. This is wholly understandable as a manifestation of what Reeve rightly characterises in the period as the feeling of 'tired horror' which followed the end of the war.[53] But it is also significant as a mode of engagement with the aesthetics and politics of modernism. Bathos performs a vital and prominent function in many major works of literary modernism: it is arguably the key mode of Joyce's rewriting of *The Odyssey*, it abounds in Eliot's *The Waste Land* as a way of juxtaposing the glorious past and the sordid present, and it is a recurrent feature of *To the Lighthouse*, as when Lily hears the word 'science' and thinks of 'sections of potatoes', for example, or even the fact that Lily completes her painting, achieves her vision, after ten years, with a 'sudden intensity' by painting 'a line there, in the centre'.[54]

In modernism, broadly speaking, bathos functions in juxtaposition with the sublime, but as Tyrus Miller has recently argued of the late modernist poets of the 1930s, that rhetorical distinction between sublimity and bathos depends upon 'intricate, multi-faceted interactions between figural language and the broader social contexts in which texts and performances are deployed'.[55] In what Miller describes as a 'general social crisis of meaning' in Britain in the 1930s, the literary registers of high and low culture may have become unstable, but in Taylor's *A View of the Harbour* culture appears to be flat. Allusions to popular culture abound, from film stars such as Cecil Beaton, Noel Coward, and Lawrence Olivier, and the cinema-inspired fantasies of romance, to seaside postcards and entertainments, children's hymns, Victorian sensation novels, and the cabaret singer Yvette Guilbert, of whom Prudence observes that her 'father has a picture of her in a book'.[56] These allusions are interspersed, but not contrasted, with references to Jane Austen, Charlotte Brontë, Tennyson, Dickens, Sterne, Woolf, and Smollett, among many others. The comedy of the interspersion of popular and high culture is acknowledged to some extent: a review of Beth's novel turns up in a fish and chip wrapper, for example, and the librarian, whom Mrs Bracey thinks symbolises 'culture, the dusty novels, the little dead worlds of other people's make believe', stamps the stigma 'For Adults Only' on *Jane Eyre* and *Madame Bovary*, and, for this reason only, the library's copies of these novels are 'full of loose leaves, black with grease, fish-smelling . . . fallen to pieces' as the 'bewildered' and 'misled' have sought in vain for pornography.[57] There is no scorn here for low culture: the novel seems to sympathise as much with those readers frustrated by the lack of pornography as with those repulsed by the censor's stamp, and to revel in the writing done in train carriages and on kitchen tables just as surely as it identifies with Prudence's concealed yawn when Geoffrey is reading poetry from a 'suede-covered book'.[58] The homage to Woolf runs cheek by jowl with the novel's frequent and playful flirtations with the conventions of popular fiction genres: the gothic scene of waxwork dummies which Lily fears look alive, the creepy, prurient librarian who censors any mention of rape and who stalks Lily back to her home, the retired sailor and amateur painter who looks more like a spy, the story of Snow White and the poisoned apple which Beth reads to Stevie on the evening that Tory has been playing 'step-mother', the various romance plots of Eddie and Maisie, or Iris, and Prudence and Geoffrey, or Bertram and Lily, or Tory, or the melodramatic possibility that Tory and Robert's affair will be revealed to Beth. The novel contains many possible sensation, romance, or adventure plots within it, all of which are quietly but decisively spurned. Here it is important to note Alice Ferrebe's argument of Taylor's 'deconstruction of the romance genre' in her novels throughout the 1950s.[59]

It is not just a pun to say that the novel refuses to harbour any of these plots, any of these sensation narratives, nor any of the modernist imaginings of visions, epiphanies, and momentous transformations. The location of the novel is central to this late modernist aesthetic of negation and risibility. By location, of course, I do not mean Scarborough, or its fictional pseudonym Newby, although Scarborough is not without significance as a basis for the novel's figuration of the seaside and harbour. Taylor's novel is skilfully loose in the details of its setting: the seaside town is within an easy train ride of London, for example, and tourists are described as 'Flashy London people' who come 'down' to Newby, yet it is also down the coast from Scotland, isolated on the coastline, and sufficiently peripheral for Robert to allude to its 'odd locality'.[60] Perhaps comparable to Woolf in her projection of St Ives as the Hebrides in *To the Lighthouse*, Taylor's lack of geographical specificity allows 'Newby' to work as a generic seaside location, and for the coast to have a significant symbolic function within its delineation of a late modernist, and postwar, aesthetic sensibility. The coastal location is by no means incidental, or decorative; indeed, we might group the novel with a proliferation of literary works which use coastal locations symbolically in and around the end of the Second World War, such as John Betjeman's 'Margate, 1940' (1945), Philip Larkin's 'The North Ship' (1945), Norman Nicholson's *The Fire of the Lord* (1944) and *The Green Shore* (1947), James Hanley's *The Closed Harbour* (1952), Dylan Thomas's *Under Milk Wood* (1954), even Samuel Beckett's *The Unnamable* (1953), in which the narrator tells us 'When I come to the coast I turn back inland'.[61] But the coast is also precisely the location, as Philip Steinberg argues, 'where civilization met "anti-civilization"', where 'Staid London ladies and gentlemen literally and figuratively "let their hair down"' and enjoyed 'risqué entertainment'.[62]

The coastal setting is important not just because of its symbolism as a protective boundary during the Second World War, nor just because of its significance in those great modernist excavations of possible sources of rejuvenation and originality. The ebbs and flows of Taylor's novel, its recurrent fascination with the tidal rhythms which provide a sense of the coast as an 'other-timed landscape', in Owain Jones's words, connect it to a moment of profound scepticism of the littoral aesthetics of the modern age.[63] As Alain Corbin's study *The Lure of the Sea* demonstrates, the coastal sea only became aestheticised as a sublime space in the Western imagination during the Romantic period, with the seaside resort emerging as the most populist and material manifestation of that process in the nineteenth century.[64] In Taylor's novel, when day-trippers arrive to experience this sublime space, however, they find 'nothing to see', merely the open sea, and a dull view of the harbour; their only pleasure is the story told to them by the lighthouse keeper of birds who are dazed by the flash of the light, and dashed to pieces against the glass, a story which 'was not true; he had merely read something of the kind in a book'.[65] All the terror, and the eroticism, of the seaside, Taylor's novel suggests, belong to books: Mrs Bracey calls out for 'A nice book about the South Sea Islands' which will show 'Some of the tricks these natives get up to, the dirty monkeys!', and tells Lily of the dangers of her husband going overseas to 'brothels of the Orient . . . which she had read about in a book the curate had lent her'.[66] It is through such an exotic prism that the seaside comes to have its romantic, sensationalist associations, and the narrator at one point corrects this vision, pointing out that Mrs Bracey, who imbues every liaison she witnesses from her window with erotic or adventurous meaning, fails to see the truth that in such desperate attempts to find love or pleasure, there is in fact 'no romance, no delight'.[67] Instead, the novel repeatedly punctures the possibility of romance, reminding us of the wrecks and corpses thrown up by the sea, the hard materiality of fishing for a living, and the quiet, desperate, and forlorn hope that a newcomer might bring romance, whereas, as Teddy Foyle thinks when he emerges on the harbour at the end of the novel, 'Nothing has changed'.[68]

'AN OLD RACE DRIVEN BACK ON ITSELF':
ISLANDNESS AND THE RETREAT FROM EMPIRE IN
BRENDA CHAMBERLAIN'S *TIDE-RACE*

Mollie Panter-Downes's novel *One Fine Day* (1947) sighs in relief that war is over, that England has survived, that life and love can go on. Set between the Sussex Downs and the coast, the novel attends to the landscape for slow signs of recovery from the wounds of war and the threats of invasion. The village of Wealding is close to the sea, but 'turned its face away from the blue towards the green', so that 'the presence of the sea could be felt only as a sort of salty vibration in the air, like a watch ticking in the pocket, reminding the landlubber of his islander's destiny'.[69] The village gives the illusion of perfect peace, nestled in trees, but 'Coils of barbed wire [were] still rusting among the sorrel', with 'Sandbags pouring out sodden guts from the old strong-point among the bracken', and the deserted remains of a 'bombed cottage'.[70] Not so long ago, these images remind us, 'the nearness of the sea had been no watch ticking comfortably in the pocket, but a loud brazen question striking constantly in the brain, When? When?'.[71] The novel shrinks from the sea, and the heroine, Laura, seeks consolation among the fern and foxgloves of the downs, upon the hill-top on which 'something said I am England. I will remain.'[72] Laura and her husband Stephen belong to that class of Englishmen and women who 'had helped to make the map an English pink all over the world . . . accepting the exile which in the end would make England seem an exile'.[73]

But the war finally ends this world of empire, as it ends that most comfortable of nineteenth-century English maxims, 'Safe as houses'.[74] The decay of their own house, the slow invasion of their garden with weeds, the shortage of servants and gardeners to maintain their house, are signs of contraction on a domestic scale which mirror the geopolitical contractions of empire. Like Woolf's *Between the Acts*, and Taylor's *A View of the Harbour*, then, *One Fine Day* asks what does remain of England, and what will become of England, when it has contracted within its own shores and its own borders?

The war had evidently heightened this sense of England as an island, that geographical misnomer so biased towards the view from the Sussex Downs. Winston Churchill used the phrases 'this Island' and 'our Island' repeatedly in his celebrated wartime speeches, even clustering such phrases for rhetorical effect in his speech to the House of Commons on 4 June 1940 after the evacuation of Dunkirk, in which he famously vowed:

> We shall go on to the end, we shall fight in France, we shall fight on the seas and oceans, we shall fight with growing confidence and growing strength in the air, we shall defend our Island, whatever the cost may be, we shall fight on the beaches, we shall fight on the landing grounds, we shall fight in the fields and in the streets, we shall fight in the hills; we shall never surrender.[75]

As Richard Toye argues, Churchill's speeches were made for 'immediate political needs', and are remembered now as evidence of a national unity which they were in fact striving hard to forge.[76] In the same speech, rarely quoted now by historians, Churchill commented on the stringent measures necessary to curtail dissent and punish traitors. So too, in the postwar mythology of the stoic little island which never admitted the possibility of defeat against the might of Nazism, the passage quoted above is frequently cited, but not the sentiment which immediately follows it, in which Churchill states that even if 'this Island or a large part of it were subjugated and starving, then our Empire beyond the seas, armed and guarded by the British Fleet, would carry on the struggle', until, finally, he hopes that the 'New World' (a quaintly colonial term for America) would liberate the 'old'.[77] In full, the closing passage of Churchill's speech captures the changing political realities of an 'island' which still ruled over five hundred million people around the globe, but which was rapidly losing power and influence to the rising empire from the other side of the North Atlantic.

As Wendy Webster argues, when Churchill died in 1965, 'the victory celebrated at [his] funeral . . . more or less erased the imperial war effort'.[78] Churchill's military and political careers were forged in the colonial enterprise, fighting wars in India and Sudan, and serving as Indian Secretary and

Colonial Secretary in the British government. It was the Empire, and a large part of the former Empire, which Churchill told the British people would save their island should a Nazi invasion succeed. Yet Churchill's own plans for his funeral had no place for imperial history or Commonwealth nations, but emphasised the Anglo-American alliance of the war and the postwar world. Webster argues too that the national cult of Churchill, which really developed in the 1950s, chose to elide the 'different national identities within Britishness', celebrating him as an English leader.[79] Moreover, the cult of Churchill followed suit with 'the eclipse of a "people's war" and the shift to an exclusive image, focusing on élite white martial masculinity', a shift which can be steadily traced through the proliferation of postwar British war films which celebrated a succession of white upper-class male heroes as the epitome of national identity.[80] As the Empire disintegrated, therefore, and the cold winters of the postwar years set in, the 'island' to which Britain had contracted was being redefined in intensely racialised, gendered, and Anglocentric terms.

Robert Colls traces the modern significance of Britain as 'an island race . . . half-maritime, half-rural' to the end of the nineteenth century, and the beginning of the decline of the Empire.[81] The concept was given its fullest geographical explanation in the work of Halford Mackinder in *Britain and the British Seas* (1902), and this was the basis for Winston Churchill's description of 'our island story' in *A History of the English-Speaking Peoples* (1956). Churchill saw the protective insularity and Anglocentrism of Britain as inevitable consequences of the lie of the land, for the 'island' was 'not widely sundered from the Continent, and so tilted that its mountains lie all to the west and north, while south and east is a gently undulating landscape of wooded valleys, open downs, and slow rivers'.[82] It was a landscape which at its most populous and wealthy was accessible to the continent, but the narrow strip of water called the Straits of Dover meant that the islanders could give 'every practice, every doctrine that comes to it from abroad, its own peculiar turn and imprint'.[83] As the English Channel distinguished 'Britain' from Europe, so too for Churchill the geology of 'our island' distinguished the English 'home-land' in the south and east from its other parts, and again this followed Mackinder, who had written:

> The contrast between the south-east and the north-west of Britain, between the plains and low coasts towards the continent, and the cliff-edged uplands of the oceanic border, with all the resultant differences – agricultural, industrial, racial, and historical – depends on a fundamental distinction in rock structure.[84]

It was Britain's position as 'a group of islands' off the shores of a continent, Mackinder argued, which determined its 'complementary' qualities of 'insularity and universality', qualities which were distributed to different degrees geographically and historically. Geographically, 'England' could be the root of a universal empire while Scotland and Ireland remained more insular. Historically, in Mackinder's words, 'Before Columbus, the insularity was more evident than the universality',[85] whereas perhaps an uncomfortable thought for Churchill, seeking to celebrate the legacies of empire in the global spread of 'English-speaking peoples', was that after the Second World War, the insularity would prevail over the universality once more.

What, then, did it mean to be an island once again? What did it mean to belong to what Brenda Chamberlain characterised in *Tide-race* (1962) as 'an old race driven back on itself along the sea-margin'?[86] *Tide-race* is Chamberlain's account of the fourteen years she spent living on Bardsey Island, off the coast of the Llyn peninsula in Wales, between 1947 and 1961. For Tony Conran, Chamberlain's work is exemplary of the modernist fascination with the 'primitive', and is indicative of the artistic search for alternative visions and perspectives in times of upheaval and turmoil.[87] *Tide-race* is certainly a reaction to turmoil, gathering together poems and drawings to accompany the prose narrative which Chamberlain used to record her experiences on an island to which she had, in part, retreated, after the break-up of her marriage, and the desolate aftermath of the war, although, as her biographer Jill Piercy argues, she was also drawn to the island and the seascape, to seek the 'hermit-life' in the 'great depths of the living sea'.[88] For Damian Walford Davies, it is an experiment in mapping a cultural landscape of a Celtic archipelago, in which Bardsey (unnamed in *Tide-race*) is a 'palimpsest' of 'Synge's cartographies of Aran, Wicklow and Mayo', and yet too is inflected by European and Mediterranean models which would become more important to Chamberlain in her later work on the Greek island of Ydra.[89] Chamberlain's mapping of the meanings of islandness, however, is also a kind of psychogeography of a postwar condition much more general to the 'British Isles', on an island very close to their geographical centre. It may also be noted that Bardsey is a kind of reverse image of the topography of Britain as described by Mackinder above, with its mountain on the north-eastern side, and the gently sloping plain facing away to the south and west. From the Llyn peninsula, hardly any of its habitable land can be seen, and the inhabitants of Bardsey face out to the Irish Sea and, at its southern end, as Chamberlain colourfully suggests, 'in the direction of South America'.[90]

Chamberlain's postwar retreat to Bardsey is conceived from the outset as both a psychological journey and a mystical quest. It begins with the promise of island healing: 'LISTEN: I have found the home of my heart. I could not eat: I could not think straight any more; so I came to this solitary place and lay in the sun.'[91] It is the promise, one might say, upon which much of the postwar boom in 'sunshine' holidays to the Balearic archipelago was built: an island in the sun, which offers solitude, peace, and replenishment. From the beginning, Chamberlain teases the reader with this conception of islandness as the 'psychological space' of the tourist brochure, as Steven Roger Fischer describes: 'An island? It's warmth bathed in surfeit and wrapped in security. No matter that this only exists in the mind: the tourist who imports these notions invariably "discovers" them.'[92] Bardsey is also an island steeped in ancient history and mysticism, an island 'to which three pilgrimages equal one to Rome', and which bears the legend of a mythical treasure island:

> The treasures of Britain are to be found in the fertile earth of the fields or in the bays of the southwest or in the seal-cave to the east; for Merlin buried or planted here in some secret place certain mystical properties. If they can be found, you shall learn from them.[93]

Chamberlain draws here upon the name of Britain for its ancient, mythical form of Arthurian legend, to play upon the possibility of a spiritual rejuvenation which will not be personal, in the manner of a holiday, but national, perhaps even racial. It is a quest for which she is 'eager', and yet also 'mortally afraid', for the 'sort of adventurous Robinson Crusoe-type of existence' she ponders has the obvious constraint of being associated entirely not just with men, but with powerful myths of masculinity.[94] She cannot dare to live on the island alone, as a woman, and therein lies the complex gendered symbolism of islands in the national imagination. The 'island home' may be home to a wife or daughter, but not to a woman alone.

As an account of island living, with all of the hardship, solitude, and catalogue of natural life which such an account entails, *Tide-race* was not without recent precedent, of course. Ronald Lockley had published a series of such accounts of his life on Skokholm, off the Pembrokeshire coast, in the 1930s and 1940s, including *Dream Island Days* (1930), *Island Days* (1934), *Islands Round Britain* (1935), *I Know an Island* (1938), and *Letters from Skokholm* (1947). The last work, in particular, took on special resonance because the letters were written to Lockley's brother-in-law who had been captured by the Germans in Norway in 1940, and therefore, at 'a critical moment in history', the island was important as a 'place apart' from this turbulent, modern world, and as an idea of life 'in its simplest terms' which might be a radically new model for living in nature after the war.[95] So, too, Frank Fraser Darling had pioneered new ideas about human ecology, and about the conditions of human life in island environments, in his wartime publications *Island Years* (1940) and *Island Farm* (1943), accounts which detailed the problems and endurance of isolation, and the difficulties of re-establishing a sustainable environment for human life on Tanera Mòr in the Summer Isles. Both Lockley and Fraser Darling had lived on their islands alone and with their young families, and so in part their narratives appealed to readers as contemporary versions of both *Robinson Crusoe* and *The Swiss Family Robinson*. Chamberlain's narrative might be regarded as analogous to, or even within a similar tradition of island writing, or even nature writing, as, Lockley and Fraser Darling, with the important exception that *Tide-race* encounters the island, from the outset, as a social space already determined as masculine. That she wishes to go there alone, but cannot, begs the question about the seemingly implacable equation of island territory with male psyche.

As Damian Walford Davies suggests, *Tide-race* is explicitly concerned with 'the forceful gendering and eroticization of space', and the island becomes a site of introspection for Chamberlain's own sense of 'gender crisis'.[96] While much of the academic and social focus of debates about gendered space has been on urban public and domestic environments, Chamberlain's narrative explores islandness as an exemplary material and symbolic manifestation of gendered exclusion. Women such as Nans, the wife of Chamberlain's bullying nemesis, Cadwaladr Tomos, are defined by their duties as housewives and mothers, fearful of domestic violence, and worn down by the daily struggle to maintain life on the island. She dies 'before she was more than middle-aged'.[97] The gendered domain of island life is made even more explicit in the case of Dic Jones and his wife, Leah, who had four children all under the age of five when a fifth child is born:

> No sooner had one been born than the next one conceived. It was a hard life for Leah, being tied to a primitive farmhouse, with babies tumbling about her feet wherever she moved. She had no escape, no relaxation. Dic, being of a roving, unstable disposition, liked the freedom of the place, for here he was his own master; whereas on the mainland, he would have been a farm servant or a road-mender.[98]

The island is no space of freedom for women, but a microcosm of the gender ideologies which dominate mainland society, made all the more intense on the miniature scale of an island which was cut off from the mainland for long periods throughout the year. Bardsey is not distant from the mainland, but it is imprisoned in poor weather by the treacherous currents in the 'tide-race', and thus Chamberlain's title advertises the space which forms the barrier between the island and the mainland, the barrier which defines the insularity of the island, especially for island women who rarely cross it. Dic and Leah leave the island shortly after the death of their fifth child in infancy:

> Life here had always been impossible for her, with no chance of ever getting away from the children for an hour's peace. Now, having been found by Dici one night trying to hold her head underwater in the well

in the mountain, the man was at last forced to take her and the children off the island.[99]

Chamberlain's text abounds with a fascination for porous boundaries – between human and animal, land and sea, man and woman, sanity and madness – but in her charting of the lives of the women around her, these boundaries are hard-edged, and dangerous. She records how one night, when the men are out fishing, a 'black storm' hits suddenly, and while the children stare out to sea, Nans 'moaned into the folds of her shawl', and cries out to her children: 'Stop looking . . . that old green grave . . . That whore out there wants all our men and won't be content till she gets them.'[100] It is in the context of these island women, and the particular constraints which island life sets upon them, that Chamberlain dwells upon her own gendered existence, upon her childlessness, upon her sexuality, upon the ways in which she is made to feel a woman in socially prescribed forms.

The pains of maternal desire seem to stir in her a series of highly charged encounters with seals, with the seal-cow, for example, who speaks to her and accuses her of stealing her baby-seal: 'It screamed with the voice of any human child. The bereft cow roared and came up from the surf to beat my door and windows with her flippers.'[101] There is little in Chamberlain's account of the stolen seal-pup, its death, and its mother's 'mournful eyes' to betray the limits of dream and reality, sense and madness. She prefaces her tale of being married to a stranger, who goes absent for long periods until he is discovered 'resting on a rock', singing 'I am a man upon the land, I am a silkie in the sea', by writing that it is 'Rooted deeper still in legend', but she roots the story too in the observation that bull-seals show 'sexual interest in women': 'There is often so strong a link between woman and seal that it would seem almost normal for them to co-habit.'[102] Martin Puhvel concludes his study of seal folklore in Northern Europe by arguing that 'the stories of the breeding of humans with seals are clearly nothing but an off-shoot of the wider tradition of the connections between humans and merfolk', but Chamberlain gives no such hint of any sense of incredulity.[103] Nor is her narrative of these anthropomorphised seals always attributed to other island dwellers, as was the case, for example, in Fiona Macleod's *The Washer of the Ford*, in which tales of seals morphing into men or women, and vice versa, are reported as collected folklore.[104] In *Tide-race*, the seals are associated with Chamberlain's sense of vulnerability. When she is drifting dangerously in a fog close to the island shore, unable to find a safe passage home, she encounters what appears to be the same seal-cow, beckoning her to 'salt death' in the sea, and yet the seal is also a 'gentle visitant' who watches over her as she sleeps before finally finding her way to a landing.[105] For Chamberlain, the mythology of seals as drowned humans, or of humans descended from seals, is not gathered up as an anthropological curiosity, but woven into the psychological fabric of her account, as manifestations of a deeply personal, gendered crisis of identity and belonging. The seal appears to Chamberlain particularly when she is overwhelmed by feelings of guilt, of sin, and these are tied explicitly and repeatedly to the prescriptions of gendered identity: 'what does my fate matter? For I want to be fulfilled like other women. What have I done to be lost in winding sheets of fog?'[106]

As with every facet of island life, the fog in which Chamberlain drifts, afraid of getting lost, is both real and metaphorical. The islandmen, she writes, 'would sooner face a storm than a fog', and this is entirely practical, yet also indicative of the psychological preference for the turbulence and drama of the storm, rather than the limbo and dissolution of the fog.[107] The existential crisis explored in *Tide-race* is located across several geographical scales, from the physical and psychological threats to her own person, through the struggle of the islanders to survive, and out to a global scale in which the fate of one individual is barely significant: 'Perhaps it's wrong to be happy when half the people in the world are chain-bound and hungry, cut off from the sun.'[108] But it is at this global level that Chamberlain articulates her most explicit gender critique, hardly surprising given the conditions of the postwar world:

> If you scratch below the surface of men's minds, you find that they are bleeding inwardly. Men want to destroy themselves. It is their only hope. Each one secretly nurses the death-wish; to be god and mortal in one; not to die at nature's order, but to cease on his own chosen day. Man has destroyed so much that only the destruction of all life will satisfy him.[109]

These de Beauvoiresque observations posit the idea of a planetary crisis which is the consequence of a gender crisis, and although the island promises a place of retreat, of hermitage, for Chamberlain, it is always a microcosm of the same psychic drama of gender relations. The closest Chamberlain comes to seeing any potential in islandness as a heterotopic space of gender lies in her depiction of some of the children, in particular Siani, the daughter of Cadwaladr and Nans. 'She had never learned to read or write or in fact to do anything but the roughest man's work; the result being that she was devoid of any femininity.'[110] Yet this is hardly potential to be admired, for it is the consequence of neglect, 'brutal ill-treatment', and the lack of creative stimuli: 'She seemed to see the world as an animal does.'[111] Siani is depicted as existing in that state of 'bare life' in which her ungendered being comes at the cost of her humanity. This is what is at stake in fictions of islandness as the new starting points of a post-apocalyptic world also, a state of innocence which is bought at the price of sensibility and sentience.

Chamberlain's ultimate vision of Bardsey Island is not the ecological vision of a small, sustainable community, nor the romantic myth of the island retreat and haven, nor yet the island home from which life might begin again in a harmonious coalescence of territory and identity. Chamberlain's Bardsey, like the larger island which lies to its east, was a graveyard of past lives and past dreams, upon which its barely existing inhabitants performed 'the danse macabre, the fatal play of life and death'.[112] If the dance performed on Bardsey offered any particular insight into human life, it lay in the image of the feet that 'leap over our own future grave-plots'.[113] The island is a place of ghosts, apparitions, and the bones of the dead beneath the soil or washed up on the beach. At every turn, Chamberlain encounters the powerful presence of the past, and ponders the meaning of the sacredness of life on an island of saints and pilgrimage, at precisely the point in history when humanity has forsaken any pretence to a connection with the sacred. Above all, her narrative scours the myth of island primitivism of its romance. The legendary figure who dominates the island, Cadwaladr, is a Caliban figure, the 'native genius of Prospero's island; of mine; of any island', who is 'primitive and self-reliant', but entirely absorbed in his own rage.[114] He is not the figure of revivalist heroism, then, but the petty tyrant intent on casting his own will as a shadow over the whole island and all its inhabitants. This is what makes Cadwaladr exemplary for Chamberlain of the fate of 'an old race driven back on itself along the sea-margin', not the insular dream of heroic rejuvenation in the homeland, but the existential and gendered crisis of a desolate island retreat in a thoroughly interdependent and precarious globe. *Tide-race* is, in that sense, a pilgrimage narrative which strips bare the cosy idealism of island life as in itself a kind of deliverance from the toils and reproaches of modern life.

'A SINGLE INSIGNIFICANT ISLAND':
MIGRATION AND BELONGING IN THE ATLANTIC ARCHIPELAGOS

Perhaps one of the most striking aspects of Brenda Chamberlain's *Tide-race* is its self-conscious striving towards a depiction of island life in which questions of indigenousness are almost completely elided. The island is a distinctive place, without doubt, but for Chamberlain its aesthetic and emotional appeal is partly that it is 'a fragment of earth lived on by men and women who curse and laugh in gusts of spray'.[115] Chamberlain demonstrates no interest in the genetic or ethnic provenance of this 'old race driven back on itself'. She elides the linguistic barrier between the mainly Welsh-speaking inhabitants and her English-speaking friends, for example, and although her account is densely versed in the history and mythology of the island, she does not dwell upon the longevity or continuity of human habitation in any manner which might lend itself to racial characterisation.[116] As Kate Holman observes, this is partly because the inhabitants were all comparatively recent migrants, and were mostly 'stubbornly Welsh, yet disconcertingly foreign'.[117] The theme of migration to and from the island, then, seems to be decoupled from ideologies of race or nativism (although, as we have seen, it is not free of questions of gender and social hierarchy).

'Who cares, who should care when a winged thistle seed drifts over the sea? There is happiness to seize, loneliness to bear.'[118] When Chamberlain asks this question, therefore, about the interest or care one might, or might not, show for the fate of a 'winged thistle seed' drifting over the sea, it relates intimately to the crisis of identity and belonging in the neighbouring isles of the British and Irish archipelago. Biological metaphors for human migration have long been identified by cultural geographers as an insidious means of policing perceived social, national, and racial boundaries.[119] Metaphors such as weeds, germs, and disease which figure migrants as 'out of place' and unwanted have their origins in late nineteenth-century colonialism, according to Laura Otis, who argues that 'While they were happy to expand outward, Westerners became horrified when the cultures, peoples, and diseases they had engulfed began diffusing, through their now permeable membranes, back towards their imperial cell bodies'.[120] This anxiety intensified in the postwar period with the arrival of significant numbers of migrants from Britain's former colonies. As a recent study of the media representation of an outbreak of tuberculosis in Leicester in 2001 has shown, migrants are frequently pathologised as the bearers of social ills, either literally in the form of disease, or metaphorically in the form of crime, poverty, drugs, and violence, and have been throughout the postwar period: 'This post-imperial hazard was closely linked with refugees, asylum seekers, the homeless and poverty, inspiring an imagery of Britain invaded with foreign migrants bringing disease into the country.'[121] Islands are frequently associated with ideas of immunity and insularity, of being protected from disease and contamination, and thus the mythology of Britain (or its potent and slippery metonym, England) as an 'island home' has always been based upon an exclusivist and protectionist concept.

The Empire did not disappear at the end of the Second World War, and Britain continued to fight increasingly desperate rearguard colonial wars in Egypt, Aden, Malaya, Guyana, and Kenya. Yet, as Paul Gilroy argues, these have become the 'forgotten wars', evacuated from 'national consciousness' in favour of the 'overarching figure of Britain at war with the Nazis'.[122] The 'island home' as a stoically defended sanctuary from fascist aggression has become the dominant image of the nation, but this idea has prevailed at the expense of any attempt to understand how the warm glow that results from the nation's wholesome militarism has combined pleasurably with the unchallenging moral architecture of a Manichean world in which a number of dualistic pairings – black and white, savage and civilized, nature and culture, bad and good – can all be tidily superimposed upon one another.[123]

The mythology of the stoic stand against the Nazis has thus been used to bolster the persistence of a neo-colonial military-industrial global role for Britain (in which military equipment and armaments remain a key export industry), and at the same time, on the home front, it lurks as the nostalgic and illusory image of a once great, and once homogeneous, society threatened from within by the cultural effects of postcolonial migration. One response to this perceived threat which immigrants pose to the moral whitewash of Britain's postwar solution is visible in the spatialisation (as well as racialisation) of migration. Thus, a morbidly nostalgic version of 'white' Britain persists in the teashops and 'real ale' pubs of the countryside, and the tattoo parlours and fish and chip shops of the seaside, as if a new front line has been drawn against the ceded multicultural territories of the cities and towns.

In the literature of postwar migration, this drama of racial and national conflict is frequently played out in scenes of arrival and encounter, which become increasingly strained and anxious. The ship, the coast, the port, the railway terminus, and later the airport become the sites at which access to the nation was tested and determined, at which the borders of the 'island home' were made visible and contested. In her poem 'Colonization in Reverse' (1966), Louise Bennett joked that after the war it was Jamaican immigration which might be the cause of England's downfall, and that the migrants would 'turn history upside dung!'.[124] It is a witty work of irony, of course, for the allusions in the poem to the dole and the struggle to 'box bread / Out a English people mout' acknowledge that the mass migration of Caribbean workers to Britain is only in the mere sense of geographical displacement a 'reversal' of colonisation. Yet the trope of reversibility proposes that, even if the power relations between 'De seat a de Empire' and its far-distant colonies are not interchangeable, one island might be read in relation to the other; one archipelago might make sense of the other. To begin with, this notion has its roots in the cultural legacy of empire, that 'England' is the centre, the origin, which defines its colonial peripheries. The radical displacement of this idea can be read most clearly in the work of Sam Selvon and George Lamming in the 1950s. In his largely neglected second novel, *An Island Is a World* (1955), Selvon follows the fate of two brothers who choose different destinations to which to emigrate from Trinidad, one to America, the other to Britain. But far from finding London 'the centre of the world, where we have nearly everything we want, books, music, art', as his girlfriend puts it, Foster is disillusioned by the 'threads of West Indian lives' in 'the frenzied bustling of London' who 'worked at anything they could get ... living in cheap, dirty rooms'.[125] Supposedly at the centre of the world, Foster discovers that he is just one 'among millions who don't know why they live'.[126] The rejection of London as the solution to his problems, however, compels Foster to think again about the possibilities of 'some creed to hold on to, some culture, some doctrine that offered hope, something worth dying for' in Trinidad itself. The novel begins with Foster's habit of waking up in the morning to the despondent recognition that the island was 'a mere dot on the lobe', but having felt the same despondency on the other side of the 'endless Atlantic', a re-scaling of the geopolitical relations between Trinidad and the rest of the world seems inevitable to Foster by the end.

Selvon had emigrated to England in 1950, and travelled on the same ship as fellow writer George Lamming. The ship was a French transatlantic steamer, the *Misr*, which hauled in to half a dozen ports in the Caribbean before crossing the Atlantic to Plymouth, where it docked on 18 April.[127] Lamming wrote memorably of the voyage on two occasions, in fictional form in the opening section of *The Emigrants* (1954), and in factual form in *The Pleasures of Exile* (1960). In both versions, the fiction curiously more accurate than the factual version, Lamming records how as the ship got closer to England the sea turned ominously turbulent, and 'a punishing wind' prevented them from looking at the land.[128] The crossing of the ocean registers upon the passengers as both an environmental and a psychological displacement. In *The Lonely Londoners*, Selvon uses similar climatic markers of alienation such as the London fog, the 'smoke' that comes from his characters' mouths on cold days, and the sun with no heat, 'just there in the sky like a force-ripe orange'.[129]

In *The Emigrants*, however, these changes are observed and felt on the ship. Beyond the Azores, as the ship heads towards the mouth of the English Channel, the men on deck are bewildered by the sun, which they can see as light, but cannot now feel as warmth. For Lamming, this is experienced as a physical and psychological shock, as if they have entered a new mode of existence:

> It seemed possible that the habit which informed a man of the objects he has been trained to encounter might be replaced by some other habit new and different in its nature, and therefore creating a new and different meaning and function for those objects. It seemed that this could happen even in a man's waking life: that change which deprived the object of its history, making it a new thing, almost unknown, since all the attributes of presence would be destroyed, leaving what was once a thing with certain fixed references, a kind of blank. This seemed possible.[130]

This is the 'better break' which the emigrants hope will be possible by travel-ling to England, that they will be able to reverse history, destroy the 'fixed' meanings and attributes of the past, and start anew. The key ingredients of a classic depiction of modernism are given here – the scorching of tradition, the purging of aesthetic habit, the liberation of form and meaning, in order to make 'a new thing'. Yet Lamming playfully situates this modernist epiphany on the deck of an ocean steamer as it crosses into a perceptibly less hospitable climate. The sea becomes rough, the storms lash up and batter the ship, and the wind prevents the emigrants from seeing the first signs of England. At this point, they huddle around the ship's chart, studded with pin flags which mark their journey, and they follow the 'line of punctures from where the pin stuck back to the Azores, the empty sea, the islands, Guadeloupe, Martinique, Barbados, Trinidad':

> and as they followed the line down and away from the point of their
> destination they recalled what had happened in the dormitory, on the
> deck, in the dining hall at various times. There was neither excitement
> nor nostalgia in their recollection, just a neutral resignation to incidents
> that couldn't be reversed.[131]

By the time the emigrants dock in Plymouth, hope has given way to fear, to the dawning realisation in the grey light of a former slaving port that the unemployment and housing shortages which they have read about in English newspapers on the voyage might just mean starvation and death for them. In their quest for a 'better break' they have been solely preoccupied with the ambition 'to be in England', but on arrival in Plymouth, as one man spots a building that 'looked like the old plantation windmills of the tropics', it becomes clear that this land means nothing new.[132]

In late modernism, Tyrus Miller argues, 'the vectors of despair and utopia, the compulsion to decline and the impulse to renewal, are not just related; they are practically indistinguishable'.[133] In *The Emigrants*, Lamming brings these vectors together in the third-class dormitory of a ship which is bound for England only as a waypoint, and after his characters disembark at Plymouth, the ship is waved off by an 'impotent flutter' of handkerchiefs as it continues on to 'another port'.[134] Their voyage has been one of neither hope nor defeat, but just another aimless movement of migrants between peripheral ports. The arrival of the West Indian migrants in Plymouth is met with bewilder-ment by the English officials who struggle to see how 'England of all places' might be the object of anyone's dreams or ambitions.[135] Lamming articulates this sense of England as just another small, marginal island from the perspec-tive of the dockside customs officials to focus attention on the post-imperial despondency of England itself, a condition manifest in the drab grey skies, tawdry commercial advertisements, and rows of red-bricked houses which are the emigrants' first visual impressions of the country. For both Lamming and Selvon, the significance of this recognition lay in a re-conception of the archipelagic relations of the West Indies, in a newly imagined community of the islands. But this understanding that 'De wahter between dem islands doan' separate dem' is only possible in the re-scaled, de-centred view of the relations between the Caribbean islands and those north-east Atlantic islands at the other end of the Gulf Stream. Just as in Derek Walcott's poem 'The Schooner *Flight*', then, a voyage which begins as the 'vain search for one island that heals with its harbour / and a guiltless horizon' ends with a melancholic sense of a restless movement between islands which are all upon 'one / island in archipelagoes of stars'.[136]

The migration of Caribbean men and women to Britain in the postwar period is not just significant for the many ways in which those migrants have enriched the social, cultural, and political meanings of life in contemporary Britain, as has also been the case with many other groups of migrants from all around the world. Caribbean migration was particularly significant because of the special trope of islandness which pertained in the colonial imagination. In Jean Rhys's *Wide Sargasso Sea* (1966), this tropology of islandness is staged in the dream-like way in which the narrative moves between Jamaica, Dominica, and England, as if all are interchangeable, as if all are fantastical. Whereas Lamming's novel devotes much attention to describing the material and psychological transformations which take place upon the voyage between the Caribbean and England, in Rhys's novel one would hardly know a voyage had taken place at all. There is only Antoinette's uncertain memory of a troubled scene on board a ship, in which she 'smashed the glasses and plates against the porthole . . . [and] hoped it would break and the sea come in'.[137] The comparison with Lamming has particularly gendered resonances, of course. For Lamming's male characters, the voyage is, if only at its outset, an adventure, an active quest to impose one's will upon the world, which requires the illusion that England might, as a reversal of colonial fantasy, be their treasure island. However, Antoinette is brought to England, drugged and imprisoned by her English husband, and all her dreams of the permeable boundaries between England and the Caribbean have been nightmares.

The sea which forms the title of the novel bears heavily upon Rhys's island geography. The Sargasso Sea is so named because of the sargassum seaweed which floats on its surface, and which is formed by the clockwise circulation of major ocean currents along its boundaries. The sargassum reproduces itself without any roots to the seabed, and gathers in the almost currentless centre of the sea between the great currents which form it.[138] Much of the scientific literature written before and during Rhys's lifetime was an attempt to account for where the seaweed came from, as it was believed that the seaweed had detached from the shores of the Atlantic. Just a few years after Rhys's novel was published, scientists observed that the same oceanic conditions have resulted in large floating pools of plastic debris and oil particles.[139] It was reputed to have been first recorded by Christopher Columbus, and has long been mythologised in sailing lore as a place where ships can be entangled and dragged to the ocean floor, or condemned to drift aimlessly between the currents.[140] It is believed to be unique as an accumulation of self-supporting seaweed, and is also the world's only sea not bounded by coasts.[141] The Sargasso Sea is not, then, synonymous, as it has sometimes been suggested, with the oceanic voyage between the Caribbean and Britain, but is instead a very distinctive and meaningful ecosystem within the North Atlantic which Rhys uses as a solely maritime place. It is both a spawning ground and a place associated with death; it is liberated from attachments to the land, and yet it is held to be a terrifying and mysterious snare. As a currentless centre of the North Atlantic, apart from, but filled with, the debris of its neighbouring Atlantic shores, the Sargasso Sea is a displaced, heterotopic form of the circum-oceanic historical relations between Europe, the Caribbean, and America.

The three islands which are the focus of Rhys's novel are beyond the boundaries of the Sargasso Sea, but they seem constantly to get lost in it. The novel begins with a former slave owner, Mr Luttrell, whose estates have become worthless after the Emancipation Act, who 'swam out to sea and was gone for always'.[142] It ends with Antoinette refusing to believe that she is in England, and that instead, somewhere out in that sea, 'we changed our course and lost our way to England'.[143] Rhys uses this metaphor of the sea as a site of loss and deviation as a counterweight to the dominant colonial idea that England found itself, its wealth, and its imperial power in the islands of the Caribbean. The English historian James Anthony Froude is the obvious target of Rhys's critique, as Froude saw England's mastery of the sea as the reason why the country had been able to build an empire on the foundations of its colonies in the West Indies:

> If ever the naval exploits of this country are done into an epic poem –
> and since the Iliad there has been no subject better fitted for such treatment or better deserving it – the West Indies will be the scene of the most brilliant cantos.[144]

The Empire succeeded, according to Froude, because England projected itself outwards upon the spaces of its colonies: 'England regards the West Indies as essentially one with herself.'[145] This notion of homology between England and the West Indies is thoroughly contested in Rhys's work, in which it is never possible to connect them. In *Wide Sargasso Sea*, this failure manifests itself at every level of society, culture, economics, politics, climate, geography, religion, and history. Antoinette experiences these differences in the most fundamental sensory ways. As a Creole woman, descended from English slave-owners, she is caught between desiring an England which can for her only ever be a 'cold dark dream', and belonging to a Jamaica in which she will always be resented and despised for the deeds of her English family, and which for her English husband will always be 'quite unreal and like a dream'.[146]

For Froude, there were serious consequences if England was not homologous with the West Indies, if England failed to read itself in those islands, for if that were so, then the 'British Empire will dwindle down before long into a single insignificant island in the North Sea'.[147] This is the anxiety which Froude strives desperately against in his extraordinary notion that the West Indies, the scene of some of the most brutal and rapacious acts of human trafficking, slavery, and repression in English colonial history, is 'one' with England. Rhys's novel concludes, of course, with Antoinette, in a dream-like state, wandering the corridors of an English home which she believes is only cardboard, haunted by the memories of her own childhood home burning in Jamaica, and shielding the flame which it is implied she will use to torch her English prison. 'As far as I know I am white', wrote Jean Rhys, 'but I have no country really now.'[148] This is the significance of the final scene in Rhys's novel, not just an anti-colonial act of retribution, but a torching of the 'cardboard house' of Englishness. It is a clearing of the rhetorical and tropological apparatus of islands, coasts, and seas upon which the ideologies of British imperialism were built. 'England,' says Christophine. 'You think there is such a place?'[149]

ULSTER SAYS NO: 1969 AND ALL THAT

'I have no country'; the phrase echoes from Woolf to Rhys, and of course has different and complex meanings for each, but for both writers the gendered expression of non-allegiance is made more intense by the historical crises figured in their work. A refusal to belong does not cost very much when there are low stakes involved: Philip Larkin's anomic relation to his birthplace ('Nothing, like something, happens anywhere') is arguably of this kind.[150] As Robert Colls has shown, George Orwell 'resisted right up to the last possible minute' the demands of his country as England went to war, and then not only joined up but proceeded to produce some of the most influential expressions of English patriotism of the twentieth century.[151] Crucial to Orwell's definition of England was a sense of durability, 'a critical mass of connecting myths and stories that are historically as well as aesthetically convincing', and this was precisely what was endangered in the early years of the Second World War.[152] Hannah Arendt argues that times of historical crises are structured by a different temporality, that a gap appears between the generations: 'the chain is broken and an "empty space", a kind of historical no-man's land, comes to the surface which can be described only in terms of "no longer and not yet"'.[153] This is, of course, the familiar modernist characterisation of the historical crises of the early twentieth century, of the space between the dead past and the unborn future. Yet a more complex and troubling temporality lay at the heart of the most serious historical crisis to affect relations between the constituent parts of the British and Irish archipelago in the late twentieth century, the war which erupted on the streets of Northern Ireland in 1969, which seemed to figure the irrepressible return of the past, and the impossibility of a future.

The war in Northern Ireland, and the fragile peace process which followed it, lies behind much of the discussion of archipelagic methodologies in Irish and British studies. It is against this background of contested identities and seemingly intractable division that any cultural work which aims to show connection and relation finds its measure. John Kerrigan expresses the hope in *Archipelagic English* that through such an approach 'literature can be re-engaged with the evolving and devolving interactivity of the Irish-British archipelago and help change the past in the future'.[154] Demographically small in relation to the archipelago as a whole, Northern Ireland is central to what historians and politicians once erroneously called 'the Irish question' or, less often, erroneously called 'the British question'. Both are errors because, as Edna Longley argues, 'The great advantage of living in Northern Ireland is that you can be in three places at once.'[155] As she wrote these words in 1990, and perhaps still today, it was very far from a consensual view that Northern Ireland's multiple relations and identifications were, and are, advantageous, but Longley was making an argument about the very gendered terms in which the political space of Northern Ireland had been imagined and contested. Longley sees literature as a space for redefinition of identities, and as inherently connective, generating 'a web of affiliation that stretches beyond any heartland – to the rest of Ireland, Britain, Europe'. The web, she argues, 'is female, feminist, connective – as contrasted with male polarisation. So is the ability to inhabit a range of relations rather than a single allegiance.'[156]

Longley's argument is an important recognition of the need for a feminist theorisation of alternative geopolitical conceptions of 'these islands', and equally a key summation of how archipelagic relations are informed by the ways in which gender crosses and complicates other forms of identification and allegiance. In short, she was right to emphasise that the political crisis of 1969 and the subsequent conflict was also both a literary crisis and a gender crisis. The sexism of literary culture in Northern Ireland at the time is perhaps the obvious source to bear out this argument. In the revolutionary month of May 1968, as Paris erupted into student and worker demonstrations, James Simmons launched his new 'magazine of revolution', as it was subtitled, although its title, *The Honest Ulsterman*, possibly suggested a less ambitious project. The contributors to *The Honest Ulsterman* were almost unanimously male, perhaps unsurprisingly given the title, and the magazine dedicated itself to the ideal of 'men talking to men'.[157] Its ambitions in terms of expressing regional identity were equally limited, as the editor looked forward to a time when 'Ulster education, politics and architecture will be as distinctive as our police force'.[158] If there was any irony intended in this statement, it is well hidden, although the events of the following few years would make it increasingly difficult to take seriously. In the previous year, *Threshold* magazine had published 'An Anthology of Ulster Writing' in its pages, which collected work by thirty writers, of which all but one were male. Perhaps more telling, however, is the gendering of the literary response to the political crisis itself. In the special issue of *Threshold* published in the summer of 1970 on 'The Northern Crisis', all of its twenty contributions were written by men. A review of the issue published in the newly formed *Fortnight* magazine chastised the general tendency of those writers included towards introspection, apathy, and voyeurism, but the only question of equality raised in the review is to ask why most of the contributors are Catholic: 'The answer to that one might reveal more about the Northern Crisis than all the words of poets and journalists.'[159] To be fair to *Fortnight* magazine, its first issue included a page, or actually what was styled 'An (anti)page', for women, which gave an account of the 'five hundred angry ladies' who met at the first British 'Liberation Conference' in Ruskin College in Oxford earlier that year, the tone of which oscillated uncomfortably between sympathetic description and faint ridicule, but which settled its 'single allegiance' quite firmly: 'But one could hardly imagine Women's Liberation happening here. Even the most militant have had to admit that liberation for women sits uncomfortably in the tradition of revolutionary struggles.'[160]

There could be little doubt that as far as the literary culture of Northern Ireland was concerned the political crisis was a male crisis, and a matter for the male conscience. In a series of three articles for the *Irish Times* on 'The Northern Writers' Crisis of Conscience', Eavan Boland interviewed five writers, all male, who probed their own childhood memories either for early unrecognised signs of the coming conflict, or for guilty feelings of complacency. Michael Longley led the confessional tone: 'The crisis for me was ignorant and complacent and self-satisfied, that as a middle-class Protestant I'd always thought this sort of thing could never happen, and here it was – it had happened.'[161] Boland did not comment in the articles upon gender issues, and indeed she adopts the masculine pronoun as neutral when talking about the problems faced by the writer generically. She has subsequently written of the sexism she encountered in her early struggle to identify and define herself as a poet, however, and specifically of an apprenticeship characterised by 'sub-jugating her own opinions to those of the men around her'.[162] One might respond in the same way that *Fortnight*'s reviewers did to the *Threshold* special issue on the 'Northern Crisis', and despair of male poetic introspection and moral hand-wringing, but the point is that at the very time when Northern Irish writers were, in Heather Clark's words, 'recuperating a Northern poetic tradition', and forging 'the idea of a distinct Ulster poetry', and when the out-break of sectarian conflict defined the role of these writers as the public con-science of the crisis, this public role was understood to be a male domain.[163] Boland gave the final word in her articles to Michael Longley, and his account of the mission of poetry in times of conflict is wholly commendable:

> The situation in the North is one of great complexity. Yet it always enacts itself on the streets and in the ordinary passions of people, in terms of brutal simplicity. I think any human activity, any human utterance which reminds people, no matter how few, of the complexity of life, must be of use.[164]

This account is also, of course, wholly compatible with Edna Longley's cel-ebration of poetry's capacity to 'inhabit a range of relations rather than a single allegiance', and to articulate connective identities rather than 'male polarisa-tion'. Although some of the poets of the Ulster Renaissance were, from time to time, seen as complicit in the tribal politics of the conflict, for the most part they did tend to uphold this vision of poetry as a manifestation of complex-ity, as a bulwark against violence, hatred, and brutality. Archipelagic thoughts abound in the poetry of the Ulster Renaissance; indeed, it may even be a defining characteristic of that generation of poets that they reach not just for the shared spaces of a divided community, but that they attempt to remind that divided community of its many allegiances, affinities, and resonances. Yet, as was evident in the literary magazines, anthologies, and media represen-tation of the literary response to the outbreak of the conflict, Northern Irish literary culture was resolutely and complacently male. The story of the Ulster Renaissance, even in its most recent iterations, is one of a male group of poets, formed by male friendships and rivalries, and influenced by male forebears.

Yet women's writing of the time performed a similar function of remind-ing readers of shared spaces, and alternative conceptions of space and relations. In 1970, Joan Lingard began her successful series of children's novels based on the characters of Kevin and Sadie, Catholic and Protestant, who live in adjacent, segregated areas of Belfast, and whose lives become entangled by the escalating conflict between their respective communities. The first in the series, *The Twelfth Day of July* (1970), begins with Sadie's father inciting his children to display their ready knowledge of loyalist and anti-Catholic history, while her mother cooks their meal and grumbles about her husband's drinking.[165] The novel retains this focus on both the sectarian spatial divide and the gendered spaces which are woven through and between sectarianism. Sadie lives in the shadow of the shipyard gantries, and is constantly reminded of the 'ships that would sail the world over, cross the Atlantic and the Pacific, call at New York, San Francisco, Rio de Janeiro . . .', ships that her father helps to build, and that her brother might when he comes of age, but that she dreams of sailing out of Belfast.[166] As tensions in the streets rise, Sadie and Kevin encounter each other as the most daring provocateurs of their respective communities, but this rivalry turns to friendship when their actions spark a riot, and Kevin's sister is seriously injured. The novel ends with both Sadie and Kevin turning away from the contentious rituals and protests of their upbringing, and choosing instead to spend the day at the seaside, where a more amorous rivalry takes the form of splashing each other, and knocking down each other's sandcastles.[167] The seaside might be regarded in this scene as an escapist device (for seaside locations are not immune from sectarian associations in Northern Ireland either), but if, as a children's novel, *The Twelfth Day of July* necessarily simplifies the political conflict, it nevertheless makes the point that the conflict has been stoked in the intimate spaces of working-class streets in which community is understood entirely in terms of territoriality. As the police repeatedly tell the rival children, 'stay away from one another. Keep in your own areas.'[168]

Perhaps Lingard was aware from an early age of the problems of such an equation of community and territoriality. Born in Edinburgh, she grew up in East Belfast, a predominantly loyalist part of the city associated closely with the history of the shipyards, before moving back to Scotland. Lingard published another novel in 1970 partly set in the same locality, *The Lord on Our Side*, which was not intended for children, and which charted the changes taking place in the city between the devastating air raids of 1941 and the rise of the political conflict in the late 1960s. As the title implies, the focus is on the pervasive and entrenched role of religious ideology in securing political consent, and Lingard's characters are aware of the ways in which religion and politics are spatialised in Ireland, with Josie observing for example that Monaghan 'looked a Catholic county . . . as she gazed out at the small lochs, small scrubby hills, poor fields strewn with rushes, clumps of thorn, willows', while she can also read the history and character of 'Plantation towns with one wide, central street, market stalls at the sides of it, houses washed rose and shell pink,

Wedgewood and sky blue, olive green, primrose yellow'.[169] The recognition that cultural identity takes spatial forms, and can be historicised in the poverty of a landscape, or the architecture of a planned town, implies a similar point to the seaside scene in *The Twelfth Day of July*, that if spaces were organised and conceptualised differently, they might lend themselves to different outcomes. In both novels, this understanding of spatial politics comes about because of the movement of characters, their transit into and through spaces beyond their own limited territorial imagination.

The same dynamic of movement into and through Northern Ireland informs Menna Gallie's novel *You're Welcome to Ulster* (1970), the title of which is comically ambivalent about whether it expresses the hospitable sentiments of the inhabitants, or the frankly disappointed response of the tourist. Gallie lived in Northern Ireland for thirteen years, during which she wrote some of her best-known work about Wales, her home country, including *Strike for a Kingdom* (1959) and *A Small Mine* (1962). *You're Welcome to Ulster* focuses on the character of Sarah Thomas, who fears that she has breast cancer, and decides to pursue a last sexual fling before she has to undergo medical treatment.[170] Northern Ireland may seem an unlikely destination for sexual tourism, but the novel as a result intertwines political and sexual geographies, and maps an Ulster which, seen through the desires and feelings of a middling-aged woman, doesn't coalesce easily with any territorial stakes or ambitions. As Claire Connolly argues,

> Sarah Thomas' ill and ageing body serves as the primary register of external political conditions: her tiredness, her hunger, her thirst for alcohol or desire for sex all at different points of the novel determine and shape her vivid account of Ulster in the week around the twelfth of July, 1969.[171]

That both Lingard and Gallie chose to set their fictions around the twelfth of July signals the common interest of both writers in the ways in which Ulster, more than any other part of the British state, ritually and elaborately staked out the spatial and historical markers of Britishness. These markers are by turns both familiar and strange to Sarah Thomas, who as someone from 'across the water' is expected to identify with loyalist sentiments, but who at times feels in Ulster that 'she might as well be in Kenya or Kerala, or in some small state in the south of North America'.[172] As Connolly suggests, while Gallie's novel does not transcend the political conditions of national conflict in Northern Ireland, there are clear indications in the novel of an alternative model of 'community founded on affects that are transnational in scope'.[173]

If Northern Ireland has frequently appeared to be an avatar of the violent histories which characterised the formation of the British and Irish states, it might yet prove to be a place in which the archipelago can be conceived differently. As Longley suggests, it may be a useful advantage in a globalised world, or at least one which is transnational, to think of the place one inhabits as 'three places at once' (and three seems a surprisingly limited number for Longley to propose, given the many other histories and identities woven into the fabric of Northern Irish society). Equally, it may prove a useful place with which to think about islands and coasts, since the contested identities of Northern Ireland pose perplexing questions about *which* 'island' its people inhabit, and whether its coasts are borders or not. For much of its troubled history, Northern Ireland has been coveted as an inalienable part of the 'national territory' of the 'whole island of Ireland', as claimed in Articles Two and Three of the Irish Constitution, *Bunreacht na hÉireann*. Yet surely when Churchill spoke of defending 'our island home', and fighting on the beaches, it was unthinkable given his own unionist proclivities that the 'island' he meant stopped at Portpatrick. The obsession with coasts as visible markers of identity and territorial integrity was ridiculed in another innovative fiction published at the outset of the conflict, Brigid Brophy's experimental novel *In Transit* (1969). Much of the novel is set in an airport lounge, one of those 'non-places' which Marc Auge characterised as a transactional space of consumerist supermodernity in which locality, history, and identity (or at least all but the most instrumental of identities as passenger, consumer, or suspect) are erased.[174] Yet the novel also recalls a childhood spent in Ireland, in which weekend expeditions were undertaken to the coast, the purpose of which was 'to stand on the coast and look out to sea or to stand on a promontory of coast and look back along the coastline towards another bit of coast':

> And, perhaps for want of an alternative, a remarkable quantity of Irish time is spent in pointing out bits of coast from which another bit of coast can, on a not too drizzly day, be seen. On days of good visibility something like ninety per cent of the population must be standing about the island, arms extended like signposts, pointing out coast to the rest of the population.[175]

This is a habit the narrator has long ceased to share. The coast-marking rituals of her childhood led her to an identification, which was either 'egomania or patriotism', of herself as the same as the nation, as 'Ireland's I'. Yet, 'Six months later I was no longer temptable to the identification Ireland equals I, my parents having been killed in a plane crash and I transplanted across the sea they had so often bid me gaze out at.'[176] Thus Brophy generates an orphan narrative of identity 'in transit', of coast-crossing and island-hopping, which refuses nostalgia for a simple equation of self and territory. This might be called postmodernism, or supermodernity, but it is equally readable in

Arendt's terms as that modernist and feminist space between the 'no longer and the not yet'.

NOTES

1. Virginia Woolf, *A Room of One's Own and Three Guineas*. Oxford: Oxford World's Classics, 1992, 313.
2. Ibid. 313.
3. Susan Stanford Friedman, *Mappings: Feminism and the Cultural Geographies of Encounter*. Princeton: Princeton University Press, 1998, 114–18.
4. Ibid. 118.
5. Woolf, *A Room of One's Own and Three Guineas*, 156, 312.
6. Virginia Woolf, *Between the Acts*. Oxford: Oxford World's Classics, 1992, 139.
7. See Richard Mabey, *Flora Britannica*. London: Sinclair-Stevenson, 1996, 58.
8. James Clifford, *Routes: Travel and Translation in the Late Twentieth Century*. Cambridge, MA: Harvard University Press, 1997, 6.
9. John Mack, *The Sea: A Cultural History*. London: Reaktion, 2011, 161.
10. Redmond O'Hanlon, *Trawler: A Journey through the North Atlantic*. London: Penguin, 2004, 3.
11. Neil M. Gunn, *Morning Tide*. London: Souvenir, 1975, 55.
12. Ibid. 84, 95.
13. Eiluned Lewis, *The Captain's Wife*. London: Macmillan, 1944, 24.
14. Ibid. 23–4.
15. Ibid. 174–5.
16. Philip E. Steinberg, *The Social Construction of the Ocean*. Cambridge: Cambridge University Press, 2001, 193.
17. Margaret Cohen, *The Novel and the Sea*. Princeton: Princeton University Press, 2010, 11, 96, 258–9n.
18. Phyllis Leffler, 'Peopling the Portholes: National Identity and Maritime Museums in the US and UK', *The Public Historian*, 26.4 (Fall 2004), 24 (23–48).
19. Valerie Burton, 'Fish/Wives: An Introduction', *Signs*, 37.3 (Spring 2012), 530 (527–36).
20. Peter Gurney, '"Intersex" and "Dirty Girls": Mass-Observation and Working-Class Sexuality in England in the 1930s', *Journal of the History of Sexuality*, 8.2 (October 1997), 269 (256–90).
21. Philip Larkin, 'Sunny Prestatyn', *Collected Poems*, ed. Anthony Thwaite. London: Faber, 1988, 149.
22. John Betjeman, 'Beside the Seaside', *Collected Poems*. London: John Murray, 1979, 128.
23. Ibid. 135.
24. J. B. Priestley, *English Journey*. London: William Heinemann, 1935, 266.
25. Doreen Massey, *Space, Place and Gender*. Cambridge: Polity Press, 1994, 7.
26. Priestley, *English Journey*, 268.
27. Philip Larkin, 'To the Sea', *Collected Poems*, 173.

28. Les Back, 'Falling from the Sky', *Patterns of Prejudice*, 37.3 (2003), 342 (341–53).
29. Ibid. 343.
30. Daniel Burdsey, 'Strangers on the Shore? Racialized Representation, Identity and In/visibilities of Whiteness at the English Seaside', *Cultural Sociology*, 5.4 (2011), 538, 541, 543 (537–52).
31. See Cohen, *The Novel and the Sea.*
32. Elizabeth Taylor, *A View of the Harbour*. London: Virago, 2006, 140.
33. Ibid. 175.
34. Lara Feigel and Alexandra Harris (eds), *Modernism on Sea: Art and Culture at the British Seaside*. Oxford: Peter Lang, 2011, 1.
35. Taylor, *A View of the Harbour*, 39.
36. Ibid. 39.
37. Ibid. 282, 289, 9.
38. Marcel Carné, *Le Quai des Brumes*. Studio Canal, 1938.
39. Virginia Woolf, *To the Lighthouse*, ed. and intro. David Bradshaw. Oxford: Oxford World's Classics, 2006, 14.
40. Taylor, *A View of the Harbour*, 19–20.
41. Ibid. 301, 235.
42. Ibid. 309.
43. Ibid. 40.
44. Ibid. 231, 309.
45. Ibid. 207.
46. Ibid. 208.
47. Ibid. 181.
48. Sara Crangle, 'Ivy Compton-Burnett and Risibility', in Marina MacKay and Lyndsey Stonebridge (eds), *British Fiction After Modernism: The Novel at Mid-Century*. Basingstoke: Palgrave, 2007, 99–120.
49. N. H. Reeve, *Elizabeth Taylor*. Tavistock: Northcote House, 2008, 15.
50. Taylor, *A View of the Harbour*, 152.
51. Ibid. 13.
52. Ibid. 11.
53. Reeve, *Elizabeth Taylor*, 8–18.
54. Woolf, *To the Lighthouse*, 23, 170.
55. Tyrus Miller, 'The Strings Are False: Bathos, Pastoral and Social Reflexivity in 1930s British Poetry', in Sara Crangle and Peter Nicholls (eds), *On Bathos: Literature, Art, Music*. London: Continuum, 2010, 49 (49–70).
56. Taylor, *A View of the Harbour*, 31.
57. Ibid. 226, 37–8.
58. Ibid. 304.
59. Alice Ferrebe, 'Elizabeth Taylor's Uses of Romance: Feminist Feeling in 1950s English Fiction', *Literature and History*, 19.1 (Spring 2010), 62 (50–64).
60. Taylor, *A View of the Harbour*, 18, 145, 289.
61. Samuel Beckett, *The Unnamable, The Grove Centenary Edition: Novels II*. New York: Grove Press, 2006, 320.

62. Steinberg, *The Social Construction of the Ocean*, 137.

63. Owain Jones, '"The Breath of the Moon": The Rhythmic and Affective Time-Spaces of UK Tides', in Tim Edensor (ed.), *Geographies of Rhythm: Nature, Place, Mobilities and Bodies*. Farnham, Surrey: Ashgate, 2010, 190 (189–204).

64. Alain Corbin, *The Lure of the Sea: The Discovery of the Seaside in the Western World, 1750–1840*, trans. Jocelyn Phelps. Berkeley: University of California Press, 1994.

65. Taylor, *A View of the Harbour*, 266.

66. Ibid. 43, 48.

67. Ibid. 219.

68. Ibid. 312.

69. Mollie Panter-Downes, *One Fine Day*. London: Virago, 1985, 1.

70. Ibid. 2.

71. Ibid. 2.

72. Ibid. 3.

73. Ibid. 81.

74. Ibid. 81.

75. Winston Churchill, 'Wars are not won by evacuations', *Never Give In! The Best of Winston Churchill's Speeches*. London: Pimlico, 2003, 217.

76. Richard Toye, *The Roar of the Lion: The Untold Story of Churchill's World War II Speeches*. Oxford: Oxford University Press, 2013, 1–11.

77. Churchill, 'Wars are not won by evacuations', 217.

78. Wendy Webster, *Englishness and Empire 1939–1965*. Oxford: Oxford University Press, 2005, 189.

79. Ibid. 191.

80. Ibid. 191.

81. Robert Colls, *Identity of England*. Oxford: Oxford University Press, 2002, 243.

82. Winston Churchill, *A History of the English-Speaking Peoples*. London: Cassell, 1956, viii.

83. Ibid. viii.

84. H. J. Mackinder, *Britain and the British Seas*. London: William Heinemann, 1902, 63.

85. Ibid. 11.

86. Brenda Chamberlain, *Tide-race*. Bridgend: Seren, 2007, 94.

87. Tony Conran, *Frontiers in Anglo-Welsh Poetry*. Cardiff: University of Wales Press, 1997, 166.

88. Chamberlain, *Tide-race*, 16. See Jill Piercy, *Brenda Chamberlain: Artist and Writer*. Cardigan: Parthian, 2013, 126, 150.

89. Damian Walford Davies, *Cartographies of Culture: New Geographies of Welsh Writing in English*. Cardiff: University of Wales Press, 2012, 78–171.

90. Chamberlain, *Tide-race*, 218.

91. Ibid. 16.

92. Steven Roger Fischer, *Islands: From Atlantis to Zanzibar*. London: Reaktion, 2012, 254.

93. Chamberlain, *Tide-race*, 16.
94. Ibid. 16.
95. R. M. Lockley, *Letters from Skokholm*. Stanbridge, Dorset: Little Toller Books, 2010, 23, 28.
96. Walford Davies, *Cartographies of Culture*, 110.
97. Chamberlain, *Tide-race*, 201.
98. Ibid. 187.
99. Ibid. 192.
100. Ibid. 130.
101. Ibid. 37.
102. Ibid. 37–8.
103. Martin Puhvel, 'The Seal in the Folklore of Northern Europe', *Folklore*, 74.1 (Spring 1963), 333 (326–33).
104. Fiona Macleod, *The Washer of the Ford, and Other Legendary Moralities*. Edinburgh: Patrick Geddes, 1896.
105. Chamberlain, *Tide-race*, 167.
106. Ibid. 167.
107. Ibid. 165.
108. Ibid. 167.
109. Ibid. 167.
110. Ibid. 97.
111. Ibid. 97.
112. Ibid. 221.
113. Ibid. 221.
114. Ibid. 221, 94.
115. Ibid. 110.
116. See Walford Davies, *Cartographies of Culture*, 103, 230n.
117. Kate Holman, *Brenda Chamberlain*. Cardiff: University of Wales Press, 1997, 33–4.
118. Chamberlain, *Tide-race*, 90.
119. See Tim Cresswell, 'Weeds, Plagues, and Bodily Secretions: A Geographical Interpretation of Metaphors of Displacement', *Annals of the Association of American Geographers*, 87.2 (June 1997), 330–45.
120. Laura Otis, *Membranes: Metaphors of Invasion in Nineteenth-Century Literature, Science and Politics*. Baltimore: Johns Hopkins University Press, 1999, 5.
121. Morag Bell, Tim Brown, and Lucy Faire, 'Germs, Genes and Postcolonial Geographies: Reading the Return of Tuberculosis to Leicester, UK, 2001', *Cultural Geographies*, 13 (2006), 586 (577–99).
122. Paul Gilroy, *Postcolonial Melancholia*. New York: Columbia University Press, 2005, 89.
123. Ibid. 88.
124. Louise Bennett, 'Colonization in Reverse', *Selected Poems*, ed. Mervyn Morris. Kingston: Sangster's Book Store, 1982, 106–7.

125. Sam Selvon, *An Island Is a World*. Toronto: Tsar, 1993, 153.
126. Ibid. 154.
127. Inwards Passenger Lists, Board of Trade: Commercial and Statistical Department and Successors. National Archives (Kew): BT26 – 1264 – 163.
128. George Lamming, *The Pleasures of Exile*. London: Allison and Busby, 1984, 212, and *The Emigrants*. London: Allison and Busby, 1980, 95.
129. Sam Selvon, *The Lonely Londoners*. Harlow: Longman, 1985, 23, 35, 42.
130. Lamming, *The Emigrants*, 83.
131. Ibid. 96.
132. Ibid. 106, 99.
133. Tyrus Miller, *Late Modernism: Politics, Fiction, and the Arts Between the World Wars*. Berkeley: University of California Press, 1999, 14.
134. Lamming, *The Emigrants*, 110.
135. Ibid. 107.
136. Derek Walcott, 'The Schooner *Flight*', *Collected Poems 1948–1984*. London: Faber, 1986, 361.
137. Jean Rhys, *Wide Sargasso Sea*. London: Penguin, 1997, 117.
138. G. E. R. Deacon, 'The Sargasso Sea', *The Geographical Journal*, 99.1 (January 1942), 16–28.
139. Edward J. Carpenter and K. L. Smith Jr, 'Plastics on the Sargasso Sea Surface', *Science*, 175.4027 (17 March 1972), 1240–1.
140. Deacon, 'The Sargasso Sea', 16.
141. David Freestone and Kate Killerlain Morrison, 'The Sargasso Sea', *The International Journal of Marine and Coastal Law*, 27 (2012), 647–55.
142. Rhys, *Wide Sargasso Sea*, 5.
143. Ibid. 118.
144. James Anthony Froude, *The English in the West Indies, or the Bow of Ulysses*. London: Longman, Green and Co., 1888, 10.
145. Ibid. 364.
146. Rhys, *Wide Sargasso Sea*, 49.
147. Froude, *The English in the West Indies*, 364.
148. Jean Rhys, *Letters 1931–1966*, ed. Francis Wyndham and Diana Melly. London: Andre Deutsch, 1984, 172.
149. Rhys, *Wide Sargasso Sea*, 70.
150. Philip Larkin, 'I Remember, I Remember', *Collected Poems*, 82. See Robert Lance Snyder, '"Elbowing Vacancy": Philip Larkin's Non-places', *Papers on Language and Literature*, 43.2 (Spring 2007), 115–45.
151. Robert Colls, *George Orwell: English Rebel*. Oxford: Oxford University Press, 2013, 136.
152. Ibid. 151.
153. Hannah Arendt, *Reflections on Literature and Culture*, ed. Susannah Young-Ah Gottlieb. Stanford: Stanford University Press, 2007, 121.
154. John Kerrigan, *Archipelagic English: Literature, History, and Politics 1603–1707*. Oxford: Oxford University Press, 2008, 90.

155. Edna Longley, *The Living Stream: Literature and Revisionism in Ireland*. Newcastle: Bloodaxe, 1994, 195.
156. Ibid. 194–5.
157. James Simmons, 'Editorial', *The Honest Ulsterman*, 1 (May 1968), 2 (2–6).
158. Ibid. 5.
159. 'Books', *Fortnight*, 2 (9 October 1970), 22.
160. 'An (anti)page for women', *Fortnight*, 1 (25 September 1970), 24.
161. Eavan Boland, 'The Northern Writers' Crisis of Conscience – 2. Crisis', *Irish Times*, 13 August 1970, 12.
162. See Heather Clark, *The Ulster Renaissance: Poetry in Belfast, 1962–1972*. Oxford: Oxford University Press, 2006, 29.
163. Ibid. 12.
164. Eavan Boland, 'The Northern Writers' Crisis of Conscience – 3. Conclusion', *Irish Times*, 14 August 1970, 12.
165. Joan Lingard, *The Twelfth Day of July*. London: Penguin, 1989, 7–8.
166. Ibid. 9.
167. Ibid. 125–7.
168. Ibid. 102.
169. Joan Lingard, *The Lord on Our Side*. London: Hodder and Stoughton, 1970, 206.
170. Menna Gallie, *You're Welcome to Ulster*. Dinas Powys: Honno, 2010, 7–9.
171. Claire Connolly, 'Four Nations Feminism: Una Troy and Menna Gallie', in John Brannigan (ed.), *Reconceiving the British Isles*. UCDscholarcast: Series 4, 2010: <www.ucd.ie/scholarcast/scholarcast19.html> (last accessed 25 April 2014), 13.
172. Gallie, *You're Welcome to Ulster*, 13, 235.
173. Connolly, 'Four Nations Feminism', 16.
174. Marc Auge, *Non-Places: Introduction to an Anthropology of Supermodernity*. London: Verso, 1995.
175. Brigid Brophy, *In Transit*. London: GMP, 1989, 15.
176. Ibid. 17.

Epilogue: Coasting

In 'The Coasters' (1969), John Hewitt understood that the blame for the resurgence of political violence and sectarian murder in Northern Ireland could not simply be attributed to politicians, soldiers, paramilitaries, or preachers, but also lay with the comfortable, affluent middle classes, the 'coasters' of his title. 'You coasted along', he wrote, 'to larger houses, gadgets, more machines', while all along 'the old lies festered'.[1] Hewitt was a passionate advocate of regionalism as the source of an alternative solution to the divisions and insecurities of Northern Ireland. For most of his lifetime, Northern Ireland had its own regional government, but the blatant failings of its political mandate mirrored, in Hewitt's depiction, the flaws of its class-riven society, and the dangerous inadequacies of its cultural imagination.

Like many of the writers discussed in this book, Hewitt wrote as if both the nation and the union were already exhausted and redundant as political, social, and cultural forms, and indeed as if the failures of Northern Irish society were not anomalous, but emblematic of the failures of both the Irish and British political systems. In their wake, Hewitt proposed an alternative Ulster:

> Ulster, considered as a region and not as the symbol of any particular creed, can, I believe, command the loyalty of every one of its inhabitants. For regional identity does not preclude, rather it requires, membership of a larger association. And, whether that association be, as I hope, of a federated British Isles, or a federal Ireland, out of that loyalty to our own place, rooted in honest history, in familiar folkways and knowledge, phrased in our own dialect, there should emerge a culture and an attitude individual and distinctive, a fine contribution to the European

inheritance and no mere echo of the thought and imagination of another people or another land.[2]

Hewitt wrote these words in 1947, just a few years before Patrick Kavanagh would make a similar plea for each Irish writer to generate confidence in 'the social and artistic validity of his parish'.[3] Kavanagh's particular frustration arose from the disparity between a country which had the political independence to follow its own will, as it had demonstrated by declaring neutrality in the Second World War, and the same country which still appeared to be gripped by cultural subservience to London. 'The metropolis is not interested in the imaginative reality of provincial society,' wrote Kavanagh, 'it only asks the provincial to perform.'[4] For both Kavanagh and Hewitt, neither Irish Ireland nor British Ulster, and by extension the other 'provinces' orbiting around the metropolis, would resolve their social and political problems unless they could first achieve cultural integrity and confidence, and this would only be possible with a hard-won imagination of the distinctiveness and the relatedness of the 'region' or the 'parish'. In Hewitt's understanding, any solution to the crises of identity in twentieth-century modernity would have to be social, and not individual, and so the problem lay in identifying alternative, smaller units of social relationship which would satisfy this human need where 'once valid religions', individualist psychology, and a primitivist retreat to nature would fail.[5]

'Coasters', therefore, were part of the problem, the silent majority who allowed the wounds of a divided society to fester, and the blithe subservience of the provincial to remain. Yet, as a self-declared 'coaster', Jonathan Raban adopted an alternative, and more subversive, conception of this term in his narrative of a voyage around the shores of Britain which was undertaken as 'a reckoning, a voyage of territorial conquest, a homecoming'.[6] In Raban's narrative, coasting is 'a happy metaphor for a life on the fringe', and its derogatory connotations of idleness – 'to proceed without great effort', or, to the disdain of ocean-going sailors, 'to skirt, to sail from port to port of the same country' – are embraced as metaphors of a critical recalcitrance towards the pillars of an England which was 'my father's land, not mine'.[7] Raban is conscious of growing up in an England of ruins, dust, and nostalgia, in which the education system continues to prepare England's middle classes for an empire which no longer exists. *Coasting* is Raban's narrative of his decision to live on the fringes of this decaying society, and at the same time to explore its remnants as if it was unnamed and uncharted terrain. The England he discovers is a country which has 'run out of symbols' and is in need of a new identity, a new role, a new purpose, until it finds a war to fight in the Falklands, a 'phantasmal imperial exercise', which stirs its right-wing press into long-cherished analogies with the war against Nazi Germany.[8]

In Raban's account of the Falklands war, it is clear that it is not simply an imperial or martial motive which drives the war, but a morbid psychological compulsion to imagine the South Atlantic islands as a museum of 'the whole web and texture of being British', a 'miniature inverted cluster' of the British Isles, with the strange coincidence that 'they occupied precisely the same latitude in their hemisphere as the British Isles did in theirs: at 51°46'S, Port Stanley was the Hemel Hempstead of the southern world'.[9] The war is simply the occasion for a national drama, with ministers standing to make Churchillian speeches in parliament, soldiers writing letters home which imitate the pathos of the movies, and islands to re-capture which look like the wet, windy hillsides of Wales. The drama of putting the 'Great back into Britain', as the prime minister Margaret Thatcher claimed, is all for effect: Raban's voyage takes him onwards around the coast of a country where the dockyards and the coal mines are closing and the unemployment queues are reaching the same levels as during the Great Depression, and when he goes in search of the oil boom in Aberdeen as a happy ending, he finds instead the main sewerage pipe from the town, discharging its contents into the sea before a waiting, excited flock of seabirds.

Writing about the condition of England, and the demise of the British state, from the perspective of its coastline became something of a national pastime for writers in the 1980s and 1990s. It is something of a speciality in the work of Graham Swift, in *The Sweet Shop Owner* (1980), *Waterland* (1983), and the final scene of *Last Orders* (1996), in which the ashes thrown into the sea from Margate pier seem like those of a generation, and not just one man.[10] In Penelope Fitzgerald's *Offshore* (1979), the boat-dwellers living on the reaches of the Thames read like ironic subversions of Conrad's sailors, moored to a mudbank and going nowhere.[11] Kazuo Ishiguro sets the final scene of *The Remains of the Day* (1988) on a seaside pier, at which his butler-narrator, Stevens, learns the value of looking forward to the evening, as the sun sets on his career, as well as on 'the great houses of England'.[12] In *White Chappell, Scarlet Tracings* (1987), Iain Sinclair's narrator also ends up at the coast, or more specifically the intertidal grazing marshes of Thorpe in Essex, where he strives for release from a nightmare of violence and murder which seems to leak from Victorian London into the contemporary city, a dystopian take on Thatcher's desire to revive Victorian values.[13] Even while Raban was coasting from port to port, Paul Theroux was making a similar journey, which he records in *The Kingdom by the Sea* (1983). In his account, Theroux notes the withering away of the British state from the evidence of its eroding cliffs, littered beaches, and unemployed ports: 'The endless mutation of the British coast wonderfully symbolized the state of the nation . . . The British seemed to me to be people forever standing on a crumbling coast and scanning the horizon.'[14] 'Coasting', in Theroux's sense, notably suggests both of the meanings proffered by Hewitt and Raban, of standing idly by while the coast is eroded beneath our feet, and, at the same time, of seeking out the cultures of borders, peripheries, and the hidden spaces of the archipelago from which perspectives we might learn to re-imagine and re-inhabit the places we happen to live in.

These writings were not symptoms of the post-imperial English malaise taking place on the shoreline. They were returning to an overburdened symbolism of the nation as beleaguered island in order to read the archipelago anew. Raban summarised this rejuvenative mood towards the end of his voyage when he observes that 'For people who live on islands, especially on small islands, the sea is always the beginning'.[15] Raban's narrative charts the signs of social crisis, the troubled landscapes, the sense of fading glory and omnipresent gloom, but his voyage is intent too on finding new bearings among the ruins of this lost England which has never been his. It is a kind of pilgrimage, one which was shared by other refugees from the vestiges of late modernism. Among them we might include Iain Sinclair's psychogeographies of London, intent on finding dormant within the city's infrastructure and architecture 'a subterranean, preconscious text capable of divination and prophecy'.[16] Patrick Keiller's *Robinson* trilogy of films (*London*, *Robinson in Space*, *Robinson in Ruins*) explores a similar modernist understanding of suppressed signs beneath the surface of urban modernity. Tim Robinson left behind such 'artistic projects for bringing into consciousness London's suppressed geography' to take up a pilgrimage of discovery and testimony on the Aran islands, and later in Connemara.[17] It is in this rich flowering of the offshoots of late modernism that we can see the earlier modernist preoccupation with anthropology, primitivism, and evolution become more discernibly part of an ecological imagination of localities and environments.

Robinson's pilgrimage is resolutely secular, and rigorously oriented towards thinking of an ethical relation to place and environment. His compulsion to write, he explains, came from the desire to find a human form for the 'alert, reactive self-awareness' which he observes in dolphins swimming near the shoreline:

> a dolphin may be its own poem, but we have to find our rhymes elsewhere, between words in literature, between things in science, and our way back to the world involves us in an endless proliferation of detours. Let the problem be symbolized by that of taking a single step as adequate to the ground it clears as is the dolphin's arc to its wave. Is it possible to think towards a *human* conception of this 'good step'?[18]

This is no simple projection of the possibility that human beings might recover or create a sense of unity or harmony with our environment, for, as

Robinson writes, every step we take across 'our craggy, boggy, overgrown and overbuilt terrain . . . carries us across geologies, biologies, myths, histories, politics, etcetera, and trips us with the trailing *Rosa spinosissima* of personal associations'.[19] Every step measures out another, and another, and has consequences, here and elsewhere, but the step is proposed as a metaphor for living against the entanglements and hazards of roots. 'Roots are tethers', Robinson writes, 'and too prone to suck up the rot of buried histories. I prefer the step – indefinitely repeatable and variable – as a metaphor for one's relationship to a place.'[20] Robinson's books about Aran and Connemara are profound engagements with the material specificities of place, but they are also about the ways in which places inhabit language, their geographies sprung carefully and delicately upon words. The formal patterning of the narrative attempts, in lithe prose, to efface the presence of the narrator as barely more than a witness. The naming of the landscape is always understood in its contingency, as temporary a human mark upon the landscape as any sculpture, any field boundary, any furrow. If there is a politics to the landscape, there is no easy dismissal of the stakes invested in that politics when Robinson measures it against an island geology of hundreds of millennia, and writes that 'the geographies over which we are so suicidally passionate are, on this scale of events, fleeting expressions of the earth's face'.[21] Yet, it is 'on this scale of events', immeasurably greater than any nation, language, or religion, that what we choose to call home, or community, or society, is both precariously provisional and richly particular.

Robinson's celebration of the particularities of the Aran islands and Connemara belongs to that tradition of ecological writing about place and the environment in the archipelago which has antecedents in Gilbert White, Richard Jefferies, Robert Lloyd Praeger, Edward Thomas, Ian Niall, and Frank Fraser Darling among others, and which has contemporary fellow travellers such as Sue Clifford, Angela King, Richard Mabey, Andrew McNeillie, Kathleen Jamie, Roger Deakin, and Robert Macfarlane. Jos Smith makes the case for considering this genre of environmental writing in the British and Irish Isles as 'archipelagic literature' on the basis of its concerns for the politics of place and social identity, and the correspondence of these concerns with contemporary devolutionary processes.[22] In all of these writers, what Clifford and King called the 'conspiracy of nature and culture' in defining place, 'the accumulation of story upon history upon natural history', is the focus of an ecological engagement which resists the centralising and homogenising tendencies of modernity, and which functions below the level of the nation or even the region.[23] In some cases, their writings amount to a literary mapping of a bioregion, such as machairs, downs, an island, or a river course. In others, it is about a way of experiencing and looking at environments in which they cease to be 'a view'. Kathleen Jamie, for example, goes to St Kilda with archaeological surveyors, and explains that 'It was like the difference between looking through a window pane and looking at it. Look through the window, and you'd see the sea, wildness, distance, isolation. Look at it, and you saw utility, food security, domestic management.'[24] Robert Macfarlane writes of the paths, tracks, and footways which tell of both ancient and contemporary patterns of living, and reveal 'the habits of a landscape'.[25] They seldom make claims to assembling alternative geographies, or aspiring to alternative forms of social identification, and yet this tradition of writing is a rich resource for how we might think about responsible and responsive new ways of belonging.

It is not the only literary tradition to form such an important resource, of course. In *Local Attachments*, Fiona Stafford argues for the significance of a distinguished tradition of the poetry of place in these islands, from the Romantic period to the work of Seamus Heaney, for championing the validity and virtue of local truths.[26] Nick Groom makes an argument for the role of culture in defining and defending our environment by calling attention to the folklore of the English festive year: 'The generations of verses, songs, and proverbial sayings that have been in different ways passed down to us represent the accumulated story of our relationship with the natural environment over millennia.'[27] For Groom, as for Stafford, it is important to stress that these traditions are living, fluid, and dynamic, and are readable for the intimate connections which they have expressed, and continue to express, between human community and the natural environments of which we are part. In this sense, renewing a sense of belonging to the locality – however locality is defined: housing estate or village, suburb or parish, a street or an island – is as vital for ecology as it is for democracy. Both are gravely threatened in a world governed for the benefit of international capital, in which profit is the single aim of politics, and not the common welfare of people and the environments they live in.

The archipelago described in this book is plural and connective; its islands are interrelated and often interdependent, while at the same time they face in different directions, experience the same winds differently, and bear the legends of different, though tangled histories. It looks, sounds, and feels different depending on the location from which you take your bearings. There is no unity, and the archipelago is not self-contained: each part of the archipelago connects to other peoples, seas, and lands. This is the local truth which much of the literature described in this book witnesses, articulates, and celebrates. There is no utopian vision offered in those writings. As Sue Clifford and Angela King write, 'The philosophising that builds the ideal usually imagines that nothing has been there before, and that life and culture will evolve no further.'[28] Coasting is hardly a word which suggests the utopian, even as the faintest heading. Yet archipelagic modernism represents a sense of coasting as a transitive verb which we would need to recuperate from obsolescence: 'To make the round of, traverse all parts of, explore, scour', or 'To lie along the border or coast of; to border upon, adjoin, bound' (*OED*). As a border literature, archipelagic modernism finds resonances, pluralities, unlikely alliances, and shared spaces, and seeks out the alternative scales and perspectives with which we might begin to 'coast' new ways of belonging, new ways of exploring a politics of common welfare.

The most renowned poem in modern English to explore the implications of a post-utopian sensibility, perhaps, is Matthew Arnold's 'Dover Beach' (1867), which laments that the 'land of dreams' which appears to be 'So various, so beautiful, so new, / Hath really neither joy, nor love, nor light, / Nor certitude, nor peace, nor help for pain'.[29] Arnold's poem famously articulated concern for the grim scuffling and terror of a post-theological world. Situated on the same beach one hundred and forty years later, Daljit Nagra imagined the perspective of a newly arrived stowaway, 'unclocked by the national eye', and destined for illegal, low-paid employment.[30] The daily struggle for existence in this apparent 'land of dreams' has its dark coastal stories too. There is the daily battle of migrants to enter the United Kingdom and Ireland through their ports, in often desperate and hazardous conditions, sometimes alone, sometimes in groups trafficked by gangs. Nagra's stowaway dreams of freedom for 'my love and I, / our sundry others' in the only way imaginable to someone who works night shifts for low pay, as sunshine and cash: 'we raise our charged glasses over unparasol'd tables / East, babbling our lingoes, flecked by the chalk of Britannia!'.[31] But this dream is haunted by the recent contexts of migrant deaths, in particular the fifty-eight Chinese migrants who were found dead in the back of a truck in Dover in June 2000, as commemorated in Philippe Cherbonnier's play *58* (2004), and the twenty-three Chinese cockle-pickers caught by the incoming tide on the treacherous level sands of Morecambe Bay in February 2004, which forms the focal narrative of Nick Broomfield's film *Ghosts* (2006). Most of these migrants came from the same Fujian province in eastern China, and made long, arduous, and costly journeys in the hope of finding better lives and earning money to send to their families. They must have believed in the 'land of dreams', but found instead Arnold's nightmare. These coastal stories show us another bearing for archipelagic thought, another urgent reason why we need to re-think and re-imagine our existing social and political geographies. Only when we can articulate the local distinctiveness and plurality of these islands as a geography of inclusion, connection, and openness can we truly begin to imagine an archipelago 'so various, so beautiful, so new'.

NOTES

1. John Hewitt, 'The Coasters', *The Collected Poems of John Hewitt*, ed. Frank Ormsby. Belfast: Blackstaff Press, 1991, 135–7.
2. John Hewitt, 'Regionalism: The Last Chance', *Ancestral Voices: The Selected Prose of John Hewitt*, ed. Tom Clyde. Belfast: Blackstaff Press, 1987, 125 (122–5).
3. Patrick Kavanagh, *A Poet's Country: Selected Prose*, ed. Antoinette Quinn. Dublin: Lilliput, 2003, 237.
4. Ibid. 191.
5. Hewitt, 'Regionalism', 122.
6. Jonathan Raban, *Coasting*. London: Picador, 1987, 22.
7. Ibid. 17, 20.
8. Ibid. 113, 117.
9. Ibid. 101, 113.
10. Graham Swift, *Last Orders*. London: Picador, 1996, 286–95.
11. Penelope Fitzgerald, *Offshore*. London: Fourth Estate, 2009.
12. Kazuo Ishiguro, *The Remains of the Day*. London: Faber, 1989, 231–45.
13. Iain Sinclair, *White Chappell, Scarlet Tracings*. London: Granta, 1998, 209–10.
14. Paul Theroux, *The Kingdom by the Sea*. London: Penguin, 1984, 360.
15. Raban, *Coasting*, 299.
16. Iain Sinclair, *Lights Out for the Territory*. London: Granta, 1997, 1.
17. Tim Robinson, *My Time in Space*. Dublin: Lilliput, 2001, 16.
18. Tim Robinson, *Stones of Aran: Pilgrimage*. London: Faber, 2008, 19.
19. Ibid. 20.
20. Tim Robinson, *Setting Foot on the Shores of Connemara, and Other Writings*. Dublin: Lilliput, 2007, 213.
21. Robinson, *Stones of Aran: Pilgrimage*, 7.
22. See Jos Smith, 'An Archipelagic Environment: Re-Writing the British and Irish Landscape, 1972–2012'. Unpublished PhD thesis, University of Exeter, 2012.
23. Sue Clifford and Angela King, *England in Particular: A Celebration of the Commonplace, the Local, the Vernacular, and the Distinctive*. London: Hodder and Stoughton, 2006, ix.
24. Kathleen Jamie, *Sightlines*. London: Sort Of Books, 2012, 158.
25. Robert Macfarlane, *The Old Ways: A Journey on Foot*. London: Penguin, 2012, 17.
26. Fiona Stafford, *Local Attachments: The Province of Poetry*. Oxford: Oxford University Press, 2010.
27. Nick Groom, *The Seasons: An Elegy for the Passing of the Year*. London: Atlantic, 2013, 322.
28. Clifford and King, *England in Particular*, xiii.
29. Matthew Arnold, 'Dover Beach', *The Penguin Book of English Verse*, ed. Paul Keegan. London: Penguin, 2004, 762.
30. Daljit Nagra, 'Look We Have Coming to Dover!', *Look We Have Coming to Dover!* London: Faber, 2007, 32.
31. Ibid. 32.

Bibliography

Adelman, Juliana and Éadaoin Agnew (eds), *Science and Technology in Nineteenth-Century Ireland*. Dublin: Four Courts Press, 2011.

Alaya, Flavia, *William Sharp – 'Fiona Macleod': 1855–1905*. Cambridge, MA: Harvard University Press, 1970.

Alexander, Edward, '*Fin de Siècle, Fin du Globe*: Yeats and Hardy in the Nineties', *Bucknell Review*, 23.2 (1977), 142–63.

Alford, Norman, *The Rhymers' Club*. Victoria, BC: Cormorant Press, 1980.

Allen, Nicholas, *1916: Ireland, Empire and Rebellion*, forthcoming.

Allen, Nicholas, *George Russell (AE) and the New Ireland, 1905–1930*. Dublin: Four Courts Press, 2003.

Allen, Nicholas, 'Synge, Reading, and Archipelago', in Brian Cliff and Nicholas Grene (eds), *Synge and Edwardian Ireland*. Oxford: Oxford University Press, 2012, 159–71.

Allison, Jonathan, 'W. B. Yeats, Space, and Cultural Nationalism', *ANQ*, 14.4 (Fall 2001), 55–67.

Alt, Christina, *Virginia Woolf and the Study of Nature*. Cambridge: Cambridge University Press, 2010.

Arendt, Hannah, *Reflections on Literature and Culture*, ed. Susannah Young-Ah Gottlieb. Stanford: Stanford University Press, 2007.

Arnold, Matthew, 'Dover Beach', *The Penguin Book of English Verse*, ed. Paul Keegan. London: Penguin, 2004, 762.

Ashley, Scott, 'Primitivism, Celticism and Morbidity in the Atlantic *fin de siècle*', in Patrick McGuinness (ed.), *Symbolism, Decadence and the Fin de Siècle: French and European Perspectives*. Exeter: University of Exeter Press, 2000, 175–93.

Attis, David and Charles Mollan (eds), *Science and Irish Culture: Why the History of Science Matters in Ireland*. Dublin: Royal Dublin Society, 2004.

Auden, W. H., *Collected Poems*, ed. Edward Mendelson. London: Faber, 2007.

Auden, W. H., *The Enchafèd Flood: or The Romantic Iconography of the Sea*. London: Faber, 1951.

Auden, W. H., *The English Auden: Poems, Essays and Dramatic Writings, 1927–1939*, ed. Edward Mendelson. London: Faber, 1986.

Auden, W. H., 'Introduction', *The Oxford Book of Light Verse*. London: Clarendon Press, 1938, vii–xx.

Auden, W. H. and Louis MacNeice, *Letters from Iceland*. London: Faber, 1967.

Auge, Marc, *Non-Places: Introduction to an Anthropology of Supermodernity*. London: Verso, 1995.

Back, Les, 'Falling from the Sky', *Patterns of Prejudice*, 37.3 (2003), 341–53.

Baldacchino, Godfrey, 'Editorial: Islands – Objects of Representation', *Geografiska Annaler: Series B – Human Geography*, 87.4 (2005), 247–8.

Ballard, J. G., *The Drowned World*. London: HarperCollins, 2008.

Barkan, Elazar, *The Retreat of Scientific Racism: Changing Concepts of Race in Britain and the United States between the World Wars*. Cambridge: Cambridge University Press, 1992.

Barkan, Elazar and Ronald Bush (eds), *Prehistories of the Future: The Primitivist Project and the Culture of Modernism*. Stanford: Stanford University Press, 1995.

Bartholomew, Michael, 'H. V. Morton's English Utopia', in Christopher Lawrence and Anna-K. Mayer (eds), *Regenerating England: Science, Medicine and Culture in Inter-War Britain*. Amsterdam: Rodopi, 2000, 25–44.

Bartholomew, Michael, *In Search of H. V. Morton*. London: Methuen, 2004.

Bate, Jonathan, *The Song of the Earth*. London: Picador, 2000.

Baucom, Ian, *Specters of the Atlantic: Finance Capital, Slavery, and the Philosophy of History*. Durham, NC: Duke University Press, 2005.

Beckett, Samuel, *The Unnamable, The Grove Centenary Edition: Novels II*. New York: Grove Press, 2006.

Beckson, Karl, *Arthur Symons: A Life*. Oxford: Clarendon Press, 1987.

Beekman Taylor, Paul, 'Auden's Icelandic Myth of Exile', *Journal of Modern Literature*, 24.2 (Winter 2000–1), 213–34.

Beer, Gillian, 'Has Nature a Future?', in Elinor S. Shaffer (ed.), *The Third Culture: Literature and Science*. Berlin: De Gruyter, 1998, 15–27.

Beer, Gillian, *Virginia Woolf: The Common Ground*. Edinburgh: Edinburgh University Press, 1996.

Behan, Brendan, *Brendan Behan's Island*. London: Corgi, 1965.

Bell, Michael, *Literature, Modernism and Myth: Belief and Responsibility in the Twentieth Century*. Cambridge: Cambridge University Press, 1997.

Bell, Morag, Tim Brown, and Lucy Faire, 'Germs, Genes and Postcolonial

Geographies: Reading the Return of Tuberculosis to Leicester, UK, 2001', *Cultural Geographies*, 13 (2006), 577–99.

Bennett, Louise, *Selected Poems*, ed. Mervyn Morris. Kingston: Sangster's Book Store, 1982.

Benziman, Galia, '"Dispersed are we": Mirroring and National Identity in Virginia Woolf's *Between the Acts*', *Journal of Narrative Theory*, 36.1 (2006), 53–71.

Berman, Jessica, *Modernist Fiction, Cosmopolitanism, and the Politics of Community*. Cambridge: Cambridge University Press, 2001.

Berry, R. J., *Islands*. New Naturalist Library. London: HarperCollins, 2009.

Betjeman, John, *Collected Poems*. London: John Murray, 1979.

Bluemel, Kristin (ed.), *Intermodernism: Literary Culture in Mid-Twentieth-Century Britain*. Edinburgh: Edinburgh University Press, 2009.

Blum, Hester, 'The Prospect of Oceanic Studies', *PMLA*, 125.3 (May 2010), 670–7.

Blum, Hester, *The View from the Masthead: Maritime Imagination and Antebellum American Sea Narratives*. Chapel Hill: University of North Carolina Press, 2008.

Boddy, Kasia, 'The Modern Beach', *Critical Quarterly*, 49.4 (2007), 21–39.

Bogdanor, Vernon, *Devolution in the United Kingdom*. Oxford: Oxford University Press, 2001.

Boland, Eavan, 'The Northern Writers' Crisis of Conscience – 2. Crisis', *Irish Times*, 13 August 1970, 12.

Boland, Eavan, 'The Northern Writers' Crisis of Conscience – 3. Conclusion', *Irish Times*, 14 August 1970, 12.

Bold, Alan, *MacDiarmid*. London: Paladin, 1990.

Boly, John R., 'Auden and Modern Theory', in Stan Smith (ed.), *The Cambridge Companion to W. H. Auden*. Cambridge: Cambridge University Press, 2004, 137–51.

Bornstein, George, 'Remaking Himself: Yeats's Revisions of His Early Canon', *Text*, 5 (1991), 339–58.

Botar, Oliver A. I. and Isabel Wünsche (eds), *Biocentrism and Modernism*. Farnham, Surrey: Ashgate, 2011.

Bourne, George, *Change in the Village*. Harmondsworth: Penguin, 1984.

Bowers, Paul, '"Variability in Every Tongue": Joyce and the Darwinian Narrative', *James Joyce Quarterly*, 36.4 (Summer 1999), 869–88.

Bradbury, Malcolm and James McFarlane (eds), *Modernism: A Guide to European Literature 1890–1930*. London: Penguin, 1991.

Bradshaw, David (ed.), *A Concise Companion to Modernism*. Oxford: Blackwell, 2003.

Brannigan, John, 'Dreaming of the Islands: The Poetry of the Shipping Forecast', in John Brannigan (ed.), *Reconceiving the British Isles*. UCDscholarcast: Series 4, 2010: <http://www.ucd.ie/scholarcast/scholarcast25.html> (last accessed 25 April 2014).

Brett, David, *A Book Around the Irish Sea: History without Nations*. Dublin: Wordwell, 2009.

Bridges, Robert, *The Shorter Poems*. London: George Bell, 1899.

Brooker, Peter, *Bohemia in London: The Social Scene of Early Modernism*. Basingstoke: Palgrave, 2004.

Brophy, Brigid, *In Transit*. London: GMP, 1989.

Brown, Ian and Alan Riach (eds), *The Edinburgh Companion to Twentieth-Century Scottish Literature*. Edinburgh: Edinburgh University Press, 2009.

Brown, Richard, *James Joyce and Sexuality*. Cambridge: Cambridge University Press, 1985.

Brown, Terence, *The Life of W. B. Yeats: A Critical Biography*. Dublin: Gill and Macmillan, 1999.

Brown, Terence, *The Literature of Ireland: Culture and Criticism*. Cambridge: Cambridge University Press, 2010.

Brown, Terence, '"What am I doing here?" Travel and MacNeice', in Fran Brearton and Edna Longley (eds), *Incorrigibly Plural: Louis MacNeice and his Legacy*. Manchester: Carcanet, 2012, 72–84.

Bryant, Marsha, 'Auden and the "Arctic Stare": Documentary as Public Collage in *Letters from Iceland*', *Journal of Modern Literature*, 17.4 (1991), 537–65.

Buell, Lawrence, *The Environmental Imagination: Thoreau, Nature Writing, and the Formation of American Culture*. Cambridge, MA: Harvard University Press, 1995.

Bunreacht na hÉireann/Constitution of Ireland. Dublin: Government Publications, 1990.

Burdsey, Daniel, 'Strangers on the Shore? Racialized Representation, Identity and In/visibilities of Whiteness at the English Seaside', *Cultural Sociology*, 5.4 (2011), 537–52.

Burke, Mary, 'Evolutionary Theory and the Search for Lost Innocence in the Writings of J. M. Synge', *Canadian Journal of Irish Studies*, 30.1 (Spring 2004), 48–54.

Burke, Oliver J., *The South Isles of Aran (County Galway)*. London: Kegan Paul, Trench and Co., 1887.

Burrow, Trigant, *The Biology of Human Conflict: An Anatomy of Behavior, Individual and Social*. London: Macmillan, 1937.

Burton, Richard F., *Ultima Thule; Or, A Summer in Iceland*. London: William P. Nimmo, 1875.

Burton, Valerie, 'Fish/Wives: An Introduction', *Signs*, 37.3 (Spring 2012), 527–36.

Buthley, Kenneth, *Hugh MacDiarmid*. Edinburgh: Oliver and Boyd, 1964.

Caball, Marc and Clara Cullen (eds), *Communities of Knowledge in Nineteenth-Century Ireland*. Dublin: Four Courts Press, 2013.

Carné, Marcel, *Le Quai des Brumes*. Studio Canal, 1938.

Carpenter, Edward J. and K. L. Smith Jr, 'Plastics on the Sargasso Sea Surface', *Science*, 175.4027 (17 March 1972), 1240–1.

Carpenter, Humphrey, *W. H. Auden: A Biography*. London: George Allen and Unwin, 1981.

Carson, Rachel, *The Edge of the Sea*. Boston: Mariner, 1998.

Casarino, Cesare, *Modernity at Sea: Melville, Marx, Conrad in Crisis*. Minneapolis: University of Minnesota Press, 2002.

Casey, Edward S., *Remembering: A Phenomenological Study*. Bloomington: Indiana University Press, 1987.

Castle, Gregory, '"I Am Almosting It": History, Nature, and the Will to Power in "Proteus"', *James Joyce Quarterly*, 29.2 (Winter 1992), 281–96.

Castle, Gregory, 'Irish Revivalism: Critical Trends and New Directions', *Literature Compass*, 8.5 (2011), 291–303.

Castle, Gregory, *Modernism and the Celtic Revival*. Cambridge: Cambridge University Press, 2001.

Chamberlain, Brenda, *Tide-race*. Bridgend: Seren, 2007.

Child, Francis James (ed.), *The English and Scottish Popular Ballads*, Part IX. Boston: Houghton, Mifflin and Co., 1894.

Childe, V. G., *Prehistoric Communities of the British Isles*. London: Chambers, 1940.

Childs, Donald J., *Modernism and Eugenics: Woolf, Eliot, Yeats, and the Culture of Degeneration*. Cambridge: Cambridge University Press, 2001.

Churchill, Winston, *A History of the English-Speaking Peoples*. London: Cassell, 1956.

Churchill, Winston, *Never Give In! The Best of Winston Churchill's Speeches*. London: Pimlico, 2003.

Clark, Heather, 'Leaving Barra, Leaving Inishmore: Islands in the Irish Protestant Imagination', *Canadian Journal of Irish Studies*, 35.2 (Fall 2009), 30–5.

Clark, Heather, *The Ulster Renaissance: Poetry in Belfast, 1962–1972*. Oxford: Oxford University Press, 2006.

Clarke, Hyde, 'Examination of the Legend of Atlantis in Reference to Protohistoric Communication with America', *Transactions of the Royal Historical Society*, 3 (1886), 1–46.

Clifford, James, *Routes: Travel and Translation in the Late Twentieth Century*. Cambridge, MA: Harvard University Press, 1997.

Clifford, Sue and Angela King, *England in Particular: A Celebration of the Commonplace, the Local, the Vernacular, and the Distinctive*. London: Hodder and Stoughton, 2006.

Cobbe, Frances Power, *Darwinism in Morals and Other Essays*. London: Williams and Norgate, 1872.

Cohen, Margaret, 'Literary Studies on the Terraqueous Globe', *PMLA*, 125.3 (May 2010), 657–62.

Cohen, Margaret, *The Novel and the Sea*. Princeton: Princeton University Press, 2010.

Cohen, Margaret and Carolyn Dever (eds), *The Literary Channel: The Inter-National Invention of the Novel*. Princeton: Princeton University Press, 2002.

Colls, Robert, *George Orwell: English Rebel*. Oxford: Oxford University Press, 2013.

Colls, Robert, *Identity of England*. Oxford: Oxford University Press, 2002.

Connolly, Claire, 'Four Nations Feminism: Una Troy and Menna Gallie', in John Brannigan (ed.), *Reconceiving the British Isles*. UCDscholarcast: Series 4, 2010: <www.ucd.ie/scholarcast/scholarcast19.html> (last accessed 25 April 2014).

Connolly, Claire, 'Via Holyhead: Material and Metaphoric Meanings between Ireland and Wales', in John Brannigan (ed.), *The Literatures and Cultures of the Irish Sea*. UCDscholarcast: Series 7, 2013: <www.ucd.ie/scholarcast/scholarcast35.html> (last accessed 25 April 2014).

Conran, Tony, *Frontiers in Anglo-Welsh Poetry*. Cardiff: University of Wales Press, 1997.

Corbin, Alain, *The Lure of the Sea: The Discovery of the Seaside in the Western World, 1750–1840*, trans. Jocelyn Phelps. Berkeley: University of California Press, 1994.

Corry, Geoffrey, 'The Dublin Bar: The Obstacle to the Improvement of the Port of Dublin', *Dublin Historical Record*, 23.4 (July 1970), 137–52.

Craik, D. M. M., *Our Year: A Child's Book, in Prose and Verse*. New York and Philadelphia: Frederick Leypoint, 1866.

Crangle, Sara, 'Ivy Compton-Burnett and Risibility', in Marina MacKay and Lyndsey Stonebridge (eds), *British Fiction After Modernism: The Novel at Mid-Century*. Basingstoke: Palgrave, 2007, 99–120.

Cresswell, Tim, 'Weeds, Plagues, and Bodily Secretions: A Geographical Interpretation of Metaphors of Displacement', *Annals of the Association of American Geographers*, 87.2 (June 1997), 330–45.

Crotty, Patrick, 'Swordsmen: W. B. Yeats and Hugh MacDiarmid', in Peter Mackay, Edna Longley, and Fran Brearton (eds), *Modern Irish and Scottish Poetry*. Cambridge: Cambridge University Press, 2011, 20–38.

Cunningham, Valentine, *British Writers of the Thirties*. Oxford: Oxford University Press, 1988.

Cunningham, Valentine, 'MacNeice and Thirties (Classical) Pastoralism', in Fran Brearton and Edna Longley (eds), *Incorrigibly Plural: Louis MacNeice and his Legacy*. Manchester: Carcanet, 2012, 85–100.

Czarnecki, Kristin (ed.), 'Woolf and Nature': Special Issue, *Virginia Woolf Miscellany*, 78 (Fall/Winter 2010).

Czarnecki, Kristin and Carrie Rohman (eds), *Virginia Woolf and the Natural World: Selected Papers from the Twentieth Annual International Conference on Virginia Woolf*. Clemson, SC: Clemson University Digital Press, 2011.

Darwin, Charles, *The Descent of Man, and Selection in Relation to Sex*, vol. 1. London: John Murray, 1871.

Davidson, John, *St George's Day: A Fleet Street Eclogue*. London: John Lane, 1895.

Davies, Norman, *The Isles: A History*. London: Macmillan, 2000.

Deacon, G. E. R., 'The Sargasso Sea', *The Geographical Journal*, 99.1 (January 1942), 16–28.

de Selincourt, Aubrey, *The Channel Shore*. London: Robert Hale, 1953.

Donnelly, Ignatius, *Atlantis: The Antediluvian World*. New York: Harper and Brothers, 1882.

Doughty, Charles M., *The Dawn in Britain*. Six volumes. London: Duckworth, 1906.

Dowson, Ernest et al., *The Book of the Rhymers' Club*. London: Elkin Mathews, 1892.

Dowson, Ernest et al., *The Second Book of the Rhymers' Club*. London: Elkin Mathews, 1894.

Duddy, Thomas, 'The Irish Response to Darwinism', in Juliana Adelman and Éadaoin Agnew (eds), *Science and Technology in Nineteenth-Century Ireland*. Dublin: Four Courts Press, 2011, 18–31.

Dzenitis, Sigurds, *Die Rezeption Deutscher Literatur in England durch Wystan Hugh Auden und Christopher Isherwood*. Hamburg: Hartmut Lüdtke Verlag, 1972.

Eide, Marian, 'The Language of Flows: Fluidity, Virology, and "Finnegans Wake"', *James Joyce Quarterly*, 34.4 (Summer 1997), 473–88.

Eliot, T. S., *Collected Poems 1909–1962*. London: Faber, 1974.

Ellmann, Richard, 'The Backgrounds of "The Dead"', *The Kenyon Review*, 20.4 (Autumn 1958), 507–28.

Ellmann, Richard, *The Consciousness of Joyce*. London: Faber, 1977.

Ellmann, Richard, *James Joyce: New and Revised Edition*. Oxford: Oxford University Press, 1982.

Esty, Jed, *A Shrinking Island: Modernism and National Culture in England*. Princeton: Princeton University Press, 2004.

Evans, J. D., 'Islands as Laboratories for the Study of Cultural Process', in A. C. Renfrew (ed.), *The Explanation of Culture Change: Models in Prehistory*. London: Duckworth, 1973, 517–20.

Faubel, Arthur L., *Cork and the American Cork Industry*. New York: The Cork Institute of America, 1941.

Feigel, Lara and Alexandra Harris (eds), *Modernism on Sea: Art and Culture at the British Seaside*. Oxford: Peter Lang, 2011.

Ferguson, Megan C., 'Patrick Geddes and the Celtic Renascence in the 1890s'. Unpublished PhD thesis, University of Dundee, January 2011.

Ferguson, Samuel, *Congal: A Poem in Five Books*. Dublin: Edward Ponsonby, 1872.

Ferrebe, Alice, 'Elizabeth Taylor's Uses of Romance: Feminist Feeling in 1950s English Fiction', *Literature and History*, 19.1 (Spring 2010), 50–64.

Ferris, Tom, *Irish Railways: A New History*. Dublin: Gill and Macmillan, 2008.

Feshbach, Sidney, 'Literal/Littoral/Littorananima: The Figure of the Shore in the Works of James Joyce', in A. T. Tymieniecka (ed.), *Analecta Husserliana*, 19 (1985), 325–42.

Feshbach, Sidney, 'Stephen's Wavespeech', *James Joyce Quarterly*, 44.3 (Spring 2007), 557–8.

Firor, Ruth A., *Folkways in Thomas Hardy*. New York: Perpetua, 1962.

Fischer, Joachim, 'Reviews', *Irish Studies Review*, 9.2 (2001), 264–6.

Fischer, Steven Roger, *Islands: From Atlantis to Zanzibar*. London: Reaktion, 2012.

Fisher, James, *Rockall*. London: Geoffrey Bles, 1956.

Fitzgerald, Penelope, *Offshore*. London: Fourth Estate, 2009.

Fitzpatrick, David, 'Synge and Modernity in *The Aran Islands*', in Brian Cliff and Nicholas Grene (eds), *Synge and Edwardian Ireland*. Oxford: Oxford University Press, 2012, 121–58.

Flood, Donal T., 'The Birth of Bull Island', *Dublin Historical Record*, 28.4 (September 1975), 142–53.

Forster, E. M., 'Introductory Note', in Maurice O'Sullivan, *Twenty Years A-Growing*. Oxford: Oxford University Press, 1983, v–vi.

Foster, R. F., *The Irish Story: Telling Tales and Making It Up in Ireland*. London: Penguin, 2001.

Foster, R. F., *W. B. Yeats: A Life – I. The Apprentice Mage*. Oxford: Oxford University Press, 1997.

Frank, Jill, *Islands and the Modernists: The Lure of Isolation in Art, Literature, and Science*. Jefferson, NC: McFarland and Co., 2006.

Freeman, T. W., 'The Congested Districts of Western Ireland', *Geographical Review*, 33.1 (January 1943), 1–14.

Freestone, David and Kate Killerlain Morrison, 'The Sargasso Sea', *The International Journal of Marine and Coastal Law*, 27 (2012), 647–55.

Freyer, Grattan, *Peadar O'Donnell*. Lewisburg: Bucknell University Press, 1973.

Friedman, Susan Stanford, *Mappings: Feminism and the Cultural Geographies of Encounter*. Princeton: Princeton University Press, 1998.

Frost, Robert, *The Poetry of Robert Frost*, ed. Edward Connery Lathem. London: Vintage, 2001.

Froude, James Anthony, *The English in the West Indies, or the Bow of Ulysses*. London: Longman, Green and Co., 1888.

Fuller, John, *A Reader's Guide to W. H. Auden*. London: Thames and Hudson, 1970.

Fussell, Paul, *Abroad: British Literary Traveling Between the Wars*. Oxford: Oxford University Press, 1980.

Gairn, Louisa, 'MacDiarmid and Ecology', in Scott Lyall and Margery Palmer McCulloch (eds), *The Edinburgh Companion to Hugh MacDiarmid*. Edinburgh: Edinburgh University Press, 2011, 82–96.

Gallie, Menna, *You're Welcome to Ulster*. Dinas Powys: Honno, 2010.

Gardiner, Michael, *The Cultural Roots of British Devolution*. Edinburgh: Edinburgh University Press, 2004.

Garrigan Mattar, Sinead, *Primitivism, Science, and the Irish Revival*. Oxford: Oxford University Press, 2004.

Gervais, David, *Literary Englands: Versions of 'Englishness' in Modern Writing*. Cambridge: Cambridge University Press, 1993.

Ghiselin, Brewster, 'The Unity of *Dubliners*', in Peter K. Garrett (ed.), *Twentieth Century Interpretations of Dubliners*. Englewood Cliffs, NJ: Prentice-Hall Inc., 1968, 57–85.

Gibson, Andrew, *Joyce's Revenge: History, Politics, and Aesthetics in* Ulysses. Oxford: Oxford University Press, 2002.

Gikandi, Simon, *Maps of Englishness: Writing Identity in the Culture of Colonialism*. New York: Columbia University Press, 1996.

Gilligan, H. A., *A History of the Port of Dublin*. Dublin: Gill and Macmillan, 1988.

Gillis, Alan, '"Any Dark Saying": Louis MacNeice in the Nineteen Fifties', *Irish University Review*, 42.1 (Spring 2012), 105–23.

Gilroy, Paul, *Postcolonial Melancholia*. New York: Columbia University Press, 2005.

Gordon, Seton, *Islands of the West*. London: Cassell, 1933.

Gosse, Edmund, *Father and Son*. London: Penguin, 1982.

Gould, Rupert T., *Oddities: A Book of Unexplained Facts*. Glasgow: Glasgow University Press, 1928.

Greene, David H. and Edward M. Stephens, *J. M. Synge, 1871–1909*. New York: Collier, 1961.

Groom, Nick, *The Seasons: An Elegy for the Passing of the Year*. London: Atlantic, 2013.

Gunn, Neil M., *Morning Tide*. London: Souvenir, 1975.

Gurney, Peter, '"Intersex" and "Dirty Girls": Mass-Observation and Working-Class Sexuality in England in the 1930s', *Journal of the History of Sexuality*, 8.2 (October 1997), 256–90.

Haddon, A. C., 'The Aran Islands: A Study in Irish Ethnography', *The Irish Naturalist*, 2.12 (December 1893), 303–8.

Haddon, A. C., *The Races of Man and Their Distribution*. Cambridge: Cambridge University Press, 1924.

Haddon, A. C. and C. R. Browne, 'The Ethnography of the Aran Islands, County Galway', *Proceedings of the Royal Irish Academy (1889–1901)*, vol. 2 (1891–1893), 768–830.

Halloran, William F., 'W. B. Yeats, William Sharp, and Fiona Macleod: A Celtic Drama, 1887–1897', in Warwick Gould (ed.), *Yeats Annual No. 13*. Basingstoke: Palgrave, 1998, 62–109.

Halloran, William F., 'W. B. Yeats, William Sharp, and Fiona Macleod: A Celtic Drama, 1897', in Warwick Gould (ed.), *Yeats Annual No. 14: Yeats and the Nineties – A Special Number*. Basingstoke: Palgrave, 2001, 159–208.

Hardy, Thomas, *The Complete Poems*, ed. James Gibson. Basingstoke: Palgrave, 2001.

Hardy, Thomas, *Tess of the D'Urbervilles*. Oxford: Oxford World's Classics, 2005.

Harris, Jose, *Private Lives, Public Spirit: Britain 1870–1914*. London: Penguin, 1994.

Harvie, Christopher, *A Floating Commonwealth: Politics, Culture, and Technology on Britain's Atlantic Coast, 1860–1930*. Oxford: Oxford University Press, 2008.

Hay, Pete, 'A Phenomenology of Islands', *Island Studies Journal*, 1.1 (2006), 19–42.

Heaney, Seamus, 'A Torchlight Procession of One', *Parnassus: Poetry in Review*, 21.1–2 (1996), 11–29.

Hegarty, Peter, *Peadar O'Donnell*. Cork: Mercier Press, 1999.

Heidegger, Martin, 'The Origin of the Work of Art', *Poetry, Language, Thought*, trans. Albert Hofstadter. New York: HarperCollins, 1971, 15–86.

Heise, Ursula K., *Sense of Place and Sense of Planet: The Environmental Imagination of the Global*. Oxford: Oxford University Press, 2008.

Hewitt, John, *Ancestral Voices: The Selected Prose of John Hewitt*, ed. Tom Clyde. Belfast: Blackstaff Press, 1987.

Hewitt, John, *The Collected Poems of John Hewitt*, ed. Frank Ormsby. Belfast: Blackstaff Press, 1991.

Higgins, Geraldine, 'The Quotable Yeats: Modified in the Guts of the Living', *South Carolina Review*, 32.1 (Fall 1999), 184–92.

Hillan King, Sophia, 'The Note of Exile: Michael McLaverty's Rathlin Island', in Gerald Dawe and John Wilson Foster (eds), *The Poet's Place: Ulster Literature and Society, Essays in Honour of John Hewitt, 1907–1987*. Belfast: Institute of Irish Studies, 1991, 181–92.

Hillan King, Sophia, *The Silken Twine: A Study of the Works of Michael McLaverty*. Dublin: Poolbeg, 1992.

Hofheinz, Thomas, '"Group Drinkards Maaks Grope Thinkards": Narrative in the "Norwegian Captain" Episode of "Finnegans Wake"', *James Joyce Quarterly*, 29.3 (Spring 1992), 643–58.

Hogan, Gerard (ed.), *The Origins of the Irish Constitution, 1928–1941*. Dublin: Royal Irish Academy, 2012.

Holman, Kate, *Brenda Chamberlain*. Cardiff: University of Wales Press, 1997.

Horrebow, Niels, *The Natural History of Iceland*. London: A. Linde et al., 1758.

Housman, A. E., *A Shropshire Lad*. New York: John Lane, 1917.

Hughes, Linda K., 'Ironizing Prosody in John Davidson's "A Ballad in Blank Verse"', *Victorian Poetry*, 49.2 (Summer 2011), 161–78.

Huntingdon, Ellsworth, *Civilization and Climate*. New Haven: Yale University Press, 1915.

Hussey, M. O., 'Sandymount and the Herberts', *Dublin Historical Record*, 24.3 (June 1971), 76–84.

Hussey, Mark, *'I'd make it penal': The Rural Preservation Movement in Virginia Woolf's* Between the Acts. Bloomsbury Heritage Series. London: Cecil Woolf, 2011.

Huxley, Julian, A. C. Haddon, and A. M. Carr-Saunders, *We Europeans: A Survey of 'Racial' Problems*. Harmondsworth: Penguin, 1939.

Ishiguro, Kazuo, *The Remains of the Day*. London: Faber, 1989.

Jackson, Holbrook, *The Eighteen Nineties: A Review of Art and Ideas at the Close of the Nineteenth Century*. London: Grant Richards, 1922.

Jameson, Fredric, *Archaeologies of the Future: The Desire Called Utopia and Other Science Fictions*. London: Verso, 2007.

Jameson, Fredric, 'Cognitive Mapping', in Cary Nelson and Lawrence Grossberg (eds), *Marxism and the Interpretation of Culture*. Urbana, IL: University of Illinois Press, 1988, 347–60.

Jamie, Kathleen, *Sightlines*. London: Sort Of Books, 2012.

Jefferies, Richard, *After London: Wild England*. Oxford: Oxford World's Classics, 1980.

Jefferies, Richard, *Amaryllis at the Fair*. London: Sampson Low, Marston, Searle, and Rivington, 1887.

Jefferies, Richard, *The Story of My Heart: My Autobiography*. Totnes, Devon: Green Books, 2002.

Jefferies, Richard, *Wild Life in a Southern County*. Stanbridge, Dorset: Little Toller Books, 2011.

Johnson, Lionel, *The Art of Thomas Hardy*. London: Elkin Mathews and John Lane, 1894.

Johnson, Samuel, 'Discourses on the Weather', *The Idler*, 11 (24 June 1758).

Jones, Chris, 'Auden and "The 'Barbaric' Poetry of the North": Unchaining One's Daimon', *The Review of English Studies*, 53.210 (2002), 167–85.

Jones, Greta, 'Contested Territories: Alfred Cort Haddon, Progressive Evolutionism and Ireland', *History of European Ideas*, 24.3 (1998), 195–211.

Jones, Greta, *Social Darwinism and English Thought: The Interaction Between Biological and Social Theory*. Sussex: Harvester, 1980.

Jones, Olive and Catherine Sullivan, *The Parks Canada Glass Glossary*. Studies in Archaeology, Architecture and History. Ottawa: Ministry of Supply and Services, 1989.

Jones, Owain, '"The Breath of the Moon": The Rhythmic and Affective Time-Spaces of UK Tides', in Tim Edensor (ed.), *Geographies of Rhythm: Nature, Place, Mobilities and Bodies*. Farnham, Surrey: Ashgate, 2010, 189–204.

Joyce, James, *Dubliners*. Oxford: Oxford World's Classics, 2000.

Joyce, James, *Finnegans Wake*. Oxford: Oxford World's Classics, 2012.

Joyce, James, *James Joyce: The Critical Writings*, ed. Ellsworth Mason and Richard Ellmann. Ithaca, NY: Cornell University Press, 1989.

Joyce, James, *Letters of James Joyce*, vol. 1, ed. Stuart Gilbert. London: Faber, 1957.

Joyce, James, *A Portrait of the Artist as a Young Man*. Oxford: Oxford World's Classics, 2000.

Joyce, James, *Ulysses*. Oxford: Oxford World's Classics, 1993.

Kavanagh, Patrick, *A Poet's Country: Selected Prose*, ed. Antoinette Quinn. Dublin: Lilliput, 2003.

Kelleher, Margaret (ed.), *New Perspectives on the Irish Literary Revival: Special Issue, Irish University Review*, 33.1 (Spring/Summer 2003).

Kennedy, P. G., 'Bird Life on the North Bull', *The Irish Naturalists' Journal*, 5.7 (January 1935), 165–8.

Kenner, Hugh, 'Molly's Masterstroke', *James Joyce Quarterly*, 10 (Fall 1972), 19–28.

Kern, Robert, 'Ecocriticism: What Is It Good For?', *ISLE: Interdisciplinary Studies in Literature and Environment*, 7.1 (2000), 9–32.

Kerrigan, John, *Archipelagic English: Literature, History, and Politics 1603–1707*. Oxford: Oxford University Press, 2008.

Kerrigan, John, 'The Ticking Fear', *London Review of Books*, 30.3 (7 February 2008), 15–18.

Kestner, Joseph A., 'Youth by the Sea: The Ephebe in "A Portrait of the Artist as a Young Man" and "Ulysses"', *James Joyce Quarterly*, 31.3 (Spring 1994), 233–76.

Kiberd, Declan, *Inventing Ireland: The Literature of the Modern Nation*. London: Jonathan Cape, 1995.

Kiberd, Declan, *Irish Classics*. London: Granta, 2000.

Kiberd, Declan, *The Irish Writer and the World*. Cambridge: Cambridge University Press, 2005.

Kiberd, Declan, *Synge and the Irish Language*. Dublin: Gill and Macmillan, 1993.

Kiberd, Declan, 'Synge, Symons, and the Isles of Aran', *Notes on Modern Irish Literature*, 1 (1989), 32–9.

Kipling, Rudyard, *Kipling and the Sea: Voyages and Discoveries from North Atlantic to South Pacific*, ed. Andrew Lycett. London: I.B. Tauris, 2014.

Lamming, George, *The Emigrants*. London: Allison and Busby, 1980.

Lamming, George, *The Pleasures of Exile*. London: Allison and Busby, 1984.

Larkin, Philip, *Collected Poems*, ed. Anthony Thwaite. London: Faber, 1988.

Lawless, Emily, *Grania: The Story of an Island*. London: Macmillan, 1892.

Lawless, Emily, 'A Note on the Ethics of Literary Forgery', *The Nineteenth Century* (January 1897), 84–95.

Lawrence, Karen R., *Penelope Voyages: Women and Travel in the British Literary Tradition*. Ithaca, NY: Cornell University Press, 1994.

Leavis, F. R. and Denys Thompson, *Culture and Environment: The Training of Critical Awareness*. London: Chatto and Windus, 1933.

Lee, Hermione, *Virginia Woolf*. London: Vintage, 1997.

Leffler, Phyllis, 'Peopling the Portholes: National Identity and Maritime Museums in the US and UK', *The Public Historian*, 26.4 (Fall 2004), 23–48.

Lewis, Eiluned, *The Captain's Wife*. London: Macmillan, 1944.

Lingard, Joan, *The Lord on Our Side*. London: Hodder and Stoughton, 1970.

Lingard, Joan, *The Twelfth Day of July*. London: Penguin, 1989.

Livorni, Ernesto, '"Ineluctable Modality of the Visible": Diaphane in the "Proteus" Episode', *James Joyce Quarterly*, 36.2 (Winter 1999), 127–69.

Lloyd, David, 'Rethinking National Marxism: James Connolly and "Celtic Communism"', *Interventions*, 5.3 (2003), 345–70.

Lockley, R. M., *Letters from Skokholm*. Stanbridge, Dorset: Little Toller Books, 2010.

Longley, Edna, 'Irish and Scottish "Island Poems"', in Robert McColl Millar (ed.), *Northern Lights, Northern Words. Selected Papers from the FRLSU Conference, Kirkwall 2009*. Aberdeen: Forum for Research on the Languages of Scotland and Ireland, 2010, 143–61.

Longley, Edna, *The Living Stream: Literature and Revisionism in Ireland*. Newcastle: Bloodaxe, 1994.

Lyall, Scott, *Hugh MacDiarmid's Poetry and Politics of Place: Imagining a Scottish Republic*. Edinburgh: Edinburgh University Press, 2006.

Lynch, Peter, *The Emergence of Numerical Weather Prediction: Richardson's Dream*. Cambridge: Cambridge University Press, 2006.

Mabey, Richard, *Flora Britannica*. London: Sinclair-Stevenson, 1996.

MacClancy, Jeremy, 'Anthropology: "The Latest Form of Evening Entertainment"', in David Bradshaw (ed.), *A Concise Companion to Modernism*. Oxford: Blackwell, 2003, 75–94.

MacConaill, Michael A., 'The Men of Rachrai', *Proceedings and Reports of the Belfast Natural History and Philosophical Society, for the Session 1922–1923*. Belfast: The Northern Whig, 1924, 4–7.

McCormack, W. J., *Fool of the Family: A Life of J. M. Synge*. London: Weidenfeld and Nicolson, 2000.

McCulloch, Margery Palmer, *Scottish Modernism and its Contexts, 1918–1959: Literature, National Identity and Cultural Exchange*. Edinburgh: Edinburgh University Press, 2009.

MacDiarmid, Hugh, *Complete Poems 1920–1976*, vol. 1, ed. Michael Grieve and W. R. Aitken. London: Martin Brian and O'Keeffe, 1978.

MacDiarmid, Hugh, *The Islands of Scotland*. London: Batsford, 1939.

MacDiarmid, Hugh, *Lucky Poet: A Self-Study in Literature and Political Ideas*. London: Methuen, 1943.

MacDiarmid, Hugh, *Selected Prose*, ed. Alan Riach. Manchester: Carcanet, 1992.

MacDiarmid, Hugh (ed.), *The Golden Treasury of Scottish Poetry*. London: Macmillan, 1940.

McDiarmid, Lucy, *Saving Civilization: Yeats, Eliot, and Auden Between the Wars*. Cambridge: Cambridge University Press, 1984.

McDonald, Peter, *Louis MacNeice: The Poet in his Contexts*. Oxford: Clarendon Press, 1991.

McDonald, Peter, 'A Poem for All Seasons: Yeats, Meaning, and the Publishing History of "The Lake Isle of Innisfree" in the 1890s', *The Yearbook of English Studies*, 29 (1999), 202–30.

McEvoy, Brian et al., 'The *Longue Durée* of Genetic Ancestry: Multiple Genetic Marker Systems and Celtic Origins on the Atlantic Façade of Europe', *American Journal of Human Genetics*, 75 (2004), 693–701.

Macfarlane, Robert, *The Old Ways: A Journey on Foot*. London: Penguin, 2012.

MacHaffie, Fraser, 'Facilities for Transit: The Congested Districts Board and Steamship Services', *Irish Geography*, 28.2 (1995), 91–104.

McHugh, Roland, *Annotations to Finnegans Wake*, 3rd edn. Baltimore: Johns Hopkins University Press, 2006.

Mack, John, *The Sea: A Cultural History*. London: Reaktion, 2011.

Mackail, J. W., *The Life of William Morris*, vol. 2. London: Longman, Green and Co., 1899.

MacKay, Marina, *Modernism and World War II*. Cambridge: Cambridge University Press, 2007.

Mackinder, H. J., *Britain and the British Seas*. London: William Heinemann, 1902.

Maclagan, R. C., 'Ghost Lights of the West Highlands', *Folklore*, 8.3 (September 1897), 203–56.

McLaverty, Michael, *Call My Brother Back*. Belfast: Blackstaff, 2003.

McLaverty, Michael, *Collected Short Stories*. Belfast: Blackstaff, 2002.

McLaverty, Michael, 'The Green Field', *The Irish Monthly*, 60 (August 1932), 497–504.

McLaverty, Michael, 'The Prophet', *The Irish Monthly*, 64 (February 1936), 95–101.

McLaverty, Michael, 'The Wild Duck's Nest', *The Irish Monthly*, 62 (April 1934), 236–40.

Macleod, Fiona, *The Washer of the Ford, and Other Legendary Moralities*. Edinburgh: Patrick Geddes, 1896.

MacNeice, Louis, *The Agamemnon of Aeschylus*. London: Faber, 1936.

MacNeice, Louis, *Collected Poems*, ed. Peter McDonald. London: Faber, 2007.

MacNeice, Louis, *I Crossed the Minch*, intro. Tom Herron. Edinburgh: Polygon, 2007.

MacNeice, Louis, *Letters of Louis MacNeice*, ed. Jonathan Allison. London: Faber, 2010.

MacNeice, Louis, *The Poetry of W. B. Yeats*. London: Faber, 1967.

McNeillie, Andrew, 'Editorial', *Archipelago*, 1 (Summer 2007), vii–viii.

Maggio, Paula, 'Digging for Buried Treasure: Theories about Weather and Fiction in Virginia Woolf's Essays', *Virginia Woolf Miscellany*, 78 (Fall/Winter 2010), 23–6.

Mahaffey, Vicki, 'Bloom and the Ba: Voyeurism and Elision in "Nausicaa"', *European Joyce Studies*, 22 (2013), 113–18.

Manganaro, Marc, 'Modernist Studies and Anthropology: Reflections on the Past, Present, and Possible Futures', in Pamela L. Caughie (ed.), *Disciplining Modernism*. Basingstoke: Palgrave, 2010, 210–20.

Mao, Douglas and Rebecca L. Walkowitz (eds), *Bad Modernisms*. Durham, NC: Duke University Press, 2006.

Massey, Doreen, *Space, Place and Gender*. Cambridge: Polity Press, 1994.

Mathews, P. J., *Revival*. Cork: Cork University Press, 2003.

Matless, David, *Landscape and Englishness*. London: Reaktion, 1998.

Meaney, Gerardine, 'Decadence, Degeneration and Revolting Aesthetics: The Fiction of Emily Lawless and Katherine Cecil Thurston', *Colby Quarterly*, 36.2 (June 2000), 157–75.

Mendelson, Edward, *Early Auden*. London: Faber, 1981.

Milesi, Laurent, 'The *Habitus* of Language(s) in *Finnegans Wake*', in Valérie Bénéjam and John Bishop (eds), *Making Space in the Works of James Joyce*. London: Routledge, 2011, 145–54.

Miller, Hugh, *The Testimony of the Rocks, or Geology in its Bearings: On the Two Theologies, Natural and Revealed*. Edinburgh: Thomas Constable and Co., Shepherd and Elliot, 1857.

Miller, Tyrus, *Late Modernism: Politics, Fiction, and the Arts Between the World Wars*. Berkeley: University of California Press, 1999.

Miller, Tyrus, 'The Strings Are False: Bathos, Pastoral and Social Reflexivity in 1930s British Poetry', in Sara Crangle and Peter Nicholls (eds), *On Bathos: Literature, Art, Music*. London: Continuum, 2010, 49–70.

Mitchell, Breon, 'W. H. Auden and Christopher Isherwood: The "German Influence"', *Oxford German Studies*, 1 (1966), 163–72.

Mollan, Charles (ed.), *Science and Ireland: Value for Society*. Dublin: Royal Dublin Society, 2005.

Mollan, Charles, William Davis, and Brendan Finucane (eds), *Irish Innovators in Science and Technology*. Dublin: Royal Irish Academy, 2002.

Monmonier, Mark, *Air Apparent: How Meteorologists Learned to Map, Predict, and Dramatize Weather*. Chicago: University of Chicago Press, 1999.

Moore, Desmond F., 'The Port of Dublin', *Dublin Historical Record*, 16.4 (August 1961), 131–44.

Moore, George, *Hail and Farewell*, ed. Richard Cave. Gerrards Cross: Colin Smythe, 1976.

Moore, George, *Parnell and his Island*, ed. Carla King. Dublin: University College Dublin Press, 2004.

Moore, Madeline, *The Short Season Between Two Silences: The Mystical and the Political in the Novels of Virginia Woolf*. Boston: George Allen and Unwin, 1984.

Moretti, Franco, *Atlas of the European Novel 1800–1900*. London: Verso, 1998.

Morris, Jan (ed.), *Travels with Virginia Woolf*. London: Hogarth Press, 1993.

Morris, William, *News from Nowhere*. Oxford: Oxford World's Classics, 2003.

Morton, H. V., *In Search of England*. London: Methuen, 1932.

Morton, Timothy, *The Ecological Thought*. Cambridge, MA: Harvard University Press, 2010.

Nagai, Kaori, '"'Tis Optophone with Optophanes": Race, the Modern, and Irish Revivalism', in Len Platt (ed.), *Modernism and Race*. Cambridge: Cambridge University Press, 2011, 58–76.

Nagra, Daljit, 'Look We Have Coming to Dover!', *Look We Have Coming to Dover!* London: Faber, 2007.

Nairn, Tom, *After Britain: New Labour and the Return of Scotland*. London: Granta, 2000.

Ní Dhuibhne, Eilís, *The Bray House*. Dublin: Attic, 1990.

Nolan, Peter, 'Imperial Archipelagos: China, Western Colonialism and the Law of the Sea', *New Left Review*, 80 (March/April 2013), 77–95.

North, Michael, *The Dialect of Modernism: Race, Language, and Twentieth-Century Literature*. Oxford: Oxford University Press, 1994.

Ó Cléirigh, Nellie, 'Life in the Rosses, Co. Donegal, in the 1890s', *History Ireland*, 13.2 (March/April 2005), 8–9.

Ó Criomhthain, Tomás, *An tOileánach: Scéal a Bheathadh Féin*. Baile Átha Cliath: Clólucht an Tálbóidigh, 1929.

Ó Crohan, Tomás, *The Islandman*, trans. Robin Flower. Dublin: Talbot Press, 1934.

O'Doherty, J. F., 'Reviews', *Irish Historical Studies*, 2.6 (September 1940), 217–18.

O'Donnell, Peadar, *Islanders*. Cork: Mercier Press, 2005.

O'Donnell, Peadar, *Wrack: A Play in Six Scenes*. London: Jonathan Cape, 1933.

O'Dushlaine, Colm T. et al., 'Population Structure and Genome-wide Patterns of Variation in Ireland and Britain', *European Journal of Human Genetics*, 18 (2010), 1248–54.

O'Farrelly, Agnes, *Smaointe ar Árainn (Thoughts on Aran)*, ed. Ríona Nic Congáil. Dublin: Arlen House, 2010.

Ó Gráda, Cormac, 'Seasonal Migration and Post-Famine Adjustment', *Studia Hibernica*, 13 (1973), 48–76.

O'Hanlon, Redmond, *Trawler: A Journey through the North Atlantic*. London: Penguin, 2004.

O'Leary, Don, *Irish Catholicism and Science*. Cork: Cork University Press, 2012.

Orwell, George, *Inside the Whale and Other Essays*. London: Penguin, 1957.

Orwell, George, *The Road to Wigan Pier*. Harmondsworth: Penguin, 1962.

Ó Súileabháin, Muiris, *Fiche Blian ag Fás*. Baile Átha Cliath: Clólucht an Tálbóidigh, 1933.

O'Sullivan, Maurice, *Twenty Years A-Growing: Rendered from the original Irish by Moya Llewelyn Davies and George Thomson*. Harmondsworth: Penguin, 1938.

Otis, Laura, *Membranes: Metaphors of Invasion in Nineteenth-Century Literature, Science and Politics*. Baltimore: Johns Hopkins University Press, 1999.

Panter-Downes, Mollie, *One Fine Day*. London: Virago, 1985.

Patten, C. J., *The Story of the Birds*. Sheffield: Pawson and Brailsford, 1928.

Peacock, Sandra J., *The Theological and Ethical Writings of Frances Power Cobbe, 1822–1904*. Lewiston, NY: Edwin Mellen Press, 2002.

Pearson, Nels, '"May I Trespass on your Valuable Space?": *Ulysses* on the Coast', *Modern Fiction Studies*, 57.4 (Winter 2011), 627–49.

Pethica, James (ed.), *Lady Gregory's Diaries: 1892–1902*. Gerrards Cross: Colin Smythe, 1996.

Piercy, Jill, *Brenda Chamberlain: Artist and Writer*. Cardigan: Parthian, 2013.

Pocock, J. G. A., 'British History: A Plea for a New Subject', *Journal of Modern History*, 47.4 (December 1975), 601–21.

Pocock, J. G. A., *The Discovery of Islands: Essays in British History*. Cambridge: Cambridge University Press, 2005.

Praeger, Robert Lloyd, *The Way That I Went: An Irishman in Ireland*. Cork: Collins Press, 1997.

Priestley, J. B., *English Journey*. London: William Heinemann, 1935.

Puhvel, Martin, 'The Seal in the Folklore of Northern Europe', *Folklore*, 74.1 (Spring 1963), 326–33.

Quiggin, A. Hingston, *Haddon the Head Hunter*. Cambridge: Cambridge University Press, 1942.

Raban, Jonathan, *Coasting*. London: Picador, 1987.

Radford, Andrew, *Thomas Hardy and the Survivals of Time*. Aldershot: Ashgate, 2003.

Rancière, Jacques, *On the Shores of Politics*, trans. Liz Heron. London: Verso, 2007.

Ransome, Arthur, *Bohemia in London*. New York: Dodd, Mead and Co., 1907.

Ray, Martin, 'Thomas Hardy's "Geographical Knowledge"', *Notes and Queries*, 53.3 (September 2006), 343–4.

Read, H. H., 'The Metamorphic History of Unst, Shetland', *Proceedings of the Geologists' Association*, 47 (1936), 283–93.

Reeve, N. H., *Elizabeth Taylor*. Tavistock: Northcote House, 2008.

Reizbaum, Marilyn, 'Urban Legends', *Eire-Ireland*, 45.1&2 (Spring/Summer 2010), 242–65.

Rhys, Ernest, *A London Rose and Other Poems*. London: Elkin Mathews, 1894.

Rhys, Ernest (ed.), *Malory's History of King Arthur and the Quest of the Holy Grail*. London: Walter Scott, 1886.

Rhys, Jean, *Letters 1931–1966*, ed. Francis Wyndham and Diana Melly. London: Andre Deutsch, 1984.

Rhys, Jean, *Wide Sargasso Sea*. London: Penguin, 1997.

Roberts, Callum, *The Unnatural History of the Sea: The Past and Future of Humanity and Fishing*. London: Gaia, 2007.

Roberts, J. Kimberley, *Ernest Rhys*. Writers of Wales Series. Cardiff: University of Wales Press, 1983.

Roberts, Lynette, *Collected Poems*, ed. Patrick McGuinness. Manchester: Carcanet, 2005.

Robichaud, Paul, 'MacDiarmid and Muir: Scottish Modernism and the Nation as Anthropological Site', *Journal of Modern Literature*, 28.4 (Summer 2005), 135–51.

Robinson, Tim, *My Time in Space*. Dublin: Lilliput, 2001.

Robinson, Tim, *Setting Foot on the Shores of Connemara, and Other Writings*. Dublin: Lilliput, 2007.

Robinson, Tim, *Stones of Aran: Pilgrimage*. London: Faber, 2008.

Roche, Anthony, '"The Strange Light of Some New World": Stephen's Vision in "A Portrait"', *James Joyce Quarterly*, 25.3 (Spring 1988), 323–32.

Roche, Anthony, 'Yeats, Synge, and an Emerging Irish Drama', *Yeats: An Annual of Critical and Textual Studies*, vol. 10. Ann Arbor: University of Michigan Press, 1992, 32–55.

Rolleston, T. W., *Parallel Paths: A Study in Biology, Ethics and Art*. London: Duckworth, 1908.

Roper, Jonathan, 'Thoms and the Unachieved "Folk-lore of England"', *Folklore*, 118.2 (August 2007), 203–16.

Rutenberg, Daniel, 'A Study of Rhymers' Club Poetry'. Unpublished PhD dissertation, University of Florida, 1967.

St. Jean, Shawn, 'Readerly Paranoia and Joyce's Adolescence Stories', *James Joyce Quarterly*, 35.4/36.1 (Summer/Fall 1998), 665–82.

Saintsbury, George, *A History of English Prosody from the Twelfth Century to the Present Day, Vol. 1: From the Origins to Spenser*. London: Macmillan, 1906.

Sale, Kirkpatrick, *Dwellers in the Land: The Bioregional Vision*. San Francisco: Sierra Club, 1985.

Samuel, Raphael, *Island Stories: Unravelling Britain* (vol. 2 of *Theatres of Memory*). London: Verso, 1998.

Sayers, Peig, *Peig: A Scéal Féin*. Baile Átha Cliath: Clólucht an Tálbóidigh, 1936.

Sayers, Peig, *Peig: The Autobiography of Peig Sayers of the Great Blasket Island*, trans. Bryan MacMahon. Dublin: Talbot Press, 1973.

Scott, Bonnie Kime, *In the Hollow of the Wave: Virginia Woolf and Modernist Uses of Nature*. Charlottesville, VA: University of Virginia Press, 2012.

Sekula, Allan, 'Between the Net and the Deep Blue Sea (Rethinking the Traffic in Photographs)', *October*, 102 (Autumn 2002), 3–34.

Sekula, Allan, *The Forgotten Space: A Film Essay*, dir. Allan Sekula and Noël Burch. Amsterdam: Doc.Eye Film, 2010.

Selvon, Sam, *An Island Is a World*. Toronto: Tsar, 1993.

Selvon, Sam, *The Lonely Londoners*. Harlow: Longman, 1985.

Sharp, Elizabeth and William Sharp (eds), *Lyra Celtica: An Anthology of Representative Celtic Poetry*. Edinburgh: Patrick Geddes, 1896.

Shortland, Michael (ed.), *Hugh Miller and the Controversies of Victorian Science*. Oxford: Clarendon Press, 1996.

Shovlin, Frank, *Journey Westwards: Joyce,* Dubliners, *and the Literary Revival*. Liverpool: Liverpool University Press, 2012.

Sidhe, Wren, 'H. V. Morton's Pilgrimages to Englishness', *Literature and History*, 12.1 (2003), 57–71.

Simmons, James, 'Editorial', *The Honest Ulsterman*, 1 (May 1968), 2–6.

Sinclair, Iain, *Lights Out for the Territory*. London: Granta, 1997.

Sinclair, Iain, *White Chappell, Scarlet Tracings*. London: Granta, 1998.

Sisson, Elaine, '*The Aran Islands* and the Travel Essays', in P. J. Mathews (ed.), *The Cambridge Companion to J. M. Synge*. Cambridge: Cambridge University Press, 2009, 52–63.

Sloan, John, *John Davidson: First of the Moderns*. Oxford: Oxford University Press, 1995.

Smidt, Kristian, '"I'm Not Half Norawain for Nothing": Joyce and Norway', *James Joyce Quarterly*, 26.3 (Spring 1989), 333–50.

Smith, Jos, 'An Archipelagic Environment: Re-Writing the British and Irish Landscape, 1972–2012'. Unpublished PhD thesis, University of Exeter, 2012.

Snyder, Robert Lance, '"Elbowing Vacancy": Philip Larkin's Non-places', *Papers on Language and Literature*, 43.2 (Spring 2007), 115–45.

Stafford, Fiona, *Local Attachments: The Province of Poetry*. Oxford: Oxford University Press, 2010.

Steinberg, Philip E., *The Social Construction of the Ocean*. Cambridge: Cambridge University Press, 2001.

Swanson, Diana (ed.), 'Eco-Woolf': Special Issue, *Virginia Woolf Miscellany*, 81 (Spring 2012).

Swift, Graham, *Last Orders*. London: Picador, 1996.

Symons, Arthur, 'A Causerie: From a Castle in Ireland', *The Savoy*, 6 (October 1896), 93–5.

Symons, Arthur, 'In Sligo: Rosses Point and Glencar', *The Savoy*, 7 (November 1896), 55–61.

Symons, Arthur, 'The Isles of Aran', *The Savoy*, 8 (December 1896), 73–86.

Symons, Arthur, 'Memoir', in *The Poems and Prose of Ernest Dowson*. New York: Modern Library, 1919, 1–16.

Synge, J. M., *The Aran Islands*. London: Penguin, 1992.

Synge, J. M., *Collected Works, Vol. 2: Prose*, ed. Alan Price. Gerrards Cross: Colin Smythe, 1982.

Synge, J. M., *Collected Works, Vol. 3: Plays Book 1*, ed. Ann Saddlemyer. Gerrards Cross: Colin Smythe, 1982.

Synge, J. M., *Collected Works, Vol. 4: Plays Book 2*, ed. Ann Saddlemyer. Gerrards Cross: Colin Smythe, 1982.

Synge, J. M., *Travelling Ireland: Essays 1898–1908*, ed. Nicholas Grene. Dublin: Lilliput, 2009.

Taylor, Elizabeth, *A View of the Harbour*. London: Virago, 2006.

Thacker, Andrew, *Moving through Modernity: Space and Geography in Modernism*. Manchester: Manchester University Press, 2003.

Theroux, Paul, *The Kingdom by the Sea*. London: Penguin, 1984.

Thomas, Edward, *The Annotated Collected Poems*, ed. Edna Longley. Tarset: Bloodaxe, 2008.

Thoms, W. J., *Choice Notes from* Notes and Queries: *Folklore*. London: Bell and Daldy, 1859.

Thomson, A. Landsborough, *Bird Migration*. London: Witherby, 1936.

Thomson, George, *Island Home: The Blasket Heritage*. Dingle: Brandon, 1988.

Thomson, George, *Studies in Ancient Greek Society: The Prehistoric Aegean*. London: Lawrence and Wishart, 1949.

Thornton, Weldon, 'An Allusion List for James Joyce's "Ulysses": Part III "Proteus"', *James Joyce Quarterly*, 1.3 (Spring 1964), 25–41.

Tong, Pin et al., 'Sequencing and Analysis of an Irish Human Genome', *Genome Biology*, 11: R91 (2010), 1–14.

Toye, Richard, *The Roar of the Lion: The Untold Story of Churchill's World War II Speeches*. Oxford: Oxford University Press, 2013.

Tropp, Sandra, '"The Esthetic Instinct in Action": Charles Darwin and Mental Science in *A Portrait of the Artist as a Young Man*', *James Joyce Quarterly*, 45.2 (Winter 2008), 221–44.

Tucker, Herbert F., 'Doughty's *The Dawn in Britain* and the Modernist Eclipse of the Victorian', *Romanticism and Victorianism on the Net*, 47 (August 2007): <http://www.erudit.org/revue/ravon/2007/v/n47/016705ar.html> (last accessed 6 May 2014).

Waidson, H. M., 'Auden and German Literature', *Modern Language Review*, 70.2 (1975), 347–65.

Walcott, Derek, *Collected Poems 1948–1984*. London: Faber, 1986.

Waldman, Carl and Catherine Walsh, *Encyclopedia of European Peoples*. New York: Infobase, 2006.

Walford Davies, Damian, *Cartographies of Culture: New Geographies of Welsh Writing in English*. Cardiff: University of Wales Press, 2012.

Webster, Wendy, *Englishness and Empire 1939–1965*. Oxford: Oxford University Press, 2005.

Wells, H. G., *The Outline of History*. London: Cassell, 1951.

Whitworth, Michael, 'Culture and Leisure in Hugh MacDiarmid's "On a Raised Beach"', *Scottish Studies Review*, 9.1 (Spring 2008), 123–43.

Whyte, Nicholas, *Science, Colonialism and Ireland*. Cork: Cork University Press, 1999.

Williams, Alexander, 'Bird Life in Dublin Bay: The Passing of Clontarf Island', *The Irish Naturalist*, 17.9 (September 1908), 165–70.

Williams, Daniel G., *Ethnicity and Cultural Authority: From Arnold to Du Bois*. Edinburgh: Edinburgh University Press, 2006.

Williams, Raymond, *Marxism and Literature*. Oxford: Oxford University Press, 1977.

Wills, Clair, *That Neutral Island: A Cultural History of Ireland During the Second World War*. London: Faber, 2007.

Wilson, G. V. and J. Knox, 'The Geology of the Orkney and Shetland Islands', *Proceedings of the Geologists' Association*, 47 (1936), 270–82.

Wolfreys, Julian, *Thomas Hardy*. Basingstoke: Palgrave Macmillan, 2009.

Wood, J. G., *Common Objects of the Sea-Shore*. London: Routledge, 1912.

Wood-Martin, W. G., *History of Sligo, County and Town, from the Earliest Ages to the Close of the Reign of Queen Elizabeth*. Dublin: Hodges, Figgis and Co., 1882.

Wood-Martin, W. G., *The Lake Dwellings of Ireland: Or Ancient Lacustrine Habitations of Erin, Commonly Called Crannogs*. Dublin: Hodges, Figgis and Co., 1886.

Woolf, Virginia, *Between the Acts*. Oxford: Oxford World's Classics, 1992.

Woolf, Virginia, *A Change of Perspective: The Letters of Virginia Woolf, Vol. 3: 1923–1928*, ed. Nigel Nicolson. London: Hogarth, 1977.

Woolf, Virginia, *The Diary of Virginia Woolf, Vol. 4: 1931–1935*, ed. Anne Olivier Bell. Harmondsworth: Penguin, 1983.

Woolf, Virginia, *The Essays of Virginia Woolf, Vol. 4: 1925–1928*, ed. Andrew McNeillie. London: Hogarth, 1994.

Woolf, Virginia, *The Essays of Virginia Woolf, Vol. 5: 1929–1932*, ed. Stuart N. Clarke. London: Hogarth, 2009.

Woolf, Virginia, *The Letters of Virginia Woolf, Vol. 5: 1932–1935*, ed. Nigel Nicolson. New York: Harcourt Brace Jovanovich, 1979.

Woolf, Virginia, *The Letters of Virginia Woolf, Vol. 6: 1936–1941*, ed. Nigel Nicolson and Joanne Trautmann. New York: Harcourt Brace Jovanovich, 1980.

Woolf, Virginia, *Orlando*. Oxford: Oxford World's Classics, 2008.

Woolf, Virginia, *A Room of One's Own and Three Guineas*. Oxford: Oxford World's Classics, 1992.

Woolf, Virginia, *Selected Essays*. Oxford: Oxford World's Classics, 2008.

Woolf, Virginia, *To the Lighthouse*, ed. and intro. David Bradshaw. Oxford: Oxford World's Classics, 2006.

Woolf, Virginia, *The Voyage Out*. Oxford: Oxford World's Classics, 1992.

Yeats, W. B., *Autobiographies*. Dublin: Gill and Macmillan, 1955.

Yeats, W. B., *The Collected Letters of W. B. Yeats, Vol. 1: 1865–1895*, ed. John Kelly. Oxford: Clarendon Press, 1986.

Yeats, W. B., *Essays and Introductions*. London: Macmillan, 1961.

Yeats, W. B., *The Letters of W. B. Yeats*, ed. Allan Wade. London: Rupert Hart-Davis, 1954.

Yeats, W. B., *Memoirs*, ed. Denis Donoghue. London: Macmillan, 1972.

Yeats, W. B., *Uncollected Prose, Vol. 1: First Reviews and Articles 1886–1896*, ed. John P. Frayne. New York: Columbia University Press, 1970.

Yeats, W. B., *Uncollected Prose, Vol. 2: Reviews, Articles and Other Miscellaneous Prose 1897–1939*, ed. John P. Frayne and Colton Johnson. London: Macmillan, 1975.

Yeats, W. B., *Yeats's Poems*, ed. A. Norman Jeffares. Dublin: Gill and Macmillan, 1989.

Yeats, W. B. (ed.), *Fairy and Folk Tales of the Irish Peasantry*. London: Walter Scott, 1888.

Yonge, C. M., *The Sea Shore*. The New Naturalist. London: Bloomsbury, 1990.

Young, Robert, *The Idea of English Ethnicity*. Oxford: Blackwell, 2008.

Youngs, Tim, 'Auden's Travel Writings', in Stan Smith (ed.), *The Cambridge Companion to W. H. Auden*. Cambridge: Cambridge University Press, 2004, 68–81.

Index